Revaluing Ethics

SUNY series in Ancient Greek Philosophy
Anthony Preus, editor

Revaluing Ethics

Aristotle's Dialectical Pedagogy

THOMAS W. SMITH

State University of New York Press

Publsihed by
State University of New York Press

Printed in the United States of America

For information, address the State University of New York Press, 90 State Street, Suite 700, Albany, NY 12207

Marketing by Patrick Durocher • Production by Bernadine Dawes

Library of Congress Cataloging-in-Publication Data

Smith, Thomas W., 1965–
Revaluing ethics : Aristotle's dialectical pedagogy / Thomas W. Smith.
p. cm. — (SUNY series in ancient Greek philosophy)
Includes bibliographical references and index.
ISBN 0-7914-5141-0 (alk. paper) — ISBN 0-7914-5142-9 (pb : alk. paper)
1. Aristotle. Nicomachean ethics. 2. Ethics, Ancient. I. Title. II. Series.

B430.S65 2001
171'.3—dc21 2001018362

1 2 3 4 5 6 7 8 9 10

For Thomas, Christopher, and Katherine

You wake us up

Sparking wonder and delight

Table of Contents

Human beings consider the cause of happiness to be external goods—as if the lyre rather than the art were held to be the cause of brilliant and beautiful lyre playing.

—Aristotle, *Politics*

Concerning equality and justice, even though it's very hard to find the truth about these things, still it's easier to hit on the truth than to persuade those who are overgrasping. The inferior always seeks equality and justice; those who dominate them take no thought for it.

—Aristotle, *Politics*

Abbreviations

DA	*De Anima*
EE	*Eudemian Ethics*
LSJ	Liddle and Scott, *An Intermediate Greek-English Lexicon*
M	*Metaphysics*
NE	*Nicomachean Ethics*
P	*Politics*
PA	*Posterior Analytics*
R	*Rhetoric*
SR	*Sophistical Refutations*
T	*Topics*

Preface

When I was sixteen I stole a copy of the *Nicomachean Ethics* from my brother Ed, skipped work, and, on a Long Island beach, read Aristotle's account of friendship. I was hooked and still am. It's fitting that my introduction to Aristotle was through acts of injustice because a large theme of my work is that we often come to virtue through vice.

I came to Aristotle at a propitious time, for there has been a huge renaissance in Aristotelian studies over the last two decades. Yet after wrestling with Aristotle I became convinced that many contemporary interpretations mistakenly confuse the perspective of Aristotle's audience with his own considered view. Thus the title of my book has two senses. First, Aristotle's dialectic aims at a revaluation of his audience's values. The drama of the *Ethics* lies in the dialectical engagement and transformation of the valorization of a life of prestige and power. Second, my interpretation uncovers an Aristotle who prioritizes questions over answers. Thus it revalues traditional interpretations of Aristotle's ethical and political texts as didactic treatises conveying abstract moralisms to an indeterminate audience.

Over the years many students, teachers, friends, and colleagues helped me understand the *Ethics* better. In graduate school I read the *Ethics* with my good friend Jay Thompson, who first suggested to me that Aristotle's discussion of *megalopsuchia* is ironic. In turn, this suggestion bore fruit in my argument that Aristotle's account of the moral virtues is critical. As is clear from my conclusion, my understanding of the relationship of practical reason to contemplative practice also owes much to Jay's work. In graduate school and after Brad Lewis offered invaluable support and advice. Villanova University has provided a wonderful environment for a young scholar to grow. I am grateful to many people there, but in particular, to my colleagues in Villanova's Political Science Department, Jack Schrems and Colleen Sheehan, who read parts of the manuscript. Kevin Hughes, Fr. Martin Laird, OSA, and William Werpehowski read parts of the manuscript and I have profited from their conversation and friendship. Thanks also to Jack Doody and David Barrett for their advice, encouragement, and seemingly endless help. Edward Goerner of the University of Notre Dame also read the entire manuscript and his comments improved it enormously. Thanks to my teachers, Fr. James V. Schall SJ, David Walsh, John Roos, and Edward Goerner, who were models of patience and generosity. Stephen Salkever of Bryn Mawr College read parts of the manuscript and provided excellent comments and conversations over the last few years. Margaret King of the Political Science Department provided invaluable secretarial services. My wife has made a home that is a place of flourishing, teaching me countless lessons in what it means to be a good human being. My children's spirit of questioning and joyful wonder provided perfect models of what it means to be a seeker. I dedicate this book to them with love.

Earlier versions of different parts of this book have appeared elsewhere. A précis of the argument that Aristotle's *Ethics* is protreptic appeared as "The Protreptic Character of the *Nicomachean Ethics*," *Polity* 27, no. 2 (Winter 1994): 307–30. Parts of chapter 2 appeared as "The Audience of the *Nicomachean Ethics*, *The Journal of Politics* 62, no. 1 (February 2000): 166–86. Parts of chapters 6 and 8 appeared as "Aristotle on the Conditions for and Limits of the Common Good" *American Political Science Review* 93, no. 3 (September 1999): 625–36. Finally, a section of chapter 1 appeared as "Ethics and Politics: A Response to Terchek and Moore" *American Political Science Review* 94, no. 4 (December 2000): 913–18. The author gratefully acknowledges permission to reprint revised versions of these articles.

Introduction

The Return to Aristotle

There are vast disagreements about the meaning of the term "postmodern" but perhaps everyone can agree that it implies a period of rapid and revolutionary transition, when something is slowly and painfully passing away even as something else is slowly and painfully being born. In using the term, people sense that there is something unique about the time, and that this uniqueness demands a name. However, at the same time there is an incapacity to name. When we use "postmodern" we merely describe by a kind of temporal negation. We do not exactly know what we are, but we know what we are not; we are not in the modern.

The widespread feelings of disorientation and deracination attending such a time provoke a sense of crisis. Two sorts of dangers flow from this. On the one hand, there is the danger of ineffectual and often counterproductive conservative hand-wringing over the crisis. In flight from the anxiety our time brings, some demand a return to traditional or family values or religions or communities. However, part of the problem with this demand is that in a time of transition, when narratives legitimating such social and cultural institutions as families or religions are called into question, it is not at all clear what any of these are supposed to look like. All that is clear is that many have abandoned traditional conceptions of family or religion because they experience them to be discredited. So the demand for return will often seem to be reactionary attempts to ram sclerotic and oppressive structures down people's throats. Yet on the other hand, there is the danger that some will use this time of uncertainty and anxiety to assert their own brand of nihilistic irresponsibility. In my own calling, for example, I have witnessed professors who take glee in playing at ersatz bodhisattva to disaffected young people by tearing down responsible behavior and putting nothing in its place. Yet the stakes are too high for this. The astounding economic, technological, scientific, military, police, bureaucratic, political, and social powers that the modern age bequeathed us make self-promoting nihilism extraordinarily dangerous. So the postmodern time demands neither reactionary fear nor nihilistic surrender to our baser instincts. It demands a sober measuring of the human task such a time presents.

One of the most sober measurers of this task has been Vaclav Havel. In his public addresses to the West, Havel consistently argues that the contemporary period is at once a potentially dangerous and fruitful time of transition, when the old modern West is in the process of dying, and something else is being born. In one piece, for example, he points out that the term "Europe" comes from the Akkadian word meaning "sunset," and uses this etymology to reflect on the character of the time:

> I believe we are facing a great historical challenge, a challenge to grasp and put into practice at last what is implied in the word twilight. We should stop thinking of the present state of Europe as the sunset of its energy and recognize it instead as a time of contemplation when the work of the day ceases for a while and, as the sun goes down, the rule of thought sets in. This does not mean we need to be estranged from ourselves and the world we live in. It simply means taking a calm look back at what we have accomplished, assessing the meaning and the consequences of our efforts and making a few resolutions for the day to come.[1]

There are a variety of ways of dealing with one's responsibility to reflect. The contemporary resurgence of the study of ancient political philosophy can be understood as helping to fulfill our need for thoughtful reflection about the past to help us manage our transition into an uncertain future. Mainly for this reason, there has been a veritable explosion in Aristotle scholarship in recent years. Scholars of various stripes have returned to Aristotelian ethical and political thought for a similar reason: Aristotle helps us reflect on various contemporary problems.

However, the result of this revival of Aristotelianism is a bewildering variety of Aristotles, with an enormous range of possible teachings. The revival of Aristotelianism has reached a series of dead ends, for Aristotelians have set up various camps devoted to this or that account of Aristotle's conclusions. So, for example, Aristotle has emerged today as a defender and as a critic of liberal democracy; an unsystematic thinker who holds incompatible conceptions of moral and intellectual virtue, and thus of the best life for man; an immoralist ready to sacrifice ethical character on the altar of philosophy; a virtue theorist who can effectively demolish deontological rule-bound ethics; a sane alternative to the dangers of nihilistic skepticism and dogmatic foundationalism; a misogynist; a defender of women against the Ancient Greek cult of masculinity; a racist authoritarian who uses his philosophic brilliance to justify slavery; and a critic of slavery.[2] With far less frequency has he emerged as a man more interested in inquiring into problems and provoking thought than in articulating conclusions. Yet if Aristotle gives priority to questions over answers, then the current form of the renaissance of interest in Aristotle may be one of the obstacles to the recovery of his thought.

By contrast, contemporary scholarship on Plato has avoided such dead ends by rescuing Aristotle's teacher from two related but mistaken readings. On the metaphysical misreading, Plato is a dogmatic idealist who posited an eternal realm of forms. On the political misreading, he is a fascist whose recommendations in the *Republic* for a closed protototalitarian society helped pave the way for modern tyranny. Both of these readings are made possible by neglecting the implications of the fact that Plato wrote dialogues. The assumption implicit in these interpretations is that the dialogue form was a literary adornment incidental to Plato's teaching. The recovery of a new way of looking at Plato's political philosophy went hand in hand with a recovery of the dialogue form. In Leo Strauss's words, the contemporary rediscovery of Platonic political philosophy was possible with the realization that the content of the dialogue is inseparable from its form. In order to grapple with Plato's teaching, one had to deal with the hermeneutical problems that the dramatic character of the dialogue presents. This renewed appreciation for the importance of the dialogue form allowed Plato to emerge not as an enemy of thought, but rather a thinker who fosters inquiry through dialogues that force the careful reader into the kind of profitable confusion that induces wonder. Indeed, the fact that Plato never speaks as a character in any of his dialogues led Strauss to question the assumption that a reader can in a straightforward, unproblematic way glean any explicit doctrine from a reading of his work:

> We can know Aristotle's political philosophy through his *Politics.* Plato's *Republic* on the other hand, in contradistinction to the *Politics,* is not a treatise but a dialogue among people other than Plato. Whereas in reading the *Politics* we hear Aristotle all the time, in reading the *Republic* we hear Plato never. In none of his dialogues does Plato ever say anything. Hence we cannot know from them what Plato thought. If someone quotes a passage from the dialogues in order to prove that Plato held such and such a view, he acts as reasonably as if he were to assert that according to Shakespeare life is a tale told by an idiot, full of sound and fury but signifying nothing. . . . Could it be true that Plato, like Socrates, the master of the knowledge of ignorance, did not assert anything, i.e., did not have a teaching?[3]

Yet, as we can see from the above quote, Aristotle has fared less well even among friends such as Strauss, for he is said to have written treatises. While the recovery of Plato proceeded in large part by re-evaluating the literary and dramatic character of the dialogue, that reevaluation has not taken place with Aristotle. Thus, it seems that Aristotle speaks to us directly in his "treatises," laying out various straightforward teachings or conclusions on political and ethical reality. In other words, in most places in the contemporary Academy, he is read as Plato was once read.

Thus many contemporary readings of Aristotle rest on the assumption that one ought to read Aristotle's ethico-political inquiries as didactic treatises. On this view, Aristotle wrote a set of moral textbooks in which he set forth conclusions on such topics as the nature of the virtues or the best life for human beings. The implication is that since his teaching can be gleaned from his texts in roughly the same way one gleans information from an encyclopedia, it does no harm to understand his conclusions apart from their place in the overall inquiry. To understand what Aristotle has to say on a particular subject, it is sufficient to look up the appropriate heading.[4]

However, this approach runs into at least two objections. First, Aristotle insists at several places that his inquiry has a practical intent; he says his purpose is not to lay out a correct account of ethics, but to make us good in some way (*NE*, 1094b11; 1103b27; 1179b1–4; cf. 1194a22–23). One wonders what kind of book is intended to convert its readers, and whether a treatise could have such an effect. Aristotle's care to make his audience good entails that we pay special attention to audience; to the structure of the inquiry, and its intended effects; that is, to the direction or goal of the inquiry. If this is the case, however, this would preclude isolating the discussion of any particular topic from its overall place in the inquiry. This would mean that we refuse to read Aristotle's philosophy of human affairs[5] as a treatise, and rather work to understand his teaching by paying strict attention to the integrity of the whole inquiry. This conclusion is further strengthened by reflecting on the fact that at different places in the same text Aristotle makes notoriously conflicting statements about such crucial topics as pleasure and the place of contemplation in the good life. In the opening pages of the *Ethics*, for instance, he dismisses the life of pleasure as fit only for cattle. By the closing pages of the *Ethics*, he identifies pleasure with the good life. If one reads Aristotelian writings as didactic treatises, one must work to explain away such apparent contradictions.[6] By contrast, if one reads the text as a teaching, the apparent contradictions can be interpreted as pedagogical devices that foster critical inquiry.

Recently scholars have begun to challenge the conventional way of reading Aristotle. These scholars have taken what might be called a political turn in interpreting Aristotle. This body of work eschews the notion that the *Ethics* is a treatise addressed to an indeterminant audience of disinterested scientific observers that is intended to convey doctrines about the best life. Rather, these scholars are guided by Aristotle's insistence that the *Ethics* is meant to make people good. Thus, they argue, Aristotle's task is to proceed from the perspective of the active citizen-politician and to inform that perspective with his inquiry to improve practice. In order to understand the substance of Aristotle's teaching, therefore, they insist that one must take into account the political and pedagogical intent of his work, as well as the audience to whom the work is directed.[7]

I argue that Aristotle's *Nicomachean Ethics* is a pedagogy, and therefore any interpretation must proceed in light of the demands teaching and learning about politics impose. It is not an introduction to a value-neutral discipline. Rather, it is a course or teaching that means to explore the question of the best life as it appears from the perspective of one particular horizon—that inhabited by ambitious young men of the ancient Greek city-state. It is my contention that a new Aristotle emerges if one reads the *Nicomachean Ethics* as a dialectical pedagogy; an Aristotle who is interested in informing the quest for a good life by prioritizing inquiry over answers. This is precisely what is required in a time of transition. Reading Aristotle in this way does not presuppose a longing to return to a lost golden age. Rather, he articulates virtue through a kind of negative path. He argues for virtues primarily by examining reputable opinions critically and discovering what virtue is not. Aristotelian dialectic moves from the reputable opinions his audience holds about the good life to a consideration of those opinions in order to see where and how they break down on their own terms. That is, Aristotelian dialectic operates within the horizon set by the audience's commitments and seeks to expose their paradoxes and contradictions. The failures of this perspective, however, do not end in nihilistic despair. Rather, the inquiry uncovers new opportunities for reflection about what could satisfy the human heart. Thus my account rests on the view that the Aristotle behind the *Ethics* is a teacher with a profound concern for the formation of his students, rather than a philosopher who is inquiring for the sake of inquiry alone.

Aristotle himself points out the difference between acting as a philosopher and acting as a teacher and dialectician in the *Topics.* The dialectician will not treat his audience in the same way as the philosopher. While the dialectician cares for his audience,

> the philosopher and the individual seeker do not care if, though his arguments are true and known, the answerer refuses to admit them because they are close to the starting point *(arche)* and he foresees what will result from his admission. (*T,* 155b11–17)

The concern for audience means that we must read the book with Aristotle's pedagogical strategies and intent in mind. His goal is not merely to articulate in a disinterested fashion conclusions about ethics or politics. Rather, it is to refashion his audience's sense of its interest. In a real sense, his goal is the conversion of his listener; the introduction of a new way of life, which affects every dimension of the human person. This way of life has to be described as a new mode of being. So unlike its modern counterparts, the *Ethics* is not addressed to everyone. Further, even though the work is apparently theoretical and systematic, its intention is not to inform the reader of a doctrinal content. Rather its practical intention is to make the reader traverse a certain path or itinerary which will encourage personal change.[8] This journey is intended to be formative and to produce a revolution in perspective. Its detours, stops, digressions, and new beginnings are all subordinated to the overarching practical, pedagogical intention of the work. For this reason, the point of the text is not—as with a modern textbook on ethics—to be as thorough or systematic as possible in outlining a set of principles of morality or a set of conclusions about the virtues. Rather, it is meant to provoke deeper reflection on one's life in order to effect change.

For Aristotle, philosophy is not a set of doctrines articulated by the wise, but a way of life. This way of life, in turn, consists in a continual struggle to diagnose and provide therapy so that people can lead healthier lives. Philosophical dialectic aims at producing this therapy, and so it is not merely a mode of argumentation but is a way of being:[9]

> It [philosophy] is a concrete attitude and determinate life-style, which engages the whole of existence. The philosophical act is not situated merely on the cognitive level, but on that of the self and being. It is a progress that causes us to be more fully and makes us better. It is a conversion, which turns our entire life upside-down, changing the life of the person who goes through it. It raises the individual from an inauthentic condition of life, darkened by unconsciousness and harassed by worry, to an authentic state of life, in which he attains self-consciousness, an exact vision of the world, inner peace, and freedom.[10]

Protreptic

The *Ethics* is a protreptic work aimed at inviting and initiating a particular audience into this new way of life.[11] For the ancients, protreptic was a presentation of the study of some practice, art, or skill. In the hands of the philosophers it became an exhortation to the practice of philosophy, which requires the excellences of inquiry and contemplation. This persuasion proceeded by taking into account competing claims, and in particular the claims that arose from the citizenship of the intended audience. The best protreptic not only meant to persuade, however, but also to engage the audience. In other words, a protreptic text argued for the excellences it meant to instill by providing an exemplary occasion for their practice. By engaging the protreptic work, the reader is actually doing philosophy and so is given a taste of the philosophic life.[12] Protreptic endured from the period of Plato's Academy into the High Middle Ages. Platonic dialogues make extensive use of protreptic. The myth of the cave in the *Republic* may well be a protreptic and soteriological myth.[13] Socrates' conversation with Clinias in the *Euthedymus* clearly employs protreptic devices (278e–283d). It has been argued that Socrates' conversation with Meno at the beginning of the dialogue is less an attempt to grapple with the so-called "Meno problem" than a protreptic device to encourage Meno to think with greater clarity.[14] The *Metaphysics* uses protreptic devices and Werner Jaeger argued forcefully for a similarity in the openings of the *Protrepticus* and the *Metaphysics.*[15] Lucretuis' *De rerum natura* employed protreptic.[16] Early and medieval Christian writers employed protreptic as well. Augustine was deeply influenced by Cicero's protreptic *Hortensius* and used it in his *De Magistro* and *De Beata Vita.* Later, Aquinas also employed protreptic in his *Summa Contra Gentiles* and his commentary on the Book of Job.[17] And of course, Aristotle wrote the *Protrepticus.* His *Protrepticus* was either a dialogue or a text that lent itself to being recast into dialogue form (as Cicero did with his *Hortensius*). It was a hortatory text that presented a defense of the philosophic life and was addressed to Themison, a ruler somewhere on the island of Cyprus.[18]

Several common themes can be identified in the genre. First, each protreptic text is aimed not at an indiscriminate public, but at a particular audience with a specific set of interests and viewpoints. When inviting and initiating apprentices into a practice, one must first discover how they initially view that practice, and what their initial skills, potential for receptivity, and perspectives are. Second, the protreptic proceeds dialectically. Each protreptic text engages the presuppositions and commitments of its audience in order to show them that their accounts fail on their own terms, and thus stand in need of something else to complete them. In Aristotle's case, that "something else" is philosophy. Philosophy is presented in the *Ethics* not as a set of contestable doctrines but as a determinate way of life that meets the human desires that have come to light as a result of the inquiry. Third, the goal of protreptic is not merely elucidation of a true account of morality. It does not aim at persuasion on the cognitive level or to convince people of the truth of a principle; nor does it aim at a kind of political persuasion as in rhetoric. Rather, the goal is always existential. Protreptic aims at what Plato calls *metanoia*, or a kind of conversion of the whole person to new ways of acting, perceiving, and thinking. In other words, the goal of the protreptic text is a comprehensive transformation to a radically new way of life. Fourth, in order to apprentice the pupil to this new way of life, the protreptic text must do several things at once. It must not merely persuade the audience of the attractiveness of the life it seeks to present. In addition, it must invite and initiate the audience into that life. The new life calls for new excellences and abilities. A difficult transition is required. The inculcation of new habits and perceptions will be obviously painful, and so protreptic makes liberal use of exhortations and initiations in order to help the pupil work past the suffering inherent in such a transition. The protreptic must make sure that the pupil tastes the attractiveness of the new way of life in order to overcome such obstacles. For instance, as we shall see, Aristotle's presentation of *theoria* at the end of the *Ethics* is an exhortation to that practice. Further, the pupil must be given a sense of the unique demands of the practices to which he or she is being called and how to acquire the excellences needed to live the new life or practice the new skill. In the end, the goal of the protreptic text is to make the teacher obsolete, and so the pupil must be initiated into a new life by engaging a text that points beyond itself to the way of life standing behind it. Fifth, protreptic texts have a common structure. The reader must be grabbed at the beginning and told why this text will make a difference in their lives. So protreptic is usually begun with an introduction exhorting the reader to recognize the importance of the inquiry. In the *Ethics*, for example, this is accomplished by emphasizing that the goal of the inquiry is to make people happy, a problem everyone is interested in. In turn, the protreptic moves from the opinions the audience has of the theme of the inquiry and dialectically examines them in order to achieve a better account. Sixth, the protreptic not only proceeds from the audience's initial loyalties. In addition, it works to undermine the audience's notion of the alternative way of life that will eventually be presented. Plato and Aristotle employed protreptic in order to argue for the superiority of the philosophic life to the political life. Yet at the outset, their audience has a more or less deficient understanding of what philosophy is. That false account of philosophy must be undermined in the course of the inquiry so that a better account can be presented at the end. Finally, the protreptic text is always incomplete. It does not aim at the comprehensiveness of a philosophic system. Rather, since its goal is to effect change, it ends by pointing to that life and exhorting its audience to search for it themselves. The protreptic will proceed and finally conclude by setting up a series of puzzlements. By engaging these puzzlements, the reader is led through curiosity to wonder. Answers given in philosophical protreptic will always yield more questions. In this way, the philosophical protreptic introduces pupils to the love of wisdom by showing them why and where they ought to look for it.

Thus Aristotle's *Ethics* is a protreptic pedagogy which dialectically invites and initiates its audience into a new mode of life. In this sense, the results of reading the text are one with the reading itself. Aristotle's practical intent is inextricably linked to his dialectical teaching method; indeed, they are one and the same. In reading the text, we follow along with a paradigmatic inquiry and are invited to bring it to bear on our own search for happiness. For this reason, we must struggle to read the *Ethics* as we would read a Platonic dialogue, noticing such things as audience, structure, apparent mistakes, and the different ways the same theme is treated at different points in the text. We have to especially seek to understand how each particular argument is subordinated to his overall pedagogical purpose.[19]

Dialectic: A Brief Overview

In order to effect this conversion, Aristotle employs dialectic (*NE*, 1095a30–32; 1145a15). Modern scholarship has repeatedly recognized the central place of dialectic in Aristotle's *Ethics.*[20] Dialectic in the *Nicomachean Ethics* has three interrelated components: audience, method, and goal. I will briefly explicate each in turn.

Audience

According to Aristotle, dialectic *(dialektikos)* differs from demonstration *(apodeixis)* by virtue of their different starting points *(archai)* (*T,* 100a27–30). According to the prevailing interpretive approach, Aristotle's texts are treatises, seeking to demonstrate a variety of conclusions. Inasmuch as they intend to convey an abstract doctrine to a disinterested observer, the texts are meant for everyone; that is, they are meant for no one in particular. Yet Aristotle insists that dialectical inquiries are directed to a particular group with particular commitments. For Aristotle, the starting point of dialectic is *endoxa*, which he repeatedly identifies in the *Topics* as "the opinions of everyone or most or the wise—that is, of all of the wise, or most of them, or of the most renowned and well-regarded of them" (*T,* 100b2–23; also 104a9ff; 104b3–5; 1.14 generally).

Thus the translation of *endoxa* as "common beliefs"[21] lacks precision. *"Endoxa"* means beliefs which are or ought to be held in high esteem; reputable opinions. Thus, dialectic is a mode of reasoning which proceeds from the most reputable beliefs about some subject and moves to new conclusions, all the while seeking to "sustain an account *(logos)* and avoid saying anything contradictory" (*T,* 100a18–21).

According to Aristotle, in order to proceed with a dialectical inquiry one must not merely find the right kinds of arguments to use and arrange them properly in one's mind; one must also address them to a particular audience with particular *endoxa* (see especially *T,* 155b7–10). In short, the dialectician must begin the inquiry with an audience's views of the best beliefs available about the subject matter at hand and proceed using arguments they can accept. Thus understanding Aristotle's audience and its perspective is crucial to understanding the substance of his dialectical inquiry in the *Nicomachean Ethics* and *Politics.*

How does Aristotle understand and employ the *endoxa* of an audience in his discussion of ethics and politics? One cannot simply turn to the *Topics*, Aristotle's explicit treatment of dialectic, to answer this question. In the *Topics*, Aristotle emphasizes that his goal is not to give a precise account of how dialectic works in different areas of inquiry. Rather, it is to provide an outline description of a variety of matters concerning dialectic in general (*T*, 101a18–24). Because his aim is to tell his readers "in a general fashion and in outline" what dialectic is and how it will proceed, the *Topics* does not tell the reader how to apply this general sketch of dialectic to particular disciplines.

There are at least two problems here that prevent us from straightforwardly using the general discussion of dialectic in the *Topics* to illuminate the audience of the *Ethics*. First, the *Topics* merely tells us that audience is important for every particular dialectical inquiry. Yet since its treatment of dialectic is general, it does not tell us what the audience's assumptions are in any particular inquiry undertaken. In other words, the *Topics* does not tell us who the audience of the *Ethics* is and what its assumptions are. In order to understand how opinions affect a particular dialectical inquiry, the *Topics* directs us to go beyond its general treatment to the particular inquiry in which dialectic will be employed. In other words, when we turn to the *Topics* to understand the problem of audience in the philosophy of human affairs, Aristotle informs us of the crucial importance of audience, then directs us back to the *Ethics*. Second, the *Topics* does not tell us how a dialectical inquiry would operate on the audience involved in a particular subject. In order to understand the impact an audience's opinions have in a particular inquiry, the reader would have to understand how the dialectical method sketched in the *Topics* operates on a specific audience in particular kinds of discussions.

The Method of Dialectic

Dialectical inquiry begins with the reputable opinions of an audience, but how does it proceed? In brief, Aristotle tells us in the *Topics* that the method of dialectic is that which will produce the kind of assent demanded by the particular inquiry the participants are engaged in. For instance, the goal of winning a contentious argument will entail dialectical methods that differ substantially from those employed by a teacher concerned with formulating arguments that redound to the good of his or her pupils. For this reason, the mode of dialectic must be understood as subordinated to the concerns of the audience in several respects. The motivation of the audience will matter for the way the argument proceeds. In the *Ethics*, Aristotle engages in dialectic for the sake of teaching, not winning contentious argument. Thus the dialectical arguments he chooses to use must be understood as chosen for the sake of the good of his students. They must not be interpreted as the best arguments available to achieve philosophic truth for an indeterminate audience. Rather, each argument in the *Ethics* must be interpreted with Aristotle's pedagogical intent in mind.

A related point is that specific audiences are predisposed to accepting certain kinds of arguments. This means that in reading a dialectical inquiry, one must take care to distinguish the best argument available simply from the argument that will work to produce the kind of assent at which the inquiry aims. In proceeding dialectically, Aristotle may not be using the best arguments available. Rather, he may well be using arguments that reputable opinion readily accepts in order to achieve the kind of assent at which he aims.

According to the *Topics*, the dialectician must use what may be called "reputable arguments." or arguments that will allow his audience to achieve the kind of assent at which the inquiry aims. He calls these reputable arguments *topoi*.[22] The bulk of the *Topics* is devoted to setting forth *topoi*, and the point is to supply to the dialectician a vast array of arguments that will be useful to procure the kind of agreement desired in specific discussions. These *topoi* produce assent because the audience's perspective disposes them to accept their force before the fact.

At the opening of the *Topics*, Aristotle gives an indication as to why a dialectical inquiry must rely on reputable arguments that will be accepted:

> We will have the [dialectical] method in its completeness when we are in a position similar to that of rhetoric and medicine and other such powers. That is, when we carry out our purposes with all available means. For the orator will not seek to persuade and the doctor will not seek to heal by using every means. Yet if they omit none of the available means we will say they are in possession of their science. (*T*, 101b5–10)

Understanding the implications of this passage entails cashing out the distinction between "available means" and "every means." For example, a physician serving a remote, impoverished village suffering under a plague is not a good doctor if she sits around wringing her hands and wishing she had access to a recently developed but unavailable cure. This is wishing to cure by "every means." She forsakes her task if she pines for "every means" rather than treating her patients with all "available means." Similarly, an orator seeking to persuade will not use the best arguments simply, but rather the arguments available that will have the desired effect on the particular audience in front of her. Sometimes the best argument available is not necessarily as persuasive as a commonplace argument because of the views, prejudices, or limits of a particular audience. For instance, a politician seeking to persuade a group of senior citizens of the wisdom of a tax hike on their Social Security benefits may not be able to resort to an argument from justice or the common good. Rather, she may have to exploit fears of intergenerational hostility, arguing in effect that if the seniors do not accept a moderate tax now, they risk a more severe penalty later on. In a like manner, Aristotle says that the dialectician will not necessarily use the best arguments available simply to persuade. He says that the goal of dialectic is to establish agreement between discussants about some problem arising from reputable opinion. He distinguishes the philosopher who seeks truth and who does not care if the partner in a discussion accepts conclusions from good premises and arguments from the dialectician whose guiding purpose is to establish agreement and so cares deeply that at each point in the inquiry the audience agrees with the conclusion (see *T*, 155b7–17).

Because the goal of dialectical inquiry is to establish agreement, the dialectician will not necessarily use an argument that a philosopher would use when inquiring into a problem in the most extensive, comprehensive way possible. The goal of a philosophical investigation is the disinterested discovery of the truth of the matter to the satisfaction of the philosopher. Yet the goal of the dialectician is different; in the case of the *Ethics*, it is to convince the audience to change their lives. While philosophical arguments may well be the best simply, they are not the best for the quite different purposes of a dialectical discussion. Since the goal is to establish agreement, the honest participant in a dialectical discussion will employ arguments that reach the kind of agreement desired.

The fact that Aristotle's dialectical method necessitates proceeding with the *topoi* that will produce the desired agreement has large implications for how we are to read the *Nicomachean Ethics.* Not every opinion Aristotle sets forth is his own; many will be *endoxa* that provide starting points for inquiries. Similarly, not every argument Aristotle presents is the best argument available simply. Rather, he proceeds by using reputable arguments that will move the inquiry along to its desired goal: the kind of agreement appropriate for his particular audience engaging in this particular kind of inquiry. Arguments that seem to be faulty may be intended to produce agreement.

The Goal of Dialectic

If Aristotle is using arguments that work to produce assent from a particular audience, what is to prevent us from understanding this process in an utterly cynical way? How do we know that Aristotle is not manipulating his audience in the dialectic inquiry, in effect using his skill in employing reputable argument to coerce rather than persuade? After all, dialectic as presented above seems to have much in common with rhetoric as Aristotle understands it. Rhetoric, too, begins with the perspective of an audience (though rhetoric begins from the perspective of emotions and passions, not from *endoxa*). Further, rhetoric as Aristotle understands it has as its goal a political effect—to change the minds of an audience—and Aristotle's treatment of rhetoric is notorious for the argument that it can be used to produce a variety of effects, some good and others bad.[23]

As I have pointed out, in the *Topics* Aristotle emphasizes that dialectical argument can have several different possible goals. Sometimes the aim of the participants is to win a competition—to prove their superiority through argument. However, he says that this aim differs from the aim of teachers and students participating in a dialectical inquiry. In the former case, the point is not to win a competition, and the goal of the discussants will decisively affect the character of the entire inquiry. In a competition, for example, the interlocutors may hide their intentions and what they really think on a topic in order to win. However, in a teacher-pupil relationship, the learner must always state what he thinks, and the teacher must not be concerned with winning an argument, but rather with teaching what is true—for one never, Aristotle asserts, "even attempts to teach what is false" (*T,* 159a30).

In the *Ethics* Aristotle is not concerned with winning an argument. Rather, his point is to make his audience good (e.g., *NE,* 1094b11). Thus the dialectical discussion must be understood as motivated by a concern for the good of the student. The inquiry is a cooperative endeavor in which the point is not to gain mastery. The discussion is directed to helping the students acquire what they need to acquire in order to become happy. The goal of the inquiry is not to achieve a victory for philosophy or for the philosopher over the city, and the procedure is not reducible to rhetoric, which aims at convincing people to follow someone else's proposed course of action. The goal is not imposed from the outside, but from the desires of the students themselves: "Let me see if I can help you achieve what you already want." If Aristotle's inquiry is successful, at its completion students will be presented with an account of a way of life that they desired all along. In this sense,

> What is needed is *persuasion,* and for that one must use psychagogy—the seduction of souls. Even at that, it is not enough to use only rhetoric, which, as it were, tries to persuade from a distance, by means of a continuous discourse. What is needed above all is dialectic, which demands the explicit consent of the interlocutor at every moment. Dialectic must choose a tortuous path—or rather, a series of apparently divergent, but nevertheless convergent paths—in order to bring the interlocutor to discover the contradictions of his own position, or admit an unforseen conclusion.[24]

Aristotelian dialectic is prevented from degenerating into power games by having in view the truth of right action and the good of the audience. The goal of helping the student act in the presence of this truth is precisely what prevents the inquiry from degenerating into manipulative rhetoric. The point is that Aristotle's inquiry is guided by a moral purpose.

One way of making this point is to distinguish dialectic from sophistry. Both dialectic and sophistry operate by a process of distinction and division. For Aristotle, sophists distinguish falsely for their own purposes, while the dialectician distinguishes for the good of the students. The sophist resembles the dialectician. Even when a philosopher acting as a dialectician attempts to clarify a matter that has been confused and abused by sophistry, that does not put an end to the potential abuse of argument. The reason is that such abuse is a "moral matter,"[25] and so correcting the abuse entails not merely a process of clarification or correction, but of persuasion to adopt a different way of life that will enable the individual to see why such abuse ought not to be tolerated. As Gadamer argues,

> As a matter of fact, the connection between the logical and ethical aspects of true dialectic runs through the whole of Plato's work. And even Aristotle confirms this correlation when he finds the difference between sophistry and philosophy to be purely the *prohairesis tou bious* (choice of life [one leads]) (*Metaphysics,* 1004b24; *Sophistical Refutations,* 169b24, 171b8).[26]

The goal of dialectic is thus potentially radical. In the *Topics* Aristotle says that the goal is to "sustain an account *(logos)* and avoid saying anything contradictory" (*T,* 100 18–21). The task of dialectic is to uncover the contradictions hidden in reputable beliefs in order to move to better accounts. Since, as we shall see, all regimes for Aristotle are more or less defective and exhibit a partial sense of human excellence, all regimes possess internal contradictions at their heart. Dialectical argument reveals these contradictions in order to show how and why that regime's notion of human flourishing is incomplete. The failure of these notions of life clear the way for new conceptions of human flourishing.

Aristotle's conception of the goal of dialectic differs from the way it is understood today by several prominent Aristotelians. By some accounts, Aristotelian dialectic aims not at transformation of people's lives, but rather at a kind of values clarification. Nussbaum gives a good characterization of this view of the goal of dialectic:

> It [Aristotelian dialectic] holds that ethical theorizing proceeds by way of a reflective dialogue between the intuitions and beliefs of the interlocutor, or reader, and a series of complex ethical conceptions, presented for exploration.

> (This series, as Aristotle puts it, should ideally include the views of both "the many" and "the wise.") Such an inquiry cannot get started without readers or interlocutors who are already brought up as people of a certain sort. Its aim is to arrive at an account of the values and judgements of people who already have definite attachments and intuitions; these must, ultimately, be the material of the inquiry. And yet this does not mean that the outcome of the inquiry will be a mere repetition of the account of his or her view that the reader would have given at the start. For, as Aristotle stresses, . . . most people, when asked to generalize, make claims that are false to the complexity and the content of their actual beliefs. They need to learn what they really think. When, through work on the alternatives and through dialogue with one another, they arrive at a harmonious adjustment of their beliefs, both singly and in community with one another, this will be the ethical truth, on the Aristotelian understanding of truth: a truth that is anthropocentric, but not relativistic. (In practice the search for truth is rarely complete or thorough enough; so that the resulting view will be the best current candidate for truth).[27]

On Nussbaum's account, Aristotle's dialectical method uncovers the complexity of conventional accounts. His method not only begins with what we already think, but ends by clarifying what we already think. For Nussbaum, this is what Aristotle means when he says that his efforts are directed to "saving the appearances."[28] Yet if there is no way of moving beyond common belief; if the point of dialectic is not to engender conversion, but to make our own commitments more explicit in their texture and complexity, then dialectic is in slavery to its parent culture. Yet if so, then dialectic can be used by the strong to dominate the weak. It can, in effect, be used to bolster tradition to the detriment of those suffering under it.

However, this characterization of the method and goal of Aristotelian dialectic departs from what Aristotle says he will do in the *Ethics*. He does not say that his goal is merely to clarify and deepen common opinion. He says it has the much more radical goal of making us good. Appealing to such a standard entails making a potentially countervailing stance against any particular society's norms. The point, he says, is not merely to reflect our conventions and make them more intelligible or logically consistent, or even more in keeping with the best is in our commitments. Rather, the point is to change—perhaps radically—the way we live.

The goals of Aristotelian dialectic are much more robust and much more radical than Nussbaum allows. Aristotle will "save the appearances" not merely by helping us to clarify what we already think. Rather, his dialectical inquiry proceeds by producing the conviction that our usual ways of acting and perceiving are inadequate if our goal is to achieve a deeply satisfying way of life. The failures of our usual ways of acting and perceiving can point the way to more flourishing modes of being. The starting points of reputable opinion are not merely cast aside, but they are revealed to be inadequate to meet our deepest desires. On Nussbaum's account, Aristotle's method is conventionalist: there seems to be no way of transcending the blind spots our society's norms impose. Dialectic removes some and makes us more humane, but that is all. One wonders whether such conventional limits to the inquiry might blind us to the challenges Aristotle presents to conventionally respectable ways of life.

Further, given the way Aristotle's method proceeds, as we shall see, it is unfair to characterize it as some idealistic and therefore potentially smug and tyrannical attempt to justify a retreat to a secure Archimedean point outside of human experience and values. Rather, his method seeks a richer vision of human experience by taking our own commitments seriously, and inquiring into what they imply about the human condition. In short, Aristotle begins with our own reputable accounts of happiness and the accounts of happiness implicit in our actions. He then proceeds to criticize dialectically these accounts, arguing that the way we act and understand those actions is insufficient to get us what we wanted. Reputable notions of happiness break down, and these failures illuminate and thus advance a renewed search for satisfaction of desire. By understanding the ways we fail to achieve happiness through conventional ways of perceiving and acting, we may come to taste new modes of action that will make us happier.

This reading will uncover an Aristotle who skirts the charge that his virtue ethics leaves no room for social criticism.[29] On the contrary, Aristotelian dialectic proceeds by at once demanding the criticism of existing conventional opinion and practices, while at the same time exhibiting a deep care for the flourishing of the participants is in the discussion. The goal is to engender perhaps radically new ways of perceiving the world and acting within it.

PART I
The Audience

1

The Political Character of Aristotle's Pedagogy

Formation and Regimes

Aristotle wants to make his audience good. He says repeatedly that his goal is not to help us know the good, but rather to do it (*NE,* 1094b11; 1095a4–6; 1103b26–30; 1179b1–4; cf. 1194a22–23). Moreover, the range of topics he discusses in the *Nicomachean Ethics* and *Politics*—from moral and intellectual virtue, to training in music and gymnastics, and so on—makes it clear it is clear that he is aiming at a comprehensive formation of the whole person.[1] His goal demands a revolution in perspective and assumes a commitment of every dimension of our being.

However, a problem immediately intrudes. One of Aristotle's guiding insights is that every context is powerfully formative. If his goal is to change our minds about what is in our interest, he must first deal with the fact that our minds are already made up on this score. If Aristotle wants to form us, he must begin from the fact that our regime forms us first, affecting our tastes, habits, sense of justice, and who and what we look up to and emulate both as individuals and as a people. This is why Aristotle speaks not merely of politics and political things, but of regime *(politeia).* As Paul Rahe has pointed out,

> Though much may separate Plato from Aristotle, on this fundamental point they were agreed: to understand the ancient Greek *polis,* one must be willing to entertain two propositions—that the political regime *(politeia),* rather than economic or environmental conditions, is the chief deter-

> minant of what one acute, ancient observer called "the one way of life of a whole *polis*" and another dubbed "the city's soul" and that education in the broadest and most comprehensive sense *(paideia)* is more important than anything else in deciding the character of the regime.[2]

A regime for Aristotle is not merely an arrangement of political offices, or a formal legal order. While it includes offices (e.g., *P*, 3.6), and while understanding law is crucial for understanding regime, Aristotle emphasizes that these structures serve to foster or promote the end of the political organization and the society as a whole; they seek to inculcate a way of life.[3] In classical political philosophy, law *(nomos)* carries the sense both of a legal code and of unwritten rules of conduct which constitute a people's ethos. But in both senses, law is the institutionalized judgement of a community about what pleasures, pains, and activities are proper and improper (*Republic*, 636d–e, 637d, 659d). In this way law is subordinate to regime because the law follows the interests of the group which rules the regime (*P*, 1281a36; 1282b5–10; 1289a13–25, 1289a20–25; 1300a4). As one excellent study in ancient law puts it,

> [L]aw . . . is not some impersonal truth-finding mechanism which "evolves" to produce "justice" from the chaos of dispute. Though the ideology of the law typically portrays it as unchanging from time immemorial and "blind" in its judgements, legal systems are the continuing creation of human beings with various, shifting, and contradictory motivations and interests, motivations and interests which range from settling disputes to exacerbating them, from using the law as an instrument of social justice to honing it as a weapon of oppression, from making peace with one's enemies to annihilating them with the help of legal institutions. Law, rather than operating in a wholly separate realm, is enmeshed in the social sphere.[4]

Aristotle thinks that politics is architectonic because it aims at fostering and protecting a way of life. In doing so the regime decisively affects every aspect of human life, including —whether we are aware of it or not—our own comprehensive individual formation (*NE*, 1141b21; 1141b24–28; *P*, 1252a1–8;

1260a17–19). In architecture, for example, the various subcontractors and craftsmen take their cue from the architect, who decides the shape and function of the various parts of the building. The subcontractor responsible for installing air ducts has his work decisively affected by the architect's plans. The lighting subcontractor must conform her design to the architect's parameters. In a similar way, Aristotle thinks that the regime manages the overall shape and direction of the constituent parts of the political community because its participants are always acting on some conception of what is good when they pass laws or engage in typically respectable practices. Thus, for example, politics determines the kinds of science practiced, the kinds of arts permitted and encouraged, what sort of education citizens receive, and so on (*NE,* 1093a271094b10).[5]

For Aristotle, human beings aim at what appears to be good. And what appears to be good results from the way our characters have been formed (*NE,* 1114a28). Aristotle argues that we are only partly responsible for our own character (*NE,* 1114a29; 1114b22). To become good, human beings need teaching, habituation, and nature (*NE,* 10.9). The problem is that these are beyond our control. We have no control over our natural endowments given at birth. Moreover, our habits and tastes are formed not only by ourselves, but also by a host of factors mediated by our regime. According to Aristotle, while human beings require the formation our regimes provide, most regimes deform in the process of forming. All actual regimes are defective because the ruling element in each foists its own interests on everyone else and calls that "justice" (e.g., *P,* 1301a37–40 and generally 5.1; 3.9; 3.12). In fact, Aristotle thinks that most human beings identify political rule with the kind of rule masters exercise over slaves (*P,* 1252a7–9 1324b32–33). It follows that for Aristotle, most human beings are not virtuous (*NE,* 1150a15–16), precisely because we have been formed by the habits, customs, and laws of regimes that are more or less defective (*NE,* 1796b16–20).

Yet while our formation is by and large defective, it is also necessary. Nature has underdetermined us. More than any other animal, human beings desire and act as a result of habituation and reflection, rather than mere inherited instincts. In contrast to other animals, human beings can live in a thoughtful way that involves a deliberate choice of goals. However the actualization of these uniquely human qualities requires massive socialization.[6] For example, our socialization allow us to discover through deliberation the kinds of goals in terms of which we can organize and interpret our actions and our lives. So we need other human beings even in order to strive to develop some conception of what human beings should strive to be and do. So we are not in control of our formation, and thus not in control of our own tastes, habits, and characters. We require an education we cannot supply. Aristotle thinks the laws under which we live have an especially powerful formative effect, since he believes that most human beings are motivated partly by fear of punishment, and thus require some minimal amount of coercion in order to be socialized (*NE,* 1180a4–5).

If Aristotle is to help his audience become good, he has to confront this problem of prior deformation. Part of his goal is to argue for the defective character of our own formation so that we will be naturally led to question whether what we take to be good for us is really so. And the pedagogical problem that arises at this point is that one cannot make more or less defective human beings better simply through the dissemination of lawlike generalizations about right conduct. If our regime has decisively deformed our habits and tastes, we may not be competent judges of our own interests. So Aristotle must embark on a pedagogical strategy that begins from the horizons of his listeners and seeks both to undermine their own culture's conception of goodness as it works to a fuller conception of human excellence. All this is to say that Aristotle seeks to cultivate in his students a zetetic, critical stance toward their own regime. He questions the respectable opinions and practices of a particular tradition in order to cultivate the kind of questioning that can make his students better.

The Political Dimensions of the Pedagogy

The final chapter of the *Nicomachean Ethics* tells us how Aristotle responds to the problem of prior deformation. He argues that his project is not finished. His goal is not to engender knowledge but action (*NE,* 1179b1–4). The *Ethics* has been speech *(logos)* about right action, but speech is not enough. While it can urge some forward to virtue, most people are swayed neither by love of what is fair, nor by a sense of shame, but rather by fear of punishment. For this reason Aristotle concludes that he cannot convince many people of the attractiveness of virtue because most have not tasted the pleasure that comes from virtue. They are not familiar with virtue, and so have a hard time understanding what is really pleasant and fair (*NE,* 1179b15–16). These people require socialization through law.

Thus the *Ethics* has a political dimension because Aristotle thinks that any attempt to inquire into ethics must take into account the way people's characters have been (de)formed by their regime. The inquiry is political not only because of its subject matter, or object. In addition, it has a political character because the effort to make people good is inseparable from a countervailing resistance to the deformation visited upon them by their regime. The *Ethics* is a semipublic act of persuasion aimed at reforming personal and social life through the reorientation of Aristotle's students.

This countervailing thrust is not necessarily destructive of regimes. Indeed, it may be required to preserve them. The most obvious result of every regime's partial justice and deformation is civil strife *(stasis),* a persistent problem of Greek political life. A guiding question of Plato and those who more or less followed his legacy was how to reform political life (*Seventh Letter,* 326d3–6; 326a2–b4) so as to minimize this strife. Whatever his substantive disagreements with Plato, Aristotle remains sympathetic to this project. And this project requires that educative efforts produce a formation directed to developing people's critical capacity to judge rightly amid the deformation all regimes foster.[7]

Some have suggested that the *Ethics* has a political character because the object of the inquiry is to form statesmen who can achieve political reform.[8] But for Aristotle, political reform depends on having a critical attitude that will allow the statesmen to judge their regime, so that they can bend it toward excellence. Indeed, the substance of much of Aristotle's recommendations to preserve regimes is directed to making defective regimes more decent so as to avoid civil strife.[9] Thus an Aristotelian statesman's task is twofold. First, it is to form their citizens in accord with the way of life of the particular regime to which they belong. Second, it is to attempt to develop the critical capacity necessary to correct the defects of one's regime with due regard for the limits of reform, so as to bring one's regime and thus one's citizens closer to virtue.[10]

Yet the political character of the inquiry is not limited to enabling its audience to engage in politics. Even in order to develop the critical capacity needed to reform politics, one needs to address the problem of prior deformation. Aristotle thinks that while all cities form human beings decisively, most do not think about the problem of formation. He states that only in Sparta and a few other cities have lawmakers reflected on this problem; in most it is neglected and each lives as he wishes, in the style of the Cyclopes (*NE,* 1180a24–29). Aristotle's famous reservations about Sparta in the *Politics* (2.9) force us to realize that for him, in the only places where formation is attended to, it is done so badly. The same is true of households. Aristotle emphasizes that fathers generally pay no more attention to the formation of their loved ones than statesmen do to citizens. Indeed, Aristotle compares most fathers to the cannibalistic Cyclopes who lay down the law in their homes and think that is enough (*NE,* 1180a24–29).

It is only after a sobering discussion of the ways regimes and the households within them fail to form rightly that Aristotle explains fully the political character of his inquiry. Since laws are essential for us to become good, the accounts given in the *Ethics* are not enough. The *Ethics* must be succeeded by a *Politics* that will take up the question of legislation. For this reason, Aristotle says, "Our next task is to consider from what source *(pothen)* and how *(pos)* we can become practitioners of the lawmaking art *(nomothetikos)*" (*NE,* 1180b28–29). Due to widespread misunderstanding, we should be clear about this sentence. The traditional account of this passage glides over the distinction between learning what the art of lawmaking is and learning where and how to learn it. Consequently, most scholars assume that Aristotle in this passage means that he is going to speak simply about what legislation is in the *Politics.*[11] Indeed, this passage baffles many interpreters, since they say it promises a discussion of legislation that never appears in the *Politics.* Yet Aristotle never says he will discuss legislation in the *Politics.* Rather, he says his task is to inquire where and how to learn about it. Why?

The point of the inquiry is not to become good legislators. Rather, Aristotle says it is to study these questions so that "each one will be better capable of attaining virtue and leading loved ones to virtue" (*NE,* 1180a33–34). This is a reiteration of his earlier point that one who wishes "to make people better through his care, *whether many or few,* must attempt to become expert in the lawmaking art" (*NE,* 1180b23, my emphasis). We might be tempted to read these passages as a recommendation to know the art of lawmaking so that decent politicians will be able to enforce their will through law in order to make people good. But a fuller reading would pay attention to what immediately came before. Most states do not care about formation, and in the only states where it is an explicit question, that question is resolved badly. Moreover, most households are unreflective about the problems formation within a regime presents. That is, most people do not reflect on the political dimensions of the problem of formation within their households. Rather, they unreflectively lay down the law without adequately taking into account the ways the regime helps determine the structure of the home and the habits of the individuals within it.

Since human beings tend to be unreflective about the ways we have been deformed, we tend to self-righteousness by overestimating our own capacity for virtue. Yet if most of us are deformed more or less by defective regimes, our first task would be to be on guard lest we identify our own narrow interests with justice or the common good simply. Merely grabbing power and forcing society to do the right thing is not sufficient. The problem is that most societies, and thus most individuals, have a skewed understanding of "the right thing" and this makes reform from above very difficult, and perhaps even dangerous. Most of us have been deformed more or less by our regimes, and so have a hard time differentiating our own interests from the "right thing." So from Aristotle's perspective, political reformers can mistake their partisan interest with the good of society. Moreover, even if the reformer is correct, the defective formation of the larger regime entails that he or she cannot hope that decrees from above can resolve the fact that many will not see the sense in reforming policies.

So the main reason for learning the art of lawmaking is not to grab the reigns of power. Rather, it is to enable us to become more reflective about how the regime's laws deform us in order to help ourselves and our loved ones to resist that deformation more successfully. Only by achieving a sense of the way we have been deformed by our surrounding culture can we achieve some measure of thoughtfulness and genuine direction of our character. That is, since politics forms us decisively, knowledge of politics is necessary to bring us a bit closer to genuine human excellence. Admittedly this process has strict limits because the household —or indeed any community with the regime—is not self-sufficient. Because our communities rely on the larger regime for resources and protection, one cannot hope to simply withdraw from political life. And our inevitable lack of self-sufficiency entails that we cannot opt out of the fact that we require prior formation. The only thing to do, therefore, is to become more thoughtful about the realities of our own regime's assumptions and how these affect our lives.

Thus Aristotle's task is not merely to teach how to do politics. Since formation takes place within an overarching political context, in order to know how to form ourselves and our loved ones properly, we must know something about politics as a whole. In this politics differs from other human activities. For example, a bricklayer need not know anything comprehensive about architecture to do his job; in this case, knowledge of the part does not necessitate knowledge of the whole. Yet the architectonic character of politics means that knowledge of the part necessitates knowledge of the whole. Our roles as mothers or fathers or accountants or members of this or that religious community are so decisively affected by our larger regime that even in order to do these tasks well, we needs to know something about that regime. Aristotle says that we ought to give more attention to our loved ones than to our inanimate possessions, and that this attention should manifest itself above all in the inculcation of virtue (*P*, 1259b18–19). Knowledge of how to form oneself and one's loved ones on a personal level requires comprehensive knowledge of politics, because the regime is the overarching context which decisively affects each part of the city, such as households, trades, and economic life. In particular, it requires a knowledge of how law operates to subtly form and deform citizens. To resist the deformation of one's own regime, one must have as one's goal the inculcation of virtue, and in order to know how to do this, one must be acquainted with the realities of politics.

The political character of the pedagogy demands that Aristotle begin from within the horizon set by his audience's political regime. His task is to articulate that perspective so that he can then dialectically engage it. Since the audience's perspective has been decisively formed by the regime, it simply does no good merely to present an alternative view. Aristotle's reflections on formation imply that this kind of moralism is insufficient. To make his audience good, he must begin from his audience's assumptions about a successful life. He must undermine those assumptions from within, showing his students exactly why and how they break down so as to give them a vision of a new way of life. In short, he must engage in a dialectical pedagogy which pays strict attention to his audience's perspective. Further, if Aristotle is to engender a change in attitude toward virtue, some tangible motive that the audience will be attracted to must be given to them. In other words, to be successful in engendering a conversion to a new way of life, the dialectician must operate within the horizons set by his audience's *endoxa*, and show why it is in their interest to abandon their old life, with its concomitant conception of excellence, and take up a new life, with a new conception of virtue. For these reasons, we must now try to understand the perspective of Aristotle's audience.

2

The Audience of the *Nicomachean Ethics*

The Problem of Audience

In the *Nicomachean Ethics* Aristotle emphasizes his concern with the "listener" and investigates the requirements of being a participant in the inquiry (e.g., *NE,* 1.3; 1095a2; 1179b25).[1] He begins the inquiry not by postulating an overarching conception of the human good or human nature derived from metaphysics or biology. Neither does he speculate on a state of nature that drives us to set up particular social structures. Rather, he begins by asking whether his audience's way of life will get them what they most deeply want. His task is to proceed from the perspective of a particular audience—to begin with "what appears" to them (*NE,* 1095a31–b5)—and to inform that perspective with his inquiry to persuade them to become good (*NE,* 1094a26–b11; 1094b7–8; cf. *T,* 100a18–27; 100a27–30; 104a9ff; 155b7–10; *PA,* 72a25ff). For these reasons, understanding Aristotle's audience and its perspective is crucial to understanding his pedagogy. A good teacher always proceeds from the commitments of his or her audience. What were Aristotle's?

The Straussians have been the only group of scholars who have investigated this question systematically. Leo Strauss argues that Aristotle's audience is comprised of "perfect gentlemen" who uncritically accept the goodness of moral virtue and need education partly to clarify the demands of virtue and partly to show them that the limits of morality point to it.[2]

> According to Aristotle it is moral virtue that supplies the sound principles of action, the just and the noble ends, as

> actually desired; these ends come to sight only to the morally good man; prudence seeks the means to these ends. The morally good man is the properly bred man. Aristotle's political science is addressed only to such men. The sphere of prudence is then closed by principles which are fully evident only to gentlemen. In seeking for higher principles, one would raise the question, "why should one be decent?" but in doing so one would have already ceased to be a gentleman, for decency is meant to be choiceworthy for its own sake.[3]

Aristide Tessitore advanced Strauss's argument by arguing that the *Ethics* has not one but two distinct audiences. On his account, Aristotle employs rhetoric in the *Ethics* to present the philosophic life in a way that at once obscures its real character for the virtuous, politically active gentleman and illuminates its real character for the potential philosopher. On the one hand, Tessitore argues that Aristotle is writing for the potential philosopher, to give him or her some taste of the radical requirements of a life of philosophy. On the other hand, Tessitore argues that the *Ethics* is addressed to "gentlemen" who are ill disposed to philosophy but well disposed to virtue.[4] Aristotle's rhetorical presentation both obscures and illuminates for these gentlemen. It illuminates the requirements of morality and the political life, and thus seeks to improve them. At the same time, it obscures the radical character of philosophy, presenting instead a "domesticated" version that "gentlemen" can tolerate.[5] For Tessitore, this intentional obfuscation explains the apparent inconsistencies in Aristotle's account of the relation of politics to philosophy that have baffled so many readers.

There seems to be good textual evidence for the claim that the audience of the *Ethics* was fully committed to virtue. Aristotle says that in order to listen to his arguments, his audience must have been brought up nobly *(kalos)* in their habits (*NE*, 1095b4–8). He says that he will begin from this starting point, and if one accepts this starting point there is no reason to ask why one should start there rather than someplace else (*NE*, 1095b6–9). Yet the treatment of the audience's commitments that immediately follows this passage should lead us to ask whether their "noble habits" are coextensive with moral virtue. When Aristotle outlines what the audience finds attractive, he does not mention a love of virtue, but rather a commitment to noble action. While this love of noble action may have led some to value moral virtue, it led others to value power and mastery. Nietzsche, a great student of the classics, captured the character of this life in his description of early nobility, with its emphasis on beauty, physicality, life, and competition: "The knightly-aristocratic value judgements presupposed a powerful physicality, a flourishing, abundant, even overflowing health, together with that which serves to preserve it: war, adventure, hunting, dancing, war games, and in general all that involves free, joyful activity."[6] Nobility does not connote what we take to mean by "moral virtue"; rather it entails a shining vitality that demands recognition by others. And this drive for distinction can lead to mastery through self-assertive claims to superiority. Aristotle first seeks common ground with his audience by making explicit this commitment to noble action. He then links their drive to noble action to their desire for honor. Finally, he links the desire for honor to a desire for virtue.

Where the Action Is

Aristotle says that three ways of life are most "notable," and each implies a different set of goods to be pursued because they are productive of, or identified with, happiness: the life of pleasure, the political life and the contemplative life (*NE,* 1.5). Aristotle dismisses both the life of pleasure and the contemplative life without argument. By far, he spends the most energy on the life of "refined and practical people" who are active in politics. Such people want to engage in noble actions and seek praise for them. They are ambitious for political rule, since this seems to be the best way to achieve what they want (cf. *P,* 1324a25–1325a23; 1325a32–b11; 1325b14–23). Aristotle does not say that such people want virtue. Indeed, they dismiss virtue because it does not seem to produce enough activity to make them happy (*NE,* 1095b31–1096a3). So part of Aristotle's audience consists of politically active people whose upbringing leads them to valorize honorable actions and political power rather than virtue, self-indulgence, or contemplation (*NE,* 1095b19–22).

In subsequent chapters Aristotle employs a pedagogical strategy that makes explicit and develops his audience's attraction to a life of noble action. In these opening chapters Aristotle seeks a common starting point with his audience in this attraction. The argument proceeds in several stages that build on each other. First, Aristotle criticizes the Platonic notion of the Form of the Good as useless for action (*NE,* 1.6). Second, he develops the function argument, which emphasizes specifically human forms of action as the way to happiness (*NE,* 1.7). Third, he employs the language developed in these sections to articulate his audience's strong attraction to a life of action (*NE,* 1.8). Several of these arguments have been the subject of philosophical criticism, particularly the argument from function. Yet what is at stake is not the philosophical cogency of the accounts. Dialectic, recall, proceeds on the basis of the best available arguments, not the best arguments simply. These opening arguments have a pedagogical intent, and do their job if the audience accepts them and they move the inquiry forward profitably. The effect of these various arguments is to articulate and affirm his audience's commitments as a basis for the discussion as well as to invite them to do battle for the truth.

Criticizing Platonism

Aristotle's criticism of the "universal good" (*NE,* 1096a11) has the pedagogical effect of articulating and heightening the audience's commitment to action over thought. The problem the Platonists try to resolve by positing a Form of the Good is that human beings employ the term "good" in a variety of diverse contexts. So we make statements like, "Michael Jordan is a good basketball player." "Albert Einstein was a good physicist." "John is a good concrete subcontractor." "Andrea is a good doctor." These various practices are quite different. The excellences required of a good doctor differ substantially from those required of a good concrete subcontractor or a good theoretical physicist. Yet we use the same term to describe the attainment of excellence in these different practices. On first glance there seems to be no common sense of the term "good" that could encompass all these activities. It is not clear whether "good" is a univocal, equivocal, or analogical term. And this has large implications for the way we understand human action. If the term "good" is employed arbitrarily or simply has no meaning, how are we to relate our desires for goods to one another and indeed the structure of the universe? The answer

Platonists give to this dilemma is to posit the existence of a realm of Forms, which include the Form of the Good (*NE,* 1095a26–28; *EE,* 1217b2–16). Human beings apply the term "good" in diverse contexts because a practice or thing is good to the extent that it participates in the single, eternal Form of the Good.

Aristotle's various criticisms of this are well known and I need not recapitulate them here. Yet given the pedagogical character of the *Ethics*, these criticisms must be seen in light of their effect on the audience. The upshot of Aristotle's critique is that knowledge of the universal good is useless to action. When John engages the actions that make him a good subcontractor (when he deliberates about what mixture to employ on what kind of day, or when he uses his skills to pour, level, smooth, and finish the surface of a basement) he does not need a prior knowledge of the Form of the Good. Similarly, a good pitcher does not require a science of the Good. Rather, he needs practical knowledge as to whether it is best to pick this runner off here and now, or what kind of pitch to throw at this hitter; or how to grip and throw the ball for a slider. Aristotle concludes that the kind of knowledge that Platonists are speaking about is useless if one's task is to be good in particular ways. The Platonist assumption is that the Good is "out there" and must be acquired or participated in somehow to become happy. Aristotle's criticism is not merely that this is not how we understand good (*NE,* 1096b26–30). Further, if this is what the Good is, then we do not need to know it to act well. The reason people are attracted to Platonism is that they think that if we can know an absolute Good, we can attain the human good (*NE,* 1096b35–1097a5). That is, people treat this absolute Good as a kind of paradigm, and think that once they come to know it they can use that knowledge to guide their own search for the human good. However, since Aristotle emphasizes that this knowledge would be useless for action, the pedagogical effect of his criticism is to reiterate his audience's attraction to a life of action.

Yet there is subtler pedagogical effect of this criticism of Platonism. At the very outset of the *Ethics*, Aristotle engages in a devastating criticism of the doctrines attributed to his dear mentor, even though he says this is "repugnant" to him. In this way, Aristotle invites his audience to battle with him and their society for truth. He urges them to be ready to sacrifice even those near and dear to them for its sake (*NE,* 1096a11–17). This exhortation is required to begin to break the fetters of the audience's honor-loving culture, which told them to value the esteem of their loved ones and society. As we shall see, the audience does not consist of a group of risk minimizers, but of ambitious young men sometimes eager to struggle for rare and noble prizes. Aristotle urges them forward into the inquiry by framing it as a battle among competitors for the truth.

The Argument from Function

After this criticism of Platonism Aristotle underscores his point by employing the famous argument from function *(ergon).* The final good of human beings, he says, must be ascertained by looking at the function or work *(ergon)* of human beings. He argues that we share with plants the work of simply living and with animals the work of perception. However, human work must be something uniquely human, which he says is the activity of the part of the soul that has reason. He emphasizes that when people say that human work is a life in accord with this part of the soul they mean "in accord with the activity, and not merely with the possession of the reason-having part" (*NE,* 1098a5–7). Here again, common ground is sought with the audience in the commitment to a life of action.

Conclusion

Finally Aristotle gathers up the threads of these arguments by saying that all the things people strive for to make themselves happy are contained in a life of action. Even external goods are sought only because they are useful to someone who wants to act nobly (*NE,* 1099a31–b8). In the conclusion of this section he emphasizes that his account of action agrees with those who describe happiness as possession of virtue.

> However, there is a considerable difference in conceiving of a virtue as a disposition *(hexis)* or as an activity *(energeia).* For a disposition may exist without producing any result. An activity, however, must produce a result. An active person will act and act well. Thus the crown at the Olympics is not awarded to the most beautiful or the strongest. Rather it is given to those who participate in the contest. So the beautiful and

> good things in life go to those who act rightly *(oi prattontes orthos)*. (*NE*, 1098b32–1099a7)

Aristotle not only seeks common ground with his audience in their commitment to action. He also subtly begins to present a case for virtue, saying that the commitment to noble action seems to jibe with many people's account of virtue. Note that virtue and noble action are not necessarily the same for the audience. Aristotle himself has to present a case for their confluence. This is because the desire for noble action can be manifested in many different ways. Specifically, while one part of Aristotle's audience may be led to virtue through their desire for noble action, another part may be led to competition and a life of despotism.[7] This is especially true for those who think of political activity as a way of actualizing the desire for honorable action. Ambition for political rule for the sake of honor has ambiguous results, and this ambiguity is obscured if we think the whole of Aristotle's audience to be incapable of being attracted to tyranny out of a high-minded attachment to virtue.[8]

The Love of Honor and the Love of Activity

Those ambitious for noble activity think that acquiring political power will give them the means to achieve it. Moreover they want to be assured of the worth of their activity through being honored by others. Thus Aristotle says that refined and practical people attracted to politics identify happiness with honor *(time)*, and think that honor is the goal of political life (*NE*, 1095b22–24). In his criticism of the devotion to honor Aristotle explores the link between the devotion to honor and the devotion to noble action.

The main thrust of his critique is that honor is not sought for its own sake, but rather is a pointer to something more fundamental: excellent action worthy of celebration. Aristotle points out that honor depends on those who confer it rather than those who receive it. This makes honor unstable, for it can be taken away as easily as it is given. He then states that people pursue honor in order to assure themselves of their own worth, and seek moreover to be honored by people they respect and who know them and their accomplishments. Finally, he emphasizes, they want to be honored on the basis of their virtue (*NE,* 1095b23–30; cf. 1159a22–27).

This critique uncovers the motivations that spur on lovers of honor. A self-sufficient being secure in its own excellence would have no need for honor. Honor means so much to human beings because we are radically dependent on our fellows' opinions in order to help us know who we are. In addition, we are psychologically frail creatures fraught with doubts about the value of our accomplishments. For these reasons human being crave honor—not for honor's sake, but rather to know ourselves and be assured of our own goodness or virtue. The point is strengthened by Aristotle's argument that we seek honor not from just anyone, but from those we respect and who know us. We can be assured that honor points to genuine excellence only if those who bestow it really know us and are good, for only this will make them decent judges. Put the other way, since honor depends on the people bestowing it, and therefore on their values and perspectives, sometimes honor betokens vice rather than virtue. Who would accept a medal from Hitler, for example? What would deserving such a medal imply about one's character? We seek honor only from those we respect and hold dear. Implicitly we think that what they respect is good and true, and so when they honor us we think that this means we are in truth good. Thus Aristotle argues that honor is merely a pointer to something more fundamental to which we implicitly give our attachments in loving honor. For this reason Aristotle concludes that the lust for honor implies a lust for virtue, whether refined and practical people admit it or not (*NE,* 1095b30–31). In all this Aristotle emphasizes that if the commitments of those who lead a noble, political life are examined thoroughly they will be revealed as lovers of excellent action.

Virtue appears nowhere on the list of possible candidates for happiness generated by a consideration of reputable ways of life. Indeed, it is not often noticed that Aristotle himself first presents virtue as a candidate for happiness, and only does so through a critique of the devotion to honor and power. He is able to put virtue forward only because he articulated the implicit link between the ambition for honor and the desire for excellent action. The implication is clear. Since he does not include virtue on the list of reputable opinions about how to achieve happiness, Aristotle does not think that his audience associates virtue with happiness. Rather, reputable opinion identifies the good life with the possession of tanglible external goods, especially honor (*NE,* 1095a22).

By linking the ambition for power and honor with the desire for excellent activity, Aristotle is able to move the inquiry in a fundamentally new direction. He begins the *Ethics* by arguing that whatever human beings want, they want happiness *(eudaimonia)*. The Greek term *eudaimonia* meant more than a passive emotional state. A *daimon* was a semidivine being. The term *eudaimonia* thus meant something like having a good guardian angel who watches over one's life, and thus the term had quasi-religious connotations. It might be translated as a kind of blessedness, which is manifest in part in external goods and the increased range of opportunity and action that external goods make possible.[9] When attached to a noun, the term *eu* connoted "abundance," and so *eudaimonia* implies an abundance of life or blessedness or good fortune.[10] As is clear from modern scholarship, Aristotle took over the term and made it mean something like "active flourishing." The question of the *Ethics*, then is: How should the audience live to achieve the abundant action they crave?

The Ambiguous Results of the Pursuit of Honor

The pursuit of honor has ambiguous results. Aristotle's treatment of his audience's opinions shows that virtue is both hidden from and present to a person who pursues a life devoted to honor. On the one hand, virtue does not appear on the list of candidates for happiness, implying that Aristotle does not think his audience believes virtue will make them happy. On the other hand, Aristotle easily uncovers the commitment to virtue implicit in the pursuit of honor by pointing to the connection between the love of honor and the love for excellent activity. What is it about a life devoted to honor that can obscure its own implicit commitment to virtue? Why must Aristotle subtly undermine a political life devoted to honor in order to make a case for virtue? I will briefly reflect on the Greek experience of honor in order to address these problems. Uncovering the psychic motivations behind the drive for honor helps us understand how the audience's love of activity can tend either to moral goodness or to tyranny. Since as Plato points out, Homer was the educator of Greece (*Republic,* 606e), the Homeric epics are an important way of interrogating the way the pursuit of honor can lead to equivocal notions of virtue.

The Homeric epics explore both the attractions and problems in a life devoted to honor. In these poems the most basic contrast between human beings and gods is that while the gods are immortal, human beings are doomed to die. The hero's pursuit of honor or glory *(kleos)* is a way of managing the burden of his mortality. Within the poems' horizons, a life in pursuit of glory is the only way the hero has of participating humanly in the divine life of the immortals. This pursuit has two poles that are inextricably linked. The negative pole is experienced as a fear of death, while the positive pole is experienced as a lust for divine life and activity. For the Homeric hero, divine immortality is a kind of superabundant substance he shares vicariously through his shining deeds. Yet at the same time, this life of glory is inextricably bound together with the terror of death. Immortality in the sense of everlasting life after death is not available to the Homeric hero; indeed, the formless, shadowy world of Hades may be a symbolic representation of nothingness. For the hero to continue to exist as an individual after death required making a lasting impression through noble deeds that would outlast him in the memory of his society. The form and brilliance of this almost divine kind of life was necessarily contrasted with its implicit antinomy, the horror of formless death. Indeed, were it not for the fact that the hero pursues immortal existence in the face of death, his deeds would not be heroic. In pursuing personal immortality through shining deeds that outlast him in the memories of others, the Homeric hero is engaged in a kind of self-immortalization:

> If Achilles chooses to die young, it is not that he values death above life. On the contrary, he cannot accept sinking, just like anybody, into the obscurity of oblivion, merging into the indistinct mass of "nameless ones." He wants to continue forever in the world of the living, to survive within them, and remain there as himself, distinct from any other, through the indestructible memory of his name and renown.
>
> The Greek ideal concept of death is this heroic attempt to

> push away as far as possible, beyond that uncrossable threshold, the horror of chaos, the horror of what has no form and no meaning, and to affirm in the face of and despite everything, the social permanence of this human individuality that must, by its very nature, be destroyed and disappear.[11]

Consequently, in both the *Iliad* and the *Odyssey*, the drama is set in motion by the necessity of a choice between two different ways of life, each of which are at once and in different ways attractive and problematic. This point is clearest in the *Iliad.* According to Achilles, the fates have given him a choice. On the one hand, he can return to his home and lead a long happy life in obscurity, obscured to those coming after because of its ordinariness. On the other hand, he can fight and die at Troy, gaining immortal glory for his deeds. Achilles chooses to fight not merely because of his need to revenge himself upon Hector. As much as it pains him to forego a homecoming, he needs to engage in a life that will shine forever because of its excellence. He is driven by a desire for immortality—to live on in the memories of those who will come after him. So Achilles chooses death by choosing to stay and fight. But while that choice involves death, it is at the same time driven by a desire for a certain fullness of life. Inseparable from his love of honor is a lust for excellence and the fullness such a life promises. In this way immortality is not attractive merely because the hero's name will persist. In addition, it is attractive because the immortality is a sign that he has participated in the life of the immortals. Excellent action and honor and immortality and fear of death are thus inextricably bound together.

An analogous choice confronts Odysseus. At the opening of the *Odyssey*, Odysseus must decide whether to return home and die or remain with Calypso, a beautiful goddess who promises him immortality. Odysseus rejects the nonhuman immortal life offered by Calypso, who seeks to hide him (her name is taken from *kaluptein*, to hide) in her cave forever. In the most obvious sense, Odysseus is hidden from his family and friends while with the goddess. Yet, in another sense, his glory is obscured if he remains there.[12] His life is private; uninteresting; full of gratifications, but with no opportunities to pursue excellent activity. And just as there are no opportunities for excellence on Calypso's island, there is no chance for gaining immortal fame among men there. If Odysseus remains obscured with Calypso—if he forgets his home and the world of men—his story in turn will be forgotten by men, and so his heroic glory will not be revealed to the human community. Thus at the opening of the story he refuses the obscure immortality Calypso offers in order to reveal himself and insure his glory.[13] In this way the immortality Odysseus chooses is more human than the kind Calypso offers for it is based on remembering the demands his humanity imposes. Indeed, this theme of remembrance runs throughout the poem; when the hero's companions forget their humanity they degenerate into savages or animals.

Like Achilles, Odysseus's decision is a choice for death. Unlike Achilles, however, that choice is driven not merely by a thirst for renown, and an inability to bring himself to live a life not devoted to excellent action. In addition, it is driven by a desire for the life Odysseus will enjoy when he reaches home.[14] Yet the hero's immortality depends on the community that will remember him. So, Odysseus's desires for home and glory are also connected, inasmuch as he must return and reconstitute his home if his deeds are to be remembered on Ithaca.

The close connection between the horror of impending death and the glory of immortal honor drives the various conflicts of the *Iliad.* The *Iliad* is about Achilles' wrath, not about the Trojan war, which merely provides a backdrop to the problems Homer explores. It begins with the word "wrath" *(menin)* and concludes not with the end of the war but with the burial of Hektor, who bore the brunt of Achilles' wrath in the final book. This wrath comes not merely from Agamemnon's insults and Patroklos' death at the hands of Hektor. At its deepest level, Achilles' wrath comes from an inability to reconcile his lust for a glorious participation in the abundance of immortal life with the compensation for this lust that human life actually offers: a shadowy existence in the memories of those coming after him.[15]

Achilles withdraws from the battle because Agamemnon disrespected him. The only way to regain his honor is to have the king publicly apologize and make restitution. Yet after Agamemnon offers Achilles everything he wanted to rejoin the battle and much more besides, he refuses. He explains that his unwillingness to fight has a deeper motive now that he has reflected on the nature of honor:

> Fate is the same for the man who holds back, the same if he fights hard. / We are all held in a single honor, the brave with

> the weaklings. / A man still dies if he has done nothing, as one who has done much. / Nothing is won for me, now that my heart has gone through its afflictions / In forever setting my life on the hazard of battle.
>
> (*Iliad* 9.318–23)[16]

Achilles has a seemingly infinite desire for immortal life. Yet he can no longer make sense out of life, for after he has lost everything he cared about he realizes that in response to his desire for immortality, existence gives only death. And the immortality he will achieve will not actually get him anything, for while people will remember him forever, he will not be able to enjoy it. This radical unfairness is the root of his wrath.

The effects of Achilles' wrath at the insufficiency of glory as a compensation for death extend in ripples through the band of warriors, ruining their community, setting friend against friend, tempting some to exercise mastery rather than persuasion, and in the end threatening their conquest of Troy. Like Beowulf and Gilgamesh, the Homeric epics thus point to the problems inherent in the pursuit of honor by showing how it is a tragic, incomplete solution to the apparently infinite desire for life. In doing so the *Iliad* also dramatizes the potentially disastrous social effects of the pursuit of honor. The social disaster that attends the competition for honor is precipitated by the kind of self-assertion that the pursuit of honor presupposes:

> Honor is a metaphysical victory over man's mortal condition. But precisely because nothingness is an abyss ever open before man, his claim on existence acquires a narcissistic intensity, demanding constant reinforcement and reassurance by acknowledgement from others. If this is withheld, the hero's *bié* [elemental masculine force] drives him to destroy the other in ontological self-assertion. Therefore this ideological justification of the hero through honor is at the same time the elevation of force and violence to the highest moral dignity, since *bié* is the essence of the warrior's being and action.[17]

Political Effects of the Culture of Honor

The centrality of honor and its tendency to self-assertion and mastery was transmitted to classical Greece, where it decisively affected ancient politics. While the social structures in Homer's poems differ from the political practices of classical Greece, there are a variety of similar problems associated with the pursuit of honor in both contexts. The Greek political tradition was shaped by public-spirited men who competed vigorously for honor.[18] Homer traces this problem back to the fact that the pursuit of honor is a way of managing death by pursuing a fullness of life; the pursuit of honor is at the same time a flight from death. Aristotle makes the same point when he emphasizes that a life of honor is fueled by insecurity (*NE,* 1095b27). This insecurity has at its root the fear of death, the origin of all insecurities. Because on some level human beings are aware they are not the source of their own being, but are dependent on an enormous variety of contexts they did not create; because they are aware that they are in constant danger of falling out of existence, they need to assure themselves in a variety of ways of their own life and worth. Honor is one such way to self-assurance.

Aristotle expands on Homeric notions of the origin of honor, however, by emphasizing that human beings are naturally social. Part of the reason for this is that nature underdetermines us. We require society in order to actualize our capacities. Since we cannot know ourselves or come to be ourselves without the aid of others, Aristotle thinks that one of the reasons we require society is to estimate the worth of our actions. For Aristotelians, dear friends are the best mirrors. For this reason the wellsprings of the pursuit of honor are a lack of security and self-sufficiency.

Every attempt to manage the life-death antinomy is fraught with problems, and the pursuit of honor is no exception. Seeking honor is a zero-sum game. Honor is a comparative good, since the quality of honor diminishes once it is shared. An Olympic medal is precious because so few are awarded. The Congressional Medal of Honor would mean nothing if it were given to everyone. In an honor culture, cultivation of my distinction must happen at the expense of your distinction. Thus the pursuit of honor threatens competition and attempts at mastery. Another reason that the pursuit of honor tends to produce conflict stems from the limited character of human memory. Individual immortality in the memory of others requires that they actually recall and celebrate one's actions. Yet because human beings cannot remember and celebrate every great deed, honor is a scarce resource. Again, this scarcity of honor makes it a contestable good. So Aristotle says that people tend to overgrasp for scarce external goods like honor; it is one of the goods people "fight about" (*NE,* 1169a20–22; *EE,* 1248b27; *R,* 1368b12–14). Moreover, human beings place an enormous burden on honor. Aristotle points out that human desires, especially the desire for life, are not limited (*P,* 1257b40–1258a10). In seeking honor, we are attaching seemingly infinite importance to a finite thing. Since the pursuit of honor is an attempt to participate in immortal life, it will be vested with a particular intensity (see, for example, *P,* 1257b40ff; 1266a28–1267a17; 1267a31–b9). The ensuing conflicts will be equally intense. And, of course, the potential for conflict is increased in the anticipation of and preparation for conflict. This danger of conflict is also exacerbated by the fact that the pursuit of honor is fraught with anxiety not only in its origins but also in its goal. In pursuing honor we are depending not only on our own ability to perform memorable deeds. Since honor must be given by another, we also depend on those who confer it (*NE,* 1095b25). This makes honor radically unstable, since it can be taken as easily as it has been given. Indeed, human memory is so fragile that we cannot even recall all the events of our own lives, and so experience a kind of slipping away of our lives even as we live them. Yet if this is so, how much more problematic is depending on our fellows to recall our glorious actions?

The consequences of the pursuit of honor account for some of the unique contradictions that marked ancient Greek life. This culture was characterized by a fierce devotion to freedom and a vigorous suspicion of power paradoxically combined with cruel domination in public and private life. One the one hand, in city-states like Athens there was a determined cultivation of institutions that preserved the freedom of citizens from encroachment by those bent on dominating politics in pursuit of power and honor. Sensing themselves to be bound up with the public struggle for honor, these citizens were led to take the requisite political precautions. So the emphasis on freedom in Athenian political institutions can be understood as motivated in part by fear of domination. Freedom of speech in the assembly and democratic institutions, like using a lottery to determine officeholders and direct voting on law, protected the masses from honor-loving elites.[19] Private prosecution protected citizens from ambitious prosecutors, and popular juries protected them from the power that the experts in law hold.

On the other hand, in the public struggle for distinction and its consequences, we discover part of the psychic root of the civil strife *(stasis)* and domination endemic to ancient Greek like. Modern scholarship tells us that in line with a long tradition emphasizing success in agonal struggles as the criterion for humanity, political elites in classical Athens competed for influence, often in savage ways.[20] In such a context, the temptation was strong to pursue mastery over one's fellows. Such mastery seemed to promise both the extension of one's range of honorable actions and the ability to make preemptive strikes against those seeking to take away one's freedom in their own attempts to pursue power and honor (*P*, 1325a32–40). Indeed, Greek life in many ways was based on the assumption that mastery of others was a natural part of life, from the subjection of women and slaves to the use of law courts as a mechanism for competition.

Ancient sources tell the same story. In the *Politics*, Aristotle points out the seeming attractiveness of this way of life. He says that a life of mastery appears best to most, for those who possess power seem to be able to perform the greatest number of noble actions. That is, virtue appears to require vice in order to furnish materials for its action. From this perspective, he says, it seems best not to give to our neighbors but to take away from them, and to disregard ties of family and friendship in the pursuit of political power (*P*, 1325a32–40). In Plato's *Gorgias*, the politically ambitious Kallikles articulates his view that the best life is one devoted not to virtue but to despotism. Philosophy, he says, should not be pursued, for it tells us to moderate our desires in favor of virtue. So, it cannot help us defend ourselves from the injustice of men and the caprices of fortune (484b–486e).

This drive for mastery and fear of domination drove foreign affairs as well as internal politics. Thucydides, for example, points out that the Athenian empire was motivated largely by insecurity and lust for mastery. Domination was viewed as natural, and indeed, divinely sanctioned. For instance, in the Melian dialogue, when the Athenians arrive armed demanding submission, the Melians propose neutrality and friendship. The

Athenians reply that they cannot accept neutrality because "it is not so much your hostility that offends us; it is rather the case that, if we were on friendly terms with you, our subjects would regard that as a sign of weakness in us, whereas your hatred is evidence of our power." The Athenians argue that they must attack independent peoples so that their subjects will not view them as weak and afraid of conflict, thus tempting them to rebel: "So that by conquering you we increase not only the size but also the security of our empire."[21] In turn, when the Melians reject the Athenian terms, saying that they will trust in the gods, who protect those in the right against the strong, the reply is:

> So far as the favour of the gods is concerned, we think we have as much right to that as you have. Our aims and actions are perfectly consistent with the beliefs men hold about the gods and with the principles which govern their own conduct. Our opinion of the gods and our knowledge of men leads us to conclude that it is a general and necessary law of nature to rule whatever one can. This is not a law we made ourselves, nor were we the first to act upon it when it was made.[22]

A devotion to honor thus has polymorphous results. In a society dominated by a political class competing for honor, virtue becomes an equivocal term. On the one hand, the pursuit of honor is implicitly a love of glorious, quasi-divine activities worthy of celebration and remembrance. So under the right conditions, love of honor can be a spur to moral virtue. It all depends on who is conferring honor and for what they are conferring it. The consequences to one's character of pursuing honor in Nazi Germany will be obviously different than pursuing honor in a decent society. Part of Aristotle's audience may be attracted to moral virtue, if they were brought up in a context that emphasized the praiseworthiness of moral virtue. Yet the zero-sum character of honor insures that its pursuit will threaten conflicts and attempts at mastery within and without the polis. This threat encourages competitors for honor to homologize virtue with manly self-assertion. So the pursuit of honorable actions may foster genuinely excellent action or it may foster a drive for mastery and power in the elemental sense. So at least part of the audience is tempted to tyranny.[23]

The drive for honor thus tends in two different directions: a life of moral virtue and a life of mastery. While these two lives have a similar motivation, they are also fundamentally at odds. A life of moral virtue involves a sense of fairness, evenhandedness, a persistent willingness to render to others what is their due, and even to refuse to push one's just claims at the expense of social order. We could call such a conception "virtue-as-equity," since Aristotle defines the equitable person as one who has a disposition that inclines him to take fewer goods for himself even when the law is on his side (*NE,* 1137b34–1138a2). By contrast, the notion of excellence at the heart of a life devoted to mastery involves domination and exploitation. We could call such a conception of life "virtue-as-virility."[24]

To an ambitious young person living in a social scene defined by the competition for honor, virtue-as-virility would appear to be immensely attractive while virtue-as-equity would not necessarily appear to be a promising candidate for happiness. At the least, people ambitious for noble action would have heard arguments and seen actions extolling the benefits of virtue-as-virility. From the perspective of the "real man," virtue-as-equity appears weak and feminine, since it does not seem to help achieve the kind of status and power apparently required for noble action. Virtue-as-equity appears to be useless for action, unless perhaps the appearance of such virtue improves one's social standing, and thus one's chances for honor and power. Indeed, from this perspective, equitable people open themselves to manipulation, abuse, or domination by those devoted to power and glory. As the Athenians in the Melian dialogue point out, "If one follows one's self-interest, one wants to be safe, whereas the path of justice involves one in danger."[25] This means that if the person pursuing honor considers virtue-as-equity at all, he will think of it as a mere means to honor. Yet this minimizes the extent to which virtue issues in action done for its own sake. Thus virtue appears to be merely a disposition for action; it comes to be reduced to one's character. Thus virtue is valued only insofar as one's character can be developed in order to achieve honor.[26]

Plato's Case against Virtue-as-Equity in the *Republic*

Examples of the conflict between these equivocal notions of virtue abound in the Platonic dialogues. In the *Gorgias,* Kallikles challenges Socrates' notion of virtue on the grounds that it is unmanly (483a–b, 485d–e). Meno begins by expressing interest in virtue, but Socrates soon shows him to be principally interested in victory and gain (*Meno,* 70a–77d). We find an extended example of the equivocal character of virtue in the opening pages of the *Republic.* In presenting the way virtue appeared to ambitious young men eager for great actions, Plato makes it clear why his interlocutors think that virtue-as-equity is useless for happiness.

Plato makes his main case against virtue in the mouths of his brothers, Glaucon and Adeimantus. These young men remained unconvinced after Socrates demolishes Thrasymachus's argument that the just is the interest of the strong. Thrasymachus breaks in on the discussion "like a wild beast" (336a) after Socrates convinces Polemarchus to agree that it is never just to injure anyone. Thrasymachus accuses Socrates of standing in need of a wetnurse, implying that he is a baby who does not know how the real world works. For him, political rule is a technique whereby the strong structure a state of affairs which will work perpetually to their own interest and that of their cronies. It is clear that Thrasymachus's argument is a conceptual muddle. He confuses the just (as a state of affairs structured by law) with justice (as a personal virtue or disposition to engage in various kind of activities). Further, he conflates both justice and the just with rule *(arche)* (336a–348c). Socrates exposes the deficiencies of his account by playing on what might be called the "value-neutrality" of technique. He makes Thrasymachus aware that while in his view, the rulers structure the system to work in their interest, human beings are notoriously mistaken about their own best interest. If the strong have not thought seriously about what constitutes their own best interest, they are arming themselves dangerously in acquiring power (350c). They may well take actions that hurt them or make them unhappy.

However, Glaucon and Adeimantus remain unconvinced. Socrates' argument led merely to Socratic ignorance; the brothers know that justice is *not* a technique aimed at the advantage of the strong, but they still do not know what it *is.* For argument's sake, therefore, they say they will argue against justice by recreating the perspective of the leaders of their society, who urge them to injustice. According to Glaucon, such people say that it is not the strong who make the laws, but the weak. The weak are afraid of being dominated by the strong but at the same time do not have the skill or courage to commit acts of injustice successfully. Agreements about law and justice are thus the result of a contract among the weak, who are perpetually afraid of a "real man" who could rise up and overthrow their system of petty restraint (359b2). According to nature, the strong ought to rule. Indeed, it appears that nature favors and rewards the smart and the strong individuals who are willing to take the requisite risks and engage in acts of injustice successfully (i.e., without getting caught) in order to overthrow a system bent on keeping them down. The social conventions made by the weak are thus actually against nature, insofar as nature is equated with power in the most elemental sense. If virtue means primordial "manly" power, then virtue (i.e., virtue-as-virility) demands what the weak call "vice." For the naturally strong and ambitious, virtue-as-equity is not advantageous. Indeed, exhortations to virtue-as-equity are in reality a scam perpetuated by the weak on the strong. To engage in virtue-as-equity is to be duped into foregoing one's own true interests in favor of the interests of a majority of no account wimps and losers intent on protecting themselves from the designs of the strong. Adeimantus expands on his brother's presentation of popular sentiment. He argues that while the weak seek to convince the strong that injustice is shameful, in reality everyone knows in their heart of hearts that injustice is sweet and easy (364a). On the other hand, the virtue of justice is hard and difficult by nature (364a2–3). So, while according to convention justice is in one's interest, according to nature injustice is in one's interest. If justice is in reality merely a conventional opinion reached by agreement among the weak, it is best to be thought just while actually practicing injustice. Virtue is not in one's interest. Rather, the mere appearance of virtue is enough. Indeed, one's real interest is (like Gyges)[27] appearing virtuous while in reality being vicious. Whatever people say in public, in reality, virtue-as-equity does not produce happiness. Although the appearance of virtue-as-equity is sometimes useful for those practicing virtue-as-virility, this means emphasizing appearance over substance, thus reducing virtue-as-equity to a potentially useless bauble that ought to be revealed when called for and concealed when it interferes with the maximization of self-interest, narrowly understood.

Vice and crafty deception work far better than virtue-as-equity. The two brothers emphasize that they do not accept such arguments. They say that sophists like Thrasymachus and "countless others" have tried to convince them that justice is done unwillingly, and that it is far better to perform acts of injustice, provided one can get away with it (358c). This text shows that even those young men who might be attracted to virtue-as-equity are confused because of a more or less corrupt political culture that extols virtue-as-virility. Far from accepting the worth of moral virtue, they go to the philosopher for an argument on its behalf. They demand that Socrates praise justice for its own sake, apart from any rewards or punishments it might bring (358c–d).

If this was the context of classical politics, it is no wonder that virtue does not appear on Aristotle's list of reputable conceptions of happiness. If virtue is synonymous with a kind of equity; if it entails forgiving wrongs for the sake of community; if it means a refusal to push one's advantage at the cost of another; a refusal to cheat, even when seemingly profitable to do so; a desire to render joyfully to each their due; an unwillingness to be a free rider, even when it appears to be in one's interest to pile up goods by deceit or outright theft; and the lack of desire to pursue mastery over others, then practicing virtue-as-equity in such a context would seem to be madness. It is not just impracticable idealism—a kind of high-minded inattentiveness to the way the real world works. In some cases, it seems to be downright stupidity, for in opting for virtue-as-equity one is pursuing a mode of existence which leaves one open to the machinations of others who are not so decent. Practicing virtue-as-equity entails not merely foregoing the activities that lead to profit and power. In addition, it means that the practitioners of virtue-as-virility will be able to take advantage of the goodness of the practitioners of virtue-as-equity, trampling them underfoot in their pursuit of honor and mastery (cf. *Crito,* 44b–c; 45e–46b). Not only is there no reward for virtue-as-equity; it is positively punished. To paraphrase what Kallikles says to Socrates in the *Gorgias*, the real man *(aner)* does not permit himself to suffer injustice, only a slave *(andrapodon)* does that. If one pursues feminine activities like philosophy one becomes unmanly *(anandro)* and comes to avoid places where real men *(andres)* achieve distinction. Such a person lives in obscurity, whispering in corners with a few boys and is not able even to speak about freedom, greatness, or power (483a–b, 485d–e). This means that Aristotle's audience is ill-disposed to cooperative virtues and well-disposed to competitive ones:

> In law-courts, in internal politics, and in foreign policy, competitive arete prevails over co-operative excellence. Other views are beginning to be expressed [in the later fifth century B.C.], but there seems little sign of their prevailing, and little likelihood that they should prevail: the co-operative excellences are likely to resist the pull of competitive arete when there is a clash between the two; for the contribution of wealth and fighting ability to the individual's and the city's well-being is much more evident.[28]

These reflections go a long way to explaining the paradoxical emphasis on and opacity of virtue in Aristotle's account of reputable opinion. Part of Aristotle's audience seemed to be attracted to virtue. Yet they lived in a culture that celebrated a notion of human excellence limited to the political actions of a "real man." This notion of excellence is particularly manifest in the courageous defense of the homeland (*andreia*, *NE,* 3.6–9). Indeed, this seems to be why the Greek word for virtue, *arete*, bears etymological resemblance to Ares, the god of war. From this perspective, the good life tended to be identified with a vitality that its possessor thinks shines forth so brilliantly that he demands public recognition for it.

The Appearance of Virtue

All this accounts for Aristotle's strange comments when he finally presents virtue as a candidate for happiness himself. After linking the pursuit of honor with virtue, Aristotle at first dismisses virtue in a revealing way. He says that it appears *(phainetai)* that virtue is not sufficient to bring our desire for happiness to completion because it does not produce a sufficient amount of activity. A person, he says, might have virtue while asleep, or it might be inactive his whole life. Alternatively, a man might have virtue and be hugely unlucky and so be unhappy (*NE,* 1095b31–1096a3). This presentation of virtue is unintelligible unless we keep in mind that Aristotle is here laying out reputable opinion; that is, he is presenting the way virtue appears to his audience.[29] Because the inquiry is dialectical Aristotle must initially present it as it appears to reputable opinion. And for his audience, one could have virtue while asleep. Virtue-as-equity is often useless, for it does not help one dominate or pursue honor. Rather, it enjoins us to be fair and evenhanded. From his audience's perspective, since virtue-as-equity does not entail getting ahead in terms of power and glory, it seems to be a life of inactivity. Virtues would be needed as a means to honor, perhaps, since we regularly celebrate people of good character. Yet these dispositions of character need not be activated if they are pursued solely as a means to honor.

Virtue requires actions; virtue pursued for the sake of honor is inactive. From such a perspective, it would be better to have the kind of power and honor that allow us to be active amd that help us to guard ourselves from the kind of vulnerability we possess while we sleep. Further, Aristotle says, one could be virtuous but unlucky. The implication is that virtue-as-equity is not capable of warding off misfortune or of helping us to deal effectively with it.[30]

In addition, however, there may be something more subtle going on. In many ancient cultures, sleep was homologized with death.[31] For example, in Greek mythology, Hypnos, the god of sleep, was twin brother to Thanatos, the god of death. In saying that one could have virtue while asleep, Aristotle implies that if one's task is the process of self-immortalization through active pursuit of honor, virtue-as-equity will pale by comparison, even to the point of becoming a kind of sleepy death.

Aristotle's audience is not fully committed to virtue-as-equity. Rather, they hold equivocal notions of virtue—notions that are both attractive and fundamentally at odds with one another. Part of his audience harbors the temptation to a life of tyranny, which is seen as useful because it allows people to accumulate power, honor, and wealth in order to serve their desire for action. At the least, a large portion of his audience of young, virile, ambitious men would have serious reservations about the value of virtue-as-equity.

Aristotle's understanding of equivocal terms allows his treatment of reputable opinions about happiness to be true to their ambiguity. Aristotle's audience does not hold a monolithic notion of virtue; they hold several mutually incompatible notions at once.[32] In dialectically grappling with his audience's commitments to virtue-as-virility and concomitant suspicion of virtue-as-equity, however, Aristotle is able to bring to light the various unsettled meanings of "virtue" so as to clear space for his own account. This is important, for if Aristotle's audience is predisposed against virtue-as-equity, Aristotle cannot merely clarify their own dispositions to virtue-as-virility. Rather, he must argue that virtue-as-equity is in their interest, impractical as it first appears.

Pedagogical Problems: How Love of Honor Leads to Complacency

I have argued that the *Ethics* is an attempt to teach. It thus proceeds by paying attention to the demands that teaching and learning impose. What pedagogical problems confront Aristotle as he makes his own argument for virtue? The appeal to virtue is both necessary and problematic. Seeking common ground with the audience is crucial to move the inquiry forward, and Aristotle achieves this by linking noble action with virtue. Yet virtue is an equivocal term, and discussing equivocal terms is notoriously difficult. The other problem is that appealing to virtue in a culture that limits humanity to those who possess honor is inherently conservative—in the sense of preserving the status quo. Since every regime is formative, a particular appeal to "virtue" may mean "what respectable people mean when they speak about the qualities human beings require in order to be successful in this society." Since as we have seen, honor is ultimately a pointer to excellence, any culture's mode of giving honor is always an attempt to foster its own conception of human excellence. The pursuit of honor is bounded by relatively specific normative expectations that are—by the definition of honor—socially constructed. Social relations in a culture devoted to honor are evaluative and competitive. Specific social norms are employed in order to adjudicate the struggle for honor.[33] In such a context social norms are reinforced by rewarding certain actions with praise or rewards and punishing other by assigning blame or shame.

But this means that if virtue is seen as a means for achieving honor and political power, then it becomes a virtue not to rise above common opinion.[34] In this way the pursuit of honor can yield a smug complacency that impedes moral development. Struggling for honor may entail slavishly buying into one's culture's notions of human excellence, deficient or not. And winning honors can foster the kind of self-congratulation that obscures the awareness of faults—an awareness of faults that is the condition for moving away from them. So the appeal to virtue in a social context defined by the pursuit of honor can be a block to virtue inasmuch as it implies an appeal to conventionally respectable standards of success. Pursuing honor can entail an unwillingness to radically question one's own regime and one's own way of life. If so, then fostering virtue in such a context merely preserves the moral hegemony of the dominant culture, rendering personal, social, or political reform more difficult.

Aristotle must struggle to avoid the sort of conservatism inherent in the appeal to virtue even as he appeals to virtue. He must foster the genuine search for virtue by snapping his audience out of the complacency implied in the struggle for honor: If I deserve honor I must be good. If I am good I do not need to search for virtue. That is, ambitious people who strive for an active role in political and social affairs seem to think that they deserve honor and standing. In this they are confident of their wisdom and merit. Yet this confidence is the main threat to their advancement in virtue, for growth in character entails precisely doubting one's own virtue. Unless we know we do not know what virtue is, we cannot hope to attain virtue. In a like way, only a person who knows she is sick seeks a cure. Thus there is an arrogance to success and ambition that may render its possessors ineducable.

In order to help his audience become good, Aristotle must work to make his audience aware that they are unaware of what virtue really is. He must provoke a knowledge of their ignorance of virtue, for this is the only way to stir the wonder that explodes complacency and allows the search for the best life to begin. We shall see that Aristotle will argue that most human beings are not virtuous, and that virtue is much harder than the audience originally thought, partly because the struggle for virtue is always struggle against prevailing social norms.[35]

For this reason Aristotle does not begin his dialectical pedagogy by blasting conventionally accepted notions of success. This would merely turn people away. However, he does give strong indications that he is uneasy about his audience's opinions. In addition to the critique of honor, Aristotle gives other indications that his audience may need to radically revise their opinion of their own goodness. For instance, at the beginning of his discussion of happiness, Aristotle makes a broad distinction between the many *(polloi)* and the refined *(charientes).* Both these groups agree that happiness is the good life and good action. But when it comes to defining these terms, they disagree. The account given by the many differs from that given by the wise *(sophoi)* (*NE,* 1095a15–22). At first, glance, the distinction between the many and the refined seems to line up with the distinction between the many and the wise: the refined think they are wise. But Aristotle deftly undermines the distinction the refined make between themselves and the many. The many, he says, think that happiness is identifiable with some obvious, visible, and external good like pleasure, honor, or wealth (*NE,* 1095a24). The wise, on the other hand, seek an explanatory account that investigates the cause of happiness by seeking a good over and above these external goods (*NE,* 1095a26). From the perspective of the wise, the distinction between the refined and the many collapses because both groups equate happiness with the possession of tangible external goods. The refined disdain the many because they seek only pleasure and wealth. They congratulate themselves that they seek honor and political power instead. Yet from the perspective of the wise, seeking the external good of honor is akin to seeking the external goods of pleasure and wealth.

Moreover, seeking external goods is presented as a haphazard process involving blind submission to transitory desires. The problem with talking about happiness, Aristotle emphasizes, is not merely that different people think different things. In addition, "the very same person" thinks different things at different times. When sick, happiness becomes health; when poor, happiness becomes money; when ignorant, happiness becomes knowledge; when hungry, happiness becomes food, and so on (*NE,* 1095a23–26). For most of us, happiness is equated with seeking the satisfaction of whatever desires predominate at the moment. Instead of critically seeking a cause for their happiness that they could pursue thoughtfully, his audience flits from one desire to the next.

The audience of self-described refined people think that

their wisdom distinguishes them from the many. Yet from the perspective of the wise, refined people's identification of their own views with wisdom simply entails that they are not open to a critical search for happiness. Their opinion of their wisdom leads to invincible ignorance because it closes off the possibility of a search into the human good. After the discussion of the opinions of the many, the refined, and the wise, Aristotle invokes Hesiod's aphorism about wisdom: The best man works out for himself every problem; the next best man listens to those who give good accounts; and the worst man can neither work out problems for himself nor listen to others. In other words, the worst man is ineducable because he is unaware of his ignorance. The implication is that the person who thinks he is wise must be made aware of his ignorance before the inquiry can profit him. Aristotle's audience must be brought to the realization that their conception of human flourishing is defective before they can be brought to a fuller account.

Aristotle has a powerful ally in this, however: his audience's sense of shame. When Aristotle considers the life of pleasure, for example, his audience's sense of decency and superiority allows him to dismiss it as fit only for cows (*NE,* 1095b20). Yet even as he does so, Aristotle hints at powerful evidence that the life of pleasure is really quite attractive. He says that many people in stations to which the ambitious and refined aspire actually think happiness is pleasure: "Many people in high places agree with Sardanapallus" (*NE,* 1095b22), an Assyrian king known for his sensual excesses. So many ambitious people want to live a life of tyranny. Why? Apparently, the tyrant can do whatever he pleases. He is not restricted by social mores to keep his desire for acquisition or gratification in check. He can create his own context for action, for he does not need to rely on other people. He is free to maximize his pleasure and security. In fact, it seems that he can put his entire society to work on the gratification of his desires. Such a life appears to hold out hope that desires will actually be satisfied. A contemporary analogue might be the life of a rock or film star, or with the "lifestyles of the rich and famous." These people have the resources to enable them to live as tyrants do. Aristotle says that people get pleasure from excessive gain (*NE,* 1130b1–5), and he seems to argue that many people have this tendency. His collapsing of the distinction between the elite and the many implies that those who seek refined goods like honor and political power tend to be as unjust as those who seek money and pleasure. Even if the latter do not desire tyranny in the same big way, they do in petty ways—by lording it over those less powerful, by using other people as objects for various kinds of gratifications, or by overgrasping for external goods.

Aristotle can dismiss a life of pleasure because his refined audience equates it with physical enjoyment, and so believes it to be beneath them. They would be ashamed of such a life. They are attracted to noble, virile actions instead. I have argued that their attraction to nobility may also lead to a desire for mastery. Aristotle equates tyranny with a life of pleasure, thus enabling him to put off a discussion of tyranny even as he points to the reasons for its attractiveness. He has employed his audience's sense of shame to begin to turn them away from a love of despotism.

Pedagogical Strategies: Virtue-as-Equity

I have argued that proceeding dialectically entails proceeding from a particular audience's reputable convictions. And from the perspective of Aristotle's audience, virtue is an equivocal term that is in one sense attractive and in another useless or perhaps even dangerous. If part of Aristotle's audience is tempted to overgrasp for honor and perhaps even tyranny, how does one argue against this? It does no good merely to point out that they hold equivocal notions of virtue; that merely makes their commitment to virtue-as-virility more explicit. Indeed, Aristotle implies, convincing his audience to abandon their views is going to be extraordinarily difficult, for people derive their conceptions of happiness form the lives they lead (*NE*, 1095b15). The struggle to make his audience good cannot be a high-minded exercise in finger-wagging moralism. Since people are attached to their own way of life and often defend it literally to the death, they will naturally resist alternative views. If dialectic is to engender a change in attitude toward virtue, it must also engender the habit of critical questioning. The audience must be made aware that their regime's conception of a successful human life is problematic. In addition, some tangible motive must be given to engage in the search for virtue. In other words, to be successful in engendering a conversion to a new way of life, the dialectician must operate with the horizons set by his audience's *endoxa*, and show why it is in their interest to abandon their old life and take on a new one. In this particular case, Aristotle must work to show why virtue-as-virility fails to make one happy, while at the same time showing how the new way of life he is presenting will achieve what the audience originally wanted from its old way of life. Clearly, Aristotle argues for a strong connection between happiness and virtue. Yet how to lead an audience to consider the possibility of such a connection when virtue sometimes appears to be a useless, self-destructive thing?

One could approach this problem dialectically in at least two ways. First, a teacher could begin by making the case against virtue-as-equity explicit, uncovering the reasons why virtue-as-virility seems attractive and why equity appears unmanly. With the audience's views made explicit—with the cards on the table, as it were—one could then go about making a case for a different notion of virtue by showing the audience the shortcomings of their commitments by showing their implications. This may bring them around to a new way of life. This is Plato's strategy in the *Republic.* Second, one could at first ignore or dismiss the case against virtue-as-equity, preferring instead to articulate the audience's presuppositions about virtue-as-virility. Then one could, in the course of presenting the case for virtue-as-virility, show dialectically how it breaks down on its own terms; how it fails to get what the audience wants it to get. In turn, in showing how the account failed, one could point to implications in that account that were previously unseen. Perhaps the love of shining, superabundant, quasi-divine activity implicit in the desire for honor is best satisfied by another way of life—that of philosophy. This is the dialectical strategy in Aristotle's *Ethics.* Aristotle's appeal to virtue is critical and evaluative, not merely descriptive and conservative. His distinction between the good man and the good citizens radicalizes his discussion of virtue, since at any moment we may discover that virtue requires a stance countervailing to reigning notions of success.

To understand Aristotle's pedagogical strategy, one must distinguish his perspective from that of his audience and both of these from contemporary standpoints. Aristotle's audience is decisively different from an audience of individualistic risk minimizers. Consequently his pedagogical strategy has to be different from one directed to contemporary students. To convince his audience of virile, politically ambitious, honor-loving young men of the value of virtue-as-equity, he invites them to battle for the truth. As we have seen, one pedagogical effect of his treatment of Platonism was to exhort his students to honor truth more than social convention. By engaging in a "repugnant" critique of Plato, Aristotle urges his audience to be ready to sacrifice the opinion of even those nearest and dearest to them for truth's sake (*NE*, 1096a11–17). This exhortation aims to break the bonds their honor-loving culture imposes on the search for truth. Students who follow this exhortation are led through a detailed inquiry that argues that virtue-as-equity is the best outlet for noble action. Towards the end of the inquiry, he asserts that we all need the help of friends to satisfy our desire for activity. Friendship replaces honor as the best external good (*NE,* 8.7; 9.9). Aristotle tries to reorient the ambitions of his honor-loving audience in part by showing them that their desire for activity can only be achieved in and through certain forms of moral and political communities. They have an interest in preventing factional strife and domination, because these interfere with the conditions of their own flourishing. Undermining such communities in a self-assertive drive for mastery makes no sense, because it undermines the context on which one's own happiness depends. Put another way, Aristotle seeks to moderate the part of his audience prone to take competitive risks for zero-sum goods like honor by introducing them to goods that do not necessitate mastery because they are non-zero-sum and thus shareable (e.g., *NE,* 1170b10–13; 1178b34–1179a10; *P,* 1267a8–13). Aristotle's pedagogical strategy is to use his audience's notions of a successful human life to argue against the kind of activities to which they are prone. The rhetorical pitch is that their self-assertive drive for honor and political power will undermine the possibility for the very noble activity they so crave.

Pedagogical Problems: Philosophy

By the end of the *Ethics,* it is clear that Aristotle's goal is not limited to arguing for virtue-as-equity. In addition, he wants to show his audience that philosophy gets them the kind of quasi-divine life they wanted in loving honor. Aristotle writes and teaches in a context that forms the opinions of his students decisively. Thus when he takes up concepts like philosophy, he has to deal with the fact that they had already been loaded with a set of meaning he does not necessarily agree with. So, his audience may assume that in making a case for philosophy Aristotle is arguing for what they take to be philosophy. Yet, if they misunderstand what philosophy is, their own deficient notions may limit their receptivity to his argument. A contemporary teacher must struggle with the same problem, for example. In one sense, college students reading Aristotle for the first time tend rightly to reject his argument that happiness lies in a life of philosophy. This is partly because they conflate philosophy either with a set of contestable doctrines taught in a course on the history of ideas where everyone seems to be equally wrong; or with the activity of their philosophy professors. That is, when they think of philosophy they tend to think of the activities and opinions they were forced to engage in Philosophy 101. Whatever the benefit of such courses, however, it is not clear they are coextensive with what Aristotle meant by philosophy. Thus when teaching Aristotle it is often crucial to remind students both of their own preconceptions and that the way philosophy appears to them may be different than how it seems to Aristotle.

So how did philosophy appear to Aristotle's audience? When people in the presence of the wise become conscious of their own ignorance, Aristotle says, they wonder at someone who says something that goes over their heads—something big and grand (*NE,* 1095a25). However, they also seem to believe that while philosophers are wise *(sophos),* they are not practically wise *(phronimos)* because they appear to be ignorant of things that are advantageous to them. While philosophers may know many wonderful things, most people think that the things they know are useless because they do not concern the humanly good things *(ta anthropina agatha)*. Practical wisdom, on the other hand, is concerned not with such useless philosophic stuff, but with what is actually good for people in the real world (*NE,* 1141b4–10).

This attitude can manifest itself as a kind of bemused indifference to or dismissal of the philosopher. Yet it can also result in a profound hostility to what the philosopher stands for. In the *Gorgias*, Plato gives us a picture of a man with precisely this attitude toward philosophy. In that dialogue, Kallikles argues that philosophy has a limited place in a liberal education, but also insists that in the last analysis, it is useless, perhaps even dangerous, to the business of everyday living in the real world:

> Philosophy, you know, Socrates, is a charming thing, if a man does it moderately in younger days. But if he continues to spend his time on it too long, it will bring him ruin. However well-endowed he may be, if he continues to philosophize too far into life, he must necessarily find himself ignorant of everything that ought to be familiar to a gentleman and a real man [*andra*]. . . . For when I see philosophy in a young lad, I approve it; I consider it to be suitable, and I regard him as a person of a liberal mind. But when I see an elderly man still going on with philosophy and not getting rid of it, that is the gentleman, Socrates, whom I know is in need of a whipping. For just as I said now, this person, however well-endowed he may be, is bound to become unmanly [*anandro*] through shunning the centers and markets of the city (485a–d).[36]

In sum, philosophy appears to Aristotle's audience as a misguided and impractical enterprise, useless for everyday living, and perhaps even dangerous. Thus Aristotelian dialectic entails working with reputable opinion in more ways than one. In arguing dialectically Aristotle must not only show his audience why and how their own accounts of virtue fail to get them what they want. In addition, he must undermine their own preconceived notions of the way of life he is holding out as an alternative. As we shall see, in part for these reasons he does not provide an exhaustive picture of the content of the philosophic life at the end of the *Ethics*, but merely points out its advantages.

Questioning Aristotle's Pedagogical Strategy

An objection could be raised at this point to my interpretation of Aristotle's pedagogy. I have argued that his *Ethics* is not an autonomous moral treatise conveying abstract conclusions, but a dialectical pedagogy that prioritizes questions over answers. Yet his very pedagogy seems to close us off to fundamental questions. In his criticism of Platonism, he simply dismisses the question of the Form of the Good by saying that it is useless for human action. But this ignores the fundamental problem that gave rise to the doctrine of the forms. That is, by strictly delimiting the account to a consideration of what is useful for human action, Aristotle ignores the larger question of the relation of human action to the order of the universe. In this way, his pedagogy dogmatically closes us off from larger philosophical questions. Let me explain this point by contrasting Aristotle's treatment of Platonism with Socrates' turn to human action.

In the autobiographical passage of the *Phaedo*, Socrates says he turned to human action not to close off inquiry into the whole or to attain a knowledge of what is useful, but precisely to inquire into the meaning of the whole. He says that in his youth he tried to achieve a comprehensive vision of the cosmos by pursuing pre-Socratic science, which attempted to grasp the whole as a unit by reducing it to its elemental parts. He was motivated, that is, by the desire to try to understand how the various parts of the universe fit into a meaningful whole.[37]

However, Socrates says that this attempt failed. The study of pre-Socratic science could not provide a meaningful, exhaustive account of the order of the parts in the universe. In modern terms, for example, the science of biology can develop some account of organisms that reveals that they are incomprehensible unless considered teleologically as wholes participating in a stable environment that sustains them and gives them meaning and direction. Yet this ordering of parts within a whole is not the same thing as knowing the meaning of the whole. Qua biologist, the cosmos as a whole is inaccessible. The whole is not accessible, it seems, even to a discipline like theoretical physics, which sometimes self-consciously seeks to develop a grand theory of everything. Such a discipline, for example, cannot investigate the part of the cosmos called "human beings" except from a perspective that is remote from the most pressing human concerns, such as how to live or structure one's society, or what justice is. Indeed, it is not even clear whether theoretical physics or biology can explain on their own terms why this particular biological organism called "human being" wonders about physics or itself. These natural sciences thus may not be able to explain their own activity within the limits their methodology imposes. If they cannot perform such tasks, they cannot know the meaning of the whole.[38]

To put the matter in contemporary language, Socrates' realization that he is ignorant about the meaning *of* life entails that he is ignorant about any particular meaning *in* life. That is, since he does not know the meaning of the universe, he cannot say how any particular human action is intelligibly related to the meaning of the universe; and thus how any particular human action is meaningful. Thus the question of how human beings should live and act has to remain radically open. There are no settled principles of action because we cannot be sure that any human action is right or wrong, since knowing that information would necessitate knowing the order of the whole universe. So Socrates turns to the place in the universe that longs to know the meaning of the universe to see what that place will reveal about the universe. He turns to human speech and actions in order to see what they reveal about the order of the cosmos. But this turn does not appear to provide any positive morality. Socrates cannot found an ethical or political science because he has neither the requisite leisure nor the information. He is too busy to develop principles of conduct; and besides, the knowledge of the whole that such principles presuppose is beyond his grasp. His task is to consistently ask how people's speech and actions about human things reveal their underlying assumptions about the meaning of the whole in order to answer the problem he set for himself in his youth. His search for the right way of life is motivated not by some positive knowledge of how to live. Rather, it is motivated by an awareness of his ignorance about the meaning of life.

By contrast, Aristotle's emphasis that his account will be useful to human action seems dogmatic. In contrast to Socrates' turn to human things, which is open ended and zetetic, Aristotle's turn to human things is precisely a retreat from the investigation of the whole. In this sense, his inquiry into human action seems to be unphilosophic because it is autonomous. It does not reach out to ask questions about the meaning of the universe. Rather, by insisting that his account be useful to human action, it closes off the question that motivated Plato to develop his doctrine of the Form of the Good: How is my action related to the order (or lack thereof) underlying the universe? Is not Aristotle open to the very charges of complacency and smugness that he implicitly levels at his audience? The *Ethics* seems to be not a genuinely skeptical inquiry that seeks to cultivate the conditions for questioning, but an attempt to provide a set of answers about right action. This objection has to hang in the air until the character of the inquiry as a whole has come into view.

PART II
Revaluing the Virtues

3

Approaching the Virtues

Does Aristotle Accept His Culture's Notions of the Virtues?

Aristotle examines his audience's opinions in his long treatment of the virtues. His account is often interpreted to be a description or clarification of ordinary Greek conceptions of virtue. This tendency is manifest is several recent interpretations of Aristotle's account of greatness of soul *(megalopsuchia). Megalospuchia* is not one virtue among many. Rather, it is an inclusive ideal; a life in which all the particular moral virtues are present. Aristotle says that greatness of soul is a kind of crown *(cosmos),* suggesting that it is a beautifully ordered pattern of all the virtues (*NE,* 1124a1–2).[1] For this reason, any interpretation of Aristotle's account of *megalopsuchia* is an interpretation of his whole account of the moral virtues. Focusing on interpretations of greatness of soul illuminates how recent scholarship understands Aristotle's treatment of his culture's notion of virtue.

Christian Critics

Stanley Hauerwas and Charles Pinches argue that the main difference between Christian and Aristotelian conceptions of virtue revolves around their differing views of self-sufficiency. On their account, Aristotelian virtue aims at self-sufficiency. This is shown above all in Aristotle's treatment of *megalopsuchia*, where he argues that the great-souled man is characterized primarily by his effort to be self-sufficient—in particular, to be free from the necessity of being in debt to another. However, they argue, for Christians virtue is humble love, which rests on a sense of humanity's profound need for redemption and openness to gifts. For Hauerwas and Pinches, the humility and self-emptying of Jesus Christ stand in stark contrast to the pride of the magnanimous man.[2] For them, the pride of the magnanimous man and the Aristotelian insistence on equality in friendship entails that Aristotle's best man will have no willingness to aid the needy and weak—those who Christians are called to love the most. On their account, from the Christian perspective Aristotelian virtue is not virtue at all, but rather a species of pride.[3]

This account mirrors one found in John Millbank's *Theology and Social Theory.* For Millbank, Aristotle inherits the classical emphasis on honor, and so its focus on struggle, violence, domination, and exclusivity. Virtue for Aristotle entails that a strong man achieves victory over his competitors, whether in arms, politics, or honor, and the virtues are the means he uses to this end.[4] So Millbank asserts that Aristotle uncritically accepts the Greek emphasis on the possession of honor as determinative of a successful human life, and the emphasis on virility and competition that flows from this pursuit:

> A kind of giving can be exercised even in negative situations of poverty and weakness, and the charitable person is first and foremost the *recipient* of charity from God, which the magnanimous man prefers to keep in bounds. As friendship with God, and with fellow humans, charity always involves mutuality; Aristotle himself made this point about friendship, but he did not, like Aquinas, place friendship quite at the apex of civic achievement. Friends, for Aristotle, share a common love of the good, but this good is ultimately the fine economy of honour which is magnanimity. If friendship becomes the actual summit of virtue, then this suggests that virtue is itself relational, rather than a self-contained, internal matter. . . . In other words, a transitive giving of something to someone is constitutive of friendship, and therefore the thing most ultimately characteristic of virtue.[5]

These accounts mirror each other in more ways than one. It is not just that Hauerwas, Pinches, and Millbank are united in arguing that Aristotle's pagan exaltation of greatness of soul is unchristian. Further, they assert that in praising this mode of life, Aristotle is simply parroting his own culture's opinions about the excellence of a life devoted to honor. For Hauerwas and Pinches, Aristotle relies frequently on "the common judgments of his contemporaries regarding happiness as our highest good." The authors continue, "If there is a response imbedded in Aristotle's account to our query about who the virtuous person is, it is, simply, that if someone does not know then he cannot be one of us, for we know who our paragons of virtue are, just as we know that any view that denies responsibility for our character simply will not do."[6]

Pagan Praiser

In his *Pagan Virtues,* John Casey says he wishes to recover the positive aspects of ancient virtue that Christianity's emphasis on humility has papered over. He argues that the pagan virtues were built on the foundation of the "active emotions" such as anger and jealousy—emotions which encourage us to assert ourselves in a direct engagement with another person. These active emotions, especially anger, demand that we respect both ourselves and the person we are confronting. The basis of these positive emotions, in turn, is a certain kind of pride in ourselves and what is our own—our family, our history, our city—that Christianity has insisted is sinful. For Casey, Christianity dismissed as "pagan" the notion that it is good to have pride and "a desire for worldly glory, a sense that one can be a principle to oneself."[7] For him, it seems that King Lear is the representative Christian, because he is so lost in love and fantasy that he is willing to give up his pride too easily and he is "never touched by noble anger" (219). For him, Christianity's emphasis on passivity encourages not active emotions engendering respect for ourselves and others, but passive emotions which encourage debasement of ourselves and others. Casey thinks that Christianity tends to make human beings into cramped, effeminate haters of themselves and others.

Clearly, the Christian critics and the pagan praiser disagree strongly on several questions, particularly on the praiseworthiness of magnanimity and on Christianity itself. Yet for my purposes, what unites them is more important than what separates them. Both think that in presenting the magnanimous man Aristotle is praising him. In turn, this view has implications for how we are to understand Aristotle's overall approach to the virtues. If Aristotle is concerned primarily with buttressing and clarifying his own culture's notion of the virtues, then politically he is a conservative, concerned above all with preserving political regimes.

Yet Aristotle's account of the moral virtues is not a self-congratulatory list of respectable Greek behaviors. Rather, in his treatment of the moral virtues, he seeks to show where his audience's account of virtue fails on its own terms in order to present a new way of life. None of the interpretations sketched above pays attention to the ambiguities, paradoxes, ironies, and contradictions in Aristotle's account of the virtues. What are we to make of these? When modern commentators find contradictions, for example, in Aristotle's text, they often try to explain them to make the work more systematic or at least less contradictory. But this approach assumes that the text was meant to be a systematic treatise aiming at comprehensive, harmonious conclusions concerning right action. However, if the *Ethics* is a dialectical pedagogy, then perhaps the contradictions, paradoxes, ambiguities, and ironies are intentional. These can be used as effective teaching devices by illuminating the contradictions, paradoxes, ambiguities, and ironies implicit in the audience's commitments. By doing so they could shock the audience out of a self-congratulatory sense of the rightness of their opinions and cultural standards. This could move the inquiry forward by inviting them to search for more genuine conceptions of human excellence and flourishing. In this sense, the problems in the text advance its pedagogical intent by inviting the reader to think. So when a thinker of Aristotle's rank makes a mistake that would cause an ordinary professor to blush, the imperative is not necessarily to try to explain it away. Rather, it is to lay the contradictory, paradoxical statements or accounts beside each other and try to figure out what might be the intended pedagogical effect on the soul and mind of the reader. What questions or problems do the textual problems invite the audience to consider? This psychogogic effect is obscured if one explains the contradiction away in a drive for systematization:

> Although every written work is a monologue, the philosophical work is always implicitly a dialogue. The dimension of the possible interlocutor is always present within it. This explains the incoherencies and contradictions which modern historians discover with astonishment in the works of ancient philosophers. In philosophical works such as these, thought

> cannot be expressed according to the pure, absolute necessity of systematic order. Rather, it must take into account the level of the interlocutor, and the concrete tempo of logos in which it is expressed.[8]

Bifurcating the Soul; Bifurcating Virtue

Before Aristotle examines particular virtues in detail, he gives a general overview of the subject. In this treatment, he makes two broad distinctions that drive the inquiry forward. First, he distinguishes moral from intellectual virtues. Second, he distinguishes various kinds of moral virtues from each other. On closer examination, however, it is clear that these distinctions are not Aristotle's own; they are derived from the way virtue initially appears to reputable opinion. Again, the dialectical inquiry must begin from the audience's presuppositions. Aristotle does not begin his account by providing a general view of his own notion of virtue. By understanding the ways his audience's approach to virtue breaks down, we can begin to understand how Aristotle employs dialectic to undermine their accounts of virtue in order to move beyond them.

Let me begin with the first division first. On what basis are the moral virtues distinguished from the intellectual virtues? Up to now, Aristotle reminds us, the inquiry has shown that happiness is a kind of activity of the soul in accord with virtue. However, he says, since virtue is an activity of the soul, those who study politics should know something about the soul. Yet there are strict limits to this inquiry. Aristotle reminds us that he will inquire into the soul only with his own aim in view and only to the extent that the object of the inquiry demands. He refuses to go into more detail than is required (*NE,* 1102a22–26). Recall that Aristotle has reminded us of the difference between inquiring into virtue in order to know what it is and inquiring into virtue in order to become good. The object of the *Ethics* is to help us to act well, not to know what is good theoretically (*NE,* 1049b11; 1095a5; 1103b26–31). In turn, we have seen that Aristotle insists that the practical and pedagogical intent of the inquiry imposes constraints or limits upon it. The inquiry into the soul is meant to uncover what virtue is, but that inquiry will be subordinated to the pedagogical intent of the work. In other words, Aristotle's account of the soul is subordinated to a pedagogy intended to convince his audience to act in a certain way. We need not take his presentation of the soul here as his final word on the subject precisely because it is not intended to be a disinterested scientific account which aims at theoretical completeness and harmonious conclusions. Rather, the point is to teach with a view to action.[9]

Aristotle divides the soul up into two parts: the rational and the irrational. This is the basis for the division between the moral and intellectual virtues. Yet this division of the soul—upon which the division of the virtues is based—is highly suspect. Aristotle says that it does not matter for his purposes whether the soul is really divisible in this way, or whether these parts are merely complementary aspects of a single whole, as, for instance, convex and concave are different ways of looking at the circumference of the same circle (*NE,* 1102a28–32). It is clear that the latter is Aristotle's own considered view, for in his "more technical discussions" (*NE,* 1102a23), Aristotle argues that the soul is not divisible into parts in this way (*DA,* 411a10ff; 412b5–10). Our suspicions about the worth of this distinction, and thus the distinction between the moral and intellectual virtues, gains force when it is realized that in Aristotle's later treatment of character, the divisions into the different kinds of virtues are abandoned. Indeed, as we shall see, he later insists that virtue is one. So why does he divide the soul—and thus virtue—in this way? We have to look still closer into the basis of these divisions.

The main division between the irrational part of the soul and the rational part is quickly followed by more divisions. The irrational and the rational parts are each split in two. In the irrational part of the soul, Aristotle distinguishes the part that is responsible for nutrition and growth from the part that can partake in reason. The nutritive element is common with all animals and so is not exclusively human. However, in addition to this part, human beings have an irrational part of the soul that can share in reason in some way (*NE,* 1102b13). In evidence for this, Aristotle appeals to the experience of the morally strong and morally weak man. In these men, we praise the rational part of the soul, because it exhorts them to do what is right. Yet we also see another part that struggles against reason, fighting it and resisting it. In this situation, the soul behaves like the limbs of a person with paralysis: when a paralyzed man tells his arms to move right, they mover left instead (*NE,* 1102b20). Yet the movements of the body are visible; the movements of the soul are not (*NE,* 1102b22). In the morally weak man, impulses turn him aside from the urgings of reason, and he does the opposite of what it tells him. However, the morally strong man listens to reason. In turn, Aristotle continues, if the irrational part of the soul has two parts, it follows that the rational part of the soul also has two parts. One part possesses reason simply, while the other part listens to reason as one would listen to the commands of a father. Finally, he says, virtue is differentiated in line with these distinctions within the soul: the irrational element : moral virtues :: the rational element : intellectual virtues.

Moral Paralysis

Again, each of these distinctions are suspect. First, when the virtues are distinguished from each other, the appeal is not to the experience of virtue, but rather to moral weakness. However, it is unjustifiable to appeal to the experience of a morally weak man in order to delineate a table of the virtues. The justification for saying that the soul has these various elements is the experience of wanting to do the right thing, but not doing it. But this is not virtue. As we shall see, later in the *Ethics* Aristotle explicitly distinguishes the morally strong and morally weak man from the virtuous man. If he wants to speak about how the virtues are distinguished, why would he appeal to a state of character that is deficient in virtue? If he wants to divide the various virtues from each other, why does he not appeal to an experience of virtue? Why does he appeal to an experience of *wrong action* in order to elucidate the foundation of a discussion of *right action?*

This question gains force when we reflect on the guiding example Aristotle uses to illustrate the experience of the morally weak man. He emphasizes that we cannot see the movements of the soul. Since virtue involves not only external actions but also internal dispositions and motivations, it may not be visible. Aristotle employs a weird example in order to illustrate this point (*NE,* 1102b15–29). He appeals to the experience of a person so paralyzed that his limbs do not obey him; when he tells his arm to move right, it moves left instead. In acts of moral weakness, the soul behaves just like the paralyzed limbs of the body. Paralysis is not a state of flourishing health. Aristotle is writing a book on how to be happy. In his example, the analogue to happiness should be health, or a flourishing body. Surely, if one is writing a book on how to be morally healthy, one should begin by reflecting on the example of physical health rather than illness. If one wanted to explain what health was, and if one wanted to elucidate the various kinds of health, one would most definitely not begin with the example of a person who did not have control of his limbs, except by way of contrast. So why does Aristotle use the example of a paralyzed person to illustrate our experience of virtue? Why use an example of physical illness to illustrate moral excellence? Why not give an image of physical health to illuminate moral goodness?

The fact that the workings of virtue are invisible causes pedagogical problems. For instance, Aristotle says that in the arts *(technai)*, the goal is to produce some kind of product, so in order to call a craftsman "good," one merely looks at the finished product. We can say that a carpenter is a "good carpenter" if we judge her cabinets to be good, for example. Yet we judge virtue not merely by appealing to some result in the world. Rather, with virtue the how *(pos)* of the act is as important as its externals (*NE*, 1105a29). To be just—to do the just thing in a virtuous way—it is not enough merely physically to pay back one's debts, for example. This is because a person could be returning his debts in a rage, or with profound regret that he couldn't cheat his way out of having to repay a loan, or because he is trying to gain a reputation for paying back his debts so that he can swindle even more money later on. So the mere act of repaying is not sufficient for the act to be virtuous. Indeed, Aristotle lays out certain conditions that must attend the action: The actor must act with awareness of what he is doing; he must choose the act; he must do the act for the sake of itself, rather than for what results from the act; and he must do the act from a firm and unchangeable character. The most important aspects of virtue are hidden from view.

It follows that it is quite difficult to think and speak about virtue. If Aristotle begins by speaking about virtue from the perspective of the virtuous person, he may be radically misunderstood by his audience, most of whom are not virtuous and so will not have direct experience of what he is talking about. Instead, dialectic demands that he begin with his audience's own notions of action—which is an experience of moral weakness; wanting to do the right thing but being incapable of it—and work from this starting point to a fuller account of excellence. In short, the pedagogy demands beginning where the audience is developmentally.

By employing examples of physical defects to illustrate our ordinary experience of action, Aristotle implies that most people are not good. Most of our moral experience is more akin to the paralyzed person who cannot control his limbs. Apparently, according to Aristotle, we want to do the right thing, but find our passions and desires obstructing our reason and its good intentions.[10] For him, most of us are so far from virtue that our experience of right action resembles on the physical level a man who is not in control of the movement of his body.[11] On reflection, perhaps this is the only way Aristotle could have begun a dialectical consideration of virtue. If his concern is to engage in a pedagogy which will make his audience good, he must begin not with an articulation of virtue, but rather with their everyday experience of moral action. It is clear from the examples he employs that the parts of the soul and thus the various virtues come to light primarily as a result of the experience of resistance to right action. The irrational part of the soul was differentiated because we experience a tug of war within our selves, between the part that informs us of what is right and the part that wants to go its own way and satisfy our desires. If this is our most intimate experience of action, then right action will be painful; it will be experienced as a denial of our desires. For this reason, often we will not taste for ourselves the attractiveness of doing the right thing. Indeed, this will seem antithetical to our interests. To continue the medical analogy Aristotle employs, to be aware that I need a cure, I need to know that I am sick. In a like way, in order to be convinced that I need to change my way of life, I must realize that my way of life is making me unhappy. By contrast, I am incurable only if I will not admit to my illness.

The Devaluation of Reason

The experience of incontinence is also the source for the bifurcation of the soul into reason-having and non-reason-having parts. Implicit in this bifurcation is a denigration of thought. In ordinary experience reason seems impotent before desires. In the conflict within the self between reason and desires, desires sometimes follow thought—but only if they want to. Clearly, it is desires that are authoritative. In ordinary experience, desires produce action. Thought produces nothing. Thus according to initial appearances based on our ordinary moral experience (an experience of incontinence), the moral virtues are authoritative over the realm of action, while the intellectual virtues cover the realm of thought. And since thought does not yield action, it does not seem from this perspective to be active at all. Thought merely deliberates and has to hope that desire will somehow go along. Reason does nothing practical. If Aristotle is to encourage the audience to act more thoughtfully, the bifurcation between reason and action (and the consequent devaluation of thought) must be overcome. In a like way, if philosophy—a life of active thought—is to be seen as an attractive alternative, this bifurcation of thought and action and consequent denigration of thought also has to be overcome.

Slicing and Dicing the Virtues

After the bifurcation between thought and action, and the resulting bifurcation between the moral and intellectual virtues, Aristotle differentiates the various particular moral virtues from each other. Once again, the principle of individuation is highly suspect because he presents virtue not as it appears from the perspective of a virtuous person, but as it appears to his audience. Aristotle begins his differentiation of the virtues by appealing to the doctrine of the mean. Every virtue is a mean with respect to emotions and actions, he says. Yet he says that this general statement of the problem is not sufficient. Indeed, most people discussing actions give general accounts of action. However, since actions are about particular matters, particular statements are more true (*NE,* 1107a29–30), and so he must give a more particular account of the various virtues and their relationship. The various kinds of emotions and situations calling for action provide the principles of individuation. That is, the different virtues result from the kinds of temptations that people are subject to. Since we are tempted to fear, we need the virtue of courage. Since we are tempted to self-indulgence, we need the virtue of moderation, and so on.

When explicating these particular virtues, Aristotle says he used a table (*NE,* 1107a34). In order to articulate his account, it is worthwhile to try to recreate this table. Aristotle says that virtue is a mean between the extremes of excess and deficiency (*NE,* 2.7), so his table must have looked like that on the following page.

There are several puzzling things about this table. First, the principle of individuation is odd. The virtues are distinguished because of the variety of situations and emotions calling for action. Since we must react to different situations and emotions in different ways, we assume that there are distinct virtues that control or manage each one. This approach to the problem of human action seems to lead to the notion that right action can be determined by laying down principles or rules that will cover a variety of general cases. As Aristotle says, the principle of the discussion of the moral virtues is that one must act *kata ton orthon logon,* or in accord with right reason (*NE,* 1103b30). This expression has the connotation of acting in accord with a rule that governs a majority of cases. On this view, the virtues are like cattle prods. A single virtue manages a variety of similar situations in which an individual's emotions or temptations tend to lead him astray from the straight and narrow. Yet this way of thinking about action is an abstraction which flies in the face of the concreteness of Aristotle's account of practical wisdom. On his later account, practical wisdom grasps the particulars of each irreducibly unique situation in order to determine the right thing to do. But virtues do not act. Individuals do, in specific situations. On the principle of individuation employed here, every situation would demand its own virtue.

Moreover, what I will call the problems of naming is obvious from the table. In drawing up his list Aristotle repeatedly points to the problem that there is no name for a great deal of the virtues and vices he will discuss. Naming is a way of allowing something to emerge into consciousness. If we have not named something, in a sense it does not exist for us. If a specific virtue or vice has no name, it is not noticed, and therefore not practiced. For both individuals and regimes, the lack of a name for a virtue or vice implies a moral deficiency. A contemporary example might be the difficulty contemporary

Table 3.1 The Virtues in General

Greatness of Soul

(The "crown of virtues" because it describes a life that encompasses all the virtues)

State	*Vice (deficiency)*	*Virtue (mean)*	*Vice (excess)*
Fear and confidence	Cowardice	Courage/ manliness	No name* Recklessness
Pleasure and pain	No name Insensitivity	Self-control	Self-indulgence
Money	Stinginess	Magnificence	Extravagence
*Honor/ dishonor***	No name Lack of love of honor	No name Love of honor	No name Love of honor
Anger	No name Apathy	No name Gentleness	No name Irascibility
Speech	No name Self-deprecation	No Name Truthfulness	No name Boastfulness
Pleasantness in amusement	No name Boorishness	No name Wittiness	No name Buffoonery
Pleasantness in daily life	No name Grouchiness	No name Friendliness	No name Flattery
*Shame****	Shamelessness	Modesty	No name
*Pain or pleasure we feel about the fortunes of others*****	Spitefulness	Righteous indignation	Envy

* Whenever Aristotle says that there is no settled name for a particular virtue or vice, I will put "No name" in the appropriate column and then underneath write the name Aristotle coins for the virtue or vice in question.
** There are two problems here. First, people don't realize that one could love honor too much, so there is no name for the mean. For this reason, people employ the same term *(philotimos)* for both the mean and the excess. Second, the extremes lay claim to the mean (*NE,* 1107b32.)
*** Shame is a special case because Artistotle's audience does not view it as subject to education in virtue. If a person is excellent, he does not need shame. Still, shamelessness is understood to be a vice. The man intermediate in shame can be said to be modest (*NE,* 1108a30–35).
**** Spitefulness is deficiency in feeling pain at the misfortunes of others; envy is feeling pain at the good luck of others. Righteous indignation is the feeling of pain when someone profits undeservedly. But there is no name for the capacity to rejoice at the good fortune of other people when it is deserved.

citizens of capitalist societies have in speaking about virtue with respect to acquisition of material goods. Since in our context individual and social happiness are tied more or less to an ever expanding GDP fueled by consumerism, acquisitiveness is considered a virtue. From this perspective, it is not vicious to seek to acquire too much; indeed, conspicuous acquisition and consumption are celebrated. So what would it mean to be moderate in one's acquisition of material goods? It seems that we do not have a name for such a virtue precisely because it is not practiced. This is ironic, since it is arguable that the virtue that is most needed in our context is the one that is most difficult to describe. As MacIntyre has pointed out, for example,

> [T]he adherents of that standpoint [i.e., the standpoint of modern capitalist societies] recognize that acquisitiveness is a character trait indispensable to continuous and limitless economic growth, and one of their central beliefs is that continuous and limitless economic growth is a fundamental good. That a systematically lower standard of living ought to be preferred to a systematically higher standard of living is a thought incompatible with either the economics or the politics of peculiarly modern societies. So prices and wages have come to be understood as unrelated—and indeed in a modern economy could not be regulated—to desert in terms of labor, and the notion of a just price or a just wage in modern terms makes no sense. But a community which was guided by Aristotelian norms would not only have to view acquisitiveness as a vice but would have to set strict limits to growth insofar as that is necessary to preserve or enhance a distribution of goods according to desert.[12]

Perhaps this is why Aristotle repeatedly emphasizes that the mean is difficult to attain. For him, it is hard work to be good (*NE,* 1109a24). Reflecting on the problem of nameless virtues and vices is not only important for individuals, however. It is also crucial for understanding the problems presented by Aristotle's pedagogy. Since regimes powerfully inform their citizens' sense of virtue and vice, in order to lead his audience away from deficient to more flourishing notions of human activity, he must drag them in the opposite direction than the one toward which their regime encourages them to tend. And since every regime's notions of virtue and vice are more or less defective, avoiding a particular regime's deficiencies would require a consistently countervailing stance that is vigorously attentive to deformation. Aristotle's presentation of the particular moral virtues must be understood in this light. He is seeking to revalue what counts as successful notions of human activity and human life. To do so, he must struggle against prevailing notions of human excellence. In a regime that deforms its citizens to celebrate acquisitiveness, for example, virtue would demand somehow pulling individuals away from consumerism. In a regime that celebrates honor and manly self-assertion, virtue would require pulling citizens in the opposite direction. For Aristotle, human beings have to avoid the errors that have the greatest attraction for us personally (*NE,* 1109b2). And, since our regimes form us, the errors which have the greatest attraction would of course be our regime's conception of a successful human life. The test here would be what the individual and by extension, regime, feel to be most pleasant (*NE,* 2.3). This is to say that for Aristotle, there is a parallel between what the individual finds most attractive and what his or her society finds attractive. Avoiding vice personally would require investigating the presuppositions of one's regime in order to see how one was being formed or deformed by it.[13]

Conclusion

Throughout the general treatment of the virtues, Aristotle gives strong hints that his account of the virtues will be critical and evaluative; not merely descriptive. It is time to articulate in more detail exactly how he dialectically criticizes his culture's notion of virtue by considering his treatment of the particular moral virtues. In each treatment he works within the assumptions of his audience to try to get them to grasp how their notions of excellence break down on their own terms. Aristotle's own conception of virtue only emerges out of the failure of respectable Greek notions of excellence.

4
Criticizing the Moral Virtues

Questions

In his discussion of the particular moral virtues Aristotle does not aim to give didactic information about rules of conduct derived from his culture's notion of a successful life. Rather, he says that he wants to answer a set of questions: What are the virtues? What sorts of things do they deal with? How do they operate? He says addressing these questions will enable us to see the answer to a fourth: How many virtues are there? (*NE,* 1115a4–5). Aristotle says he needs to speak about particular virtues in order to answer these questions because action is about particulars, and so the discussion requires particularity.

Manliness

The first virtue Aristotle examines is usually translated as "courage." However, "courage" does not quite capture the full connotation of the term Aristotle uses. Earlier, he drew our attention to the problem with language by insisting that there were no names for many of the virtues and vices he was going to examine. Care must be taken, then, with the terms Aristotle employs. Aristotle says his discussion will be about *andreia,* which is related etymologically to the Greek term for "man." Thus the term literally means "manliness." In the city-states of Greece, manliness was so strongly emphasized that it sometimes came to be taken for virtue in its entirety. One reason for this was the external threats to the city, both from other *poleis* and from the powerful empires that threatened to gobble them up. In such a world, where one's life, homeland, and freedom depended on citizens' strength in arms, it is clear why manliness would be held in such high regard.[1] Without a successful defense of one's city, none of the other virtues would be possible; manly courage seems to be a precondition for anything else worth achieving in life.[2] Related to this is the ancient Greek emphasis on honor. A warrior culture that held the ability to struggle for honor to be the criterion for humanity would lead its participants to homologize manly self-assertion with the whole of human excellence. In taking up *andreia*, Aristotle asks, in effect, "What makes a real man?" So while it is clear that *andreia* entails courage since it implies facing death in battle, "courage" does not do justice to the full range of meaning implied in the Greek, just as "courage" does not capture all that is meant in English when we use the term "real man."

In our academic culture, the critique of manliness has gained a certain respectability. However, in Aristotle's time, criticisms of manliness would be far more problematic. Not only was the ability to bear arms like a man a prerequisite for citizenship; it was seen as the precondition for possessing specifically human qualities and thus being able to participate in public life.[3] What pedagogical strategy could be employed to shock a man's man out of his overemphasis on virility? Aristotle begins by laying out the way manly courage appears in reputable opinion. *Andreia* is a mean with respect to fear and confidence. Everyone fears evil things like a bad reputation, poverty, being without friends, and death, but these do not necessarily concern manliness. So about what is the real man *(andreios)* concerned? Aristotle says he is concerned only about the most exceedingly important things *(peri ta megista)*. Death is the most fearful thing, for it is the end of everything (*NE,* 1115a26). Yet not every death is noble/beautiful *(kalon)*, so not every death brings out the possibility of manliness. After all, a man can die by drowning or as a result of disease. Real men face a noble death without fear (*NE,* 1115a33). Aristotle concludes that such a man is only concerned with death in battle, for only in battle does a man risk the greatest and most noble kind of danger (*NE,* 1115a30–31). This is corroborated, Aristotle continues, by the way honors are given out by cities and kings, for they give the greatest honors to those who have risked all in battle. So, a real man is one who fearlessly faces a noble death and any situation that brings a sudden death, especially in battle (*NE*, 1115a33–34). This man will fear what is fearful, but will do it virtuously; that is, in the right way as reason *(logos)* directs for the sake of the noble (*tou kalou eneka; NE*, 1115b12–13). It is clear that the real man yokes the noble with honor *(time)*. This is shown by how popular opinion corroborates its reflection on manliness; the real man is given honors for braving battle. The real man, further, is revolted by the thought of a death by disease or drowning. The actions which concern manly courage are those in which a person can show his physical strength or prowess *(alke)* and die a fair death, and there are no opportunities for such things if one dies of old age (*NE,* 1115b4–6). In Aristotle's regime, death by cancer would have been ignoble because it presents no opportunity for honor.

Aristotle criticizes this notion of virtue obliquely. He says that while facing death in battle is the central case, the term *andreia* is also used to name five other states of character. He first takes up the courage of the citizen fighting for his homeland. This, Aristotle says, closely resembles *andreia* (*NE,* 1116a18; 1116a27). Citizens, Aristotle says, endure dangers because the laws take away their honor and reproach them if they do not, and honor them if they do. On account of this, among the most manly people *(andreiotatoi)*, the coward is dishonored and the most courageous people are honored (*NE,* 1116a20–21). In this Aristotle makes explicit the point that was implicit in the earlier discussion: in engaging in manly courage, the real man is seeking honor. This is what one would expect in Aristotle's culture. Yet Aristotle proceeds to criticize this notion of manliness by pointing out its disastrous implications. He says that Homer used characters like Hector to dramatize manliness. Yet when one reflects on the passage from the *Iliad* that Aristotle cites (*NE,* 1116a22–26), one sees that he is actually criticizing what I have called virtue-as-virility and its attachment to honor.

The context of the passage Aristotle points to is this: Achilles is the best warrior for the Achaians. After Achilles departs from the battle, the Trojans begin to win. Achilles' best friend, Patroklos, borrows his armor to rout the Trojans and prevent a disaster. However, Hector kills Patroklos. Everyone in the Trojan camp knows this will force Achilles back into the fighting. In the aftermath of the battle, before Achilles begins to fight again, the Trojans are camped out in the field between the city of Troy and the Achaian army. Poulydamas, the wise Trojan counselor, advises Hector to withdraw to the safety of Troy so that the army will be protected from Achilles' wrath:

> Now take careful thought, my dear friends; or I myself urge you / to go back into the city and not wait for the divine dawn / in the plain beside the ships. We are too far from the wall now. / While this man was still angry with great Agamemnon, / for all that time the Achaians were easier to fight with. / For I also used then to be one who was glad to sleep out / near their ships, and I hoped to capture the oarswept vessels. / But now I terribly dread the swift-footed son of Peleus. / So violent is the valour in him, he will not be willing / to stay here in the plain, where not Achaians and Trojans from either side sunder between them the wrath of the war god. / With him the fight will be for the sake of our city and women."
>
> (*Iliad* 18.254–65)

The appeal is obvious: we are putting our city in danger if we remain in the open. Let us retreat in order to protect our loved ones. Hector, however, ignores this advice, because he says he is tired of behaving like a coward, seeking safety behind the walls of Troy. He wants to prove his worth by finishing off his enemy. The result is a predictable disaster. In the passage Aristotle cites—one of the most famous of the *Iliad*, and surely well known to Aristotle's audience—Hector is standing before the walls of Troy as Achilles races up to kill him. His parents plead with him to come within the walls of the city but he refuses. Aristotle only cites a fragment of the full response, which reads as follows:

> Ah me! If I go now inside the wall and the gateway, / Poulydamas will be the first to put a reproach upon me / since he tried to make me lead the Trojans inside the city / on that accursed night when brilliant Achilles rose up, / and I would not obey him, but that would have been far better. / Now, since by my own recklessness I have ruined my people, / I feel shame before the Trojans and the Trojan women with trailing / robes, that someone who is less of a man will say of me: / "Hector believed in his own strength, and ruined his people."
>
> (*Iliad* 22.99–107).

The criticism is clear. Hector is an exemplar of the virile citizen who asserts himself to show forth an excellence that demands honor. Yet this self-assertion twice led Hector to refuse wise advice. Love of honor and fear of shame are flip sides of the same coin. Hector's first refusal was motivated by love of honor. He refused Poulydamus's advice because he wanted to gain glory by defeating his enemies. His second refusal was motivated by fear of shame. Hector realizes that the fate of his wife, children, and city hangs on his decision because he is the army's best hope. He knows his death will lead to the downfall of Troy. Yet he cannot bring himself to accept the appearance of cowardice by running from his impending fight with Achilles. Indeed, he knows that this loathing of shame prevents him from doing the right thing.

So Aristotle points out the contradiction in reputable opinion about manliness: ironically, the way *andreia* is actually practiced yields the opposite of what his audience wanted it to achieve. Earlier, *andreia* was identified with facing death in battle. In Aristotle's time, the defense of the homeland was crucial, for the fall of a city often led to death for the men and slavery for everyone else. *Andreia* was celebrated because it was required to defend the homeland. Yet Aristotle points out that the typical citizen is brave to achieve honor and avoid shame. A danger to the city lurks in this self-assertion. The real man Aristotle initially sketched as the exemplar of virtue (*NE,* 1116a26–29) clearly resembles both Hector and the citizen-soldier who fights for his own glory. While such a person is honored insofar as he protects the city, in pursuing honor excessively he actually puts the city in jeopardy. His "virtue" is really a splendid vice. In the end, Aristotle says, such men are like those who perform in battle only because they fear the wrath of their commanders. The citizen-solider and the real man act under constraint. Contrary to appearances, the real man pursing honor "bravely" in battle acts out of a kind of fear.[4]

By conflating the noble with honor, the typical virile citizen misunderstands what courage demands. Aristotle insists that *andreia* must come not from coercion but for the sake of *to kalon* (*NE,* 1116b2–3). Perhaps *to kalon* must not be identified with possession of honor. In the concluding discussion of *andreia* (3.9), Aristotle redefines *to kalon,* and thus the quality of *andreia.* Manly courage is about confidence and fear, but more about fear, Aristotle begins. In fact, people are called "manly" for enduring pain (*NE,* 1117a32). However, he then raises a serious problem: He says that this manly courage aims at what is pleasant, even though that pleasure is obscured by the circumstances in which manly courage shines forth (1117b1–2). Boxers, for example, must engage in a bloody fight in order to gain their prize, and that fight is so painful as to render the prize questionable. In the same way, death and wounds will be painful for the courageous man, but he will undergo them because it is *kalon.* Indeed, Aristotle emphasizes, the man of virtue finds death more painful than anyone, for he stands to lose the greatest good—his virtue. Yet he is no less brave for that. He chooses noble deeds in war in exchange for pain. Aristotle concludes, "Only insofar as it achieves its end is it true to say that every virtue is pleasant when it is practiced" (*NE,* 1117b15).

Aristotle redefines the noble in this passage by separating it from the pursuit of honor. Death makes us lose all goods, including honor. As Achilles recognized, no honor is worth the price of death, for death means one cannot enjoy the honor bestowed. However, the person of true courage fights anyway, and finds risking death pleasant, in the sense of fair or beautiful. Why does the person of real virtue choose noble deeds in war in exchange for suffering pain, according to Aristotle? This does not seem at all pleasant. It could not be for the sake of honor, for death means an end to the enjoyment of honor. Perhaps Aristotle is trying to convince his audience that acting in a noble way entails choosing in accord with the demands of the situation. It is noble to engage in the pain of battle in the sense that if one flees, one's comrades and city will be left to pay the consequences. In this sense, it is pleasant to do the right thing; at the least it would be *un*pleasant to run from battle to seek comfort and peace knowing that one's actions contributed to the death of one's loved ones. Perhaps Aristotle seeks to convey the realization that courage entails not self-assertion and grabbing for glory, which endangers one's fellows and one's city.[5] Rather, it demands setting aside one's own immediate interests and acting in a fair-minded, proportionate manner in accord with the particular realities of the situation one faces. Only then will manly courage attain its end and become genuine excellence; only then will it be pleasant (*NE,* 1117b14–15). Aristotle has revalued *andreia* and in the process begins to redefine what is *kalos*, which increasingly throughout the *Ethics* begins to mean "proportionate" or "fair."

Aristotle's pedagogical strategy mirrors Socrates' in the *Apology* (28b–30b). In his defense speech, he insists that he is not ashamed of following a life that might lead to his execution. In seeking to live the best life, no real man *(aner)* would think of the risk of death, but only focus on whether his deeds were just or unjust and those of a good man *(aner agathou)*. Socrates refers to his exemplary military service and suggests that the god who gave him his philosophic mission is like a general who assigns a soldier to his post. To leave that post because of fear of death would be unmanly. While he employs the rhetoric of virility Socrates revalues what the real man stands for. For Socrates, true *andreia* requires philosophy, especially because philosophy is the practice of dying and *andreia* is found above all in the way the philosopher manages death. In this Socrates suggests that in order to be a real man, one has to be a philosopher. Indeed, in various places Socrates suggests that he is the new Achilles who stands by his battle station in obedience to the gods.[6]

Moderation

Moderation falls next in the list of particular moral virtues. Aristotle says this has to do with pleasure. Yet since the whole book is about pleasure and pain, and since he returns to this theme several different times throughout the text, I cannot adequately discuss Aristotle's account of moderation until we have a sense of the text as a whole. So I will put off a discussion of moderation until the penultimate chapter.

Generosity

Generosity, Aristotle says, is about *chremata*. This is sometimes translated as "material goods," but has a wider application. Aristotle says that it includes everything whose value is measured in money. The range of possibilities here is apparently endless, since it is limited only by the ingenuity of money grubbers who try to put a monetary value on anything they can.[7] Aristotle includes pimps in his discussion. Since he also includes tyrants who grant favors to supporters in the discussion, *chremata* extends to such things as offices, freedom, and all the other goodies rulers bestow on their cronies in exchange for support. Neither "possessions" nor "money" capture Aristotle's range of meaning; I will use "external goods."

Aristotle begins his consideration of generosity by laying out how it appears to reputable opinion. Generosity seems to be a mean with respect to *giving away* external goods. The virtue and its corresponding vices fall out this way:

Table 4.1. Generosity as it Appears to Reputable Opinion

	Deficiency	*Mean*	*Excess*
Giving away external goods	Stinginess (*aneleutheria*, literally not fit for a free man.)	Generosity	Wastefulness or Extravagence

Yet immediately Aristotle points to the insufficiency of this account, for on this view, generosity focuses only on giving and neglects taking (*NE*, 1120a8–9). Generosity seems exclusively about giving first because virtue seems to be about doing good rather than having good done to you, and about performing noble-fair acts *(ta kala prattein)* rather than not performing base ones (*NE*, 1120a11–13). So for example, Aristotle says while we show gratitude toward someone who gives something to us, we do not praise someone who refrains from taking from us. Further, he says it is easier not to take than to give away, and people are less likely to give away what belongs to them than what belongs to their neighbor. (Of course, careful readers will recognize that the unstated flip side of this is that people are more likely to give away what they have taken from another than what they own themselves.) In fact, Aristotle concludes, generous people are more loved than anyone else because they are so helpful (*NE*, 1120a22–23). The thrust of the argument is clear: we have a difficult time evaluating generosity because we are judges in our own case. When we think about generosity, we tend to focus more on giving than taking because we love to receive gifts. Related to this is the fact that we tend to identify virtue with visible acts that we can touch and see. Giving away is an obvious external act one can see and touch; refraining from unjust taking is hidden. So we tend to focus on the former rather than the latter. Yet Aristotle has already taken pains to remind his readers that when speaking about virtue external appearances deceive. Virtue is not merely about external action, but also about how *(pos)* that action is performed.

These reflections ought to be understood within the context of classical Greek politics. The pursuit of honor has several related dimensions. Most obviously, it manifests itself in the desire to win public recognition of excellence in competitions for superiority. Yet the desire to take vengeance at slights is also present in the process of social evaluation. Revenge is necessary both to bolster one's reputation and to ward off future attacks. In addition, the constant mutual evaluation taking place leads to feelings of envy at the good fortune of others, especially if their success appears undeserved. As Aristotle points out in the *Rhetoric*, the agonistic tendency to compare entails that participants in a struggle for honor feel pain and resentment at the good fortune of their rivals (*R*, 1388a–b). In classical Athens, this led ordinary citizens to resent the power and arrogance of those who were wealthier and more successful than themselves.[8] This envy sometimes produced malicious lawsuits intended to diminish or bankrupt one's enemies or those who were seen as hubristic. The wealthy and powerful often responded by lavishing gifts on the city in order to avoid such litigation. Or, if they got sued, they used their past generosity as a legal defense before the democratic jury:

> Rich litigants commonly pointed to the material benefits they and their ancestors had conferred upon the state. Some individuals used much of the water in their clocks reciting lengthy and detailed lists of liturgies they had performed. Others pointed out to juries that their liturgies had entailed considerable personal sacrifice and that the benefactions had been in excess of what would normally be expected from an estate of a certain size. Litigants who spent part of their limited speaking time discussing their liturgies obviously expected to evoke a positive response from jurors. The performance of liturgies was one way that the wealthy individuals might hope to deflect the natural envy of the poor. Iseaus states explicitly

> that since his clients had performed liturgies it is not proper that they should be envied *(phthoneisthai);* in addition, he suggests that if the judgement goes in their favor, they will be even more eager to pay up in by the future.[9]

Aristotle seeks to move his audience to a fuller notion of generosity—one not cramped by envy, self-seeking, and self-protection. He does so by giving a sketch of what genuine generosity would require. The truly generous person will give away in the right way and for the sake of the noble-fair (*NE,* 1120a26). He will not take from the wrong source, for unjust taking is not characteristic of a person who holds possessions in low esteem (*NE,* 1120a33). The generous person will not give to everybody but only to the right people at the right time and only for the sake of *to kalon.* This draws us to a richer conception of generosity for several reasons. The generous man is more loved than anyone, recall, because he gives away. The motives for generosity as actually practiced are honor and an avoidance of the dangers of being envied. Yet Aristotle points out that real virtue is done for the sake of the noble-fair, not to curry favor with sycophants. Further, the generous person will focus not merely on giving in the right way; in addition, he will focus on right taking as well. Indeed, Aristotle points out, the truly generous man almost by definition cannot be wealthy, for one cannot have an abundance of material goods without devoting the extraordinary amount of time and effort it takes to getting them. The truly generous man will not be someone who takes indiscriminately. Rather, he will be someone who values external goods for the sake of giving. Since people obsessed with external goods are overly worried about accumulating, they may not know the real criterion of value for the very goods they pursue (*NE,* 1120b17–22). The implication is that they neither give away nor acquire virtuously. Aristotle makes this point explicit later, when he argues that the generous man will both give and take in the right way from the right sources. The practices of giving and taking are found in the same individual; if one takes rightly, one tends to give rightly as well (*NE,* 1120b32–35). However since we tend to overvalue giving and undervalue not taking, we do not praise a poor man because he refuses to take unjustly and gives away what little he has.[10] In fact, we tend to attribute poverty to bad luck rather than to virtue (*NE,* 1120b17).

For these reasons, generosity is much more complicated than it initially appeared. Most obviously, virtue with respect to *chremata* requires right giving and right taking. Aristotle's argument has resulted in a new view of the vices opposed to generosity—vices that were not named in the initial account of generosity because they were not apparent. This articulation of vices opposed to right taking gives new meaning to right giving. In reality there are several forms of extravagance and stinginess. The initial generosity table must be revised:

Table 4.2. Vices Concerning External Goods

	Giving too much	*Not giving enough*
Taking too much from the wrong source	Extravagance #1 (Most extravagant people are like this)	Stinginess #1 (Pimps and Tyrants)
Not taking too much	Extravagance #2	Stinginess #2 Two kinds: A) Those afraid to give because they don't want to be forced to do anything base if they lose what they have. B) Those afraid to take because they think it's risky and hard.

The discussion revalues how one should relate to external goods. This happens in two ways. First, the virtues of respectability and mere law-abidingness are devalued. If one looks carefully at Stinginess 2A and 2B, it is clear that while neither case involves unjust taking, neither involves virtue either. Law-abiding stingy people are revealed to be petty, overgrasping, venal people prevented from acting on their desires only because of their fear of legal punishment. On the one hand, there is the stingy person who will not give because they want to keep what they have so that they will not have to do anything base if they lose their possessions. Yet this is cowardice masquerading as high-mindedness. Such a person is not confident enough in his or her own character to do the right thing in adversity. Thus he or she avoids generosity to as a form of self-protection (*NE,*

1121b23–27). On the other hand there is the stingy person who refuses to take. Yet this person too is motivated not by virtue but by fear. He or she does not want to engage in the difficult, dangerous work of unjust taking. He or she obeys the law only out of cowardice. Respectability sometimes masks petty insecurity. It is depressing to note that Aristotle thinks most people incline to these kinds of stinginess; he says that they love external goods, holding onto them rather than giving them away. Stinginess reaches far and takes many different forms (*NE,* 1121b15–16). Aristotle thinks most people identify happiness with the possession of zero-sum goods like wealth of honor or power. It follows that if the majority can take unjustly with ease and with impunity, they will do so.

Along with this devaluation of mere law-abidingness, Aristotle devalues the life of political domination. Earlier, he said that people do not call the tyrant extravagant because generosity is relative to a person's means (*NE,* 1120b24–26). Since the tyrant owns everything, he cannot give away too much; what in an ordinary citizen would be the vice of excess in the tyrant appears to be virtue.[11] The tyrant who gives abundantly may not be seen as vicious. Indeed, if the person in power gives away a lot he will be loved and celebrated. Yet looking at the revised generosity chart, one sees that such a "generous" ruler is more like the pimp and usurer than anyone else. He engages in massively unjust taking. For this reason, the use to which he puts those goods is of no consequence. Since he took unjustly, it does not matter how much he gives away to curry favor with the people. The tyrant is analogous to the pimp living off the misfortunes of others (*NE,* 1122a1–12). This identification of pimps and tyrants devalues the life of political domination in which one holds onto power in part by giving away external goods.[12] Aristotle devalues the drive to mastery implicit in virtue-as-virility by equating it with other forms of contemptible overgrasping. While mastery may be attractive to an audience extolling virtue-as-virility, pimpery would be considered shameful.

In short, in his own discussion of generosity Aristotle argues that many people are petty tyrants who long to unfairly grab other people's things, but refrain out of fear. Occasionally, one comes across someone with the audacity and strength to engage in massive unjust taking. However, he can cover up his vice if he gives liberally at the same time. In the end, Aristotle argues that stingy risk minimizers and tyrannical maximizers are both motivated by the same desire: an overgrasping for external gain (*NE,* 1121a30–32).[13]

In addition to calling into question the inordinate attachment to *chremata*, there is a more fundamental revaluation going on. Most of us judge generosity by asking the question, "How much has been given away?" But for Aristotle, the real question is, "What is the quality of the good that has been given away?" Aristotle says that everyone has a greater love for what he has produced than what he has been given. Parents and poets, for example, have a great love for what they have made (*NE,* 1120b13–14). For this reason, people who have inherited money are held to be more generous than self-made men. This formulation is strikingly similar to a passage in Aristotle's account of friendship. The reason we love friends is that we love activity; we love being and doing. The analogy Aristotle employs to illustrate this is the affection parents have for children. Parents love children more than children do their parents precisely because of this longing for activity (*NE,* 9.7 generally and especially 1168a5–9). Good friends are our most important external possession because our self-knowledge and virtue depend on them. The audience initially thought that external goods, especially honor, constitute happiness. However, by the end of the *Ethics,* Aristotle asserts that good friends are the most important external good. When this passage about parents and poets is read in light of what comes later, the implication is that we misunderstand generosity because we misunderstand what is best for us. Our own good is not constituted primarily by the possession and enjoyment of external goods that can be bought and sold. If we focus on such a view of life, we will end either as cowardly minimizers or as base despots. What is best is to strive for the activities friendship makes possible. Indeed, I will later argue that the activities characteristic of such friendship are shareable and non-contestable, and so they constitute communities that benefit everyone involved.

Aristotle seeks to transform his audience's notion of generosity. Initially, reputable opinion identified the generous person with the rich man—or perhaps ruler—who liberally bestows external goods on people. Yet by the end of the inquiry, we realize that the rich person who gives much away is not necessarily generous but may be self-assertive and overly attached to material goods and security. The truly generous person gives excessively but does not take because he or she does not overgrasp for external goods. The generous person bestows not *chremata*, but less visible (and infinitely more valuable) goods, such as wisdom and virtue, for generosity depends not "on the amount given but on the characteristics of the giver" (*NE,* 1120b7–10).

Aristotle's revaluation of external possessions not only devalues the external goodies most of us overgrasp for. It also begins the work of showing the value of non-zero-sum goods like wisdom. For Aristotle wisdom is better than external goods, partly because in the absence of wisdom we do not even know how to use those goods to achieve happiness. The wise person who shares his wisdom extravagantly may wind up in poverty because he does not devote himself to the pursuit of external goods. Indeed, the person who shares extravagantly and does not care about acquisition, Aristotle says, is easily cheated in business, for he does not care about *chremata* (*NE,* 1121a3–6). This seems to be one of the reasons that—from the perspective of the many—the life of philosophy is not in one's interest. Indeed, it seems that to lead such a life is to open oneself to deceit and manipulation. Yet from the perspective of the person whose life has been turned upside down by love of wisdom, generosity and *chremata* can be seen in a new light. The wise person's generosity is stems not from his willingness to bestow external goods to gain honor. Rather, it stems from the wisdom he liberally shares, and this generosity may make him poor (*NE,* 1120b4–6). In the end, Extravagance #2—the virtue of the person who does not take but who gives extravagantly—is characteristic of the person of wisdom. This type of extravagance, Aristotle points out, is rare, and most think that it is also foolish, for it gives and is not concerned with taking. Indeed, such people are easily cheated (*NE,* 1121a25ff). While the goods shared by such people are not visible, they are more fundamental to human life. Because of the worth of wisdom, giving it away makes one infinitely more generous than the tyrant who dispenses money or office. Yet unless a person undergoes the revaluation that enables him to see the worth of wisdom, then the extravagant philosopher can only appear to be a worthless fool. The greatest virtue appears to the audience as a vice.

Once again, this transformation of the criteria for judging generosity recalls Socrates' defense speech in the *Apology.* The gods generously gave Athens the gift of Socrates, who is the gadfly awaking them from their slumber to the requirements of virtue. He shares his wisdom generously but is deemed foolish and dangerous. This is because in his service to the god and to the city, he has not cared for all the things most people do—moneymaking, political power, or household management (36b). Socrates says that he is poor because he is truly generous; he has spent his life giving away the most precious human possession and thus has not been able to accumulate external possessions. After he is found guilty and must propose a prize, Socrates does not apologize for his alleged misdeeds and throw himself on the mercy of the court, as is expected of him. Rather, he demands a reward for all he has bestowed on his city. He says he deserves something good, in accord with his worth. His reward should be forthcoming because he is a benefactor who requires leisure to exhort the people of Athens (36d). The philosopher who shares wisdom extravagantly should be honored more than the person in power who dispenses zero-sum goods to insure his popularity and honor. His proposal for punishment is both hilariously ironic and deadly serious. The city, however, can only see a "foolish" person who neglects all the "serious" things in life.

Magnificence

In the following discussion Aristotle links generous giving even more explicitly with the possession of wisdom and the person of Socrates. Magnificence *(megalopropreia)* is difficult to define. On the one hand, it means the virtue that is shown when citizens spend money for the benefit of the public. Greek city-states did not have the modern state's systems of taxation and bureaucracy. Public works projects, defense requirements, adornment, and the religious life of the city all needed to be funded by individual citizens (*NE,* 1122b18–23). On the other hand, Aristotle says that magnificence comes into play on occasions in which an expenditure is made only once, such as a wedding or paying for foreign visitors to be received. He even says is could be about giving a present or furnishing one's house (*NE,* 1123a1–3; 7–8). So magnificence is generosity with a public dimension, but this public dimension is not limited to spending money on political things (*NE,* 1123a2). People say that magnificence is about the "honorable things" *(ta timia)* (*NE,* 1122b18–19). In the popular mind, magnificence is especially associated with people of high birth or those who have connections, since these qualities carry greatness and prestige (*NE,* 1122b29–33). Magnificence is thus in evidence only in the upper strata of society. Poor people cannot be magnificent; the poor have little opportunity to be wondered at or celebrated because they do not have the requisite resources. The point is that when a wealthy person gives a wedding or pays for a public production or religious service, he has to have one eye on how that expenditure will be evaluated by public opinion, especially in the eminent circles in which he travels. In order to appear favorably in the ancient equivalent of the society pages, he must spend liberally, not regarding the cost. He must have in mind the intended effect. The gift that will be most honored will be one that is big and great *(mega)* and fair-noble (*NE,* 1122b15–16). In fact, the gift has to be so big that it is a source of wonder. When a magnificent man spends money, he wants to make people's jaws drop (*NE,* 1122b15–18).

Aristotle lays out various criteria for magnificence, and these help us understand the opposing vices. The magnificent man is like a knower *(epistemoni),* for he has the ability to behold *(theoresai)* what is suitable and appropriate for the *polis* and spend with good taste (*NE,* 1122a34–1122b1). The magnificent man must be wise because he has to be able to distinguish between a frivolous expenditure that makes him look good and an expenditure that will work for the benefit of the city. For this reason, he has to know what the city actually needs in order to know where his money and effort will do the most good. By contrast, he must be aware of what the city mistakenly thinks it needs and avoid that in order to avoid the temptation of spending to get flattery. A man is magnificent not when he spends on himself, but for the sake of the common good (*NE,* 1123a3–4).

But the problem with evaluating the vices opposed to magnificence is that in reputable opinion they do not appear to be vices; indeed, they seem to be virtues. It is difficult to judge magnificence for the same reason it is difficult to judge generosity: we tend to like people who give us things. The extreme is the vulgar person *(banausos)* who spends much when he ought to spend little and vice versa. He does this because he does not spend for the sake of the common good but in order to display his wealth in the hope that he will be wondered *at (thaumadzethai, NE,* 1123a24–26). In his case, it is clear that the city will not receive what it most needs. Yet it will nevertheless celebrate the vulgar man, for in his having his eye on honor, he will obviously give the city what it most wants. Love of honor tempts people to play the sycophant for popular opinion. By contrast, the deficiency opposed to magnificence is the cheap person who spends large amounts of money but then spoils the beauty of his gift by fretting over a trifle. He grumbles and complains and finds ways of economizing, always saying he is spending too much. Aristotle says that neither of these vices bring reproach (*NE,* 1123b33). Indeed, if we follow this train of thought to its logical conclusion, these vices will bring praise because they both involve giving.

If we think carefully about how magnificence is judged by people who like to be given things, we realize that in most cases, what is taken to be "magnificent" will be an act of vice. A contemporary example will perhaps drive this home. A modern analogue of magnificence is philanthropy, doled out by private individuals, corporate giving programs, and large charitable foundations like the Pew Charitable Trust and the Ford Foundation. However, when one reflects on why and how these institutions give, one sees immediately the problem with the practice of magnificence. A major portion of this giving goes to higher education, for example. However, while today's smaller private colleges have more need for external funding than large public or private research institutions, they have a much harder time competing for the cash, because more honor can be had by giving to Harvard than to a small college. Even large universities that receive gifts, however, can run into problems when soliciting funds. Since foundations and corporations are giving in large part for honor, they will give to high-profile, trendy causes. Library acquisitions (or professors' salaries) may take a back seat to funding for sports stadiums or new pools. In such cases, the desire for acclaim actually works against the better interests of the school, and indeed the nation, insofar as the nation benefits from quality education. Such excesses, Aristotle points out, do not involve spending too much on a proper object, but rather in spending at the wrong time in the wrong way (*NE,* 1122a29–34).

It is often difficult to give the city what is required for the common good. Due to the fact that most regimes are more or less unjust and therefore deform their citizens, most of us do not apprehend in all cases what is in our best interest. The expenditures we most celebrate may turn out to be bad for us. The person who gives us what we most want may be giving us what we least need. While magnificence is supposed to operate for the common good, in such cases, spending will actually operate for the private good of the man who loves honor disproportionately, and actually hurt rather then help the regime. In a like way, spending for the common good may bring censure rather than praise, since, like an addict, what we need is sometimes what is most painful to us.

Yet the results of this discussion are not simply negative; it is not merely the case that Aristotle criticizes the way public expenditure is practiced, revealing it to be for the most part *banausic.* In addition, he has uncovered the way in which the magnificent man's desire for praise points to a more fundamental desire: the desire for wisdom. In the course of the discussion, wisdom clearly emerges as the overarching criterion for evaluating what the common good requires. Again, Aristotle says that the magnificent man must be a kind of knower *(epistemoni)* who can behold *(theoresai)* what the city most needs (*NE,* 1122a34–1122b1). Aristotle consistently identifies the motivation for magnificence as the desire to produce something that will be "wondered at." Wonder is the beginning of philosophy. Earlier, he said that when people in the presence of a wise person become conscious of their own ignorance, they wonder at him because he says big and grand things that go over their heads (*NE,* 1095a25). The magnificent man wants to be wondered at in the same way. He wants to be celebrated for being a good judge; for knowing what the occasion requires. He does not merely want to be known as a good spender. His desire to be wondered at implies that he wants to be known as someone who is wise enough to spend well because he spends on what the people need. As Aristotle pointed out at the beginning of the *Ethics,* we always want to be honored in virtue of some excellence. The magnificent man's longing to be honored for wisdom points beyond itself to a desire for wisdom. However, if he is not careful, the magnificent man will be led not by what wisdom demands, but by what popular opinion demands. He risks mistaking popular acclaim as proof of wisdom. He risks becoming unwise by reverting to the standards most of us use to evaluate wisdom. By playing the sycophant, he risks becoming foolish.

As we have seen, wise people do not give away external possessions; they give away their wisdom, which the city needs even more than material gifts. Yet the problem of appearances intrudes. While people wonder at the wise person, they also seem to believe that philosophers are not practically wise *(phronimos)* because they seem ignorant of things that are advantageous to them. While philosophers may know many wonderful and extraordinary things, most think that such things are useless because they do not concern the humanly good things *(ta anthropina agatha)*. *Practical* wisdom, on the other hand, is concerned not with such useless philosophic stuff, but with what is actually good for people in the real world (*NE,* 1141b39ff). In order to be attracted to a life of philosophy, the audience must somehow revalue its conception of philosophy. Aristotle has to show them that what appears to be in their interest is not really so, and what does not appear to be in their interest actually is.

The Mean with Respect to Anger

Aristotle says that there is no name for the virtue regarding anger *(orge)*. Again, this should warn the careful reader that it is not practiced in Aristotle's society. A person is praised, Aristotle says, for being angry under the right circumstances with the right people in the right way for the right amount of time (*NE,* 1125b31–33). Such a person will be called *praos* (mild, gentle), since that is a term of praise. Yet, Aristotle emphasizes that this term is problematic, for the gentle person is also seen as prone to going in the direction of deficiency; he is held to be someone who does not stand his ground and get angry enough. The mild person, he says, is not vengeful or vindictive. Such a man is more inclined to pardon *(suggnomonikos)* than revenge (*NE,* 1162a2–3). And while the mild person is sometimes praised, he is also blamed because he seems apathetic in defense of his own causes. He tends to let his character be smeared and put up with insults against those near to him. Thus he is seen as slavish (*NE,* 1126a8). The excess regarding anger is irascibility, defined as becoming angry at the wrong persons, under the wrong circumstances, to an improper degree, too quickly, and for an unduly long amount of time. Thus, the table depicting the virtue regarding anger and its corresponding vices looks like this:

Table 4.3. Virtue and Vices Concerning Anger

Deficiency	*Mean*	*Excess*
Gentleness	Gentleness	Irascibility. Much more common than deficiency.

The problem is clear. From the perspective of virtue-as-virility, the mean appears to be a deficiency. It is no surprise that Aristotle goes on to say that the excess is more common than the deficiency. He also says that the excess is more opposed to the virtue than the defect is. Put another way, Aristotle thinks that the virtue lies closer to the defect than to the excess. That is, the virtue with respect to anger is closer to the defect of forgiving and forgetting and letting slights pass than it is to the desire for revenge. Irascible people are hard to live with, he adds (NE, 1125a29–31).

The point becomes even clearer when one reflects on the motivation for anger. Throughout the discussion, Aristotle describes anger as the reaction to slights and insults. The self-assertive man extolling virtue-as-virility simply cannot tolerate such things. The zero-sum pursuit of honor leads to a social order where men constantly jockey for positions in the social hierarchy, and these positions are doled out not in clear and obvious ways that can be measured and quantified, such as possession of discrete amounts of wealth. Rather, in social orders devoted to honor, one's position in the constantly changing social hierarchy is experienced as unstable, and therefore slights against one's honor are occasions for extreme reaction. To opt out of that whole system is to be open to the manipulation and contempt of its other participants. It is to risk seeming slavish. There are several reasons for this. As Aristotle points out in the *Politics*, the quest for honor entails a concomitant commitment to the minimization of shame. Men esteem their rivals, Aristotle says, and thus respect leads them to be particularly concerned to avoid doing anything shameful their rival will hear about (*P*, 1384a; 1385a). In such a situation, individuals engage in public actions with one eye on how those actions will be evaluated in accordance with the society's normative expectations for a man's man. The dynamic of the quest for honor and the avoidance of shame leads inexorably to cycles of assertion, insult, and vengeance. As Aristotle points out in the *Rhetoric*, according to his culture's standards,

> To take vengeance on one's enemies is more noble than to reconcile with them [*katallattesthai*], for to retaliate is just [*dikaion*], and what is just is noble. Further, a real man [*andreiou*] ought not to allow himself to be beaten. Victory and honor are also noble, for both are desirable even when they are fruitless and are manifestations of superior virtue. (*R*, 1367a24–25)

Thus according to prevailing cultural standards, failure to retaliate toward a slight or insult undercuts one's own claim to honor.[14]

In such a culture revenge does not aim merely at the avoidance of feeling disrespected. The term Aristotle uses for "slavish" is a combination of "man" *(andra)* and the root of the word for "foot" *(pod)*. The reference seems to be to the Greek practice of supplication. When in danger of death a soldier could throw himself at the feet of his enemy to beg for his life. If he humbled himself in this way—if he preferred slavishness to death—this was evidence that he was a natural slave and that it was just to take his freedom. "Slavishness" implies being at another's mercy. By contrast, if a man can acquire the reputation of someone who is very good at exacting vengeance, this reputation acts as a deterrent.[15] Thus from this perspective of virtue-as-virility, the person who gets angry in the right way at the right time toward the right person for the right duration may appear to be a wimpy chump. In forgiving and forgetting, he is opening himself up to be exploited by those eager to advance themselves at his expense. In a social context bounded by pursuit of honor, more people will be prone to vengeance than to the deficiency of letting slights pass. This cycle of revenge and retribution was a large problem in ancient Greece. Cycles of revenge were often undertaken not just by individuals but also by families and clans, with the resulting feuds tearing the city apart. Tort law was unknown, as was a neutral judiciary competent to adjudicate private disputes. In saying that the extreme of irascibility is much further from the mean than is the defect, gentleness, Aristotle is criticizing the common view of anger and vengeance and bemoaning its effects on the social order. He says that must hold fast to the mean, giving very severe blame for very great deviations from it. In other words, in his discussion of the virtue controlling anger he urges his audience on to engage in the countercultural virtue of forgiveness, not minding the blame attached to that stance.

Social Relations

Aristotle next takes up three virtues having to do with speech and actions in social relations. The problem of naming that has plagued his treatment of the ethical virtues again comes into play here. Aristotle says that there are no names for the virtues he will discuss, particularly those he calls "friendliness" and "truthfulness." All these have to do with giving other people pain and pleasure in social relationships. They are differentiated by the ways in which the pleasure and pain are bestowed. Sometimes pain and pleasure are bestowed by praise: Obsequious people praise too much; grouchy people praise too little. The mean regarding praise is a nameless virtue in which one praises other people in the right way for the right things (IV.6). He calls this *philia*, which is a kind of friendliness. Laughter must be managed as well. Some people joke too much and in the wrong way; they are called "buffoons." Others refuse to laugh or take pleasure in it; they are called "boors." The mean is wit, which is the ability to be humorous in the right way at the right time (4.8). The virtue that occupies the mean in social relations is nameless. It involves telling the truth about oneself and others (4.7). Thus Aristotle's table outlining the virtues of social relations must have looked something like this:

Table 4.4. Virtues and Vices Concerning Social Relations

	Deficiency	*Mean*	*Excess*
In speech or action	Self-deprecation	Truthfulness	Boastfulness
In amusement	Boorishness	Wittiness	Buffoonery
In daily life	Grouchiness	Friendliness	Flattery

Aristotle discusses truthfulness in the very middle of his treatment of social relations, implying that it is the keystone of the whole account. In order to understand where Aristotle is trying to lead his audience, first we have to understand the implications of the account of truthfulness.

Aristotle begins the discussion by emphasizing yet again that there is no name for the mean in regard to truth-telling. In pointing out the lack of names to describe these virtues, Aristotle implies that they are not evident because they are not practiced (*NE,* 1108a17–19). For this reason, we have to pay special attention to the implications of the account, for we may have no direct experience of the kind of activity he is speaking about. He first lays out the deficiency and the excess. The excess is boastfulness. Aristotle says reputable opinion holds that the boastful man pretends to have qualities that are held in esteem, or he boasts of qualities he simply does not have. By contrast, a person is deficient if he deliberately underestimates his capabilities. The term for the latter is *eirones,* which means self-deprecator, and connotes a person who pretends that he is less than he really is. Aristotle notes that Socrates was said to be guilty of this vice. To describe the mean, Aristotle employs the term "truthfulness" in life and speech.

This initially straightforward scheme is complicated, however, when Aristotle notes that the people who engage in the vices associated with truth-telling sometimes do so for an ulterior motive (*NE,* 1127a26–27). Sometimes a man boasts to gain a reputation or to cinch a business deal; at other times a man may deprecate himself to look good. Thus there are two different kinds of deficiency and excess. Each kind of vice is distinguished according to whether it has a motive. The complete taxonomy of truthfulness in social relations is shown in table 4.5 on the following page.

Some people lie just for the sake of lying. Others lie for the sake of a good reputation. The person who lies for honor does not usually receive too much blame. People who boast for the sake of reputation pretend they have qualities for which a person is praised. Others boast for profit. Often, those lying for profit pretend to have qualities which benefit their neighbors or boast of accomplishments that are not at all easy to judge, like prophecy, wisdom, and doctoring. This person is shameful (*NE,* 1127b9–23). It is difficult to judge qualities such as wisdom and prophecy, for they are not manifest or evident, nor are they

Table 4.5. Truthfulness in Social Relations

Deficiency	*Deficiency*	*Mean*	*Excess*	*Excess*
No motive	Honor as motive	No motive		Motives
Self-deprecator (Socrates)	Self-deprecator (Such a person appears to be refined because they don't boast so that they will get honor)	No name	No name	If honor is the motive a person is called boaster, but that is not see as bad. If money is the motive, the person is called a boaster, and that is seen as base.

subject to easy quantification. So people can successfully pretend they have such qualities. They realize that their boasts are safe from scrutiny. The defect of truthfulness about oneself is self-deprecation, and the people who engage in this are much more subtle than the boasters are. People who engage in self-deprecation with no ulterior motive want to avoid pomposity *(orgkeron)*. Aristotle mentions that Socrates was said to be this way. This kind of deception is difficult to pull off, however. If one disclaims insignificant and obvious qualities, one is held in contempt. Refined people are not so crude, however. They self-deprecate moderately by understating qualities that are not too noticeable and obvious. In this way they try to strike people as "cultivated and refined" (*NE,* 1127b25–33). (Recall that Aristotle earlier characterized his audience as "refined and practical.") So respectable people who downplay their own qualities act like Socrates in order to get a reputation for refinement and cultivation. Bragging to their social circle about their assets would be in bad taste. Yet since their self-deprecation is for the sake of honor, it is clear that they resemble the braggart who boasts for the sake of reputation. To engage in either boasting or self-deprecating is to lie for honor. Both cultivated people who do not brag as well as boasters who make grand claims in order to get money and profit are in reality motivated by the same kind of lust for reputation. Indeed, later on Aristotle explicitly says that contrary to appearances, we boast both when we self-deprecate and when we brag (*NE,* 1127b29). He then concludes the discussion by insisting that both sorts of boasting are the opposite of truthfulness (*NE,* 1127b32–33).

The question arises: If the excess and the deficiency are really the same vice (lying for honor), then what is the mean? From the perspective of the majority of people who lie to gain reputation or profit, the deficiency appears to be occupied by Socrates, who downplays his own qualities for no apparent reason. Yet the mean appears different to different people, depending on their inclinations. The refined might think that the mean is self-deprecatory lying for the sake of reputation; while the boastful might think that virtue is exaggerating one's qualities. Yet why should we allow people who lie habitually for personal gain to stake out the mean? Clearly, such people are not the best judges of truthfulness, precisely because they are habitual liars. Perhaps Aristotle is driving us to the conclusion that the nameless virtue about truthfulness is best exemplified by Socrates, who insisted that he did not know. Naturally, conniving liars would not believe Socrates' claim that he self-deprecates for no motive. Rather, since refined self-deprecators lie for the sake of reputation, they would assume that Socratic self-deprecation was also for some ulterior motive. Socrates' self-deprecation is familiar in the Platonic dialogues. For instance after having been found guilty in the *Apology,* Socrates insists that he cannot persuade the jury of his real motivations in refusing to live as he does. If he tries, he will appear to be engaged in self-deprecation *(eironeuesthai)* (38a). Socrates is also accused of this kind of false humility in the *Republic* (337a). And in the *Symposium,* Alcibiades makes the same kind of judgement: Socrates says he is crazy about beautiful boys and likes to say he knows nothing. Yet in reality he is utterly self-controlled on the inside. He doesn't care if a person is rich or beautiful or famous, or any of the other things most people admire. He considers all these possessions beneath contempt. In public, his life is a big ironic game. When one catches him revealing his true self, one finds godlike beauty (216e–217a; see also *Meno,* 71c).

The problem with popular characterizations of Socrates is that they miss the substance of the Socratic life. When people proceeding from reputable opinion accuse Socrates of self-deprecation, they assume he is pretending when he insists he does not know what wisdom and goodness are, and that this pretense has some ulterior motive. But this is merely the way his pleas of ignorance appear to people who habitually dissemble to make themselves look good. The starting point of the Socratic approach is that the condition for searching for the best way of life is the realization that one does not know how to live. One must be aware of one's own ignorance in order to be motivated to ask a question. Socratic pedagogy forces other people into the same kind of perplexity as he is in so that they too will realize their own ignorance and search for wisdom. When discussing virtue, for example, in the *Meno,* Meno says that even before he met Socrates, people told him that he was adept at reducing others to perplexity. Meno tells Socrates that he feels like he is exerting magic on him, and that under Socrates' spell he is a mass of helplessness (80a–b).[16] The typical reaction to Socratic ignorance is numbness and a feeling of helplessness, confusion, or becoming dizzy. Yet Socrates insists that the reason he produces such feelings is not that he knows the answer to questions. Rather, he infects people with perplexity precisely because he is perplexed himself. Cultivating this perplexity is the condition for engaging in a search for wisdom.

Socratic wisdom is identical with Socratic ignorance because an awareness of ignorance about how to live is the precondition for pursuing wisdom. However, Aristotle has already pointed out the problem with knowing the difference between real wisdom and the way wisdom appears. Indeed, he said that people who claim wisdom to make money—like the Sophists of his day or perhaps college professors in ours—do so because they know their boasts will not be subject to dispute. Wisdom and doctoring and prophecy are so difficult to know and judge, he says,—the evidence for their possession is so hard to find—that pretenders to these qualities can be assured that they will not be easily found out. Most people claiming wisdom are boasters who want to get a reputation for knowing how to live successfully. However, such people, it turns out, are liars because they boast in order to get a reputation for knowing how to live well or how to benefit people (*NE,* 1127b17–20). In this they merely pretend to know how to live. In doing so, they show their own closure to a genuine search for wisdom, for in lying to others about their knowledge of living, they are lying to themselves about how much they know. People who pretend to know how to live well have a hard time changing their lives. They think they are wise but are really invincibly ignorant because they do not know how to live. Truthfulness turns out to be admitting, like Socrates, that we do not know what we are talking about when we brag about how we live. It means acknowledging our ignorance and beginning to search. In this sense, knowledge of ignorance is the beginning of virtue.

Irony

Once one understands the implications of the discussion on truthfulness, one can see the discussions of praise and humor in a new light. The extremes of praise are obsequiousness and grouchiness. Yet, Aristotle says, these vices appear to be opposed only to one another—not to the mean—because there is no name for the mean. Aristotle uses the term *philia* for the nameless virtue of the person who praises and blames in the right way. Yet later we learn from the "Treatise on Friendship" that the best kind of *philia* requires looking after the good of the friend. Aristotelian friends correct each other—they praise and give blame—when necessary in order to spur each other on to virtue. Thus the concern of the friend will not be praising or withholding blame in order to flatter or to insinuate. It will be praising and blaming to cultivate the genuine good of the friend. When the good of a friend is at stake the friend is even more truthful than when nothing is at stake (*NE,* 1127b3–5).

Finally, with regard to humor, Aristotle says that the mean is a kind of nimbleness in mind that allows people to see the humor in a given situation *(eutrapeloi).* To explain this term, Aristotle makes reference to the word *eutropos,* which means "agile" or "nimble in body." Thus using humor well means being able to joke properly and gracefully (*NE,* 1128a7–9). The deficiency belongs to harsh people who exhibit a kind of rude boorishness that refuses to see humor in any situation (*agroikoi,* literally farmers from the boonies). By contrast, the excess is characterized as the buffoonery associated with vulgar clowns. The term he uses here is *bomolochoi,* which means someone who lurks around sacrificial altars looking for scraps. In other words, the term connotes someone who would do any kind of dirty work to get a meal.

Humor is one of the last virtues Aristotle speaks of in his long treatment of the moral virtues. By the end of the discussion, we realize that vice often passes for virtue and virtue for vice. Aristotle has tried to convince his audience that if they practice conventionally respectable notions of happiness they will fail to become happy. One wonders therefore whether a sense of humor is required in social relations. We human beings are so habitually slow witted and stupid; we are so small souled and self-assertive; we fall into so many different forms of vanity and pettiness and simple mistakes; we are so wrong about our own best interests, that after Aristotle's criticisms of "virtuous" practice we begin to wonder whether what is required in order to progress in virtue is a kind of ironic distance from our own thoughts and actions. This issues in a liberating ability to poke fun at ourselves and others when we claim to know the right way to live.

Aristotle's dialectical pedagogy leads to a kind of negative knowledge—he wants his audience to realize that they do not know what virtue is. In another sense, however, the concluding discussion of nimble wittiness makes the reader wonder whether Aristotle urges his audience to take an ironic perspective on human things. Vice is so woven into the fabric of my character and that of my society that the result of reading the *Ethics* cannot be a propositional set of directives. Such would appear unintelligible from the perspective of we who are morally paralyzed. Rather, one result of the reading is the cultivation of persistent questioning of ourselves and our culture. Put another way, one result is the cultivation of an ironic perspective on the tragedy of human affairs. The things we desire and pursue so often make us unhappy that human life is tragically funny. The things that most of us take with the utmost seriousness—wealth, reputation, power—are revealed to be fundamentally unserious. By contrast, the things that we ignore or treat with bemused indifference or even contempt may be the most serious of all.[17] Social reality forces us to engage them, but if we are to remain free, we must engage them playfully at an ironic distance.

One alternative is to proceed from the tragedy of human

affairs to despair, failing to see the humor in human things because they are so tragic. The morose person is boorish because he cannot poke fun at himself. The other alternative is to pretend to know how to live. The mean is to look at human life as a kind of serious play in which people do all sorts of bad things, and suffer and make terrible errors, but which is still immensely fun and rewarding, if we can only achieve the right kind of attitude toward our own failings and limits. This would require the ability to see the ways in which our own failings are not merely tragic, but also that the ironies and paradoxes that result from our perpetual stupidity allow us to poke around in a search for increased life and happiness. So Aristotelian irony is not a postmodern variety that issues in a detachment from the ways our society speaks and acts.[18] As Salkever argues:

> This liberal conception of the good life is thus inseparable from a kind of ironic stance toward oneself, an unwillingness to take any one of my present beliefs or commitments too seriously. The term "irony" can mean many different things; all would agree that speech is ironic when it contains a meaning different from its literal or apparent sense, but there are many kinds of difference. In speaking of Socratic irony as a kind of liberal intellectual virtue, I do not mean irony either as a deceitful way of tricking your enemies, or as infinite self-reflexive negativity. These are both nineteenth-century senses of "irony," conceptions that flow from the thought of Hegel, Kierkegaard, and Nietzsche. As I understand Socratic irony, it is less strategic than the first of these and less bombastically enervating than the second; rather, it is, as Wayne Booth says, the knowledge "that all literal systems mislead," and that "the true philosopher lives in self-corrective dialogue, in which the inadequacies of one attempt lead inevitably to another one, and then yet to another." As I see the term here, irony is the virtue of human self-consciousness, a sort of mean between cynicism (the mode of slaves and tyrants) and prophecy (the mode of priests and kings).[19]

Philosophic irony entails ignorance and skepticism. Yet there is a bright center at the heart of this skepticism, for it leads to the most important human act: the reflective search for the right kind of life. The problem with both alternatives—with boorish nihilism or buffoonish pretenses to certainty—is that they lead to a refusal to engage in a lifelong search for more and more adequate ways of thinking and acting because the adherents of both sides assume that they already know the meaning of the whole. For Aristotle, virtue in social relations requires a kind of philosophic ignorance and irony.

5

Greatness of Soul

Irony is required in speaking about social relations because the contradictions at the heart of every regime's notion of a successful human life produce ironic consequences. We have seen that while manliness was celebrated because it was needed to defend the homeland, the way it was pursued in Aristotle's time actually hurt the homeland. Generosity and magnificence were praised because they were ways of showing forth one's liberality and wisdom. In the end, however, the one who pursues them for honor may well end up a foolish sycophant enslaved to popular opinion. Self-assertive anger was praised because revenge was seen as required to insure one's place in the social hierarchy. But the lust for revenge undermines the very social order that is required for pursuing honor in the first place. Thus overgrasping for honor undermines the condition for achieving honor. Aristotle's dialectical pedagogy begins from the perspective of his audience and asks whether the way they practice virtue will get them what they want. Its goal is not propositional information about right conduct but the realization that the audience's conception of a good life breaks down on its own terms; ironically, it produces the opposite of what was intended. This ironic consequence is clearest in Aristotle's treatment of greatness of soul. Just as greatness of soul is the crown of the virtues in reputable opinion, Aristotle's critique of this mode of being is the crown of his critical engagement of reputable opinion. Aristotle began the *Ethics* by seeking common ground with his audience in their desire for noble action. Ironically, in the end their drive for noble action tends to an empty, sterile inactivity.

I began my account of the moral virtues by arguing that since Aristotle says that the great-souled man embodies all the moral virtues, understanding this mode of life is the key to understanding Aristotle's conception of the practice of each particular virtue. I argued that in most contemporary scholarship Aristotle is interpreted as praising the great-souled man. I argued further that this interpretation flows from the assumption that his treatment of the virtues is descriptive rather than critical. However, after seeing how Aristotle's treatment of the moral virtues is critical, we are now in a position to see how he criticizes the crown of all the moral virtues. In his treatment of the moral virtues, he seeks to show where his audience's account of virtue fails on its own terms in order to present a new way of life. He does the same with greatness of soul, and it is not a pretty picture.

Aristotle on Greatness of Soul

Scholars who have investigated Aristotle's treatment of greatness of soul have paid insufficient attention to the ambiguities and ironies in his account. To begin with, as Hardie points out, there is a strange disparity between the loftiness of the opening of the discussion, where Aristotle says that the great-souled man is concerned with the most important things, and the actual description of him, which focuses primarily on negative traits. Indeed, the negativity of this discussion has led some contemporary observers to be deeply disappointed with Aristotle's account.[1] Hardie puts the question well: "[I]f we agree that Aristotle's intention is to describe a great man dedicated to great actions, we are faced by the question how he came to give us a description which has produced perplexity, and even dismay, in so many of his readers."[2] One way of approaching this question is to see that it arises when we insist on reading the *Ethics* as a treatise that uncritically presents an account of virtue-as-virility. However, if we approach Aristotle's *Ethics* as a dialectical critique of prevailing opinion, we begin to see the ambiguities and paradoxes in his account.

According to Aristotle, the great-souled man is concerned with "lofty matters." He thinks he deserves the "greatest reputation." In fact, Aristotle says, *megalopsuchia* implies bigness, because it is derived from the word for bigness, *megas*. Just as beauty consists in a large body, this state consists in grasping for the biggest thing. By contrast, small people have charm and proportion but not beauty (*NE,* 1123b2–3). This identification of beauty and bigness and the concomitant devaluation of smallness is clearly ironic. In the *Poetics,* Aristotle emphasizes that beauty is "a matter of size and order, and so it is impossible in a very small creature or in a creature of vast size" (1450b34–40). Initially, for example, the Lilliputians found Gulliver to be horribly grotesque. This ironic view of the identification of bigness and beauty introduces the irony running throughout the account.

The great-souled man thinks he deserves certain external goods, especially honor *(time),* which is the greatest of these. In fact, this is what we pay as tribute to the gods (*NE,* 1123b20–21). In this sense, the pursuit of honor is a pursuit of a kind of divinity.[3] Thus the account of greatness of soul is bound together with the pursuit of godlike honor. It is clear that Aristotle has a difficult time speaking about how his audience should relate to honor. Here the problem of naming intrudes once again. Aristotle insists that there is no name for the virtue regarding honor. This is because in a culture celebrating honor, moderating its pursuit often appears to be a vice. Aristotle says that love of honor *(philotimia)* is sometimes held to be a vice, and sometimes held to be a virtue (*NE,* 4.4 generally, especially 1125b22; 1107b31; cf. with 1117b29, where he says that people who indulge in love of honor are not blamed for immoderation). So there is a fundamental ambiguity in how love of honor is praised and blamed. Sometimes, Aristotle says, people *blame* the lover of honor *(philotimon)* for striving for more honor than he should and for trying to get it from the wrong sources. Other times, they *praise* the *philotimon* as a real man and a lover of what is fair and noble *(philokalon).* In a like way, people often blame the person who does not love honor *(aphilotimon)* for deliberately refraining from the pursuit of honor. Yet at other times they praise the *aphilotimon* because he is measured and self-controlled (*NE,* 1125b11–14). Since there is no name for the mean, however, the extremes lay claim to the middle and dispute for the title of virtue. So the person who withdraws from the pursuit of honor considers himself virtuous. At the same time, the person who actively pursues honor identifies virtue with his virile self-assertion. This results in a horrible confusion when the audience tries to think and talk reasonably about how to relate to honor. From the perspective of the inhabitants of the extremes, the virtue appears to be a vice (*NE,* 1125b21–25). Thus it appears we cannot trust common accounts of how to relate to moderate love of honor. The muddled speech reflects an inability to think through the problem clearly precisely because the pursuit of honor is so exalted. This is the context of Aristotle's discussion of the great-souled man, who thinks he deserves the greatest honors. Clearly, the context leads us to be suspicious about the claims of the great-souled man. Indeed, in the *Rhetoric,* Aristotle lists *philotimia* as a vice that leads people to commit injustice (*R,* 1368b).

Aristotle says that the great-souled man has the right attitude toward honor, for he regards himself as worthy of honor above all else. He thinks he deserves honor because each virtue is embodied in him. For example, such a man would not run away in battle or do anything base. Why would he, when for him, *nothing is great* (*NE,* 1123b33, my emphasis)? So greatness of soul is the crown *(cosmos)* of the virtues (1124a1). This identification of greatness of soul with a crown seems to be a way of praising it, for *cosmos* sometimes refers to the crown given to the victors at the Olympics. But it is important to note that Aristotle's first mention of the Olympic crown occurs in book I, when he is trying to seek common ground with his audience by appealing to the attractiveness of a life of noble action. He says, "Just as the crown *(cosmos)* at the Olympic Games is not awarded to the most beautiful and the strongest, but to those who participate in the contest—for the victors are found among the participants—so the good and noble things in life are won by those who act rightly" (*NE,* 1099a3–6). His point is that one may have the capacity to engage in excellent activity, but never actualize that potential. If one merely has the capacity without the result, one is not good. Happiness is not a disposition to activity, but rather it is an activity itself (1169b28ff; 1098b32–1099a7).

Yet ironically, this is the opposite of what characterizes the great-souled man. Such a man thinks that he is so great, in fact, that while he desires honor, he thinks that no honor his fellow citizens could bestow on him will actually do justice to his own sense of worth. So, Aristotle concludes, the great souled man is slothful *(argon)* and a procrastinator *(mellitin),* except when there is some great honor or work *(ergon)* at stake (*NE,* 1124b23–16).

It is impossible to convey in English the ironic play on words that Aristotle employs here. Happiness is an activity *(energeia)* or a work *(ergon);* by contrast, the great-souled man is characterized by sloth *(argon)*. Some of Aristotle's translators blunt the force of this ironic critique by translating *argon* with "slow to act."[4] But *argon* means literally living without labor. being idle or lazy. In fact, in agriculture, it was used to refer to land that is lying fallow.[5] The implication is that the great-souled man is like land that is potentially fertile but that is in fact sterile because it has been set aside for later. The great-souled man has not sown so he cannot reap. For him, the activities that most people engage in are "small change," so he refrains from them. Yet often, a happy human life requires precisely an engagement of the small things that bring no honor. An excessive devotion to honor can ruin one's life because the honor seeker is constantly asking whether any proposed course of action is "great enough for me." Yet this may be the path to inactivity. Since inactivity is the opposite of Aristotelian happiness, we can conclude that his account of the great-souled man is ironic. He is restless for activity, but he remains inactive, for he is always waiting for some great project worthy of his greatness to come along. While happiness is the fullness of activity, all the great-souled man gets is the emptiness of inactivity. He will not achieve what he most desires if he pursues his own account of what makes him happy. As Aristotle pointed out at the beginning of the account, the great-souled man who loves honor desires a way of participating in the life of the gods. Yet instead of this quasi-divine fullness, he only gets emptiness.

There is more to Aristotle's ironic criticism of the great-souled man, however. *Cosmos* may mean Olympic crown, but it also means an embellishment worn by a woman, like jewelry. In employing this term, Aristotle lampoons the great-souled man's perspective on honor. The great-souled man thinks of honor as a vain woman would think of her adornments: they are things meant to serve her self-absorption. Indeed, Aristotle emphasizes, the great-souled man would rather possess beautiful and profitless objects like jewelry than objects that are profitable and useful (*NE,* 1125a11–12). For the great-souled man, honor is like a useless bauble worn by a vain woman concerned with her looks. And of course, for the great-souled man—the "real man" who is the embodiment of the ancient Greek conception of virtue-as-virility—such a parallel would have been difficult to bear. In a wonderful Socratic irony, the "real man" bent on showing forth his own greatness in possessing honor is revealed to be like a woman for whom he would have nothing but contempt.

Yet if such a life is so sterile and unattractive, what motivates it? For Aristotle, it is clearly the illusion of self-sufficiency that goes along with such a life. The long list of characteristics Aristotle provides of the great-souled man serves to underscore how his life is a pursuit of this self-sufficiency. In the end, however, he has a strange relationship with the external goods he seeks. The great-souled man is neither excessively pained nor pleased by good fortune (*NE,* 1124a13–16). He has a lofty detachment from honor itself, which makes him appear haughty (*NE,* 1124a19–20). Such a person finds it difficult to admire anything; nothing is great to him. He will not gossip. He is not given to praise or speak evil of others. He will not ask for help in misfortune. Indeed, he likes hearing about all the good things he has done for others, but hates hearing about favors bestowed on him. He will do good, but is ashamed to accept a good turn, for doing good is the sign of a superior, while being in another's debt is the mark of an inferior. So the great-souled man will recall all the favors he has bestowed on people, but will forget the favors that have been bestowed on him (*NE,* 1124a20–1124b13). The great-souled man has a moderate attitude toward wealth, power, and every manner of good and bad luck to befall him. In sum, the great-souled man is detached and pretends to independence. Aristotle later says that he desires the self-sufficiency that comes from this high-minded, superior detachment (1125a13). He likes to feel he does not need anything.

What is the cash value of such an attitude? This question must be answered with reference to the psychic motivations that underlie the desire for honor because Aristotle emphasizes that the desire for honor is the driving force of greatness of soul. We have seen that negatively, the pursuit of honor is a way of fleeing death. Positively, it is a desire pursue a quasidivine life. We have also seen that Aristotle points out at the outset of his treatment that the great-souled man wishes to achieve the honor the gods have; in a sense he wants to be like a god. Within the Greek tradition, one way of dealing with the longing for divine life in the face of death was by reconciling oneself to the limits on the possibility of human happiness in a cosmos which seems mute or positively hostile to human desires. Homer, for example, tried to manage the conflict that resulted from the problem of death by insisting on limits. The great-souled man seems to take the Homeric emphasis on limits to heart; indeed, perhaps he takes it too much to heart. Perhaps Aristotle is saying that in adopting this view of life, the great-souled man is led to the sterility of a high-minded form of despair. He is a man incapacitated—unable to engage in the kind of activity that is happiness—because he has learned the lesson of Homeric culture all too well.

THE *ILIAD* ON HUMAN LIMITS

Homer not only provides a dramatic sketch of the motivation and problematic character of honor. In addition, he hints at a resolution to the political and social problems caused by the pursuit of honor. How does he address those problems? And how does he deal with the questions about life and death implicit in a devotion to honor? He dramatizes the disastrous consequences of opting for extremes, thus pointing to the necessity to accept limits on the possibility of human happiness. Through acceptance of limits lies moderation, some measure of genuine human excellence, and community. Through pursuit of extremes lie madness, strife, obsessive concern with self, a false sense of self-sufficiency, and a view of excellence that recognizes only brute force. One extreme is represented by the gods; the other is represented by Achilles. Yet both extremes are made possible only by neglecting the reality of human limits. In short, in the *Iliad* Homer shows the consequences of acting as though human limits did not exist.

Let me explore the extreme of the gods first. The theme of strife *(eris)* dominates the *Iliad*, and Homer traces the root of the conflict back to the gods. Strife among human beings is not sent into the world as an atonement for humanity's misdeeds. According to the traditional myth, despite the human longing for peace, the gods send strife. At the behest of Zeus, Eris (personified strife) interrupts the wedding of Peleus and Thetis by causing a quarrel among Hera, Athena, and Aphrodite as to who is most beautiful. Following Zeus's orders, Hermes brings the goddesses to Mt. Ida where Paris is to judge among them. Aphrodite promises Helen to him if he decides in her favor. With Aphrodite's help, Paris and Helen commit adultery and leave Sparta, setting off the war. To take another example, just as the nine year Trojan War seems on the verge of resolution with the trial by combat of the two people most involved in the issue—Paris and Menelaos—the gods interfere again, insuring more fighting. The strife the gods foster grows in violence as the *Iliad* proceeds, reducing people more and more to the level of brutes, eliminating the capacity for compassion and mutual respect.[6] This is shown most clearly in how human corpses are treated throughout the book. Early in the story, the two sides agree to a truce in order to take care of their fallen comrades. By the end of the story, there are at first threats to abuse corpses, and then there is actual abuse. At one point, Achilles has become so debased that he wishes that he could hack away meat from Hektor's body and eat it raw (22.346–47).[7] Why do the gods insist on introducing such wanton strife among human beings? Homer does not offer any explicit hypotheses. Clearly, the gods are fundamentally flawed beings. They are vain, jealous, selfish, petty, and contentious. Zeus is not the guarantor of justice and right in the cosmos. Neither is he a loving provident father. Rather, Zeus himself makes clear that the basis for his rule is brute force alone.[8]

Perhaps the gods' love of strife can be traced back to their immortality. Immortality renders the gods profoundly unserious and therefore decisively inhuman. By contrast, human life attains its seriousness precisely as a result of the constraints imposed by our mortal condition. Constraints of time and place that result from our bodies and our mortality dictate that our choices be made with a seriousness that an immortal being need not have.[9] Why learn French; why take a trip; why investigate String Theory if it can be put off five or six billion years? Our ephemeral nature makes our thoughts, actions, work, and experiences precious. Our knowledge of death, for example, makes us willing to have children in order to carry on our legacy and that of our kind, and in raising children we must sort out with renewed seriousness what needs to be passed on and what needs to be abandoned. Awareness of our mortality makes us long for peace and harmony. Strife is detrimental to us precisely because our time is so short and our lives so fragile. The immortals have a radically different perspective. For Homer, human beings need a consciousness of death and the limits it imposes to be rendered humane. For Homer, paradoxically, human beings need a mindfulness of the limit of death in order to be happy. Thus one of the lessons of the *Iliad* is that if we pursue an extreme sort of happiness–if we act as if we are immortal, forgetting the limits and demands of our mortal existence—we will be rendered less than human.

The pursuit of immortality through honor leads to human disaster. As we have seen, Achilles' wrath results from his inability to reconcile his lust for immortal life with the reality of death. His consequent wrath leads him to an obsessive concern with himself that destroys his community and thus himself. For Homer, human life is unremittingly harsh and limited, and only attention to these realities can save human beings from disaster. This is shown, among other places, in the speech of Phoinix, Achilles' mentor. After Achilles rejects Agamemnon's apology and gifts and refuses to return to the battle because of his obsession with death, Phoinix tells him a parable (*Iliad,* 9.502–512), the upshot of which is this: Human beings are plagued by a temptation to be obsessively concerned with themselves. This self-possessing madness is called *ate.* Because of this obsessive concern with self, human beings are quick to be overtaken by their own destructive emotions and slow to repair the damage by forgiving, binding up wounds, and moving on to restore community that has been destroyed by their individualism and selfishness. Phoinix warns Achilles that his obsession with death is a manifestation of his neglect of human mortality, and that if he does not reconcile himself to his condition, his life will be ruined, partly because his wrath will destroy those he loves.

Of course, Phoinix's parable is prophetic. Achilles' self-obsession and rage at the limits of his condition lead directly to the death of his best friend Patroklos.[10] Only after Patroklos dies does he realize how good the community he destroyed really was, and only then does he make amends. Achilles seeks forgiveness and tries to bind back his community through the funeral games he holds in honor of his friend. The games are stylized contests that test fighting skills. But their competition is not violent; they preserve and indeed strengthen the community even in the midst of the competition. Thus the funeral games that bind the community back together parallel and displace the feud between Achilles and Agamemnon, which was itself a ritualized game or contest. In agonistic societies, a challenge to honor was often adjudicated by a ritualized game that was played out according to more or less rigid community expectations. As Cohen points out in his discussion of the relationship between the pursuit of honor, feuding, and games,

> [A] feud involves an institutionalized relationship of hostility between two individuals or groups. Once begun, feud follows its peculiar social logic through a series of aggressive acts which may or may not result in settlement. Anthropologists often note that "feuds resemble games," because feuding typically follows a course of move and counter-move according to a complex set of rules which participants generally take pains to follow (or at least take pains to appear to follow). The principal objective of this game is honor. In highly agonistic societies the honor and prestige gained through the feud provide the basis for claims to leadership within the community.[11]

The Funeral Games in the *Iliad* restore community and so replace the feud games that tore it apart. In the Funeral Games, the selfishness and self-absorption of the participants in the feud is replaced by a sense of fairness and generosity and active care for the community. The reconstitution of community flows directly from the way a reformed Achilles oversees the games. He manages them with a generosity and justice that heals old wounds and uncovers a new mode of excellence. In so doing, he evinces a concern for the common good that repairs the damage done by his own self-absorption. In confronting his friend's death, he finds a new way to deal with his own impending death; namely to grab for whatever excellence and friendship that can be had in this life, even in the midst of its limits and grief.

Finally, Achilles' wrath is broken completely when Priam, Hektor's father, comes to his camp to beg for the body of his son. Achilles' rage is overcome by commiseration with Priam about their common fate. Just as Priam grieves for Hektor, Achilles' father will grieve for him. So Achilles discovers that life is hard for all human beings, and therefore his self-obsessive neglect of community is irrational. In a like way, since he realizes his own father will grieve for him as Priam grieves for Hektor, he finds a kind of community even with his enemy that allows him to be fair to the old king as well. His wrath at the limits of the human condition did not grant him the immortality he longed for. Rather, his pursuit of extremes ruined what he loved. Achilles learns by the end of the *Iliad* that if one does not live by the limits and conditions set by mortality, one ruins what little chance for excellence is within one's grasp.

Ultimately, Achilles' new conception of limits and how to live within them is built upon the theology he articulates at the close of the book:

> There are two urns that stand on the door-sill of Zeus. They are unlike / for the gifts they bestow: an urn of evils, an urn of blessings. / If Zeus who delights in thunder mingles these and bestows them / on man, he shifts, and moves now in evil, again in good fortune. / But when Zeus bestows the urn of sorrow, he makes failure / of man, and the evil hunger drives him over the shining / earth, and he wanders respected neither of gods nor mortals.
>
> (*Iliad* 24.526–33)

For Homer, good things happen to bad people; bad things happen to good, and to pretend to be able to see some ultimate rationality in the process is an illusion. In the end, human beings are limited by the fact that the order of the whole is inaccessible to us. Yet once Achilles accepts the limits of his condition, he is able to discover a middle way between the gods' love of strife and the extreme pursuit of immortality. In this way he is able to become a decent human being. Homer was the educator of Greece because he not only pointed out the problems with honor; he dramatized a way of maintaining one's humanity in the face of the force and brutality to which the zero-sum pursuit of honor tends.

The great-souled man heeds Homer's lessons to a fault. He wants divinity, and thinks that the pursuit of honor is his only vehicle. Yet in the end he knows that possession of honor is not enough to satisfy his heart. So the great-souled man is more or less contemptuous of even honor. His attempt to become self-sufficient is the attempt to become insulated from the harshness of a world that eventually will defeat him utterly by forcing him to submit to death. And since he knows he will be defeated in the end, he refuses to join the fight. He simply withdraws from life, and so from the pursuit of any activity that could satisfy. To be sure, as Millbank, Hauerwas, and Pinches have seen, this high-minded withdrawal is in reality competition on another, much loftier level. But it ends in the pursuit of a stoic self-sufficiency that masks a deep restlessness and sterility—perhaps a kind of despair.

In drawing this picture of the great-souled man, Aristotle sees this temptation lurking at the heart of classical culture. Indeed, by showing the implications of greatness of soul, he argues strenuously against it. The stoic withdrawal from activity was the attempt to limit human desire so as to protect oneself from the harshness and limits of the human condition. So it is not only the case that pursuit of honor leads to competition, civil strife, and the celebration of the "virtue" of the strongest. It can also lead to a high-minded despair; a giving up on life so as to be free from the potential damage life might inflict. The great-souled man's experience of limits drives him to seek a self-sufficiency that closes him off from action. Such a man gives up the zeal for divinity and settles for the dispiriting consolation that in the useless because ultimately fruitless competition to determine the "real man," he is above the crowd. Ironically, while his culture celebrates the nobility of virtue-as-virility, it winds up praising one who tends to sterile inactivity. Aristotle is severely critical of the embodiment of his culture's notion of virtue, for in its pretense to self-sufficiency, it leads to precisely the kind of complacent, congratulatory sense of one's own excellence and superiority that makes both community and individual reorientation impossible. If he wants to make his audience good, Aristotle must undermine this conception of human excellence in order to force his audience to the conclusion that they stand in need of a radical kind of conversion.

Moreover, the desire for self-sufficiency would render philosophy impossible. The philosopher's activity is born from wonder, which requires a kind of radical wakefulness to reality—a reality that we ourselves do not make, but rather discover as existing "out there," much to our wonder and delight. In other words, philosophy is born from an awareness of our radical need for something we cannot ourselves supply. In Plato's *Symposium*, for instance, in contrast to all the other speakers who praised Eros for his beauty or charms, Socrates emphasizes that love involves always a lack or a need for fullness. For him, the eros that characterizes philosophy is born from a union of Poverty and Resource (203bff). Philosophy gets its characteristics from Eros:

> He [Eros] is in-between wisdom and ignorance as well. In fact, you see, none of the gods loves wisdom or wants to become wise—for they are already wise—and no one who is wise already loves wisdom; on the other hand, no one who is ignorant will love wisdom either or want to become wise. For what's especially difficult about being ignorant is that you are content with yourself, even though you're neither beautiful and good nor intelligent. If you don't think you need anything, of course, you won't want what you don't think you need.
>
> In that case, Diotima, who are the people who love wisdom, if they are neither wise nor ignorant?
>
> "That's obvious," she said. "A child could tell you. Those who love wisdom fall in-between those two extremes. And Love is one of them, because he is in love with what is beautiful, and wisdom is extremely beautiful. It follows that Love must be a lover of wisdom and, as such, is in-between being wise and being ignorant. This, too, comes to him from his parentage, from a father who is wise and resourceful and a mother who is not wise and lacks resource.[12]

In this Plato says that an awareness of our own ignorance and need for the fullness of knowledge are the preconditions for engaging in philosophy. The drive in philosophy is not for self-sufficiency. For the same reason, Aristotle hints that the great-souled man's pretense at self-sufficiency guarantees that wakefulness to need will never occur. And if philosophy holds out the hope for satisfaction of desire, the great-souled man's pretense at self-sufficiency will close off the possibility of his own satisfaction. By obscuring his awareness of need, the great-souled man remains invincibly ignorant. His smug sense of his own virtue and thus honorability insure that he is closed to the ways he has to improve morally and philosophically. Thus he is closed to happiness. As Aristotle pointed out, the great-souled man, in asserting his own self-sufficiency, will not praise or delight in reality. He assumes that reality is so harsh that it will not meet his heart's desire, and so he must struggle to protect himself from it. He does not see that he needs to be open to reality even in order to know whether it is hostile or not. And in closing himself off from community and reality, he is closing himself off from the delight in communion that may just constitute the source of his deepest satisfaction.

However, Aristotle is not merely saying that the cultivation of greatness of soul will mean a loss of happiness. Furthermore, he shows the disasters that may befall us if we fall into this kind of high-minded despair. Recall that for Aristotle, the great-souled man is unwilling to recall favors he has received, but not favors that he has bestowed. As an example of this, he refers to the scene in the *Iliad* where Thetis petitions Zeus to help the Trojans win the war (*NE,* 1124b15). The scene to which he refers is famous: Achilles is disrespected when Agamemnon takes his token of honor, Briseis. Indeed, he is so wounded and angry that he withdraws from the fighting. The way he decides to settle the dispute is to pray to his mother Thetis, a goddess, to intervene so that his comrades will begin to be slaughtered by Trojans. Then they will come crawling back to grovel and beg his forgiveness, restoring to him—the greatest of the warriors in the army—the honor that is due him. Thetis petitions Zeus to have Achilles' friends killed. How are we to understand this reference? To illustrate the implication of the great-souled man's haughtiness, Aristotle chooses an example where an honor-seeking man is led to pray for the death of his comrades for his own greater glory. In the face of the harshness of the world, Aristotle is saying, one way of responding is to assert one's claim even at the expense of one's friends and community, high-mindedly insisting on one's own greatness as a way of managing the insecurity of the human condition. One way of reading this allusion is that no matter how hard we try to act as if we were self-sufficient and independent, our various insufficiencies and dependencies remain. The only compensation for neglecting them or seeking to destroy them for the sake of self-sufficiency is a violence that causes misery to ourselves and tears apart our communities. Aristotle seeks to revalue this conception of life by showing why it leads to failure. Aristotle seems to be saying this: limit or bury your desire and it resurfaces as a self-obsessed sterile stoicism that masks a tendency to violence or fanaticism.

This stoic withdrawal contributed to the other great temptation of the Hellenistic era, which arose partly from dissatisfaction with the kind of sterile stoicism that the pursuit of glory tends to: Gnosticism. The sense of futility stemming from the turmoil and dislocation of ancient Greece and the rise of the Hellenistic world also seems to have been responsible for the rise of various Gnostic sects. A pervasive sense of the world's indifference, and the dread that indifference engenders, gave birth to movements emphasizing the possession of special knowledge as a way to escape humanity's woes.[13]

Conclusion

Paradoxically, given its emphasis on noble action, the Greek conception of virtue as love of honor ultimately tends to inactive sterility that may issue in violence and fanaticism. What is true for individuals is also true of cultures. Classical culture and its emphasis on honor may tend to the sterility of Stoicism and the fanaticism of Gnosticism. The Greek striving for self-sufficiency so as to avoid the insecurity of life ends with the ideal of a high-minded withdrawal from and contempt for social life that is untrue to our situation as social animals who are dependent on others. Aristotle seeks to revalue this way of life by appealing to a new notion of virtue. This new notion proceeds from the fact of human dependence and interdependence. It is practically wise to do the things the equitable person does—forgive wrongs, cut fellow citizens a break, refuse to push the letter of the law to one's own advantage in recognition of the flawed character of all actual politics and people. Since we depend on our society for our flourishing, individual sacrifices for its sake are in our interest. Virtue-as-equity proceeds from a recognition of our dependence on others:

> What we need from others, if we are not only to exercise our initial animal capacities, but also to develop the capacities of independent practical reasoners, are those relationships necessary for fostering the ability to evaluate, modify, or reject our own practical judgments, to ask, that is, whether what we take to be good reasons for action really are sufficiently good reasons, *and* the ability to imagine realistically alternative possible futures, so as to be able to make rational choices between them, *and* the ability to stand back from our desires, so as to be able to enquire rationally what the pursuit of our good here and now requires and how our desires must be directed and, if necessary, reeducated, if we are to attain it.[14]

6

Justice, Injustice, and Equity

Different Starting Points

The last moral virtue Aristotle takes up is justice, and this discussion is difficult for us to understand for at least three reasons. First, Aristotle's pedagogy takes for granted typical Greek assumptions about the meaning and purpose of law. Yet citizens of modern liberal democracies have quite different notions of these matters. Since the point of departure is so different, effort is required to understand the ancient assumptions in order to see the direction of Aristotle's pedagogy. Second, contemporary political philosophy gives a different account of the motive for particular injustice than Aristotle does. Yet since Aristotle undermines his audience's assumptions about law and justice in part by articulating an account of particular injustice, we have to understand these differences in order to understand his account. Third, the way liberal regimes respond to the circumstances of justice differ radically from Aristotle's response. In this chapter I will first articulate these differences in order to make Aristotle's pedagogical strategy manifest.

Law and Neutrality

Aristotle makes a broad distinction between universal justice, which aims at the whole of virtue (*NE,* 1129b26–27), and particular justice, which is a particular virtue like courage or generosity or self-control. He links universal justice with law *(nomos).* Law seeks universal justice, "for the lawful is what the art of legislation has determined to be just. The laws make pronouncements on everything" (*NE,* 1129b13–15).

Nomos referred not only to statutory law but also to usage and ancient custom. Thus it was thought to embody the ethos of a polis.[1] Thus success follows acting in accord with *nomos*.[2] Pericles' Funeral Oration is the classic account of the connection between virtue and *nomos*. Before praising the dead, Pericles lavishes praise on the forebears whose wise laws are the real source of Athenian greatness. Indeed, these customs are so great that they have become an education not just to the citizens of Athens but to the entire Greek world.

The emphasis is on the fact that the city passed judgements on every sphere of human life and in so doing sought to cultivate a certain kind of citizen.[3] In this sense, ancient lawgivers tried to encourage every virtue and discourage every vice in order to foster what the city held to be good. For example, by forbidding running away in battle and providing rewards for bravery, law encouraged courage and discouraged cowardice. Thus citizens of ancient cities had a very different notion of the nature and scope of law than does modern liberal political theory. The guiding assumption of liberal theory and practice is that individual human beings are the best judge of their own good; only we ourselves can know what really makes us happy. There are a variety of different ways of phrasing this perspective in liberalism. In early modern liberal individualism, for example, the argument was that our natural liberty is to dispose of our person and possessions however we see fit. As Locke says,

> To understand Political Power right, and derive it from its Original, we must consider what State all Men are naturally in, and that is, a *State of perfeect Freedom* to order their Actions, and dispose of their Possessions, and Persons as they think fit, within the bounds of the Law of Nature, without asking leave, or depending upon the Will of any other Man.[4]

Due to the fact that human beings have this natural liberty, every human being has the right to define happiness for himself or herself, without the interference from an overbearing majority or religious or secular elites, or any other form of external authority which sets itself up in opposition to natural freedom. From this perspective, the only law that is legitimate to obey is a law to which one had already given one's assent beforehand.

The image of contract is consistently used in liberal theory to represent this notion. The theoretical architects of liberalism such as Locke knew that an actual signing of the social contract could not be historically proven. Locke emphasizes that the state of nature was so backward that writing and history had not been invented yet.[5] Yet the social contract persists as the guiding image in liberal theory because it works so well to describe the process whereby a citizen submits to the rule of law only because it is in his or her interest, thus both obeying and preserving the original freedom to define happiness autonomously. This social contract is interpreted to mean that people sign onto a society in order to secure their own interests, whatever those interests might be. According to much liberal political theory, therefore, the just political order aims not at a public conception of the good, but at something like neutrality which "does not favor any comprehensive doctrine."[6] Or as political scientist Theodore Lowi has argued, liberal politics must be an instrumental politics which does not foster morality. For this reason, he insists, liberalism is "individualist" and "against morality."[7] Thus on this account, far from seeking the common good or virtue, law becomes the neutral means that allows individuals to pursue private lives free from interference from the city and other individuals. Justice, therefore, becomes identified with protecting prepolitical rights, which safeguard our own preferred projects.

Aristotelians would argue that this kind of neutrality is simply not possible. The city is much more than a mere alliance or contract as described by Hobbes or Locke (*P*, 3.9.1280b5–12; 1280a31–34 to take but a few examples). All regimes—liberal regimes included—cultivate a way of life by formation in *nomos*. This conclusion is resisted by liberal theorists, for liberals are (rightly) suspicious of substantive conceptions of the human good, for those conceptions could (and often are) used as justifications for all sorts of oppression. So the traditional way liberal theorists read Aristotle's insistence on the architectonic character of politics is to see it as a dangerous kind of normative prescription which issues in a teleologically justified perfectionist state. Such a conception is dangerous, it is asserted, because it risks trampling the rights of the weakest in pursuit of a teleological ideal posited by some idealistic philosopher-king. Yet given Aristotle's insistence that most of us are not good; and given his insistence that most rulers equate political rule with despotic rule over slaves by foisting off their own defective, limited conception of justice on the whole, his point about universal justice could just as easily be read as a stern warning to pay strict attention to the inevitable. Aristotle seems to be saying something like this:

> Rulers pass laws aimed at some particular conception of the human good. Given the architectonic character of politics, the question is not, '*Should* we form human beings through law?' Rather, the question is, '*How* do we form human beings through law?' Formation is inevitable. So in calling attention to this aspect of law, I am not straightforwardly making any substantive recommendations as to how to form people or how to produce a 'perfectionist state.' I am merely pointing out that political regimes form their citizens and their communities. If citizens assume that they lead radically private lives unaffected by the architectonic practice of politics they live blindly and thus in peril. Since you are formed by your regime, pay attention to that or pay the consequences of your lack of reflection.

So Aristotle's conception of law aiming at universal justice is better read as a stern warning of the inherent serious implications of all political activity than as a straightforward normative prescription for this or that particular policy which could promote public virtue. This reading is only strengthened by his later reflections on how politicians actually operate through law, as we shall see. Aristotle's pedagogical strategy is to begin with the audience's assumption that the laws of their city foster some particular kind of human excellence and point out that this identification of law and personal excellence works only if the *nomoi* are perfectly just. He then argues that since all rulers aim not at universal justice but rather at their own partial interests, the *nomoi* they create do not actually cultivate comprehensive excellence, the rulers' arguments to the contrary.

The Motives for Injustice

The second reason Aristotle's account is difficult to understand is that he has a very different account of the motivation for injustice than liberal political philosophy does. Aristotle distinguishes particular justice from universal justice. In keeping with his dialectical method, he appeals to common speech in order to draw the distinction. People use different terms to describe different motivations. For instance, if a married man has an affair with his secretary, people say he lacks of self-control. Such a man is not overgrasping for external goods. Indeed, he may have to waste external goods to keep his mistress happy. By contrast, a man who has an affair with a married woman in order to blackmail her is motivated by love of profit or gain *(kerdos)* (*NE,* 1130a15–30). In practicing some vices, people strive for smaller shares—of giving (when they are stingy), for example, or of pain (when they are cowardly). In other cases, however, people strive for larger shares. Consequently, there must be a special kind of temptation or vice that motivates this particular kind of unjust overtaking. This is particular injustice, as distinct from universal justice (the general tendency to be a lawbreaker). The unjust person in the former sense takes more than his fair share of external goods involved in "good and bad fortune" (*NE,* 1129b4–6).

Aristotle's account of the motive for injustice is strikingly different from that presented by liberal theorists. The guiding hypothesis of liberal political theory is that no one is a better judge of my own good than I am myself. It follows that I possess certain prepolitical rights that I can hold as a trump against individuals, groups, or power structures that force me to act contrary to my own will. The problem becomes how to provide individuals a motive to act for the good of others. On this account, the origin of injustice is the inability or unwillingness of people to be "other-regarding." In some contemporary ethics injustice is due to a lack of sensitivity. The unjust person is prone to violate another person's rights or conception of the good because he does not respect or value others as he should. Often, the cure for this is some form of sensitivity training, wherein the offender is immersed in the worldview of those he is offending. For example, Philippa Foote asserts,

> Virtues such as justice correspond not to any particular desire or tendency that has to be kept in check but rather to a deficiency of motivation. If people were as much attached to the good of others as they are to their own good there would no more be a general virtue of benevolence than there is a general virtue of self-love. And if people cared about the rights of others as they care about their own rights no virtue of justice would be needed to look after the matter.[8]

By contrast, Aristotle thinks that the subject of particular injustice is the contestable goods that we can gain from each other, especially external goods like honor, money, and security. Human beings are unjust insofar as they are tempted to take more than their fair share of these. Looking back to Aristotle's treatment of generosity, for example, we realize that the problem with stinginess was not merely an inability to give away. It was also the temptation to take excessively. And both stinginess and unjust taking are manifestations of a similar psychic misorientation—both vices are manifestations of an overvaluation of external goods. In sum, for Aristotle the pleasure that comes from profit motivates particular injustice (*NE,* 1130b5). The unjust are not merely insensitive to the rights and claims of others. Rather, they desire honor and gain so much that they tend to injustice (*P,* 1302a32–24). Human beings love these goods so much that they fight with one another in order to acquire them (*P,* 1302a39). And they become envious of the honors and privileges others enjoy, which also leads to conflict (*P,* 1304a33). Aristotle calls this tendency to take more than one's fair share *pleonexia,* which means literally "having more," and so connotes overgrasping or overreaching.[9] *Pleonexia* is the root of injustice in Aristotelian political thought.

Pleonexia is bound up with the insecurity of the human (*NE,* 1129b4–6). That is, overgrasping individuals seek honor, power, money or possessions for security. In the *Rhetoric,* for example, Aristotle argues that people see social relations primarily in terms of competition for scarce resources. Such a context is full of danger, for rivals are capable of exploiting any momentary weakness or lapse of vigilance. Since most men are bad and slaves of gain, being at the mercy of another is something to be afraid of (*R,* 1382b). In his presentation of respectable opinion in the *Rhetoric,* security is found not in a stable political order or flourishing friendships, but rather in power and external goods. Thus Aristotle points out that the very rich do not seem to experience fear, because they think that their wealth prevents them from having to suffer anything (*R,* 1372b–1373a).[10]

It is clear why these scarce resources have to do with fortune. We depend on a range of contexts we do not create and have little control over. We are subject to bodily limits, disease, natural disasters, unjust treatment by our fellows, and so on. The external goods Aristotle identifies as the subject of injustice apparently enable us to maximize our potential for good luck and minimize our potential for bad (or at least soften its blows). For instance, a multimillionaire has many more options if his loved one comes down with malignant cancer than does a poor person. A universally honored person has many more options if she is sued by a rival than a universally reviled person. A knowledgeable person with powerful connections has many more options in resisting a new tax law that would devastate his business than a poor person does. Aware of our own insecurity, and longing to protect our lives in the face of it, we tend to overgrasp for these scarce resources in order to be free from a terrifying dependence on fate.[11]

The Supply Problem

The scarcity of these resources makes them the subject of intense competition and conflict, and often prompts the desire for mastery. For this reason, Aristotle consistently calls these scarce resources the goods people "fight about" (*perimacheta agatha* [*NE,* 1169a21–22; see also *EE,* 1248b27; *R,* 1368b12–14]). Material possessions are scarce. This was especially true in ancient economies where—in contrast to modern economies of growth—wealth was fixed. The scarcity of economic resources and the difficulty of providing for them led to strife and domination in the ancient city. Factional conflict in these cities usually occurred between the rich and poor. Moreover, citizens thought it necessary to exercise mastery over slaves and women whose time would be spent in providing for their material needs, in order to have leisure for politics and culture. The difficulty of providing for material resources led ancient Greek communities to see hierarchy and domination as central to their life (*Politics,* 1278a10–11; 1329a1–3; 1334a19).[12] We have seen that honor is also a limited resource. Being honored requires that people actually recall and celebrate one's excellent deeds. Yet because human beings can remember and celebrate only a few activities and individuals, honor is scarce. Finally, what conduces to people's security and preservation is also scarce, insofar as power and prestige are scarce. Clearly, such goods protect us from fortune, and political elites therefore compete vigorously for power and prestige. The ambition for these scarce resources creates a host of political problems.

The Demand Problem

Yet for Aristotle, the scarcity of these resources is not the only reason we overgrasp for them. In addition, human beings are unjust because we desire far more than we strictly need. In Aristotle's own terms, people overgrasp for the scarce goods involved in good and bad fortune because of the pleasure that comes from excess profit (*NE,* 1130b4–5). Since fortune leads us to demand much more than we strictly need, Aristotle argues that human desire is one of the intractable motivations for injustice. In the first book of the *Politics,* Aristotle explores the motivations behind the unlimited acquisition of wealth. His account of the motive for this scarce resource indicates the general character of the problem.

In his discussion of acquisition, Aristotle distinguishes two ways of meeting human needs. The first, he says, is the true art of business expertise, which he identifies with household management. This aims at a limited goal—self-sufficiency in the household with a view to the good life *(pros agathen zoen)* (*P,* 1256b31–32). However, the sham art of moneymaking (*P,* 1257b2) is also a typical response to human neediness. Proponents of the latter view insist that business has no limit, and strive for unlimited acquisition of wealth and property (*P,* 1257a1–2).

Natural forms of trade arose out of the division of labor, as a result of which some people acquired or made more of what they needed, and others less. The art of trade initially arose as a way of making mutually beneficial exchanges for an adequate supply of necessary goods. Yet since necessary goods are not always portable, money was invented in order to facilitate trade. The trade involving money is according to nature, Aristotle says. Yet over time and with the benefit of experience, trade degenerated into the technique of making the biggest profit (*P,* 1256b40–1257b10). In the end, Aristotle's standard for differentiating the true art of acquisition from its sham counterpart lies in his articulation of limit *(peras).* Put another way, he differentiates household management from its sham counterpart by articulating their different goals.

While the goal of household management is the self-sufficiency that makes flourishing family life possible, moneymaking strives for wealth and possessions without limit. Aristotle says that this maximization of profit initially seems to be the goal of a true art, because the goal of any art is without limit, in a sense.[13] Yet if arts are not directed by practical wisdom, which grasps the shape of a flourishing human life, then their ordering principle will be the practitioner's own desires. In other words, Aristotle argues that if we treat sham arts as architectonic we paradoxically destroy the goods we sought through the sham art in the first place. For example, according to Aristotle, household management is the architectonic practice that guides the use of the goods which business expertise makes or acquires. For him, business expertise is directed to a flourishing life in the household, and for this reason it makes no sense to seek unlimited wealth. If a businessperson seeks unlimited wealth, she is treating moneymaking as architectonic and thus subordinates all the activity of her household to moneymaking (*P*, 1257b30–33). However, that pursuit might well preclude the possibility of a flourishing life within the household. It simply makes no sense to destroy one's life in the pursuit of unlimited wealth and possessions, for these goods exist as a means to the good life, not the other way around. In this way, household management sets limits on the practice of business. When people forget those limits, at the same time they forget the purpose of the household, and the sham art of trade takes over their lives (*P*, 1257b30–35), with ruinous effects.

For Aristotle, the motivation to pursue scarce resources like unlimited wealth is the desire to escape the conditions of mortality. Aristotle says that the reason people seek wealth without limit is that they are eager for life *(to zen)*, but not for living well *(to eu zen)* (*P*, 1257b40–1258a2). Since their desire for life is without limit, they also desire what produces unlimited things. Moreover, for most of us, living well is equated with bodily pleasure, and this also leads people to pursue unlimited acquisition because pleasure seems to be available in and through external possessions. Aristotle concludes this discussion with the sobering observation that if people cannot acquire what they want through the art of moneymaking, they will try some other way (*P*, 1258a9–10; cf. *NE*, 1095b19–22). For Aristotle, the human tendency to overgrasp for external goods like honor and wealth and power over others is related to the radical insecurity of the human condition. In a variety of ways, we feel ourselves to be relatively helpless before that on which we depend, and therefore seek to control it by acquiring external goods that seem to be able to ward off the vagaries of fortune. For Aristotle, we are unjust not because we are unaware of other people's right to self-respect. We are afraid of death; the motive of injustice for Aristotle is the pervasive insecurity that drives us to acquire more than our fair share of the goods that make our insecure lives more secure.

The motivation for particular injustice is personal misorientation to scarce resources; people are unjust because they value scarce resources more than they should. If the unjust person were not so devoted to goods like honor and money, the community would be much better off, for such overgrasping inevitably leads to social disorder and mastery (*NE,* 1169a21–2; *EE,* 1248b27; *R,* 1368b12–14). Conversely, from an Aristotelian perspective justice will not mean merely a sensitivity to other people's rights and conceptions of the good, but rather the disposition to engage in cooperative ventures which foster the non-zero-sum, shareable goods which constitute a satisfying common life. The Aristotelian insistence on the connection between friendship and justice stems from his assumption that there is no divergence between intrapersonal virtues like temperance and courage, and interpersonal virtues like justice and friendship. Personal misorientation to honor, profit, or power leads both to personal vice and to social conflict:

> Aristotle does not think of justice and other interpersonal virtues (such as *philia*) as having a different aetiological basis from the particular virtues concerned with pleasure and pain. He does not see two realms of virtue, but one fundamental kind of human excellence viewed from two perspectives. Injustice and other breaches of community are not caused by a special incapacity linked to egoism (such as a poorly developed sense of justice). They are the "political" or interpersonal symptom of psychic or intrapersonal misorientation. Someone with an insatiable desire for money or honors will necessarily find himself at odds with others. Thus for Aristotle the self-indulgent man is at least potentially the unjust man, and the cure for his self-indulgence would also be the cure for injustice. The only guarantee of good citizenship is

> the proper psychic disposition toward the pleasures and pains that motivate human action.[14]

The vicious person misunderstands his own best interest, and this intrapersonal problem has disastrous interpersonal consequences.

Liberal Theory's Responses to the Supply and the Demand Problems

Liberalism applies Enlightenment natural science, economics, and political science to the supply and demand problems in order to create a stable, materially prosperous, and secure political order. This solution has two related thrusts. First, there is the attempt to educate human desires away from the scarce good of honor to security and material plenty. Second there is the attempt to create the economic and political conditions for the desire for material plenty to be satisfied. To this end, early modern political theorists like Hobbes and Locke embarked on an ambitious and radical project of revaluing traditional conceptions of appropriate human activities and desires in order to pave the way for their new conception of life.

Hobbes's *Leviathan* is a paradigmatic instance of this attempt at revaluation. Since the new ethics is built on a careful articulation of the passions as the building blocks of human conduct, it can be subsumed under physics, which studies all motion with certainty.[15] Hobbes begins the account by making a broad distinction between the passions inclining people to war and those inclining to peace. In order to achieve his stable society, he needs to minimize the passions inclining to war and maximize those inclining to peace. The following chart conveys his taxonomy of the passions:[16]

Passions Inclinng to War	Passions Inclining to Peace
1) Competition for	1) Desire of ease
riches	2) Love of sensual delight
honor	3) Fear of death and wounds
command	4) Desire for knowledge
2) Neediness	5) Desire for arts of peace
3) Hardihood	

Hobbes's passions inclining to war do so either because they are limited in supply or are in great demand because of the insecurity of the human condition. As we have seen, riches, honor, and power are in short supply and thus are the cause of conflict. Neediness also inclines to war because people in dire need are in such an insecure condition that they will do practically anything to survive. Finally, hardihood also leads to injustice because it is the manifestation of excessive desires, or what I have called the "demand problem." Hardihood is the willingness to take enormous risks—to overgrasp for some lofty goal such as power or prestige; or the desire to have much more than one needs—and so it can lead to massive injustices like tyranny.

To address the supply and demand problems Aristotle argues that human desires can be educated and thus moderated in a very different direction. His pedagogy aims at forming human desires away from goods that lead to personal and social disharmony. However, the English speaking liberal tradition took a different tack.[17] It sought to resolve the supply and demand problems by increasing the supply of the scarce goods whose supply could be increased, and downplaying the desire for scarce goods whose supply could not.

Increasing the Supply of Scarce External Goods

Liberal political theory tries to resolve the distributive justice problem by creating politically the conditions for unlimited economic growth; it addresses the problem of limited supply by creating more supply. So in effect liberal regimes try to grow their way out of the need for distributive justice between rich and poor. Yet the difficulty understanding Aristotle's account of justice is not merely that the liberal solution to the supply problem is unavailable to Aristotle because ancient economies were economies of scarcity. Aristotle assumed that wealth was stagnant, and this assumption was demolished by modern economics. But the real difficulty lies in Aristotle's articulation of the problem of unbounded desire itself. Aristotelian dialectic uncovers at the heart of human endeavors limits, contradictions, and tragic ironies. If Aristotle were alive to look at contemporary liberal solutions to the justice problem, he would surely be true to his own procedure of negative dialectic.

For Aristotle, external goods are clearly not bad things in themselves; indeed, they provide the material conditions for virtues such as generosity. He is, however, sober about the problems inherent in pursuing these goods. He insists that these things are not good in an unqualified sense, but are rather only good insofar as one uses them well. People have been known to be ruined by power and wealth, for example. So people should struggle to know what is good for them before they go chasing after goods which may or may not contribute to flourishing (*NE,* 1129b2–7; compare this with the same kind of reflections found at the opening of the *Ethics,* 1094b17–29).[18] So for Aristotle, economic activity cannot be an end in itself. Rather, it is a means to create the external goods that are needed to live a flourishing life. Aristotelians insist that economic systems must be embedded in and thus limited by the social and cultural practices of the larger regime.[19] Thus Aristotle would be critical of the tendency in liberal individualist regimes to compare the workings of almost every area of human culture to the model of the marketplace. In doing so we risk other goods cherished by our regime, like individual rights and dignity or the goods of local communities that cannot compete in the market.

The goods produced by the market, to be sure, are really good, but it is a question of knowing how to put them to appropriate human uses, and how and when to limit the drive for acquisition and consumption in order to preserve and foster countervailing goods. The problem is not merely that money cannot buy happiness. Most mature people know that already. Rather, it is the nagging, often inarticulate sense of an incommensurability between the desires of the human heart and the realities of comfortable self-preservation. To take an obvious example, the market economy depends on consumerism; it expands in part by cultivating acquisitive habits. In order to buy into this acquisitiveness, the consumer must be convinced that the world is cruel and inhospitable to the human heart's longings. Advertisers must convince their customers that their lives are somehow inadequate so that they will purchase things that they do not really need. This is true most obviously in the cosmetic industry, where the attempt is made to convince women that they must "make up" for some lack. Advertisers consistently attempt to manipulate the passions; inflating the anxiety at the heart of our mortal condition so as to inflate the passion for consumption that they hold out as the palliative to the anxiety they help foster. But the result of all this manipulation of desire is paradoxical: the source of the success of such an economy is also a source of danger to the society it inhabits. Such an economy creates wealth and comfort by encouraging the formation of cowardly, vicious, small-souled individuals best described by the commercial culture exploiting them not as free, rational citizens, but rather as "consumers." Yet a consumer is merely an alimentary canal. In this way the cause of the success of the economy may be the source of the decline of the larger culture, insofar as these vices degrade the conditions for the exercise of citizenship. Of course, such a vision of life—if there are no attractive countervailing tendencies—leads many to a kind of strange anxiety or hopeless despair in the midst of plenty.

Thus liberal individualist political economy has costs and benefits. Locke, for example, seems to have had an awareness of the costs as well as the benefits of the new order he was helping to promote. This is clear in his articulation of the transition to the use of money. Before the invention of money, he argues, infinite human desire did not exist. People were too busy providing for the necessities of life to do much else. In particular, they were far too busy to allow their imagination free reign, so they could not speculate about what they lacked or how their lives could be improved, or compare themselves to their neighbor and, coming up short, indulge in the desire for accumulation. But this all changed with the invention of money. Money for Locke is not merely an invention that allows for easier trade. Rather, it is symbolic of a certain level of social progress, for it presupposes a moderately divided labor force, the leisure and trust necessary to invent the scheme of money, and so forth. With the invention of money, the rough-and-ready justice of the original human condition was lost. That justice arose because human needs in the state of nature were limited. Inhabitants of the state of nature were satisfied—happy, in a sense—because there was a perfect fit between their desires and their satisfactions. Yet leisure and the possibility of accumulated wealth gave free reign to desires. Thus for Locke the price we pay in modern societies for our prosperity and security is a deep restlessness that is vented—without final satisfaction—in infinite acquisition. In a like way, Hobbes emphasizes that his conception of human life will not result in final happiness or satisfaction. Rather, happiness for him is a dreary process of desire to desire. The point of this process is not a final state of rest, but rather a pursuit of power so that we will be able to successfully pursue desire later, whatever those desires happen to be.[20] These early modern thinkers know that increasing the supply of riches exacerbates the problem of demand, for to engage in the new economics is to put human desires on a treadmill, running after an infinite accumulation of finite goods that can not satisfy the longings of the human heart.[21]

The ancient Greeks possessed a static economy and did not value technological innovation. Since scarcity and poverty were such a natural part of everyday life, it was thought that people could minimize their desires by restricting their needs. Thus one goal of household management would have been to minimize consumption in order to lessen neediness.[22] In an expanding, technologically dynamic economy, however, such a solution does not seem as attractive. So we have a hard time understanding Aristotle's denigration of excessive desires for external goods such as money because this excessive desire is precisely the mark of a good consumer-citizen. But perhaps Aristotle has a point. Early liberal theorists attempted to get people to sign onto their contracts. Like any good businessman making such a pitch, they did this through a brilliant rhetorical strategy: to make the contract rational, they played up the benefits of the contract and played down its costs. To play up the benefits of the contracts, they needed to play up the danger of its alternative, the state of nature. The point of articulating the state of nature is not to provide a theoretically satisfying developmental account of the origin of modern societies. Indeed, both Locke and Hobbes admit that their accounts of the state of nature are nonverifiable. The point of such articulations is to give a portrait of what the real world is like. For Locke and Hobbes, life in the state of nature is the only real alternative to liberal society, and that life is solitary, poor, nasty, brutish, and short (Hobbes), or at the least extraordinarily inconvenient (Locke). The reality of the human situation is that radical insecurity lies at the heart of every human undertaking. The world is not generous enough to provide for activities that are not subordinated to accumulating wealth and security. Indeed, even in those relationships where disinterested love seems to reign—the family—Hobbes and Locke find narrow self-interest to operate. Early liberal theory rested its pitch for comfortable self-preservation by emphasizing the terrifying insecurity faced by all human beings.[23] This process is most clearly at work in advertising: human beings are manipulated into doubting their own worth and the worth of their bodies and looks in order to be convinced to be acquisitive.[24]

Liberalism operates in part by convincing people of the insecurity of life and arguing that the most attractive alternative to this is comfortable self-preservation. In decisive ways it addresses the supply side of the problem by creating more wealth and security. I love my indoor plumbing and laptop and appreciate the fact that modern medicine has saved my wife's life several times. We all know the enormous advantages of living in a materially prosperous nation. Yet the cost of modern economics from an Aristotelian perspective is that it exacerbates the demand side of the circumstances of justice. Aristotle might argue that an expanding GDP necessarily inflates the human temptation to engage in *pleonexia*, thus not really solving the problem of justice, but merely lessening one dimension of the problem and exacerbating another. At the least, Aristotle will emphasize that in the midst of the plenty created by the liberal economy, *pleonexia* still exists. For him, even the promise of infinite acquisition will not resolve the insecurity at the heart of the human condition, if only because "you can't take it with you." So even when human beings have enough external resources to meet their basic needs—indeed, even when they have more than enough—they still are tempted to grab for more. To take the most obvious examples, in the richest country in the history of mankind, our economy is rife with instances of excessive love of profit fueled by the pleasure that comes from taking: wealthy moneygrubbers dislocating employees for even more profit; exploiters who pay absurdly low wages to workers in developing countries to make shoes they sell at ridiculously inflated prices to youngsters who can't afford them; advertising people who demean public spaces and public life in order to manipulate people so that they will be disposed to buying into the latest fad . . . Such depressing examples could go on and on. An Aristotelian response to these examples is to point out that we have not resolved the problem of justice by increasing the supply of scarce resources. We have merely put off addressing the side of desires.

Honor

I have argued that the pursuit of honor created a host of problems in classical societies. Realizing this, liberal theory engaged in two strategies to minimize the risk honor poses. First, Hobbes seeks to transform love of honor by equating honor with the possession of power.[25] This includes the "small power" of wealth. If the worth of a man is what people are willing to pay for him, then honor is a token attached primarily to wealth.[26] We are worth what people are willing to pay us. Hobbes insists that money rather than social approval is the best token of excellence, and when ambition can be vented through business practices in an economy of unlimited growth, honor is more easily accessible. The second move liberal theory made was to transform honor from a good that society bestows to a good that the individual gives himself or herself. For example, John Rawls has extolled self-respect as the most basic human good. Self-respect is the right to feel that one's own projects and conceptions of the good are worthwhile.[27] Yet if no one can shame me and no one can give me honor—if only I can give myself honor—then it is no longer a scarce commodity.

The Demand for Power

Liberalism's successful reinterpretation of the res publica as an artificial construct for the benefit of individuals who contract into it has the implicit effect of denigrating the pursuit of public office. The res publica is not seen as a natural unit in which people find their end, but is rather seen as an artificial construct that enables people to pursue private gratifications. But this means that since politicians pursue their necessarily private desires by seeking status in an artificial public realm, by definition they become in the public mind a form of parasite. There is no such thing as nobility of statesmanship in liberal politics, because politics has been defined in such a way as to preclude noble public motives. Ambition for political power is thus unseemly, with the result that many of the naturally ambitious will seek honor elsewhere, such as in business. This denigration of political office is buttressed by these regimes' ethos of equality. Striving for distinction through politics is inherently inegalitarian.[28]

Comfortable Minimizers versus Needy Risk-Takers

Aristotle's accounts of justice and injustice proceed from two notions foreign to our usual way of thinking about politics. First, he assumes that the laws of a society will engender some determinate conception of virtue in human beings. Second, he takes it for granted that many external goods are scarce and that social problems will be created if citizens desire them excessively. To put this a different way, he assumes that at least some people in his society will take great risks to accumulate power and prestige. This means that ultimately Aristotle's audience may have a different notion of rationality than is assumed by liberal theory. To the extent that liberal theory has assumed that comfortable self-preservation is the most attractive human life, liberal rationality has come to be identified with risk minimization. To take an obvious example, in *A Theory of Justice* John Rawls wants us to imagine a group of individuals trying to determine what social rules they will live by before knowing what position they will occupy in the society they are founding. In this "original position" they would agree on the following principle, among other things: inequalities in wealth will be considered just only if they result in compensating benefits for everyone, and in particular for the least advantaged members of society.[29] In this Rawls takes as his central case of rationality the person who is a calculating risk minimizer. Everyone in his original position is assumed to be adverse to risk, and so each actor wants to make sure that if he winds up on the bottom of the heap, that place is as attractive as possible. Yet it is a measure of the success of the liberal tradition's denigration of the ambition for honor and power that Rawls never seriously considers the person who would distain this kind of risk minimization. That is, he never seriously considers the perspective of a risk taker who might revel in the opportunities such a high stakes proposal presents. Such a person might reply to the problem of the original position this way: "I will structure principles of justice to benefit the *most* advantaged. To be sure, in the society we are constructing I may wind up being one of the least advantaged. But if so at least I risked all for power and status and have the comfort of knowing that I am not a coward. Yet if my gamble pays off, I will enjoy all the privileges my society offers, with no corresponding duty to take care of those who are beneath me." Even in liberal societies, there are people who value goods other than material comfort, security, and self-respect. There are people who favor of honor or lordship or holiness or moral virtue or philosophy, and these people act politically.

The problem a risk minimizer has with understanding Aristotle's point of departure in discussing justice and injustice is that it takes for granted an audience that consists precisely of people who would take great risks for honor and power. Since liberal rationality such as Rawls espouses cannot encompass audacity, we must drop this perspective if we are to understand Aristotle's pedagogical strategy in dealing with audacious people.[30] What would an ambitious, virile young Greek say when told by a liberal theorist that his perspective violates the rights of others because it goes against the rule that individuals value the perspective of the other? Would such an argument dissuade him from tyranny?

In contrast to Rawls's presentation of the circumstances giving rise to the problem of injustice, Aristotle's does not presuppose risk minimization, nor an abundance of external goods nor a preference for material comfort and security. Rather, he begins by assuming two things about his audience. First, they equate law and justice, and so assume that their city cultivates genuine comprehensive excellence. Second, they entertain the possibility that risk for glory and power is the mark of a real man, and so are tempted to arrogance and despotism.

The Problem with Law

Now I am finally in a position to explore the pedagogical strategy Aristotle employs to introduce his audience into a wider conception of justice than the one their culture offers. Again, Aristotle begins his account of justice by emphasizing that universal justice is associated with law and encourages all the virtues and discourages all the vices, thus promoting a comprehensive excellence. The way Aristotle disabuses his audience of this notion is to argue that all actual law is passed by politicians who have only a partial sense of justice. Since the laws they pass in reality reflect their own partisan goals—to promote the strength of their own class, or to reward themselves or their cronies, and so on—the conception of excellence that their laws encourage will consequently be partial, not comprehensive.

However, the deeper argument is that even just law fails to achieve comprehensive excellence. This is not a defect of the lawgiver, but rather a fundamental limit of law itself. Once it is realized that law does not in truth aim at comprehensive excellence, the audience is shocked out of its self-congratulatory notion that their culture is comprehensively best and are ready for an argument about how to improve their own deficient practices. Let me examine these points in more detail.

The Partiality of Law

Aristotle thinks that all regimes are more or less defective because all regimes aim not at the advantage of all their members, but rather at the advantage of the ruling element. Aristotle insists that all ruling groups structure the laws so that they will benefit only themselves and their cronies, leaving the rest of the society behind in the allocation of scarce resources. As Aristotle says in his discussion of justice, it looks to the advantage of the rulers *(archonti)* or to his fellows *(koinono)* (*NE,* 1130a3–5). As evidence, he points to the saying of Bias that "Rule shows the real man" *(arche andra deixei)* (1130a1–3). This statement can be read in two ways. One way is that ruling shows what a person is really like, for with rule comes the power to do as the ruler wills and to set the priorities he wishes to set, to act with impunity, and to be free from social stigmas and laws against certain sorts of conduct. Yet read another way, the statement is ironic. "Bias" comes from the root word *bia,* which means "elemental, manly strength" or more generally, "force." Thus given the context, the phrase could easily have the connotation, "Only the real man can rule." That is, the person who achieves power is the man who has the guts and strength to lord it over others so as pursue his own interest (cf. *Republic,* 343c).

Aristotle elaborates on this later in the *Ethics* and the *Politics.* Most human beings, he says, equate rule with the lordship masters exercise over slaves. Political rule is thus usually seen as a certain kind of mastery (*P,* 1252a8–17). To most people, the life of mastery appears best, for those who possess power seem to be able to perform the greatest number of noble actions. Thus virtue might require vice in order to furnish materials for its deeds. From this perspective, it seems best not to give to our neighbor but to take away, and to disregard the ties of family and friendship in the pursuit of political power (*P*, 1325a322–40). So when people come to power they generally structure their laws to benefit themselves and their own faction. So while all actual regimes have a certain kind of justice; they are "in error simply" (*P*, 1301a37–38). Everyone agrees that justice consists in rendering equal things to equal people. Yet since people disagree about what equality entails, their conceptions of justice will be different. And these different conceptions of justice will yield different regimes, each exhibiting only a partial sense of justice as a whole (*NE*, 8.10–11). Indeed, if laws are systematically organized with a view to a way of life, they are generally ordered to war and mastery, as in the Spartan case (*P*, 1324a38–1324b15).

It is clear that Aristotle's pedagogical strategy throughout the philosophy of human affairs is to draw parallels between contemptible cases of *pleonexia* such as pursuit of wealth, and more conventionally respectable ambitions, such as desire for honor and political power (e.g., *P*, 1311a5–8; 1321a34–1321b1). Once the audience realizes that tyrants and powerful politicians overgrasp in a way similar to the money grubbers they despise, perhaps they can question the devotion to virtue-as-virility, and its concomitant emphasis on mastery. Since law is the product of overgrasping rulers, the conception of excellence fostered by every actual regime is partial or defective. And since we are all decisively formed by the regimes we inhabit, our own characters are consequently partial and defective. One cannot achieve comprehensive excellence merely by following the *nomoi* of one's own regime.

Equity

The second problem with law as a guide for comprehensive excellence has nothing to do with the defects of regimes. Rather, it involves the inability of a law to comprehend the particulars of right action. This is made clear in Aristotle's discussion of equity (*epiekeia*; *NE*, 5.10). Aristotle begins the discussion of equity by pointing out that common opinion about it seems muddled, for it is said to be both the same as and different from justice (*NE,* 1137a33). He addresses this dilemma by arguing that equity is in one sense a kind of justice, but in another sense it is better than legal justice. Equity in the first sense comes into play when the law needs "straightening out." Laws sometimes require correction because they are universal statements, and it is impossible to provide for the practically infinite variety of all possible cases under such universal statements. This is not the fault of the lawgiver, but is rather due to the variability of human affairs. For this reason, even a well-made and perfectly just law will sometimes cause an injustice if it is followed to the letter without regard to the particularities of the case at hand. Such cases call for equity. These corrections, Aristotle says, ought to correspond to the lawgiver's will; to what he would have done in the unique situation that his law could not foresee. This is not an insight unique to Aristotle's political theory. It is a consistent theme of Western theory and practice that law is an insufficient guide to human conduct.[31]

Yet at the end of the account of equity Aristotle complicates the discussion. He suddenly states that not all things are determined by law. He cryptically compares equity to a flexible piece of lead which, when molded around the irregular surfaces of stones of a building under construction, told the builders which stones would make the best fit with the ones already in place. He states that in cases like this, the indefinite *(aoristos)* is the standard *(kanon)* (*NE,* 1137b29–30). So equity can be taken in two ways. First, equity can be understood to be a kind of particular excellence, insofar as it is a corrective to legal justice, which is required when the law breaks down due to its generality.[32] Taken in this sense, equity would be bounded by the law, at least in the form of the intention of the lawgiver. It would not transcend the law but rather perfect it by insuring justice in its attempt to apply the spirit of the law to the particulars of the case. However, the cryptic statement about the lead pipe—the indefinite standard—makes us uneasy about this account. Perhaps there is another sense of equity. This question gains additional force when we note that the statement about the lead molding arises in the context of a discussion about lawmaking, and whether all things can be determined by the making of a law (*NE,* 1137b25ff). The thoughtful reader must reflect on the fact that the law on which this "particular equity" is based must be made at some point with no existing guide. By definition, the first legislators had no rules to guide them. So where does law come from in the first place? When a society's laws are being laid down, there seems to be no universally valid set of rules that could guide the process. So while it is fine to insist that in difficult cases we ought to refer to the intention of the lawgiver, we cannot state this intention exhaustively in any universally applicable set of rules or principles that we could bring to bear in sorting through the particulars of the case in question. Perhaps equity must be understood not merely as a corrective to legal justice. In this section, Aristotle argues for a second, more robust sense of equity—stronger and better than partial justice because it is the standard for law and thus justice.

Taken in this second sense, equity—not law—is the whole of excellence. It consists not merely in the ability to correct law when law needs correction. Indeed, from this perspective, decent laws are precisely the rules of thumb determined by those who possess virtue-as-equity.[33] Equity in this second sense transcends law and provides the reference point for all the particular excellences by being their standard. Indeed, in this sense, equity is the whole of virtue, and thus is the standard for law itself. This point gains additional force when it is noticed that from this point on in the *Ethics*, Aristotle uses the term *epieikeia* not to connote "equity" but rather as a synonym of "goodness." Aristotle began the discussion on justice by arguing that in a sense justice is the whole of virtue because it commands every act of virtue and forbids every act of vice. By the end of the discussion, however, we realize that equity is the whole of moral virtue.[34] Further this sense of virtue-as-equity implies a willingness to forgo one's own apparent interest in the short term for the sake of the community, for a flourishing community is the condition for one's own long-term flourishing.[35]

Conclusion

At this point there is a problem. By the end of the treatment of the moral virtues, Aristotle argues that genuine human excellence consists in virtue-as-equity rather than in virtue-as-virility. Yet this was revealed partly by arguing that all actual regimes promoted defective conceptions of excellence. Since we have all been deformed by our regimes, however, how do we know what equity entails, apart from simply experiencing it? How could we retreat to some Archimedian point outside the limited perspective of our own culture so as to achieve a glimpse of what true virtue requires? Aristotle's answer comes when we consider anew his dialectical examination of the particular moral virtues from the perspective that his account of virtue-as-equity provides. Aristotle's dialectic is revealed as a negative dialectic. That is, he has uncovered a hint of what virtue might require by examining systematically the way his audience's practice of virtue failed on its own terms. By exploring the way human practices go wrong, we can achieve some insight into how to go right. There is no transcendent point outside of our own cultural perspective that we can retreat to in order to judge the worthiness of our practices and beliefs. In order to educate human desire, Aristotle employs it as both a starting point and a point of reference in his inquiry. He examined what ordinary opinions had to say about the object of human desire to see where and how they broke down. I have argued that these opinions failed on their own terms: the practice of virtue-as-virility failed to achieve the noble action extolled by its practitioner. The way virtue was practiced did not satisfy in the way initially thought. Indeed, instead of noble action, it led to overgrasping, petty lies, ignoble stinginess, and ultimately to inactive sterility. These failures are articulated in order to shock the audience out of their attachment to honor and the concomitant attachment to the prevailing ethos of their culture. This failure not only clears the ground for further inquiry by sparking the realization among the audience that they are in ignorance about where genuine virtue lies. In addition, it implicitly points in a new direction. Comprehensive moral virtue does not lie in self-assertion, individualistic overgrasping to insulate the self from insecurity, or mastery. Rather, it seems to lie in the countervailing practices contained in virtue-as-equity.

If one looks at the way the term is employed throughout the rest of the philosophy of human affairs, one sees that *epieikeia* connotes a range of dispositions which are not valued by practitioners of virtue-as-virility. As I have pointed out, in an honor-loving culture, personal slights were occasions for cycles of retribution that often tore the city apart. By contrast, those who practice virtue-as-equity do not take revenge for slights. Since all regimes have only a partial sense of justice, the common good requires that individuals refuse to push their "just" claims too far. It is not enough for people to render legalistically to others what is their due and insist on the same from their fellow citizens. Rather, they must refuse to push their advantage at the cost of another, even when the law is on their side (*P*, 1301a38). So, for example, Aristotle argues that while equitable people have the most claim to rule because of their virtue, they are precisely the ones who refrain most from factional strife to assert this claim (*P*, 1301a38–40). So virtue-as-equity entails a generosity of spirit and evenhanded dealing. Along with this willingness to forgive and forget, to cut one's fellow citizens a break, and to refuse to push one's own claims too far, *epieikeia* connotes a preference for thoughtful fairness in one's dealings. The equitable person realizes that while law lays down rules for conduct, there are no rules for laying down such rules. Thus *epieikeia* demands the cultivation of thoughtfulness and reasonableness in a way that was not at all apparent when Aristotle first explained how common opinion bifurcates thought and action. For this reason Aristotle turns to the relation between thought and action in the next book.

7

Turning Reputable Opinion Upside Down

Reassessing the Relation of Thought to Practice

At the opening of the *Ethics*, Aristotle remarked that his procedure is to begin with the way phenomena appear to his audience and ascend by way of dialectic to what is first in itself (*NE*, 1095a31–1095b4). So Aristotle began with the way right action initially appeared to his audience. Recall that his audience's experience of action is analogous to the physically paralyzed person whose arm is so deformed that it moves right when commanded to move left. This leads both to a bifurcation of thought and action, and to a denigration of the role of thought in action. Book 6 revalues the place of thought in action in a way that unites the virtues. After the long treatment of the way the audience's notion of moral virtue breaks down, this revaluation comes as no surprise. Aristotle showed how extraordinarily difficult right action is by showing how respectable notions of virtue fail to achieve happiness. His dialectical criticism of reputable account of the virtues provokes the realization that the audience has to be much more reflective about their own actions than they initially thought. They cannot rely on conventional models of conduct, since the regime's conceptions of excellence have proven deficient. Contrary to popular belief, thoughtfulness is required to be good (*NE*, 1138b20–34). So Aristotle opens *Nicomachean Ethics* 6 with a set of questions: What is right reason *(orthos logos)?* What is its standard *(oros)?* (1138b34–35). To answer these questions he will take up the intellectual virtues, especially practical wisdom *(phronesis)*.

The prologue of his discussion of practical wisdom (*NE*, 6.1–2) begins the revaluation of the relation of thought to virtue. Aristotle differentiates two kinds of thought based on their respective work or function: practical and theoretical. The goal of practical thought, he says, is an act to be done *(to prakton)*. The goal of theoretical thought is something necessary and unchanging. The work of both parts, Aristotle emphasizes, is truth. The truth of practical thought is an action which is right, or in agreement with right desire. The motive of this action he calls forechoice *(prohairesis)*. Moreover, he says, forechoice is desiring intelligence *(orektikos nous)* or thoughtful desire *(orexis dianoetike)* (*NE,* 1139a36–1139b6). Because forechoice moves us to act, and because the beginning of forechoice is a combination of desire and reason that aim at something experienced as good, doing well *(eupraxia)* requires both virtue in thought and virtue in character. In other words, right actions require an agreement between reason and desire (*NE,* 1138b35–1139b7). This prologue points to a more robust conception of the place of reason in discerning right action. The bulk of the rest of Book 6 clarifies practical wisdom by a process of elimination. Aristotle divides intellectual virtue into its parts, showing what practical wisdom is by differentiating it from what it is not.

Practical wisdom is not science *(episteme),* because it is not about eternal, unchangeable things; it is not technical knowledge *(techne),* because it is about acting rather than making; it is not intelligence or insight *(nous),* for insight deals with the apprehension of starting points *(archai)* for inquiry or knowledge; it is not wisdom *(sophia),* for it deliberates about things that could be otherwise. Rather, practical wisdom is the capacity to know what is good and advantageous to oneself. It is the capacity of acting in a way whereby we achieve truth about what is good and bad for human beings to do (1140b4–6). Practical wisdom sees to it that a person acts well amid all the particularities of the situation. It deals not only with universals, but also with actions, particular things to be done (*NE,* 1141b14–16). The example Aristotle uses in this regard makes his point clear. If we want to become healthy, we need to eat well. Universal knowledge about health would be the knowledge that light meat is good for you. Particular knowledge would be that eating this chicken is good for you. It is best, Aristotle says, to have both universal and particular knowledge, for the combination of these is practical wisdom, and if one has both, one will eat in a healthy way. Yet, for Aristotle, if one has to choose between universal knowledge and particular, it is better to know particulars (*NE,* 1141b17–18). Thus one will not become healthy if one knows only general principles like "Eat more vegetables," and "Eat less red meat." In addition, one must know that these particular lima beans are vegetables and as such, are good for health. Yet there is more. In order to taste for oneself that these vegetables produce health, one must have the experience of consistently eating them and realizing through lived experience that they make you healthy. The person of experience knows how to achieve flourishing because he or she flourishes in the concrete. Such a person may not be aware of rules or maxims that, if followed, produce health. Rather, they know what works because it has worked for them.

It follows that *phronesis* is a rigorously practical mode of knowledge. We go wrong if we interpret it as a speculative mode of knowing. Often when we think about "knowing," we conceive of the ability of a subject to know objects or facts "out there" in the external world. If we proceed by analogizing *phronesis* with this kind of propositional knowing, however, we think of practical wisdom as the dispassionate "knowledge of the right thing to do in particular instances." That is, the image we get of *phronesis* is of an actor seeing various alternatives and determining which is the best. On this model, the ethical theorist is the one who possesses *phronesis* because she can discern in various cases the right choice in the same way that we know the capital of South Dakota. Yet *phronesis* cannot be understood merely as "propositional knowledge about the right thing to do in specific instances." This phrase does not capture what *phronesis* does because it relies on a subject-object dichotomy between the knower and what is known. For Aristotle, *phronesis* is not a speculative virtue because it does not theoretically contemplate right action as a subject might contemplate a knowable object. Rather, *phronesis* produces an act done. Thus in its central manifestation practical wisdom is the capacity of doing a particular right act. Aristotle says that *phronesis* regards the last concrete thing, for the *praktikon,* the thing done, is the *eschaton,* or the last thing (*NE,* 1142a24). *Phronesis* is the acting person's awareness of right action in the process of the action itself. The action and the knowledge are inseparable and thus the subject-object model cannot be applied.

Aristotle emphasizes this point by distinguishing *phronesis* from right understanding *(sunesis)* and right judgement *(eusunesia)* (*NE,* 6.10). *Sunesis* has the same scope as *phronesis* but is not identical to it, for *phronesis* commands; it tells us what is to be done and what is not to be done. Yet *sunesis* is merely the virtue of right judgement and understanding, and does not necessarily result in any concrete action or thing done. The person of good judgement, Aristotle says, knows how to assess what is to be done correctly, but he does not in this way become a *phronimos,* a practically wise person, for his assessment does not necessarily issue in an action.[1] *Phronesis* always issues in a particular act. It is not practical because it is judges matters of practice. Rather, it is practical because it specifies an act to be done.

Let us follow Aristotle's example of healthy eating. Speculative knowledge can be conceived as a kind of seeing. Practical knowledge can be understood as a kind of tasting. I may know the capitol of South Dakota or know the cause of a planetary alignment. My way of knowing here is to view them—I can see them in a book or in the sky through my telescope. In such knowledge, there is a distinction between myself and the object I am knowing. But when I act in the external world, I employ another mode of knowledge. If I am hungry and have to choose between an excellent steak and a fast food hamburger, how will I decide which is best for me? In one sense there is no real choice in the matter. I have tasted both and from these tastings, I know the steak is better. My experience of tasting has led to an awareness of the respective qualities of these two meats. The kind of knowledge this choice demands is an experiential knowledge, not a propositional knowledge. It is the kind of knowledge that comes about when one "tastes" for oneself the attractiveness of certain actions and modes of life. And when one tastes an action, the subject-object model of knowing simply does not apply. One simply knows how it tastes. I may know, for example, that acting unjustly or cowardly "left a bad taste in my mouth." Or I may taste that when I have quit smoking or exercised regularly, a new healthy lifestyle produces flourishing in a myriad of ways. This means that taking particular courses of action depends on what I have tasted. How will my choice between hamburger and steak be different if I have never tasted steak?

We make distinctions between people who are qualified to judge some area and those who are not. I am perfectly willing to defer to a concert level cellist in her judgement about the technical proficiency of another cellist's performance. I am willing to do so because her whole life is a tasting of music and with this tasting goes a profound capacity to assess excellence. She has a level of judgement that I am not able to grasp.

Someone will raise the question as to whether one has to taste cowardice to know that courage is better (or any vice in order to know that its correlative virtue is better). Part of Aristotle's answer to this question is that as we gain awareness of virtue, we will naturally wish to move beyond vice; for virtue is happiness. So his dialectical strategy is to give his audience a taste of virtue by giving them reasons why their own account of virtue is insufficient. By extension, perhaps an Aristotelian would have to say that there is a vicarious tasting, by imaginative re-creation or observation of the lives of others. So we could "experience" the lot of the vicious and virtuous by wondering on the fruits of their respective ways of life. A deeper answer to the question stems from Aristotle's argument that even vicious actions have something good about them. For him, every action is chosen under the aspect of some good; we are always motivated by a desire for something good whenever we act, however mistaken we may be about the good. So tasting virtue can also be a matter of putting a vicious act in some broader context in which it can be seen that the act is wrong. For instance, we might eat some very sweet candy just before drinking orange juice. Though the orange juice is sweet in itself, it tastes bitter after the much more intense sweetness of the candy so that the snack as a whole becomes unpleasant. In a like way, perhaps virtue demands an awareness of the entire context of the action—an awareness that may give us an intimation that an act that appears virtuous is in reality vicious. A generous citizen of Nazi Germany may be given pause when he reflects on the broader context of his action. Hopefully, the realization that his wealth is being used to bolster a regime devoted to a hatred antithetical to a generous spirit, will leave a bad taste is his mouth.

For Aristotle, the practically wise person is the measure of right conduct. She knows the right thing to do because her everyday tasting of right action has made her proficient at judging the quality of different sorts of actions. Is such an account irrational because it is unobjective or unverifiable? To be sure, the knowledge of the *phronimos* is unverifiable for someone who has not tasted the attractiveness of practical wisdom, in the same way that the judgement that "This is a good cellist" is unverifiable for someone who has never heard music. However, the question of verifiability is different from the question of whether particular individuals are adequate to make some particular kind of practical judgement, whether that occurs through direct experience or acts of imaginative insight. Aristotle thinks we must we must try to be adequate to what we want to receive. In *De Anima*, he says that the activity of perception *(aisthesis)* is one with the activity of that which is perceived (*DA,* 3.1.425b26ff). He likens the process of perception to the way in which a sealing wax receives the impression of a ring; that is, by being receptive to its mold (2.12). Right action, too, is a perception *(aisthesis)* of the particular action done for Aristotle.[2] Understanding the attractiveness of right action requires us to be adequate to right action; our tasting must form us to realize its inherent attractiveness. Such knowledge is not objective or scientific in the Cartesian sense, and therefore not verifiable apart from the process of becoming adequate to understanding right action by engaging in virtue or acts of imaginative wonder. Indeed, this is a fundamental limit set on the inquiry from the beginning: each person can be a competent judge only of what he knows; and lack of experience of action—whether the result of youth or immaturity—renders us incapable of participating adequately in the discussion (*NE,* 1094b32–1095a10). We are not adequate to understand that which is above us; to understand the intelligibility and attractiveness of the Aristotelian complex "right action/practical wisdom/virtue," we must struggle to act aright as best we can on each particular occasion so that we may become adequate to understand. Aristotle's pedagogy points beyond itself to a way of life. The question is whether we can become adequate to that mode of being. In this sense, reading the *Ethics* is an existential exercise because implicit in the argument is the notion that we have to change our lives to understand the text.

Phronesis is the practical knowledge that this action I am doing here and now is right. For this reason, *phronesis* is not one virtue among many, or even the predominant virtue. Rather, it is virtue in toto, for in an act of practical reason the whole person acts on a specific occasion as the reality of the situation demands. Aristotle thus moves beyond his audience's initial conception of virtue as a set of cattle prods. On Aristotle's understanding of action, what motivates human beings to act is some object or action experienced as good. In this sense, the beginning or motive of *(arche)* action is its purpose *(telos)*. We act when we think that some good will accrue. That good both initiates the action and is its goal. Many of us experience right action as painful because we have become habituated by our deformation to behave badly. Since the initiating principles and objects of our acts are habitually disordered, we may not see the attractiveness of goods that may be in our interest. Thus pursuing these goods appears nonsensical and painful. Thus for Aristotle we sometimes cannot understand the reason why right action would be in our interest because we have not tasted for ourselves the joy of right action. Vice destroys the initiating principle of or motive for right action (*NE,* 1140b15–20) because it truncates our experience. By contrast, for Aristotle, virtue-as-equity and practical wisdom go together because they are the same thing.

The Place of Thought in Action

Aristotle's audience was wrong about the place of thought in action in part because they neglect the irreducible uniqueness of every situation. Early on in the *Ethics* (1107a28ff), Aristotle follows a discussion of the mean with reflections on the limited value of such generalities if the goal of the inquiry is action itself. In ethics, he says, the general principles may be more widely accepted, but specifics are more true, for in action we deal with concrete things *(hekasta);* that is, specific actions. As Eric Voegelin comments,

> [E]thics is not a matter of moral principles, nor a retreat from the complexities of the world . . . but a matter of the truth of existence in the reality of action in concrete situations. What matters is not correct principles about what is right by nature in an immutable generality, nor the acute consciousness of the tension between immutable truth and its mutable application (possibly even with tragic overtones), but the changeability, the *kineton* itself, and the methods to lift it to the reality of truth. The truth of existence is attained where it

> becomes concrete, i.e., in action. The *kineton* of action is the locus where man attains his truth.[3]

Human practice emerges in *Ethics* 6 as a comprehensive category that includes all human activity (theoretical and practical) because *phronesis* is articulated as the capacity that allows human beings to see the right thing in each unique situation. Each situation demands a thoughtful assessment of what action is required amidst all the particularities of the situation being confronted. The bifurcation of thought and desire is overcome by calling attention to the particularity of all human activity and thus to the need we have for thoughtful assessment of particulars each time we act. This is the logical conclusion of Aristotle's discussion of equity, inasmuch as equity was needed because law required the excellence of thoughtfulness about particulars in order to remain just.

One way Aristotle emphasizes this point is by differentiating the various dimensions of *phronesis*. *Phronesis* is one virtue, but it can be manifest in different ways. Simple *phronesis* has to do with one's own interests. Yet one also needs to deliberate about wholes which are comprised of different parts, like homes and politics. Household management *(oikonomia)* is the capacity of deliberating about matters affecting the entire family. Further, there is deliberation about matters affecting the city. This might be called "political practical wisdom." And Aristotle divides this sort of practical wisdom into a variety of capacities, depending on what is being considered. Good lawmakers must show practical wisdom in the art of making laws *(phronesis nomothetike)*. And when people deliberate in the Assembly or in the courts about practical matters, they exhibit still different kinds of *phronesis*: deliberative practical wisdom *(phronesis bouleutike)* and judicial practical wisdom *(phronesis dikastikae)*. Thus one could order Aristotle's treatment of the dimensions of *phronesis* in table 7.1

To illustrate the way *phronesis* requires deliberation about particulars, let us say that a contemporary couple with two children want to buy a house. Their decision is bounded by a host of factors over which they have very little control: neighborhoods in their price range, local schools, the housing market; the way the national and global market impinges on their choice of careers and the places where they can or cannot earn a living; their particular taste in housing, which has been decisively

Table 7.1. The Types of *Phronesis*

With respect to individuals	With respect to the household	With repect to the city
Simple *phronesis*	Household management	Legislative practical wisdom *(phronesis nomothetike)* Political practical wisdom *(phronesis politike)* Two kinds: 1) deliberative practical wisdom 2) judicial practical wisdom

formed by their experience in the homes in which they grew up, as well as by their own personal taste; what they can can and cannot afford; whether they have been able to conceive children, and so forth. In making their decision, they have to pay attention to the intricate relationship between the choices they will make and the contexts that flow from those choices. Making a decision to buy a large house and be house rich and cash poor, for instance, leads to a host of constraints that in turn drives a host of choices about career, time spent with children and each other, child care, dual incomes, where and how to vacation, and so on. Any decision to buy any home, in other words, will create an encompassing context that both creates some practical choices and limits others. Since any decision presents unique opportunities, every choice extends the capacity to make others.

In addition, we can easily see how overgrasping for money or status could ruin the couple's flourishing. If, for instance, they decide to overextend themselves financially in order to have a terrifically expensive house to impress their friends, they may have to make changes in their work habits and financial practices that would have profound implications for how they raise their children or care for an elderly relative. In the effort to appear successful they may make choices which drive them to neglect those they love the most. So the practically wise choice may demand the conscious effort to clear away an excessive attachment to external goods such as status and wealth. Becoming practically wise would demand not only the effort to make decisions that benefit oneself and one's loved ones. In addition, it would require an acknowledgment of the realities of the situations one both confronts and creates out of one's choices, as well as a willingness to take them as they come and do the best one can with them. Finally, it would mean the cultivation of the peace of mind that is the condition for clear headed decision making inasmuch as that peace comes from the proper valuation of the scale of human goods and activities. Thus ethical virtue is required for practical wisdom and vice versa. If one has not formed one's ethical character so as to value love, fairness, generosity, and wisdom, one will be unable to grasp why one should not overgrasp for wealth and status. In a like way, if one cannot deliberate about the particulars in a given situation, one will not be able to apply one's rightly formed desires in order to generate right actions.

Grappling with one's interest in such cases demands thoughtful reflection on the context of the choice as given: How do we want to raise our children? What do we want to give them? How will a choice of housing affect the lifestyle we lead and thus the kind of time and effort we can spend on our children? Will buying this particular home force me to become more dependent on my car and thus help ruin the earth? How will the decision to buy this particular home in this particular area affect our relationships with our family and larger community? One cannot see all the implications of buying this particular home because one has little or no control over neighbors, local politics, or local or national economies. Rather, in such a situation, choices are driven by a host of contingencies that we simply have to react to as well as we can if we want to do well. To refuse to be thoughtful in the name of practicality is to be massively impractical. Since the decisions we make as household managers and citizens in political regimes decisively affect our lives, we have to react to them thoughtfully using practical reason if we are to flourish. And if the relatively uncomplicated and straightforward process of one couple buying a home demands this kind of thought, how much more thought will reforming Social Security or passing campaign finance laws require?

Thought as an Action

Aristotle's audience was wrong to equate thought with inaction. It is not merely that thought is required for moral activity. Aristotle insists that thought itself is an activity. *Phronesis* is the comprehensive virtue, seeing to the coming to be of every particular human act. Intellectual activity is just as much an activity as moral activity. Indeed, the question of whether to engage in intellectual activity on particular occasions is itself a moral decision that *phronesis* must adjudicate. The practical decision to set aside some time to reflect on the particular demands of a situation in order to insure that one acts rightly is a moral decision which *phronesis* must provide for. In *Ethics* 6 Aristotle reminds his audience that "the realm of practice is encompassing of all pursuits, of all human activities as chosen and performed."[4] As Thompson has argued, Aristotle's delineation of *phronesis* cuts both ways. Neither the practical man of politics who has a hand in everyday affairs nor the philosopher who leads a life of reflection and pursuit of wisdom is exempted from the need to develop the virtue of *phronesis*, for their activities must be brought into being by determination of the right thing to do on specific occasions.[5]

Aristotelian Rationality, the Human Good, and Life-Plans

If my account of *phronesis* is correct, several contemporary interpretations of Aristotelian rationality are mistaken. According to some interpreters, the goal of Aristotelian practical rationality is to articulate an account of the human good or goods. In turn, happiness is identified with the successful implementation of a lifeplan that maps out a strategy for acquiring these goods.[6] As John Cooper puts it, "According to Aristotle, it [flourishing or happiness] is a person's conception of what it is to flourish that he is, if fully in control of his life, putting into effect in all his actions . . . ."[7]

Yet this way of viewing practical rationality leads to the kinds of sterile and insoluble debates that have plagued recent Aristotelian studies. If the goal of rationality is to develop an account of the human good which must be instantiated though activity, then virtues are the means to an end. So virtues become strategic necessities that help us implement our life plan to acquire the basic human goods. But this leads to a host of questions: If virtues are merely the means to the human good, what keeps people from attempts at getting the human good(s) directly by theft or trampling on the less fortunate? Sometimes, such dilemmas lead to a proliferation of rules that are directed to the deontological demand to refrain from acting directly against one of the basic goods.[8] Further, if the goal is the good of the intellectual life, what prevents that life from being amoral, since such a life does not seem to require moral virtue?[9] Does Aristotle think happiness is the maximization of the good of intellectual activity over a life of practice or vice versa?

These problems only arise if one abstracts from the phenomena of action by conceiving of rationality as a means to the human good and not an end in itself. Aristotle never issues a decision rule: "Maximize intellectual (or any other kind of) activity." Practical wisdom does not operate by developing an abstract set of goods that are to be pursued in a life plan. Rather, it is the capacity to act aright on particular occasions. For Aristotle happiness is not the enjoyment of a successfully implemented life plan; nor is it the appropriation of a set of basic goods. Rather, happiness is right action *(eupraxia)* itself. As we move to this right action, we become more virtuous. Virtue is not a means to the human goods that can be skirted to attain them. For Aristotle, virtue is the human good. Since this is so, the job of practical reason is not to articulate a life plan or set of goods, but to do right here and now.

This holds for intellectual action as it does for moral action. Theorizing is a practice. While practical reason cannot make the realities that theory contemplates, still it must determine where, when, and how to theorize. Considering activities not in themselves, in their nature as *energeiai*, but as particular acts chosen and performed, practical reason and its excellences are comprehensive (compare *NE,* 6.12.1144a1–9, and 6.13.1145a2–6). While Aristotle argues for the superiority of theory (*NE,* 6.12.1144a2–6; 10.7.1177a–1177b26), he nowhere suggests that from this teaching one can deduce a decision rule or a life plan that would determine action in any particular case. He does not do this because his teaching on the superiority of theory is a theoretical teaching that cannot be straightforwardly applied to practice. That is, it is a teaching on the nature of human being or the nature of the human good. Yet the human good does not act; particular human beings do, and they do so in situations that are irreducibly unique. Moreover, the human good is not something that can be done; only particular actions can. If, as Aristotle says, practice is concerned with ultimate particular actions, then a theoretical teaching on human nature and the human good cannot straightforwardly determine action if only because it cannot be enacted. As Thompson notes,

> Practically speaking, Aristotle will say that the end of action is doing well *(eupraxia)*. Doing well is happiness *(eudaimonia)* concretized, rendered practical. The task of practical reason is to discern which particular action, of the many that might possibly be done, should be done, is appropriate in and for the particular circumstances in which one acts. Practical wisdom perceives and commands that particular action which constitutes doing well in the here and now.[10]

The contemporary tendency to identify the human good with the maximization of a set of contestable goods in a life plan would strike Aristotle as dangerous for at least two reasons. First, as we have seen, human finiteness means that we cannot in a strict sense choose a life or do the human good. Happiness for Aristotle is neither possession of the human good nor the successful implementation of a life plan. Rather, happiness is doing the right act itself. Indeed, a life comes into view only through reflection on the accumulation of these discrete actions. We can plan a life, but such plans are notoriously subject to failure because of the vicissitudes of fate. A life really only emerges through recollection. Thus a life does not emerge as a unity until after death. Aristotle makes this point at the opening of the *Ethics.* Happiness, he says, only emerges over a whole life, and since a life is subject to so much misfortune, we cannot really judge a man happy until after his life has emerged as a whole; that is, until after it has been bounded by death.

Aristotle does not think that human beings are not the most important things in the universe (*NE,* 1141a22). Since we make neither human life nor the context on which it depends, Aristotle will say, we simply have no right to think that our main task is to implement our preferred plans on a more or less recalcitrant reality. Such a conception of life is dangerous because in principle it may subordinate reality to the dictates of the human will. If we take our imperative to be the maximization of our own interests or the maximization of the human good, typically, the weak pay a heavy price. Ironically, deontological ethicists insist that Aristotelian accounts be abandoned precisely because in their effort to maximize the human good they risk trampling on the rights of the weak. But as John Cooper has pointed out, Aristotle is not a teleologist, if we take that term in its usual meaning:

> [I]n the dispute which has raged in moral philosophy since Kant between "teleological" and "deontological" theories of right action, Aristotle does not stand with the teleologists, as is generally assumed, but is in fact in certain respects closer to Kant and the deontologists. For if the distinguishing feature of a teleological theory is that in it [quoting Rawls] "the good is defined independently from the right and then the right is defined as that which maximizes the good," then Aristotle's theory of virtuous action is not a teleological theory. For although he does hold that virtuous action is a means to *eudaimonia*, or human good, *eudaimonia* is itself not specified independently of virtuous action; on the contrary, *eudaimonia* is conceived as identical with a lifetime of morally virtuous action.[11]

Aristotle's task is to convince people that doing the right action on each particular occasion is in their interest. In the end, an Aristotelian ethics that insists on right action amid the particulars of a given situation may protect the weak better than a deontological ethics that insists on maximizing life plans.

For Aristotle, the virtue of practical wisdom is reactive, not merely proactive. *Phronesis* does not formulate a set of external goods like honor, conventional success, and power, and then figure out ways of acquiring these. Rather, practical wisdom is partly reactive because its task is to determine the best course of action in the situations that have been handed to us. In the vast majority of cases, the context of our choices has been set by a host of factors over which we have very little control. I cannot control the kind of children I get; I can only try to raise them right. I do not solely determine the colleagues I have in my department, I can only try to be collegial to the ones in front of me. I did not decide who would be my parents or neighbors. Some of the most difficult practical decisions we must make are terrifying partly because we have no hand in framing them or their outcome. How am I to react to a terminal illness, for instance? But this is the stuff of a human life. Like it or not, we all have family, friends, neighbors, coworkers, talents, or limitations not of our own choosing. In a decisive sense we depend on all these in order to live a flourishing life. Part of the task of practical wisdom is to react well to them. In addition, since our regime deforms our habits and tastes so decisively, Aristotelian practical wisdom will consist partly in clearing away from our souls the excessive desire for the external goods related to fortune. That is, much of what practical wisdom must do is minimize the tendency to be distracted from right action by overgrasping for money, status, and power. Practical wisdom must to struggle to create a peaceful detachment from such distractions so that we can get on with flourishing. But this means that from the perspective of respectable opinion, what Aristotle considers to be practical wisdom might appear to be quietude and lack of ambition for the good things in life. Practical wisdom is always more or less countercultural. Since this is so, a wise person may well be misunderstood by his or her larger society.

A New Start

In *Ethics* 6 Aristotle argues for a much more robust conception of the place of reason in right action. Since this differs so markedly from the way reputable opinion initially understood that relationship, Aristotle says that a new start is needed (*NE,* 1139b14). In order to understand the pedagogical effects of *Ethics* 6, it is necessary to understand the ways its conclusions differ from the audience's initial conception of virtue. Aristotle opens the concluding chapter of Book 6 by saying that he will investigate virtue again, taking back or contradicting what was previously said about it.[12] And he is right to emphasize the extent to which his conclusions contradict what came before, for he introduces three new conceptions of virtue. I will take each in turn.

The Two Kinds of Arete

The discussion of practical wisdom allows Aristotle to articulate a new distinction between two kinds of virtue. Recall that previously, he proceeded from the common experience of morality to a bifurcation of thought and action. This led to the articulation of two kinds of virtue: moral and intellectual. In turn, each of these broad categories was further subdivided into various particular moral virtues: manliness, self-control, magnificence, and so on. This schema drove forward the first half of the *Ethics.* But after his account of *phronesis* as the whole of virtue, Aristotle drops this scheme entirely. After Book 6, the audience's distinction between moral and intellectual virtues is not the dominant paradigm. The two kinds of virtue discussed are no longer moral and intellectual virtue, but rather natural virtue *(phusike arete)* and authoritative virtue (*kurios, NE,* 1144b3–4; 15-16).[13] To explain the difference between the two, Aristotle offers an analogy:

Natural virtue : Cleverness :: Authoritative virtue : Practical wisdom

The term "nature" has a wide variety of meanings, but it is clear from the context that Aristotle is using the term to connote a natalistic conception. That is, "natural" is identified with sheer endowments or potentials given at birth and uninformed by practical wisdom. From the time of our birth, he says, we tend to exhibit certain kinds of character traits, such as self-control, manliness, and justice. Yet we search for something more than this called the "authoritative good" *(to kurios agathon)* (*NE,* 1144b7–8). Children have natural capacities but it is clear that they are harmful without intelligence *(nous).* Great natural endowments like strength and intelligence can be terribly misused if not ordered properly, for they might allow one to become a tyrant or thief. Once a person acquires intelligence, however, it makes a great difference to action (*NE,* 1144b13–14). When this happens, natural virtue will become authoritative virtue, which previously it only resembled, as a young girl full of potential resembles the flourishing woman she eventually becomes.

Initially, the audience identified virtue merely with potential—one could possess virtue while asleep. Yet Aristotle points out that the term "virtue" can be used in more than one sense. It can mean both *potential* (natural virtue) and *act* (authoritative virtue). As our potential becomes actualized by desiring thought, human beings become more active and flourishing. The audience's initial conception of virtue is merely the natural kind, for it was both divorced from guiding intelligence and was seen to be merely a potential for action; not action itself. Thus the initial conception of virtue did not go beyond an assessment of natural endowments.

Socratic Virtue

Linking virtue with intelligence leads to the articulation of a second new problem for the *Ethics.* Recall that Aristotle analogized natural virtue with cleverness and authoritative virtue with practical wisdom. He concludes that this authoritative virtue cannot come about without practical wisdom (N *NE,* E 1144b17–18). The question that arises here is the relation of virtue to knowledge. Aristotle immediately brings up Socrates. Some people, he says, maintain that all the virtues are really forms of practical wisdom. Indeed, Socrates identified all virtue with the possession of this practical wisdom *(phronesis, NE,* 1144b17–25).[14] Aristotle goes on to say that reputable opinion follows Socrates' lead. People say that virtue is a disposition guided by right reason *(kata ton orthon logon).* And what is right *(orthos)* is what follows practical wisdom *(kata ten phronesin).* But, Aristotle adds, it is necessary to go a little beyond this:

> Virtue is not merely a characteristic that is guided by right reason *(kata ton orthon logon),* but rather is a characteristic that is united with right reason *(meta tou orthou logou),* and right reason in these practical matters is practical wisdom. (*NE,* 1144b26–28)

For Aristotle, right action entails a participation in or possession of reason that was not at all apparent from the start. This goes way beyond the requirements of following rules. Right action initially appeared to be equated with following a set of commands.[15] Yet by the end of Aristotle's discussion of practical wisdom, he insists that right action entails not merely following or implementing a set of rules and commands, but rather a possession of reason that informs all of one's actions. This leads to a series of puzzlements that drive the inquiry forward. In particular, it leads to the investigation of *Ethics* 7, which inquires into the relationship between character, right action, and knowledge. But for our present purposes, it is enough to stress Aristotle's revaluation of the place of thought in right action.

The Unity of Virtue

This point leads to the final and perhaps most astounding of Aristotle's taking back what the audience initially thought. By the end of *Ethics* 6, the reader realizes that authoritative virtue and right action require the possession of practical wisdom. Aristotle has made it clear that we cannot be good without practical wisdom, and that we cannot have practical wisdom without ethical virtue (*NE,* 1144b30–32). This conclusion, he says, refutes the argument that the virtues exist separately.[16] The assumption that there are many virtues stems from a natalist conception of virtue-as-natural endowment: a single person is not equally well endowed by nature for all the virtues, so that at one point in time he will have acquired one but not another. For instance, we could easily imagine a person like Achilles who embodies courage but not patience.

Aristotle uses his distinction between natural virtues and authoritative virtue to argue against this. He says that the natural virtues can indeed exist independently from one another, but authoritative virtue is one (*NE,* 1144b35–36). That is, if one sees virtues to be natural endowments given at birth, then one person could appear to have courage but lack self-control, and thus it could be argued that virtues exist independently. But this is only true if one reduces virtue to natural capacities. For example, a little girl might be naturally immune to loud noises and so appear to have courage, while her brother might not and so appear cowardly. Yet the girl might like candy and be apt to steal it while her brother does not. Thus the boy appears to be a cowardly, just person while the girl appears to be a courageous, unjust person. Yet for Aristotle, virtue is not reducible to natural endowments, and if we use this analogy to guide our account of virtue, we will fail in decisive ways to understand what authoritative virtue is.

Seen from the perspective of virtue-as-potential, there are many virtues corresponding to the many different kinds of human capacities. But if we want to call a person good simply *(haplos legetai agathos),* this way of viewing things is inadequate (*NE,* 1145a1). Aristotle identifies virtue not with endowments given at birth, but with the flourishing action that is only possible with the possession of practical wisdom. Aristotelian teleology takes its bearings not from the natalist case, but from the most flourishing case. For Aristotle, authoritative virtue is the most flourishing case because it means "action" and not "potential for action." This means that virtue is not divisible in the way it initially appeared in reputable opinion, for our various capacities are integrated and unified by the action of practical wisdom as it reacts well in each specific case. As a person moves toward authoritative virtue, she *acts well* in each particular case as the situation demands. Acting well depends on practical wisdom directing our natural capacities in each case. Since acting well depends on the activity of this one ordering virtue, virtue is one. Thus after *Ethics* 6, there is no more talk of the different kinds of virtues, and the broad distinction between moral and intellectual excellence is dropped. As soon as a person possesses practical wisdom and attains authoritative virtue, he possesses all the virtues (*NE,* 1145a1–5).

Virtue initially appeared to be sliced into a variety of different kinds of excellence, corresponding to different natural capacities and to different situations calling for action. Yet, Aristotle takes all that back. Authoritative virtue requires the possession of practical wisdom in a way that was not at all evident to his audience initially, precisely because their accounts articulated the experience not of right action but rather of a kind of moral paralysis. So the pedagogical effect of *Ethics* 6 is to revalue the place of thought in action. Specifically, Aristotle asserts three conclusions that directly contradict the way virtue initially appeared. First, virtue is not divisible into moral and intellectual virtue, but rather into natalistic virtue and authoritative virtue. Second, Socrates was right to identify all of virtue with the possession of practical wisdom. Third, virtue is one, not many, for practical wisdom is the same as authoritative virtue. As we have seen, *Ethics* 6 began by asking, "What is right reason?" and "What is its standard?" Aristotle answers, "In practical matters, right reason is coextensive with right action." Indeed, this link is so strong in Aristotle's thought that I am tempted to say that for Aristotle right action is right reason incarnate.

Moral Weakness

These startling conclusions demand a new start to the *Ethics.* Appropriately enough, after it is clear that the prevailing accounts have broken down, Aristotle announces at the opening of Book 7 that he must make a new beginning (*NE,* 1145a15). The contrast between authoritative virtue and the way virtue initially appeared forces the realization that most of us fall away from authoritative excellence, more or less. Book 7 outlines and investigates the range of possible states of character that come to light with this realization. Real virtue is practical wisdom, and this is bound up with knowing one's own interest. However, at this point in the inquiry we have no direct experience of what that might be. What we know is that the audience's initial account of virtue is not virtue. This knowledge leads to a new framework for understanding our moral experience. Aristotle uses the concepts of moral strength *(egkrateia)* and moral weakness *(akrasia)* in order to articulate the dimensions of moral experience.

In keeping with his dialectical procedure, Aristotle begins his examination of these concepts by inquiring how they appear in generally accepted accounts. It seems that the morally weak man does not stand by what he has deliberated but rather abandons the decision resulting from his deliberation; while the morally strong man holds to what he has deliberated (*NE,* 1145b10–12; 1150b19–21; 1152a18–19). That is to say, the morally weak man and the morally strong man both have the same knowledge of the right thing to do. They each come to the same forechoice *(prohairesis)* of the proposed action. Yet one acts against this forechoice whereas the other does what he decided he should do (*NE,* 1151a5–7; 1152a15–17). Thus on the prevailing account, moral strength is praiseworthy and virtuous, but moral weakness is vicious.[17]

Aristotle undermines this prevailing account by articulating a series of puzzlements *(aporia)*. How, he asks, can a person be morally weak when he somehow knows what is best for him? Some people say, for example, that it is impossible to be morally weak if one has knowledge of what is best to do (*NE,* 1145b22–23). Aristotle here returns to the Socratic insistence that moral weakness does not exist, for according to Socrates no one acts against what is best *(to beltion)* except on account of ignorance *(di'agnoian)*. On the one hand, Socrates seems correct, for it would be strange if someone had actual knowledge *(episteme enousues)* and something like passion overpowered it and dragged it about like a slave.[18] On the other hand, Socrates' account seems at variance with what appears to us *(phainomenos)*, for all of us have the experience of knowing on some level that what we are doing is wrong and doing it anyway. Finally, Aristotle says, we ought to inquire into the passions and if bad acts come about as a result of ignorance, we ought to ask what kind of ignorance it is (*NE,* 1145b24–29).

Aristotle initially sides against the Socratic contention that virtue is *phronesis.* Yet by the end of the inquiry, he reiterates the Socratic line, saying that virtue is the possession of knowledge. The way Aristotle generates this agreement with Socrates is to explain the analogical character of human knowing. Analogical terms are those which resist both definition and the application of a single account that does not vary from one context to another, yet still demand employment in diverse contexts in spite of acknowledged differences in meaning.[19] In short, analogical language is necessary for realities that are both different and alike. This is the central thrust of *NE,* 6.3, where Aristotle explains the variety of different cases that demand the use of the same concept "knowledge." It is worthwhile recalling these arguments in detail.

First, Aristotle distinguishes two kinds of knowledge. A man is said to know both when he does not use the knowledge he has as well as when he uses the knowledge he has (*NE,* 1146b33–35; cf. *PA,* 71b6–9 and 1.2 generally). Aristotle says that it would be surprising if a man acted against knowledge when his knowledge is in act; that is, when he actually possesses it in the full sense. Second, Aristotle distinguishes two kinds of premises for action: a universal and a particular. Nothing, he says, prevents a man who has both premises from acting against the knowledge he has of right action. Yet this can only happen if he is aware of the universal premise and the particular premise is present to him potentially but not in the sense of being aware of it when he acts. In this case, he knows that a certain kind of act *(X)* is wrong but does not realize that this particular act in front of him *(x)* is a case falling under the kind of act *(X)* he knows is wrong. An example of this kind of moral syllogism would look like the following:

Major Premise: All adultery is wrong.
Minor Premise: Sexual intimacy with Matilda, who is not my wife, is adultery.
Conclusion: As attractive as she is, I am not having, nor will I ever have, sexual relations with Matilda.

Thus on Aristotle's account, a married man may know the major premise that adultery is wrong, but his lust renders him incapable of bringing to mind the minor premise, the realization that this particular sexual act with Matilda is adulterous and therefore wrong. According to Aristotle, it would be understandable if the morally weak man knew in the latter sense (i.e., with one term of the syllogism nonspecific), but it would be amazing if he knew all the premises of the syllogism but still acted wrongly (*NE,* 1147a9–10). Third, Aristotle calls to mind the analogical character of knowledge by explaining the different senses of "having" knowledge. He asserts when we say a man has knowledge but does not use it, we must realize that "having" is a capacity with several different meanings. For example, someone who is asleep, mad, or drunk both has and does not have knowledge. This is also the condition of people in the grip of the passions *(pathe).* Aristotle does not believe in a mind that is separable from the body. We act with our whole being, which is inescapably bound up with our physical existence. For him, desire produces physiological changes that decisively affect our mode of knowing. In his own words, spiritedness *(thumos),* desire *(epithumia)* and "the things of Aphrodite" produce changes in our bodies and even a kind of "madness" (*NE,* 1147a15ff). These physiological changes affect our mental capacities. The fact that a morally weak person under the influence of such factors appears to speak reasonably and in accord with knowledge of right and wrong does not matter. People can repeat geometrical demonstrations they have memorized when they are drunk or talking in their sleep, and beginning students in some subjects can reel off words they have heard without really knowing what they are talking about. In such cases, they are speaking like a parrot, Aristotle says, for the knowledge which produces this speech is not actual knowing in the full sense, but only a pale imitation. For Aristotle, to know something in the full sense it is necessary to grow into the subject matter. The subject matter has to become like second nature *(sumphuenai)* and this takes time. In the *Ethics* the subject matter is right action, and Aristotle insists that unless we experience right action for ourselves we do not possess the awareness of right action that is *phronesis.* Our knowledge of the right thing to do is merely a pale imitation of the central case: the person of practical wisdom doing the right thing, knowing she is doing the right thing, and enjoying the right thing as she does it. Fourth, Aristotle says that we may look at the cause of moral weakness according to its nature. As we have seen, in a practical syllogism, one premise is universal while the other is about the particular action to be done. Sense perception *(aisthesis)* is authoritative *(kurios)* over the latter but not over the former. When an opinion is generated out of these, it is clear that the conclusion is affirmed from necessity. In practical matters, however, the conclusion of a syllogism is not an opinion but an action (*NE,* 1147a27–28). When, therefore, two opposing major premises are present and a sense perception is present, we will choose the major premise that follows the sense perception. In this particular instance, what we know is that satisfaction of desire is better than the alternative. Let us give an example of what Aristotle means:

> *Major Premise:* I must limit sweets to lose weight.
> *Competing Major Premise:* Sweet things are very good to eat.
> *Minor Premise (i.e., a sense perception):* Here is a bowl of sweet M&Ms, the tastiest mass-produced candy I know of.
> *Conclusion (in practical matters, always an action):* Here I am eating M&Ms.

In retrospect the action which concludes the syllogism may be experienced regretfully. In hindsight, one can say, perhaps with spirited anger against oneself, "I am a weak-willed person, for I ate despite my previous determination." Yet, for Aristotle, this knowledge is different from the kind of practical knowledge that drove the actor to eat. That knowledge was reducible to the practical experience that "M&Ms are certainly tasty and it is a very good thing for me to eat them." Right action demands for Aristotle, as we saw before in his articulation of practical wisdom, a practical knowledge of all the particularities of the situation the actors faces. Right action demands not merely the possession of universal knowledge of moral principles. It demands more than a theoretical articulation of a variety of human goods, as helpful as that articulation often is to the practical determination of what is to be done. Right action demands a specifically *practical* mode of knowledge: this action here and now is right or wrong.

In practical knowledge the knowing subject is the object known; the actor is in a sense what is acted upon. Practical wisdom is an experiential knowledge or a kind of tasting knowledge, for right action is an event in which the virtue of the actor is coextensive with the fullness of actualized awareness of doing the right thing. Thus Aristotle ends up vigorously disagreeing with the reputable account of moral strength and moral weakness. The difference between them does not lie in the fact that both have the same knowledge but the morally strong person acts on the knowledge while the morally weak person does not, as common opinion states. Rather, for Aristotle, the difference between moral weakness and moral strength is a really difference of knowledge. The morally weak person fails to know the content of right action on the occasion demanding action. He may know it prospectively as a duty ("I should refrain from eating this cake, because I am on a diet"). He may know the content of right action retrospectively ("I shouldn't have eaten that cake because I am on a diet"). But when the morally weak person is actually eating the cake, he knows that this eating is good for him at the moment. If he had practical knowledge that this particular eating was not in his interest at the time he was eating, he would not have done it. Aristotle agrees with Socrates that virtue is knowledge. On an ascending scale, the morally strong person and the virtuous person know more and more of the reality of right action; and this really means they know more and more of their own interests each time they act.

New Distinctions

The rest of Book 7 is built on a few large distinctions between types of character. Aristotle employs these states of character as diagnostic tools to make sense of the audience's experience of virtue. The various states of character can be ordered in a chart, proceeding downward from best to worst:

Good States of Character

1. A kind of heroic and godlike excellence *(heroiken tina kai theian)* that is beyond our excellence (hyper hemas aretas)
2. Virtue *(arete)*
3. Moral Strength *(egkrateia)*

Bad States of Character

4. Moral weakness *(akrasia)*
5. Badness, vice *(kakia)*
6. Brutishness *(theroites)*

Much of Book 7 is simply an examination of these various states. However, it is important to note the way Aristotle does not proceed. He does not begin from a preconception about the nature of the highest good, proceeding downward from godlike excellence to brutishness. These two extremes are rare, according to Aristotle, and he puts off a consideration of them. Rather, he begins by examining the intermediate states of character, moral strength and moral weakness. That is, he does not begin from an a priori Form of Good and impose it on everybody. Rather, taking into account the failure of prevailing accounts of excellence, Aristotle concludes that most of us are in between *(metaxu)* moral strength and moral weakness. Indeed, he emphasizes, most of us incline toward the inferior states such as moral weakness and badness (*NE,* 1150a15–16). Since Aristotle is explicit that neither moral strength nor moral weakness are states of virtue, the conclusion is obvious: most of us are not good. Indeed, it seems that for Aristotle, our most intimate experience of excellence is a more or less conscious falling away from virtue. Book 7 turns out to be a sober consideration of the extent to which we are deceiving ourselves when we call ourselves "virtuous" and our societies "good." This consideration is possible not only because the dialectical inquiry has uncovered our deficient accounts of excellence, but also because it has pointed to the inkling we have of a fuller, more authoritative excellence. The inquiry has revealed more or less inarticulate desires for comprehensive virtue and goodness by uncovering the ways our ordinary ways of acting do not satisfy. These desires urge us forward to search for more deeply satisfying ways of acting and comprehending action. In Book 7 Aristotle embarks on a new kind of negative dialectical inquiry, seeking to understand authoritative excellence by contrasting it with our own experience—the way we actually behave.

A cardinal principle of Aristotelian ethics is that pleasure and pain are the test of virtue. Virtue is not coextensive with the externals of an action since part of virtue is in *how* the act is done. In Book 7, Aristotle seems to invite us to examine our own lives using the standard of pleasure and pain. Let me take the following example. Walking in a mall one day, I happen upon a wallet with one thousand dollars in cash inside. For Aristotle, my character is revealed only in part by the external action I take. It is also revealed in the pleasure and pain that attend my act. I may decide to return the wallet to its owner. If I do so with pleasure, I am virtuous. If I do so with regret, I am merely morally strong. By contrast, if I decide to keep the wallet and my decision gives me pain, I am morally weak. And if I decide to keep the wallet and enjoy my unjust taking, I am vicious. This is the worst state for Aristotle because in doing this I am incurably bad. The pain that attends wrong action is a kind of punishment, and so it may cause regret and reform of character. Feelings of pain and shame are important factors for human growth, for unless we can admit we have done wrong there is no possibility for reform.[20]

Godlike excellence is beyond our usual view of human activity. The person of godlike excellence is so astounding as to be almost beyond our reckoning. Perhaps Aristotle means people like Socrates, Confucius, the Buddha, Moses, Mohammed, or Christ—the exceptional human beings ordinary people take their bearings from. By contrast, at the bottom of the scale lies "brutishness," to which he attributes three causes: physical disability, disease, or insanity; a debilitating failure of nature *(mochtheras phuseis);* or habit (1148b17–10). The examples Aristotle employs of brutishness make it clear he is speaking of severe mental illness.

By considering the ways human beings go wrong, we uncover a glimmer of excellence; by showing how our desires for goodness are frustrated by our own deficient actions, the inquiry casts light on their structure and direction. Book 7 seeks to make the audience aware of its lack of experience with right action and virtue, forcing them to wonder about what would most deeply satisfy. This realization is necessary for self-improvement, because unless one knows one is sick, one cannot seek a cure. So Aristotle wants his audience to learn the inadequacy of their usual understanding of the human good.

I do not think that his emphasis on the fact that most of us are not good makes Aristotle moralistic and intolerant. This interpretation would be possible only if he insisted that he is exempt from his conclusion and that he therefore condemns people from his superior perspective. He does neither. In fact, given the fact that he thinks equity is necessary for human affairs, we could read his conclusion in another way. Recall that equity entails forgiveness, evenhandedness, a generous capacity to refuse to push one's own advantage even when in the right. Perhaps this is necessary precisely because we are all more or less deficient. Far from producing a moralistic intolerance, the realization that most of us are not good could issue in the injunction to be generously tolerant of our neighbors' faults, precisely because we are so faulty ourselves. Before telling anyone else what to do, Aristotle might argue, our first task is to mind our own business, which for him is to seek above all wisdom rather than power and honor.

Standing Virtue on Its Head

Aristotle wants to make us good. By the end of Book 7 we have a variety of ways to describe this process. To become good we have to reorient ourselves to our own best interests. We have to realize that we stand in need of goodness and follow our desires for it wherever they lead. We have to make what is really pleasant appear to us as such. Yet the question remains: How do we know what is good for us if we cannot trust our own initial conception of excellence? We do the work Aristotle has been doing all along. His pedagogy is not merely an invitation and exhortation to a new way of life. It is also an initiation into that life. By following along with the inquiry, we experience what is necessary in order to become good. In order to have a better grasp on what might be good for us, we employ dialectic ourselves. We do not begin by articulating some theoretical conception of the human good derived from moral theory or metaphysics and then map its conclusions onto our lives by developing and implementing a life plan. We have too little experience with comprehensive excellence to be confident of our ability to do such a thing. We simply do not know what human goodness requires. Rather, we begin from respectable conceptions of excellence and see where and how these break down. Aristotle dialectically examines his regime's conception of excellence in order to see where it leads. This allows him to argue that his audience's conception of virtue was not comprehensive excellence, but only an immature capacity.

Yet this does not mean that the inquiry fails. Rather, through dialectic Aristotle is able to uncover a fuller, authoritative conception of excellence. Thus the dialectical inquiry helps us uncover the scope and direction of our own desires. The reorientation Aristotle seeks cannot be effected by sublimating desires, but rather by searching for activities adequate to them. After this long dialectical inquiry, we are ready to consider new conceptions of virtue in order to search for what truly satisfies. In the end, the results of the inquiry are a kind of negative knowledge. Clearly, the inquiry does not result in theoretical propositional knowledge of a set of rules or duties. Rather, it reveals a failure which allows us to see that most of us are not as good as we think, and that dominant conceptions of virtue serve to conceal deeply flawed human activities and institutions. In short, we learn that we make mistakes. This realization is needed if we are to change our own lives; if we are to be made good. In the end, Aristotle's negative dialectical criticism of the virtues is inseparable from his positive attempt to make us good.

This line of thought ought to be taken to its logical conclusion. Aristotle does not draw out for us explicitly the implications of what he has accomplished. But that should not stop us from investigating those consequences. Since the *Ethics* is a pedagogy, we ought to take Aristotle's invitation to think and draw the conclusions when it is warranted by the evidence. Of course, by Book 7, Aristotle has left behind the notion that right action can be analyzed by looking at particular virtues. Yet at this point, it is helpful to return briefly to that earlier language to understand what Aristotle has accomplished. In modern terms, he has accomplished a revaluation of values. Aristotle flips his audience's conception of the order of the virtues on its head.

Let us return briefly to the moral virtues in order to explain this point. At first glance, Aristotle's list of the moral virtues appears to be in random order with no ranking. However, with the realization that his regime's conception of virtue is defective, we can understand his presentation of the moral virtues in a new way. In line with his dialectical procedure, he proceeds from what his audience considers the most needful and most praiseworthy virtues to what they consider to be the least needful. Recall that Aristotle's treatment of the moral virtues began with manliness and ended with the virtues having to do with social relations, such as friendship *(philia)*. Shame was treated last, for the audience thought that the good man did not need it; shame follows upon bad action. If one is virtuous, shame is absent from life. One could rank the virtues from the perspective of Aristotle's audience of virile, assertive Greeks thus:

Most needful for success in social life: Manliness.
Least needful: Virtue in various social relations: wit and irony; gentleness, friendship
To be avoided: Shame

Yet we have seen that Aristotle thinks that the commonly received account of a successful human life is in reality the result of a deficient understanding of our own best interests. Indeed, if we look ahead to his discussion of friendship, we see the way Aristotle turns upside down his audience's vision of happiness. There Aristotle rejects the notion that honor is the goal of human activity (*NE,* 1095b23), the idea that the life of honor is most divine and the greatest of external goods (*NE,* 1123b19–20), and the concomitant denigration of friendship, gentleness, and truthfulness about oneself. Rather, he insists that a good friend rather than honor is the greatest external good (9.9). The denigration of self-assertion in pursuit of honor is accompanied by the elevation of the activities pursued by friends who care for each others' good. The refined and practical men who comprise Aristotle's audience assume they are virtuous and superior. Yet they initially thought of their own virtue instrumentally, as excellences whose sole purpose is to appropriate the most important external goods, especially honor. They aspire to be like the magnanimous man who is self-confident in his own goodness and self-sufficiency. Aristotle breaks down reputable accounts of excellence in order to foster our awareness of a need for personal reorientation. This reorientation proceeds in part by reevaluating one's own formation.

In the end, Aristotle's dialectical pedagogy turns the reputable opinion of virtue upside down. What is most needed is not self-assertive manliness and confidence about our own virtue, but an ironic stance to our own formation that realizes the need to be truthful about our own limitations and faults. Put another way, what is most needed to improve ethically is a kind of shame. This is not the destructive pathological shame of people who are ridden by unproductive guilt, but rather a thoughtful awareness of one's own failings. Human goodness requires an ironic distance from one's own actions and a persistent willingness to scrutinize one's life in order to discover better and better ways of acting. For this reason, the most important external good is not the honor that comes with self-assertive virility but rather friendship, because friends help us become good by correcting, exhorting, and generally caring for us. Finally, the least needful thing in a society like Aristotle's is a manly, self-assertive life in pursuit of power and honor. Indeed, the last moral virtue Aristotle treats is equity, as that connotes an evenhanded willingness to forgive and let slights pass. If one proceeds from the realization of one's own tendency to wrongdoing and cultivates the kind of ironic distance between one's actions and one's attitude toward them that is the criterion of real truthfulness, then one is even more willing to render what is due. While virtue-as-virility leads to self-assertion, wounded pride, and anger at slight offenses, virtue-as-equity would entail the attempt to smooth over social relationships that have been wrecked by self-assertion. The virtue of *philia* is most important, not least important, as it initially appeared. And this *philia*, as we shall see, depends on radical conversion and issues in a willingness to forgive each other's faults for the sake of the common project of one's community. Aristotle's revaluation of his culture's values results in a new vision of the ranking of the virtues:

Most needed: Shame rightly understood that entails a truthfulness about oneself. This is like Socratic irony, and it leads us to realize the need for improvement.

Leads to: Formation of friendships in which two good people can mutually care for each other and help each other grow in seriousness and wisdom.

Least needed: Manly self-assertion which issues in confidence in one's own goodness and social disorder.

This new perspective allows Aristotle to turn to his long examination of friendship. After the devaluation of manliness and honor, friendship can emerge as the most important external good, for friends allow us to participate in shareable, non-zero-sum activities that constitute our best interest. It is no wonder, therefore that many in their societies complained about the ancient political philosopher's radical reassessment of human priorities (*Gorgias* 485a–d).

The failure of the prevailing account of excellence can be liberating, for recognition of failure clears the way for new and better ways of acting more in harmony with our desires. In particular, we have learned that our deepest longings are satisfied by the pursuit of an excellence the reality of which we only experience through the desires that spur us on. At this point, we know the context of that excellence only negatively; we know it only by knowing what it is not. As yet, we know it only through our desire for it. The result of the inquiry to this point is a reiteration of Socratic ignorance and eros. Indeed, since Aristotle's account of knowledge is analogical and since he is driving us to the conclusion that we know excellence in part through our longing for it, Aristotle must begin to speak of love as a mode of knowledge and excellence.[21] The inquiry therefore turns to a consideration of *philia*—usually translated as "friendship" but really connoting relationships based on love.

PART III
Friendship and Philosophy

8
Analogous Communities

Introduction

The "Treatise on Friendship" is by far the largest section of the *Ethics.* It is a response to the ignorance of and eros for a new kind of authoritative virtue. It gives a motive for this virtue by providing a sketch of its attractiveness. Making this clear entails clarifying the character of Aristotle's inquiry into friendship *(philia). Philia* has a wide range of connotations that render "friendship" a necessary but inadequate translation. Nussbaum identifies several problems:

> The first is extensional: *philia* includes many relationships that would not be classified as friendships. The love of mother and child is a paradigmatic case of *philia;* all close relationships, including the relationship of husband and wife, are so characterized. Furthermore, our "friendship" can suggest a relationship that is weak in affect relative to some other relationship, as in the expression "just friends." Aristotle deals with relationships of varying degrees of intimacy and depth; a few of them may be weak in affect. But *philia* includes the very strongest affective relationships that human beings form; it includes, furthermore, relationships that have a passionate sexual component. For both of these reasons, English "love" seems more appropriately wide-ranging . . . . A second translation problem is more intractable. In English, partners to a love relationship are linguistically divided into the active and the passive: we have "lover" or "person who loves," and we have "loved one." Greeks *philos* makes no active/passive distinction. And mutuality will in fact be an important part of Aristotle's conception of *philia* and the *philos.* (In this respect, English "friend" is better off).[1]

So when Aristotle uses the term *philia*, he is referring to a host of relationships involving mutual benefit and affection, from families to business partnerships, to what we take to mean friendship. Most of the literature recognizes the translation problem. Often missing, however, is an emphasis on the moral and political dimensions of Aristotle's discussion. He uses *philia* to describe not only what we understand to be "interpersonal relationships," but also relationships between citizens within political regimes. The question for human beings according to Aristotle is, "What focus should I give my life? How should I orient myself?" Since one's relationships affect and are affected by how one responds to this question, they involve morality. Furthermore, for Aristotle, insofar as familial, erotic, business, friendly, and political relationships are each constituted by love, they are decisively alike. Yet insofar as the quality of that love differs in each case, they are also decisively unlike. The various kinds of communities he discusses in this section of the *Ethics* are thus analogical. By inquiring into one relationship, Aristotle is shedding light on all the others. In seeking to reform one of these relationships through his reversal of values, he is seeking to reform them all.

The "Treatise on Friendship" is often read as a didactic treatise. The goal of the treatise appears to be to articulate and explore the relationship between the three kinds of *philia.*[2] Yet Aristotle never says that the burden of his discussion is the articulation and explanation of these. Rather, his inquiry into *philia* is a continuation of the overall practical inquiry. At the beginning of his account, Aristotle poses a series of disagreements: Some say *philia* arises due to likeness. Others say opposite attract. Some ask questions about *philia:* Can it develop in all people? Can wicked people become friends? Is there only one kind or more than one? Then Aristotle reiterates the fundamental problem raised in Book 1: Do human beings love what is actually good or only what is good for them? (*NE,* 1155b21–22). Aristotle states that the answers to these questions will become clear only if we know what is worthy to be loved *(ton phileton)* (*NE,* 1155a33ff). So the object of the inquiry is to grasp what is most worthy of our love. The differentiation of the various kinds of *philia* is not the focus of the discussion. Rather, Aristotle explicitly subordinates his treatment of them to the question of what is most lovable. That is, the different types of *philia* are articulated in order to find out what people actually love on the way to ascertaining what they ought to love in order to flourish. The discussion is dialectical for it begins with common ways of talking and acting in order to transform our activities. The focus of our love determines who we are for Aristotle. For instance, when someone asks the existential question, "Who are you?" we generally respond by referring to our roles in relationships ordered by our love. That is, I may respond by saying, "I am a Catholic. I am a husband. I am a father. I am a friend. I am a teacher. I am a son. I am a brother." In each case, our responses refer to the relationships we have formed or cultivated with our love.

It is not merely that Aristotle is enjoining us to form affective relationships. We are already enmeshed in them. Since we are social animals, it is inevitable that we have familial, social, and political relationships. The question is not whether we will have them. Rather, the question is, How will our inevitable relationships be affected by the quality of our love? Most of the relationships Aristotle discusses are beyond our choice. We do not choose our parents, siblings, coworkers, neighbors, or in-laws. In a strict sense, we do not choose our lovers, for we fall in love, and this implies that the process is not wholly in our control. Since our lives are given shape and meaning in these relationships; since in many cases we depend on them to actualize our specifically human potentials, the question is how to improve the affection that animates them so that we can flourish. Aristotle brings us to the realization that we belong to a series of analogous communions constituted by love. If we love what is most lovable, these communions will flourish.

Thus the treatment of *philia* advances the pedagogical intent of the *Ethics;* it helps make us good by seeking how and what we ought to love to make our lives flourish. The discussion addresses the problems raised at the end of Book 7. There we learned that most of us are not good, and Aristotle argued that this realization spurs us on to search for a more authoritative kind of excellence. The discussion of *philia* advances the pedagogical aim of the text in several interrelated ways. It becomes a powerful argument for the new orientation hinted at in the end of *Ethics* 7. This reorientation to a new life requires an articulation of the benefits that will accrue if it is adopted, and the discussion of *philia* provides a sketch of those benefits. In this way, the discussion of *philia* is a hortatory picture of the content of the new life to which Aristotle invites his audience. The discussion is both an invitation and an initiation. In sketching the attractiveness of a new mode of being, the discussion invites us into that new life by giving us a motive for its pursuit. Moreover, since this new life consists partly in the search for the best way of life, the discussion initiates us into that search by articulating a paradigmatic inquiry.

Equality is a major theme in Aristotle's treatment of *philia*, and it seems that for him, all relationships involving *philia* must be constituted on the basis of equality. However, I will argue that for Aristotle, equality is not the foremost consideration in the best kinds of friendships. Indeed, for him, the most intimate and important human relationships do not involve equality. The "Treatise on Friendship" is a dialectical inquiry in which Aristotle moves from a consideration of reputable views to more considered conclusions. This entails that he moves from the way most people experience and talk about their relationships of *philia* to a more flourishing account. Aristotle's audience begins from the presupposition that relationships of *philia* are defined by equality. As Aristotle himself puts it,

> The usual view is that friendship should be more like a business partnership: those who contribute more should also take more of the proceeds. The inferior partner who stands in need takes the reverse position. It is the mark of the good friend, he argues, to come to the aid of the needy. What is the use of being a friend of a morally good and serious person *(spoudiaos)*, they ask, if you get nothing out of it? (*NE*, 1163a30–35).

Equality is the dominant motif in the audience's account of *philia* because they tend to value relationships as a way of acquiring and protecting the contestable zero-sum goods to which most are devoted. Put another way, they tend to insist on equality in relationships as a way of protecting their investments in them. If people give more than they take from such relationships, they feel exploited and dominated. So people jealously guard their investment of time and energy, expecting something commensurate from their partner for their commitments. Human beings often insist on equality as a way of managing and protecting our freedom. Yet, as Aristotle points out, this likens such relationships to business partnership where the goal is a kind of tangible common advantage. I hope to show that Aristotle seeks to substitute a more profound and flourishing conception of the basis for relationships of *philia.* He argues that in engaging in such relationships, our motivation should be neither to dominate nor to protect ourselves from domination. It should not even be to protect our investment of time and resources. Rather, Aristotle argues that *philia* should be understood as flowing from interdependence. Our need for flourishing activity is only met by realizing that we need each other's different talents, strengths, and perspectives. Aristotle wants to reconceive *philia* in order to move from associations aimed only at common advantage to associations aiming at a common good.

From Having to Being: Equal versus Unequal Relationships

The opening of the inquiry is a panegyric to *philia.* Aristotle begins with an exhortation to the study that proceeds from the audience's commitments. It was common in protreptic genres to begin by emphasizing the importance of the discussion. No person would want to live without friends, Aristotle insists. Rich men and rulers above all need friends, for friends help them to do good things. Even the poor and the unfortunate take refuge in their friends. Friendship also holds the polis together, and lawgivers pay more attention to it than they do to justice, for friendship drives out civil strife *(stasis).* Finally, friends enhance our power to think *(noesai)* and act *(praxai)* (*NE,* 1155a15–16).

This recalls Aristotle's earlier assertion that "it appears that happiness requires external goods, for it is impossible or at the least not easy to do noble/beautiful things if one does not have the wherewithal, for many actions can only be done with instruments such as friends, wealth, and political power" (*NE,* 1099a31–33). The inquiry into *philia* explores the connection between *philia,* activity, and happiness. Friends, it seems, are useful and good because they help us to engage in the noble activities that constitute our flourishing. However, since the early statement of the problem, the inquiry has revealed that the way reputable opinion conceives of noble action is problematic. Reputable opinion held that noble action can be achieved through the accumulation of the external goods of wealth, honor, and political power. Yet Aristotle has argued that the overvaluation of such goods is a root of personal and social unhappiness. The point of the inquiry into *philia* is to revalue our relationships in line with this conclusion. A certain kind of friend emerges as the most important external good (*NE,* 1169b10). Yet this revaluation depends on a dialectical inquiry into commonly accepted views of *philia,* with a view to overcoming them and allowing a new conception to emerge.

All friendships are understood to be useful to the participants. The reason friendships are formed is because the participants are devoted to some good or activity or practice they find attractive. We become friends in order to be useful to each other, and Aristotle argues that the affection we give each other results from their experience of being mutually useful. The question for Aristotle is, Useful for what? That is, in order to understand the best kind of friendship, we must struggle to understand what is really in our interest; we ought to try to find out what is most useful to our lives. Aristotle articulates three types of *philia:* for the sake of the pleasant, the useful, and virtue. The first two types are quickly set aside as lesser manifestations of *philia,* for in these the participants feel love not for each other, but for the good that comes from the other. Such friendships are merely chance events *(sumbebekoi)* because they are based on a coincidence of interest. Thus they are easily dissolved when the common interest dissolves (*NE,* 1156a10). These relationships are ephemeral because what is useful and pleasant does not stay the same, but is always in a state of becoming (*NE,* 1156a21). By contrast, reputable opinion insists that real *philiai* ought to be lasting. However, while these lesser varieties of *philia* fall away from the best, Aristotle argues that friendships for utility and pleasure are also similar to the best (*NE,* 1157a1). People speak of friendship for the sake of the pleasant and useful as real friendship, just as poleis do when they speak of alliances that aim at mutual advantage *(sumpherontos)* (1157a28). The example is telling. These kinds of friendship are compared to states coming together in the world of power politics for common advantage to protect their own interests. The lesser kinds of friendship which are based on utility for common advantage are both like and unlike the best kind of *philia* and therefore they both are and are not *philiai* (*NE,* 1158b6). They appear to be friendships insofar as they are similar to friendship that comes to be as a result of the love of virtue, for virtue friendship is both useful and pleasant. However, the lesser kinds of *philia* have only usefulness or pleasure or some combination of the two; they are not based on the mutual love of virtue. So they both change quickly, and are based not on the partner's interest but on our own (*NE,* 1156b6–10). Friendship for the sake of virtue is the central case of *philia* because it comprehends the rest. Again, Aristotle's treatment of *philia* is analogical; the central case is virtue friendship, and the lesser kinds are both like and unlike it.[3]

Yet after all these clarifications, Aristotle still has not discussed the central case. He emphasizes that the relationships he has discussed up to this point are based on equality. The reason equality is emphasized in the lesser kinds of relationships is that both partners want the same kind of thing from one another, so they exchange commensurable goods, such as pleasure or material advantage (*NE,* 1158b1–4). If the *philia* is for money, they both exchange money. If the *philia* is for the sake of laughter, they both exchange laughter. In these varieties of *philia,* Aristotle says, there are often disagreements because each partner is out to maximize his or her share of the goods sought. Yet, there are other kinds of *philia* which involve a superiority of one of the partners (*NE,* 1158b11). Interestingly enough, these include the most intimate bonds between people: children and parents and husband and wife. Also included is the political relationship between ruled and ruler. In unequal friendships the partners do not receive the same things from each other and should not seek to (*NE,* 1158a20–1). While pleasure friendship and usefulness friendship emphasize equality so as to protect the partner's investment in the zero-sum goods to which their relationship is ordered, in these unequal relationships there is a different kind of affection and therefore a different view of equality. For Aristotle, one of the main differences between equal and unequal relationships lies in the character of the goods exchanged.

However, in the kind of unequal *philiai* Aristotle is speaking of now, the partners do not give and receive the same goods from each other. For instance, parents bestow life on the children and give them everything that is due to them as children. In turn, children do not bestow the same gift—indeed, they cannot bestow life on their parents. So in return for the gift of life, people say, children ought to give affection to their parents. In fact, in reputable opinion, affection seems to be a kind of currency that guarantees a kind of equality even in such relationships. For it appears, Aristotle says, that the inferior partner should give more affection to the superior in return for favors bestowed.

This insistence that unequal relationships be equalized somehow is quite understandable. After all, the unequal relationships Aristotle speaks about are the ones most open to abuse. Households can be places of enormous cruelty. Children can be broken by physical, sexual, or emotional abuse. They can be exploited for their labor. Parents can simply neglect their duties and refrain from developing the child's capacities. Political relationships are subject to tremendous abuse of the strong by the weak, and examples are so obvious that I do not need to go into them.

Yet there are obvious problems with the notion that affection can guarantee equality. Children cannot bestow any gift to their parents commensurate with what their parents have given them. In giving their children life, parents give them literally everything, for contained in the gift of life is every experience, joy, sorrow, and love that a person ever has. For this reason, no gift a child gives to a parent could possibly restore equality between them, for it is impossible to match what has been received with what can be given back. Children do in fact give affection to their parents, but Aristotle insists that this affection cannot cover their debt (*NE,* 1163b13–17). Filial relationships are not a matter of justice—of keeping a balance sheet on affection given and favors bestowed. To conceive of them so is to invite disaster, as King Lear learns. To return what is owed to their parents, paradoxically, children must have children of their own and love their children as their parents loved them. In order to be flourishing, the love that is bestowed in these relationships must be unconditional, not for the sake of equality. As MacIntyre has argued,

> For to participate in this network of relationships of giving and receiving as the virtues require, I have to understand that what I am called upon to give may be quite disproportionate to what I have received and that those to whom I am called upon to give may well be those from whom I shall receive

> nothing. And I also have to understand that the care that I give to others has to be in an important way unconditional, since the measure of what is required of me is determined in key part, even if not only, by their needs.[4]

This is why Aristotle says that real *philia* consists in giving rather than receiving affection. The sign of this, he says, is that mothers enjoy giving affection to their children. Indeed, he says, even in cases where a mother is forced to give her child away she may still feel affection for him yet does not try to get the child to return that feeling. It is sufficient for her to love the child and see him prosper, even if the child does not return her love because he does not know her (8.8). Nitpickers can take issue with this case by issuing counterexamples of mothers in such situations who behave differently. Yet that would be to miss Aristotle's point. The example is an extreme meant to illustrate the central case. Genuine *philia* consists in giving rather than receiving affection. In fact, Aristotle later says, mothers and fathers love their children more than their children love them (9.7).

Aristotle explains the emphasis on equality by pointing to misorientation to the zero-sum goods that reputable opinion identifies as the way to happiness. Due to the fact that most relationships involve excessive devotion to zero-sum goods, the partners involved seek not to give away affection and external goods but to receive them. For example, Aristotle argues that the desire for honor manifests a desire for affection. "Being loved and receiving affection is closely related to being honored, and honor, of course, is the aim of the many *[oi polloi]*" (*NE,* 1159a12–17). In loving honor, people want to be honored for their goodness, and thus seem to attach more value to goodness than to honor. People especially enjoy getting honor from those in positions of power because they think it means that they will be able to get what they want. Yet Aristotle devalues this common attachment to honor. Unlike honor, he says, love is enjoyed for its own sake. "So receiving love seems to be better than receiving honor, and *philia* would seem to be desirable for its own sake" rather than for the sake of something else, as honor is (*NE,* 1159a25–26).

Aristotle picks up this theme of the relationship of inequality to affection again later in Book 9. The introduction is an account of *pleonexia*, the tendency for human beings to grasp for more than their fair share of contestable, zero-sum external good. Aristotle seeks to show why it is not in one's interest to engage in *pleonexia*. Bad people, he says, cannot be friends, for they aim at more than their fair share *(pleonexias)* when it is profitable and fall short in situations calling for sacrifice (*NE,* 1167b9–12). These people have narrow wishes only for themselves. They are jealous and suspicious of their neighbors. Thus they will tend to create a community rife with mistrust which will destroy the possibility of flourishing. Indeed, in a society full of such people, civil strife *(stasis)* will become prevalent because bad people will have to force each other to act justly, despite the fact that nobody in such a society will want to behave that way (*NE,* 1167b12–16). Immediately after this depressing picture of the personal and social costs of *pleonexia*, Aristotle returns to the question of relationships between unequal partners in order to argue against the conception of life that emphasizes constant attempts to overgrasp for external goods. Indeed, the goal of the discussion is to show why it is better to give and act than to get and have.

Unequal *philiai* are both a limit case and a central case. They are a limit case, for a superior person seems to derive fewer benefits from such a partnership than the inferior person does. If Aristotle can show why unequal relationships constitute the happiness of each partner, he has thereby shown us why every kind of decent friendship contributes to our own flourishing. He has given us a motive to engage in loving relationships because he has given us a motive for the extreme case. Yet there is more. As we have seen, the unequal friendships he speaks of include the most intimate human relationships. Indeed, since they include the family, unequal relationships constitute the majority of our everyday experience. Aristotle especially focuses on the unique bond between mothers and children to illustrate his point. In illuminating this bond in the deepest and most lasting kind of *philia*, where nature conspires to foster in decent parents a devotion to the good of the child, Aristotle sheds light on all the other analogous kinds of *philia.*

Throughout Book 8, Aristotle returns again and again to the opinion that all friendships must be based on equality. Indeed, reputable opinion insists that unequal friendships must have this same basis, for in such relationships the superior partner must be loved more than the inferior, so that the unequal exchange of affection can equalize the relationship. However, when Aristotle finally explicitly takes up the motive for these unequal friendships, he argues strongly that the opposite is true: benefactors love the recipients of their favors more than vice versa. He says that this appears unreasonable to most people, and they seek an account *(logos)* which could explain it. When people search for the cause, they analogize the situation to usury, wherein the lender likes being owed and the debtor hates owing. The desire to give so as to receive is probably universal; but it was especially strong in Greece, as Ober has pointed out.

> In classical Athens, the interaction between giver and recipient never developed into a formal system of patronage on the Roman model, but the Athenian relationship based on *charis* was overt nonetheless. The individual who had received a gift owed his benefactor not mere thanks but a favor in return. The benefactor could legitimately demand that the return favor be rendered. With the institutionalization at a national level of the charis relationship into the system of liturgies there were some changes; especially important was the introduction of the idea that the corporate recipients had the right to judge the spirit in which the gift was given. Yet the essential concept of the recipient's duty to repay the donor was retained.[5]

Yet Aristotle dismisses this argument. He argues that the real answer lies "more in the nature of things" *(phusikoteron)*. In doing so, he devalues the ethos of honor which insists that every exchange of gifts entails a return of favors in order to respect the honor of the giver. Aristotle says that the analogy to usery does not make sense because there is no affection between the creditor and debtor. Rather, there is only the wish that the debtor should continue to live so that something may be gotten out of him. Yet Aristotle insists that benefactors have love for the recipients of their favors even if they are not useful to them at the moment. Such a relationship is more analogous to the love craftsmen have for their work, the love poets have for their poems, or the love parents have for their children. The passage that explains the cause of this is the dramatic center of the entire *Ethics:*

> The cause of this is that being is choiceworthy and lovable to all. We all exist in activity for [we exist] by living and doing.

> Now in a way, the work is the maker in act. So [the benefactor] loves the work [i.e., the recipient] since he loves being. And that is natural, for that which is potentially the work discloses in activity. (*NE*, 1168a5–9)

In the end, Aristotle's is an ethics of being, not having. This passage completes the revaluation of the common emphasis on acquiring and having external goods by emphasizing the centrality of being and activity for human beings. Aristotle began the inquiry by seeking a common ground with his audience in their devotion to a life of noble action. Many sought honor and political power as ways of achieving this. He examined their conception of moral virtue in order to show how the devotion to external goods such as honor did not give them the kind of activity they wanted; indeed, pursued to its limit, honor gave only sterile inactivity. This led him to articulate a new view of the role of practical wisdom in action. The activity of practical wisdom animates our natural capacities, turning them into authoritative virtue. As our potential virtue is actualized, we become more active, and thus *become more.* In this passage, Aristotle provides a philosophical explanation of his audience's drive for noble action. This drive is in reality a manifestation of the deeper love of being. The human mode of being is being in certain kinds of activity. So we become happy when we bring our potential into act; we discover who we are by becoming what we are. We long for existence, and this longing manifests itself in the desire to actualize specifically human forms of flourishing activity in the world. This overflow of good deeds apart from ourselves allows us to *be* more fully, to *be* more in act, and so satisfies our thirst for life and being. Indeed, for Aristotle, as we become more active, we become more divine, since the divine seem to be most active. His audience's longing for a quasi-divine fullness of life is satisfied not through a pursuit of honor but rather a pursuit of right action. It makes no sense to pursue a life of power and status that detracts from this orientation.

Aristotle's is an ethics of being, not having. As we have seen, for him the appropriate question for human life is not, "Which goods should I instantiate in a rational life plan?" Rather, the appropriate focus is the search for activities that will satisfy. Aristotle wants to move beyond the notion that relationships must be conceived as a choice between equality and despotism.

He gives us a motive for the reorientation of our loves by arguing that our flourishing depends in part on the quality of our relationships. Since our flourishing entails relying on the people in these relationships—since we are interdependent beings—we must decide whether we are going to be responsible with our dependencies or not. If we decide against responsibility we only hurt ourselves, since our neglect erodes the condition of our own happiness.

Interdependence and Human Flourishing

Aristotle provides several different accounts of the ways our individual flourishing depends on surrounding communities. In one case he argues that happiness can be pursued with good friends who make possible and reciprocally contemplate each other's activities. We want to be active because we exist in activity, but we need friends to help keep us in act (*NE,* 1170a5–7). Living with good people provides us with a kind of training we need to lead an active life. Good friends make possible the variety of actions that constitute flourishing. None of us likes to be bored or lonely. Friends help us overcome these states of inactivity by providing stimulation and conversation. Running a business or a family is in many cases impossible (or at least more difficult) without friends and loved ones. Friends help us remain active in our work and are necessary for all sorts of play. In each case, we enjoy increased activity by relying on the different talents and perspective of others. My business does better if my partner and I have different talents. My softball team plays better if one person can show me and my teammates how to improve our swings. My life flourishes if I have a loving spouse who can help me understand my strengths and weaknesses and help me improve my life in areas that need improvement. For Aristotle, most of us are not good, so he argues that we require a truthfulness about our own life that would allow us to grow. The best kinds of friends provide precisely this kind of self-knowledge because they care for our good. Thus the best kind of friendship involves mutual loving correction that aims at the flourishing of the other. Without these various relationships, we cannot be as humanly active as we could be otherwise. The condition for my flourishing is my reliance on my loved ones.

Yet is it is not only the case that friends provide a means for self-improvement and activity in the world. In addition, they help make thought possible. Whereas in animals life is defined by a capacity for perception, Aristotle says, in human beings it is defined by a capacity for perception and thought *(noesis)*. Capacities, however, are traced back to their corresponding activities *(energeia)*. While activities for the sake of what results are fundamentally important for human flourishing, Aristotle also argues that "in the authoritative sense *[kurios]*, life *[to zen]* is perceiving *[to aisthanesthai]* or thinking *[noein]*" (*NE,* 1170a18). If life in the authoritative sense is a kind of wakefulness and perceiving, Aristotle says, we must not take "life" to mean a wicked or corrupt life, or a life spent in pain. Rather, for Aristotle, human life is wakefulness to specifically human modes of activity. As he says, when a person sees, he perceives that he sees. When he hears, he perceives he hears. When he walks, he perceives that he walks. In a like way, in all our other activities there is something in us that perceives we are active. It follows that in the act of perception, we perceive that we perceive, and in understanding, we perceive that we understand (*NE,* 1170b1). Thus life is especially good for the good person *(epieikeis),* for he will be self-consciously aware of the abundance of his good activities when he does them (*NE,* 1170b3-5).

For Aristotle, our own awakeness to or perception of human activity, especially the activity of thought, is a kind of abundant quasi-divine activity that constitutes our own flourishing. Thus for him, the rage for an abundant divine life that drove Achilles—and his own culture of honor generally—is best satisfied by a life of *philia.* This is why friends are the greatest external good *(ektos agathon megistou)* (*NE,* 1169b10). The benefits that good friends bestow are not the zero-sum kind that diminish in the sharing and are thus the cause of strife and envy. Rather, they mutually contemplate and complete each other's activities. These activities are nonmaterial goods that only increase with the sharing. This joyful sharing and mutual awareness of abundant activity is the motive for engaging in the highest form of *philia.*

One of the more profound dramatizations of this point in Aristotelian ethics is the children's classic, *Charlotte's Web.* All of the great Aristotelian themes are present: amazement at the beauty and regularity of nature, the reality of death in life, the desire for honor, the ways of managing our knowledge of mortality. The book is about a friendship between Wilbur, a pig, and Charlotte, a spider. Charlotte saves Wilbur from being butchered by his owner, Zuckerman, by writing about him in her web. As she tells her friend that she is about to die she reveals the meaning and motive for Aristotelian friendship:

> "I feel peaceful. Your success in the ring this morning was, to a small degree, *my* success. Your future is assured. You will live, secure, and safe, Wilbur. Nothing can harm you now. These autumn days will shorten and grow cold. The leaves will shake loose from the trees and fall. Christmas will come, then the snows of winter. You will live to enjoy the beauty of the frozen world, for you mean a great deal to Zuckerman and he will not harm you, ever. . . ."
>
> When he [Wilbur] recovered from his emotion, he spoke again.
>
> "Why did you do all this for me?" he asked. "I don't deserve it. I've never done anything for you."
>
> "You have been my friend," replied Charlotte. "That in itself is a tremendous thing. I wove my webs for you because I liked you. After all, what's a life, anyway? We're born, we live a little while, we die. A spider's life can't help being something of a mess, with all this trapping and eating flies. By helping you, perhaps I was trying to lift up my life a trifle. Heaven knows anyone's life can stand a little of that."[6]

More in the Nature of Things

Aristotle also explains the cause of the benefactor's affection by appealing to a certain conception of nature. These appeals illustrate the fact that human happiness depends decisively on interdependence. At the beginning of the inquiry into *philia*, he says that the most profound investigations look more into the nature of things (*phusikoteron; NE,* 1155b2). For instance, Euripides speaks of the parched earth as loving the rain and of the majestic heavens loving to rain upon the earth. In a like way, Heraclitus says that opposites help each other, and that these different elements produce the most beautiful harmony. Empedocles says that like strives for like. Aristotle says he will not investigate these accounts, even though they are more profound. Yet, he emphatically returns to these metaphors when he later discusses unequal friendships.

Recall that for Aristotle, the reason most people insist on equality in friendship is that in *philiai* based on zero-sum goods like pleasure and utility, what is taken by each partner is the same as what is given. Thus, most people tend to look on *philiai* as they look on business partnerships (*NE,* 1163a30–35). Further, he says that in most friendships, people want to be recipients of good deeds, but avoid doing them. It seems that most of us would like other people to be virtuous, but do not want to be so ourselves, if we can help it (*NE,* 1163a27). However, like the passage I have said is the dramatic center of the *Ethics*, Aristotle's examples from nature explain *philia* not by emphasizing equality between partners and sameness in what is given and what is received. They point instead to mutuality and complementarity as the conditions for the highest kind of *philia.* Such relationships involve not grasping for zero-sum goods, but rather the mutual meeting of natural needs and dependencies. Just as the earth loves the heaven for the rain it gives, the heaven loves the earth precisely because it receives the gift. Just as the child loves the mother for the gift of life, the mother loves the child because he receives her gift. Or using Aristotle's own more philosophical terms which have the same meaning, being is loved by all, and we achieve our being in activity. This is why the benefactor loves his work, for his work is in a sense his activity. And we must rely on the different talents and perspectives of our friends to help us achieve this action.[7]

Analogical Communities

Aristotle employs the concept of *philia* as both a diagnostic and a normative tool of analysis. Aristotle uses "community" *(koinonia)* as a generic term for all social groups. Thus the term comprises families, business partnerships, trade organizations, and the different kinds of political communities.[8] Aristotle differentiates political communities by describing the kind of *philia* which predominate in them (*NE,* 1159b30–32).[9] The final chapters of *Ethics* 8 are a kind of miniature *Politics* in which Aristotle uses the concept he has developed to differentiate and rank regimes.[10] Here he consistently compares relationships within the city to relationships within the household.[11] Since *philia* is an analogical concept, illuminating one of these communities partly illuminates the others. Aristotle's pedagogical strategy is to begin with our experience of affection in our friendships and homes and then to point to the conditions for and limits of political reform in the analogous community of the city.

A large part of Aristotle's treatment of the different regimes is devoted to showing the similarities between political regimes and relationships within the household. Kingship, for instance, is like the paternal rule fathers exercise over sons, although in Persia, where there is tyranny, paternal rule is tyrannical. In democratic families everyone is on an equal footing, and so on. Why does Aristotle go into detail about the similarities between households and regimes? Clearly, part of the story is that Aristotle is presenting what we would call a sociological analysis of how relationships within the household are affected by the larger regime. A guiding assumption of Aristotelian social and political theory is the formative power of contexts. The inability of the household to be self-sufficient entails that the regime it inhabits will decisively form it. Yet Aristotle emphasizes that most cities do not think about the problem of formation (*NE,* 1180a24–29). Only in Sparta and a few other cities do legislators attend to the way their activities affect the formation of their citizens. Aristotle's famous reservations about Sparta in the *Politics* (2.9) force us to realize that for him, in the only places where formation is fostered, it is done so badly. By implication, he thinks that most households are *de*formed more or less by the regimes they inhabit. Moreover, Aristotle thinks that human socialization requires the force of law, since we are motivated more by fear of punishment than anything else (*NE,* 1179b1–17). So even where paternal rule possesses the intelligence and order required to form character properly, it lacks the strength necessary to form human beings. In short, Aristotle thinks that both regimes and homes are more or less defective substantively and in their lack of care for formation. In fact, most fathers live as the Cyclopes do, laying down laws for their spouses and children (*NE,* 1180a24–29).[12]

It is important to emphasize Aristotle's sociological account of the household because it prevents us from jumping to conclusions about his examples from the family. I will argue that

Aristotle employs these examples to illustrate the conditions for a common good in politics. Yet in doing so he is not making abstract normative statements about which family structure is best. Since regimes differ, Aristotelian recommendations for reforming household life would always have to take into consideration how this particular family with its unique needs and strengths could improve, given its dependence on this particular regime which tends to (de)form its households in these particular ways. For Aristotle, there are different kinds of good households because of the uniqueness of the individuals comprising them and the uniqueness of the regimes on which they depend. So in contrast to those in our time who extol family values, Aristotelians would insist both on the variety of good households, and on the fact that good households are a necessary but not sufficient condition for the proper formation of human beings. Since the household depends on the larger economic and political structures of the regime, an Aristotelian could never speak about family values in the abstract. Thus rather than seeing his discussion of familial relationships as intending to make potentially oppressive recommendations, one must interpret his examples in light of their pedagogical intent. In keeping with his goal to make us good (*NE,* 1094b11; 1103b27; 1179b1–4), the account of *philia* is an inquiry into what is most lovable. Once the guiding purpose of the discussion is brought to light, the examples he employs from family life can be seen as part of a pedagogical strategy that draws on our experiences of affection between parents and children to investigate whether analogous affections could inform analogous communions between friends or fellow citizens.

In line with his analogical treatment of *philia*, Aristotle draws our attention to the similarities between familial and political relationships. As we have seen, familial and political relationships are similar to each other because the goods the partners exchange are not commensurable. For example, sexual differences between men and women make procreation possible. In politics, the goods exchanged are also different, for the interdependence of the political community is based on recognition of different talents and abilities (*NE,* 1161a10–15; 8.11 generally).

Right after the sketch of regimes and households, Aristotle says that children are the good common *(koinon agathon)* to parents (*NE,* 1162a28–29). This example reinforces what he previously said about how individual happiness depends on heterogeneous community, and it is important to draw out its implications. Sexual differentiation is not merely a source of difference for human beings. It is at the same time a manifestation of our need and dependence. In our sexuality, we discover that we are incomplete and need the other. One of the many possible ways this difference can be transformed from a wound dividing us from ourselves and each other to an opportunity for flourishing is through loving procreation. Healthy sexual partnerships are not characterized by the individualistic pursuit of contestable zero-sum goodies, but by mutual love and respect. The dominant concern between loving partners is not equality in what is given and taken. Rather, it is complementary self-giving. When such partners procreate, they aim for the creation of a mutually beloved good. In procreation the partners' differences can become the means by which they complete each other by bringing forth a new life that provides an occasion for increased joint activity. The new life is both a mutual gift and a common work. In thinking about how to raise the child parents are forced to step back and evaluate anew what is true and good and beautiful and what is not. The child thus presents parents with opportunities to grow in seriousness, wisdom and goodness. Further, in a sense the parents' activity is present in whatever good the child accomplishes through her life. The gift and work of having and raising children becomes a way for people within a family to mutually complete each other. In this sense, it is not merely that the parents give to the child in return for affection. In loving families, children give back a host of different and intangible gifts often without being aware of it. Differences and mutual dependence are the basis for the common good in a household. In this way, the household can become a loving, disciplined, mutually perfecting school for virtue where each partner is valued because each contributes through their differences to the common good. The particular example of parental love draws our attention to the general fact that diversity is the necessary condition for mutual completion.[13]

Aristotle immediately draws the analogy between the common good in the family and politics. After identifying the child as a common good of the parents, he says, "How a man is supposed to direct his life toward his wife and his love toward his friend, appears no different from inquiring how to act in a just way *(pos dikaion)*" (*NE,* 1162a29–30). For Aristotle, justice is an essentially political term (NE 1129a35–1129b1). In comparing familial relationships to the political problem of justice, he points to the political implications of his discussion of common good in the family.[14] Justice and friendship are about the same things and involve the same people (*NE,* 1155a18–22; 1159b25–26). People engage in communities for some common advantage *(koine sumpheron),* and the political community is no different (*NE,* 1160a10–11). Aristotle calls *homonoia* the political form of *philia. Homonoia* implies a certain unity of vision about what is advantageous for the community (*NE,* 1167a26–29) and means agreement on anything from how to elect officials to what a typical citizen ought to value. In a flourishing political union fellow citizens will see no advantage in overgrasping for more than their fair share, for this would destroy the web of community that renders possible the cooperation for mutual benefit in the first place. Indeed, people in such communities who are aware of what their common life is about will see no profit in accumulating more than their fair share of scarce resources, since they are oriented to what is lovable. In sum, citizens in such regime have an incentive to act justly toward one another, for just actions guarantee the relationships that make possible the striving for common advantage.

For Aristotle, the partners in every community are united by some common agreement on the objects of their love. The quality of every community's *homonoia* thus fluctuates with the quality of what it strives for. In each political community, justice and *philia* mirror each other and fluctuate together, for both depend on the vision of the good the community shares (*NE,* 1159b6–7; 1159b30). In tyranny, the worst of all regimes, there is almost no *philia,* since the ruler and ruled have nothing in common (*NE,* 1161a31–33). However, as citizens strive to make their regimes more just, their *homonoia* improves in quality (*NE,* 1167b2ff). Just as problems of justice diminish on personal levels as we become friends with people, problems of justice diminish on public levels as citizens become friendlier. Political community is for the sake of mutual advantage, and thus the specifically political form of friendship is an advantage friendship. Clearly, this political form of friendship cannot be transformed into virtue friendship for Aristotle, and it may sometimes be dangerous to try.[15] But by asking what the political community finds lovable, Aristotle asks what it finds advantageous. His point is that flourishing becomes much more difficult in a community of people who overgrasp because they think it advantageous to be devoted to zero-sum external goods. The question is whether he thinks it is possible to reorient citizens to a more flourishing conception of what is advantageous for the political community. Is a common good possible?

The Common Good in Aristotelian Thought

The common good is notoriously difficult to define, and has fallen into disrepute in contemporary political theory. Indeed, in the twentieth century, practically the only thinkers who paid it any attention were Catholic political thinkers.[16] Recently even self-professed Catholic political thinkers have backed away from the notion of a substantive common good.[17] While the term has been used in many ways, it is generally acknowledged to have Aristotelian roots and to refer to "a good proper to, and attainable only by, the community, yet individually shared by its members."[18]

The ascendance of liberal theory led to the decline of interest in the common good. For a variety of reasons liberal theorists suspect that the common good cannot be sustained politically because the "common" good is always someone's bad. Some liberal theorists argue that since no one is a better judge of what is ultimately good for us than we are ourselves, neither moral nor religious elites nor any community has the right to enforce their conception of ends on us.[19] Others are antiteleological, insisting that no summum bonum exists which could provide a nonarbitrary, nondespotic foundation for a common good.[20] Still others insist that science cannot reveal any uniquely human function that could provide a universally attractive image of human flourishing.[21] In a different vein, Rawls argues that the diversity of opinions about what is good entails that the liberal community must be based on overlapping consensus rather than the kind of deep agreement that the common good would seem to require. Contested comprehensive doctrines should remain private, partly because they are unable to provide reasonable public claims to the community's allegiance.[22]

Leaving the common good behind, liberal theorists articulated a constellation of concepts to manage the tension between the individual and the community. Liberal theory generally requires political neutrality so as to provide for universal means that allow equality in pursuit of individual ends.[23] This neutrality flows from the community's social contract that enables individuals to pursue their preferred good free from coercion. Thus, the basis for political authority and legitimacy in liberal theory is not the common good but rather a free contract among rational individuals for the protection of their natural rights. Since the common good always seems to be someone else's bad, and since Aristotle believes that most people are not good, how could he possibly argue for a notion of the common good? Can an Aristotelian account of the common good meet the kind of important objections that liberal theory makes to arguments for the common good?

For Aristotle, the cure for injustice is reorientation. So if the common good is to come about, each citizen must undergo a kind of conversion. According to Aristotle, moderation is the cure for excessive desires (*P*, 1267a10). This cure entails forming reasonable people *(epiekeis)* so that they will not want to overreach for external goods (*P*, 1267b6–8).[24] That is, moderation involves not merely limiting, but reorienting desire. The question is whether citizens can somehow transform themselves from individualistic competitors fighting over scarce resources to partners in a flourishing community. If such a community were possible, overgrasping would not be in one's interest, because it would destroy the conditions of one's own satisfaction.

Since injustice stands in the way of personal and social flourishing, the common good would require meeting two conditions. First, to address the supply problem of justice, it would have to be possible for the community to attain non-zero sum goods that do not diminish in the sharing. Thus the pursuit of these goods would not issue in competition and mastery. Second, a common life devoted to such goods would have to be more satisfying than overreaching individualistically for power and profit. Only if these two conditions are met could political life be improved in the direction of the common good.

The problems are obvious. Aristotle thinks that most of us are unjust, and the sources of injustice—the scarcity of the world's resources and the strength and problematic character of human desires—are more or less intractable. So it seems unreasonable to think that people will actually reorient their lives. Moreover, since the common good requires a shared life devoted to cooperative activities, it would necessitate surrendering control of our lives to other people in the community. Yet given the way Aristotle says most of us behave, we have little reason to trust that we would be treated fairly if we did. Rather, any sacrifice for the community exposes us to exploitation and domination. Given Aristotle's account of the motivations for injustice, how is it possible to argue for—much less actually bring about—a common good and the reorientation it would require?

Aristotle's pedagogical strategy is to work from the example of the family, where affection receives a boost from nature, to politics. In comparing familial relationships to the political problem of justice, Aristotle points to the political implications of his discussion of common good in the family. The common good requires politically active people to pursue practical wisdom *(phronesis),* rather than reputation and power. For Aristotle, practical wisdom is a single virtue with several manifestations; the personal disposition that makes *phronesis* possible is the same for the familial and political communities (*NE,* 1144b31–35). However, the goals the practically wise person has for her family must be different than those she has for her political community, since these communities are analogous rather than identical. So Aristotle says household management is *phronesis* directed to matters affecting the entire family. When directed to politics, it is called "political wisdom" (*NE,* 1141b23–24; 1141b29–35). In the family, the common good arises when each person is valued because they contribute through their differences to the common good. In a like way, political wisdom involves the capacity to arrange the parts of a political community into a beautiful and proportionate whole. That is, political wisdom involves weaving the different talents of each citizen into the fabric of a community that provides the context for the flourishing of each of its members. Since this work requires a familiarity with and concrete care for its participants, such a community would be necessarily small. For this reason, Aristotle would insist on the principle of subsidiarity and emphasize that if the common good is possible politically, it could only happen in local communities. One of the most pressing problems for a contemporary Aristotelian is thus whether it is possible to pursue policies that respect and foster local common goods on the national level.

Due to the connection between interpersonal and intrapersonal virtues, the common good in a political community also requires the cultivation of a certain kind of self-love. Self-love is often used in the pejorative sense because those so named want a larger portion of nonshareable external goods like material things, honors, and bodily pleasures (*NE,* 1168b17). Yet for Aristotle, there is another sense of the term. The real self-lover would gratify only the most authoritative part of herself. The good or equitable person's *(epieikes)* self-love is radically different from the common notion of it.[25] If everyone, Aristotle says, were to compete not for external goods like money and honor but rather for noble-beautiful actions, "all the needs of the community would be met and each individual would have the greatest of goods, since that is what virtue is" (*NE,* 1169a11). MacIntyre's account of external and internal goods helps to illuminate this passage:

> It is characteristic of what I have called external goods that when achieved they are always some individual's property and possession. Moreover characteristically they are such that the more someone has of them, the less there is for other people. This is sometimes necessarily the case, as with power and fame, and sometimes the case by reason of contingent circumstance as with money. External goods are therefore characteristically objects of competition in which there must be losers as well as winners. Internal goods are indeed the outcome of competition to excel, but it is characteristic of them that their achievement is a good for the whole community who participate in the practice.[26]

Aristotle says that the mature person will freely give away the zero-sum external goods like money or honor that people usually fight over to gain a much better prize (*NE,* 1169a20–22). This reorientation of perspective reflects the shift that would be required in individual citizens to reform political life. Advantage communities would have to redefine what they take to be advantageous. Further, since the common good would depend on cultivating this self-love, political communities would have to attend to the problem of formation of their citizens. To take one obvious example, since Aristotle thinks that injustice stems from a defective self-love which overgrasps for external goods, he might urge contemporary citizens to think about how to protect themselves from an economy that depends in large part on reducing human beings to consumers with artificially inflated desires for external goods.

Moreover, one would have to accept joyfully the fact of our interdependence in order to treat it responsibly. The fact that other people have different talents than we do can foster jealousy rather than conviviality. So in order to rely on the different capacities and perspectives of other people in order to flourish, we have to respect and be grateful for their differences. As Aristotle says of spouses, each satisfies the other's needs by contributing to the common store. Each partner has his or her own excellence, and they can "take joy" in that fact (*NE,* 1162a25–26).

Finally, the common good requires equity. Aristotle thinks that the partiality of all actual conceptions of justice and of law entails that political community is as much the site of competition and conflict as of harmony.[27] Since this is so, the common good demands the cultivation of equity, which Aristotle says is the most comprehensive political virtue. Equity is justice plus an awareness of when more or less unjust laws require straightening out, and thus when they should be followed strictly or not. This noncompetitive virtue inclines people to take fewer external goods for themselves, even when they have the law and its partial justice on their side (*NE,* 1137b34–1138a2). Since all regimes have only a partial sense of justice, the common good requires that individuals refuse to push their legal claims too far. It is not enough for people to render joyfully what is due. Moreover, they must refuse to push their advantage at the cost of another, even when in the right (*P,* 1301a38). Since Aristotle thinks there are very few such people (*P,* 1302a1), he seems quite pessimistic about the possibility of a common good. Yet the alternative to striving for it is frightening. In contrast to equitable people, bad people aim at more than their fair share when it is profitable and fall short in situations calling for sacrifice (*NE,* 1167b9–12). Such narrow individualistic people foster a community rife with mistrust that will undermine the possibility of their own flourishing. In a society full of such people, civil strife *(stasis)* will become prevalent (*NE,* 1167b12–16).

In sum, Aristotle's pedagogical strategy is to ask whether it is possible to address the problem of overgrasping for scarce resources by reorienting desires away from contestable zero-sum goods to noetic goods which satisfy more. That is, he wants to resolve the problem of supply and demand by directing our attention to shareable goods that satisfy our demand and are in abundant supply (*P,* 1323b10–29). He seeks to moderate the pursuit of scarce resources like honor and the concomitant temptations to competition and mastery by reorienting human desire toward goods that do not necessitate mastery because they are non-zero-sum and thus shareable (e.g., *NE,* 1170b10–13; *NE,* 1178b34–1179a10; *P,* 1267a8-13). In this way, the demand problem is addressed by giving people a flourishing life that actually satisfies their desires. The supply problem is addressed because the goods shared in such a life increase when pursued in common, and so do not result in competition or factional strife. Thus, Aristotle argues that friendship rather than honor is the most important external good (*NE,* 7.7; 9.9). He provides a variety of political recommendations intended to preserve states by moderating the excessively partisan stance of their rulers (*P,* 5). Finally, he argues that the best kind of regime will not seek domination of its neighbors in foreign affairs (*P,* 7.14).[28] In short, Aristotle argues that his audience will become happier if only they can redirect their desires for money, status, and power. The common good flowing from this reorientation would lessen factional strife because the resulting community would be collaborative and convivial rather than competitive and exploitative.

Theory Informing Practice

What would modern political communities look like if they were infused with the kind of affection present in analogical relationships like virtue friendship or flourishing families? Since I have argued that Aristotle is relatively pessimistic about the possibility of the common good, what criteria could he come up with to help us discern when a political community should strive for the common good and when it should not?

I want to provoke these questions. Yet insofar as I agree with Aristotle's characterization of the way theory informs practice, I cannot answer them in an abstract, universal way. A common good would have to be made present in some irreducibly unique political community. There is no common good in the abstract. There are only common goods present in particular contingent regimes. Since each community is unique, addressing these questions requires not merely theoretical prescriptions but rather thoughtful deliberation in the concrete (*NE,* 1140a25–1140b4). That is, knowledge of "ultimate and particular things" (*NE,* 1143a25–1143b5) is required to discern whether and how to bring about the common good. The common good in an American inner city neighborhood would look vastly different than that in a farming community in Tibet because of their different economies, cultures, citizens, problems and opportunities. Just as there are a variety of good households for Aristotle, there would be a variety of common goods, depending on the particular community in question. For an Aristotelian, since it is disastrous for different regimes to follow the same path, abstract prescriptions for the common good could not be put forward. Indeed, Aristotle says that virtue is extremely hard precisely because the variability of human affairs renders it difficult to find the mean in particular situations (*NE,* 1109a24–32).

Yet Aristotelian theory can improve political practice by cultivating the thoughtfulness required to address these questions. Aristotle does not set out to answer a set of specific political problems systematically in the *Ethics* and *Politics.* Still less is he interested in supplying the theoretical ground for a set of universally applicable rules. Rather, he wants to make people good (*NE,* 1094b11; 1103b27; 1179b1–4). For Aristotle, in order to become good, human beings must persistently ask themselves certain kinds of natural questions. His *Ethics* values questions above answers in order to provoke a zetetic way of life that will inform practice with wisdom. Specifically, he uses dialectic to question the most respected opinions *(endoxa)* of a given human community to foster the habits of critical reflection needed to deliberate well about politics. Since *endoxa* set the terms of political debate in a given regime, questioning them clears the ground for new ways of speaking and acting. Thus Aristotle's political theory aims to supply us with a set of questions and revisable standards for examining our lives and the political regimes we inhabit. The critical awareness of our presuppositions and blind spots shocks us out of the self-satisfied complacency that stifles thought. In this essay, for example, I argue that Aristotle brings to light our overgrasping for external goods like honor, power, and wealth and the way this overgrasping undermines political community. This encourages thoughtfulness insofar as it makes us aware of our lack of justice. In doing so it provides the conceptual tools we need to explore better ways of acting in particular situations. In short, theory helps us raise and interrogate political questions so that we can deliberate about them well in the concrete. For instance, deliberation about whether and how to achieve the common good is improved once theory makes us aware of its conditions and limits.

Indeed, the conditions of the common good point to its strict limits. The common good is inseparable from the reorientation of desires. Thus it is impossible for a well-meaning nation-state to impose rules on recalcitrant citizens through a large bureaucracy in order to make them good. As MacIntyre has pointed out, the common good would be very difficult to attain on the level of the nation-state because it requires some deep common vision about what constitutes flourishing, and this vision is impossible to achieve in interest-group politics:

> Modern nation states are governed through a series of compromises between a range of more or less conflicting economic and social interests. What weight is given to different interests varies with the political and economic bargaining power of each and with its ability to ensure that the voices of its protagonists are heard at the relevant bargaining tables. What determines both bargaining power and such ability is in key part money, money used to provide the resources to sustain political power: electoral resources, media resources, relationships to corporations. This use of money procures very different degrees and kinds of political influence for different interests. And the outcome is that although most citizens share, although to greatly varying extents, in such public goods as those of a minimally secure order, the distribution of goods in no way reflects a common mind arrived at through widespread shared deliberation governed by norms of rational enquiry.[29]

Reflecting on the conditions for political reforms is important because it is the only way we can deliberate thoughtfully about how and whether to achieve it.

Aristotle is not a pie-in-the-sky dreamer. He emphasizes again and again that a vision of common interest is no easy thing to insure. Since Aristotle insists that the common good depends on a reorientation of desire, if he teaches anything, he teaches that it cannot be imposed from above by a authoritarian ruler who will force his subjects to submit in order to make them good. Aristotle does not justify oppression by arguing for the maximization of some state of affairs teleologically justified as best. The critique of Aristotelian politics as authoritarian does not do justice to his emphasis on sharing shareable resources. For an Aristotelian, the best kind of political community will be defined by mutual exchange of differing talents. In this way each person's strength can be used for the common benefit. Since every individual is dependent on a political and social context she or he did not create, this reorientation must be done in reciprocal relationship with one's larger regime. Formation would be especially important, therefore, for a political regime devoted to the common good.

Yet if we return to the previous discussion of formation, we realize the Aristotelian problem. On the one hand, Aristotle wants to reform personal and political life by dialectically arguing for a reorientation of perspective. Yet given his realistic assessment of most actual regimes and their defective formation, and given his pessimistic assessment of the possibility of genuine reform, how might he answer, for example, the argument of *Federalist* #10 about the limits of political reform? Publius thinks that it is impractical to eliminate faction through an educational process that gives everyone the same opinions and passions for virtue, though for different reasons than Aristotle.[30] The reason Publius sees such an educational scheme to be impractical illustrates the character of the problem Aristotle faces.

> As long as the reason of man continues to be fallible, and he is at liberty to exercise it, different opinions will be formed. As long as the connection subsists between his reason and his self-love, his opinions and his passions will have a reciprocal influence on each other; and the former will be objects to which the latter attach themselves. The diversity in the fac-

> ulties of men, from which the right of property originate, is not less an insuperable obstacle to a uniformity of interests. The protection of these faculties is the first object of government. From the protection of different and unequal faculties of acquiring property, the possession of different degrees and kinds of property immediately results; and from the influence of these on the sentiments and views of the respective proprietors ensues a division of the society into different interests and parties.[31]

From Publius's perspective, the differences between people's passions and natural endowments result in different kinds and degrees of property. The drive to acquire contestable zero-sum external goods (i.e., "property," which has a more extensive connotation than in our use of the term) leads to the formation of distinct interests and classes that tend to engage in factional strife to protect and extend their interests. The notion that these diversities in people's natural endowments might become the source not of conflict but rather of interdependence does not cross Publius's mind. It follows that the goal in *Federalist* #10 is not to eliminate the cause of faction through an education of desire motivated by the awareness of interdependence. Rather it is simply to manage factional strife through long-term damage control. Since factions are inevitable, the strategy is to minimize their bad effects on the republic through a variety of constitutional devices and institutional arrangements that keep people from doing the worst to each other.

By contrast, Aristotle asks whether it is possible to minimize factional strife through a reorientation of priorities. So in one sense an Aristotelian might emphasize that even the mechanical solutions devised by the American Founders depend in some fundamental sense on the character of the people inhabiting the offices and those voting for them. Law is not enough; virtue is required even in order to sustain the law. Yet in another sense, Aristotle seems to share Publius's notion that reorientation in most actual regimes will be almost impossible, and so institutional arrangements ought to be made that will balance opposing selfish interests in order to minimize the danger of factional strife. Indeed, Aristotle's "best regime" is a mixture of two kinds of bad ones—democracy and oligarchy.[32]

Aristotle is hesitant to use the expression "common good" *(koinon agathon)* with reference to politics. He uses it only with reference to the love parents have for children and argues from this experience to delineate the condition of a flourishing politics. *Philia* is an analogous term, and this means that political *philia* is decisively similar to *philia* in the household. This is especially true because Aristotle says they are relationships wherein the goods shared are different. Up to now I have been emphasizing the similarity of political *philia* and *philia* in the household. However, analogical terms are employed for realities that are both like *and different.* So while the analogical character of Aristotle's discussion means that the *philia* found in flourishing family life is like political *philia*, it is also decisively different as well. If a real common good were practicable in politics, it would have to be on the basis of highly localized communities in which people can actually see and act upon each other. This is because acting in common with other people is the precondition for engaging in a substantive common good. That is, the necessary (but not sufficient) condition for a common good is being able to pursue mutually perfective, shareable actions.

Why Bother?

Since, as I have argued, Aristotle does not hold out much hope for personal reorientation to have much widespread social effect, substantive political reform seems next to impossible. Why, then, does he bother to make the argument? Is not such an articulation of a common good in fact the useless dreamings of an ivory-towered philosopher? This question is inseparable from the further question of why Aristotle decided to write the *Ethics* in the first place, if even personal reorientation is extremely unlikely.[33]

Perhaps one hope is to give the kind of active, ambitious people that comprise Aristotle's audience an incentive to be a bit more thoughtful about their own political activity. As I have pointed out, one of the goals of Aristotle's pedagogy is to train legislators to be more concerned with the formation of their fellow citizens and to be more reflective about the implications of their own activity. Indeed, one of the pedagogical thrusts of the treatment of *philia* and virtue is to give practical people a new view of their own political activity. Aristotle's audience is comprised of people who think that honor is the most important external good because they value it as a token of their noble action. Yet this conception of political activity is obviously profoundly dangerous to one's fellow citizens.

As an example, let us take a passage from Lincoln's "Address to the Young Men's Lyceum" (entitled, "The Perpetuation of Our Political Institutions"). In this speech Lincoln wants to identify the problems that will face the United States now that the founding generation has passed away. The problems will come not from external enemies, but rather from a tendency to irrational rule, both on the part of the mob and the part of highly ambitious rulers. The founding generation was full of ambitious people who loved honor and wanted immortal glory. Yet in that generation, ambition was not destructive but rather was supportive of political institutions because attaining honor was linked to the success of the founding effort. Lincoln's assessment of the dangers of ambition follows from the demise of the founding generation and the problems resulting from the separation of ambition for honor from political stability:

> If they [the founding generation] succeeded, they were to be immortalized; their names were to be transferred to counties and cities and rivers and mountains; and to be revered and sung, and toasted through all time. If they failed, they were to be called knaves and fools, and fanatics for a fleeting hour; then to sink and be forgotten. They succeeded. The experiment is successful; and thousands have won their deathless names in making it so. But the game is caught; and I believe it is true, that with the catching, end the pleasures of the chase. The field of glory is harvested, and the crop is already appropriated. But new reapers will arise, and *they*, too, will seek a field. It is to deny, what the history of the world tells us to be true, to suppose that men of ambition and talents will not continue to spring up amongst us. And, when they do, they will as naturally seek the gratification of their ruling passion, as others have *so* done before them. The question then, is, can that gratification be found in supporting and maintaining an edifice that has been erected by others? Most certainly it cannot. Many great and good men sufficiently qualified for any task they should undertake, may ever be found, whose ambition would aspire to nothing beyond a seat in Congress, a gubernatorial or a presidential chair; *but such belong not to the family of the lion, or the tribe of the eagle.*

> What! Think you these places would satisfy an Alexander, a Caesar, or a Napoleon? Never! Towering genius disdains a beaten path. It seeks regions hitherto unexplored. It sees *no distinction* in adding story to story, upon the monuments of fame, erected to the memory of others. It *denies* that it is glory enough to serve under any chief. It *scorns* to tread in the footsteps of *any* predecessor, however illustrious. It thirsts and burns for distinction; and, if possible, it will have it, whether at the expense of emancipating slaves or enslaving freemen.[34]

Lincoln links the thirst for honor to deeds which, by shining for all time, confer immortality on the doer. Yet he points out that often from the perspective of the politician craving such distinction, the quality of the deeds pales in comparison with whether a particular action will bring the kind of glory he desires. This kind of ambition is dangerous because in the attempt to outshine all other human actors, the person of ambition is tempted to evil as well as good.

In emphasizing the satisfying quality of thoughtful action—rather than just any kind of action—Aristotle's account of *philia* shows ambitious people the implications of their own desires. His point is that the ambitious drive for noble action can be fulfilled only through loving certain modes of satisfying activity. This love flows from our love of being. How much better, Aristotle seems to say, to satisfy that rage for a kind of abundant, quasi-divine life by engaging consciously—not in just any kind of frantic politicking—but rather in serious, thoughtful action which reflects one's own capacity for activity and thus fundamentally completes the individual. Such political activity would be much more in our interest, partly because it would be much more interesting and actualizing of our potential.

Yet I also emphasized that the practical intent of the *Ethics* is not exhausted merely by the attempt to influence ambitious political leaders. I argued that since most actual regimes are more or less defective, virtuous action will always be more or less nonconformist. Part of the task of the dialectical pedagogy is thus to enable us to understand the ways in which our regime tends to deform us so as to resist that deformation. If this interpretation is correct, there seems to be no straightforwardly unproblematic practical context for virtue. Virtue is ill at home wherever she lives. This is a serious problem, for virtue must be embedded in a context if it is not to be complicated forms of self-hating denial. Virtuous actions only make sense within a social environment that gives them life and substance. As MacIntyre has forcefully argued, virtues become intelligible and pursuable only within the context of specific practices. As he defines it, "A virtue is an acquired human quality the possession and exercise of which tends to enable us to achieve those goods which are internal to practices and the lack of which effectively prevents us from achieving any such goods."[35] Fidelity, for instance, is not viscerally attractive and joyful to engage in apart from a particular relationship experienced as good and beneficial in a myriad of ways. Collegiality in an academic department must rest on a community of scholars devoted to each other because they are devoted to the truth. That collegiality must be experienced every day as beneficial for those in the community if it is to be upheld. Otherwise, collegiality will be a mask for libertarian mutual neglect. Perhaps one reason for Aristotle's account of *philia* is to make virtuous action attractive by providing a context for it, even if this context is only created through a work of sympathetic imagination. In this sense, the classical drive to develop a city in speech is related to the need to provide a context for virtue. The city in speech has a critical function insofar as it is a measure from which one can evaluate all actual regimes. But perhaps the articulation of the best city also has a hortatory function insofar as it is intended to provide courage to those struggling daily with the disheartening spectacle of more or less vicious contexts in which virtue is not practiced, not understood, and often positively punished. We are deeply compromised individuals living in deeply compromised communities. So a sketch in speech of a context for right action would be necessary as a kind of goal toward which people should strive. Since most actual regimes are defective, it follows that if people take Aristotle's advice and try to reorient their perspective, they will be engaging in acts which are viewed by many in the regime to be strange, impractical, or even potentially subversive. That work is necessarily difficult and stands in need of encouragement.[36] Perhaps this is another part of the motive that drove Aristotle on to write the *Ethics*. If human happiness is an activity which issues in works that complete the actor because they complete what he is acting upon, then in writing the *Ethics* Aristotle is encouraging others to reorder their activities, thus increasing his own. In this sense, the *Ethics* is an astounding act of *philia* that has lasted through the ages.

Virtue-as-Equity, Virtue-as-Fairness

I have argued that virtue is always embedded in a context to which it reacts in order to discern the right thing to do on particular occasions. Aristotle's teaching on *philia* is meant to convey a sense of the embeddedness of practical wisdom. Virtue has to be seen within the context of a whole that informs it and animates it, justifying its very difficult practice. In order to be attractive the difficult work of virtue must be embedded in intelligent, flourishing rhythms of work, family life, politics, sexuality, and liturgies surrounding important events in life such as marriage, birth, death, celebrations, and so forth. One could imagine community contexts in which each part flourished. Perhaps one could imagine human associations in which each part did its work well and contributed to a whole replete with mutuality and self-giving. Such a context would require the cultivation and practice of virtue-as-equity. Equity involves a sense of fairness or proportionate weighing of the particulars of a situation. Aristotle, true to his dialectical method which begins from what is first for us, begins his articulation of this embeddedness with what is closest to our experience: family life. Reading his texts, we could imagine a flourishing home where each part is valued and each part mutually contributes to the good of the whole. We might think of a home with a substantive common good defined by a sharing of the most important things rather than a grasping for scarce goods. Such a place would be full of joyful activities, mutual giving, and interdependence. By analogy, we could conceive of ever widening circles of analogous communions, radiating out from the family: neighborhoods, social and civic organizations, religious communities, and political organizations. Since practical reason is partly a reactive discerning of right in given contexts, right action must be understood with reference to these encompassing wholes. Human life is lived in the midst of a series of encompassing wholes to which each individual's action is inextricably bound. Beyond all of these lies the Whole in which we all mysteriously participate.

Yet this brings us back to the problem of Socratic ignorance. In order to act well, one must be practically wise on each occasion. Being practically wise means assessing the particular demands presented by one's own context and reacting as best one can. Yet the various wholes to which one must react present our limited human intellects with a practically infinite number of considerations. We belong to a series of wholes on which we depend. Part of the work of practical reason is to act well in response to the demands these wholes place upon us. However, our limited intellects cannot foresee all the implications of our actions on these wholes. We have very little knowledge of the way our actions will affect our children or spouses, for example. How much less do we know how our actions will affect a much larger whole like the environment? And when we reflect on the immense complexity of the universe as a whole, defining practical reason as the discernment of the right thing to do amid the complexities of the particular situation seems to imply that it is impossible to become practically wise. Does not human ignorance entail that much of what we take right action to be will be in reality a kind of guesswork? Is not this especially true, since the meaning of the encompassing whole that bounds our actions is not accessible to us as a whole?

As I argued in chapter 2, Socrates realizes that he does not know how to live because he is ignorant about the meaning of the whole. He examines human speech and action to see what these reveal about the meaning of the cosmos. But since he is ignorant about the ultimate meaning *of* life, he is also ignorant about any particular meaning *in* life. That is, since in order to be meaningful each human action would have to be related back somehow to the meaning of the whole in which it participates, one can never tell with certainty whether any particular human action is right or not. We simply cannot be sure about the right way to live and act. Yet this means that any genuine political philosophy is not merely countervailing to each society's more or less deficient standards of justice. In addition, it means that political philosophy is ultimately disruptive since it calls every kind of life into radical question but refuses to offer any real alternative. Can Aristotle actually develop an ethics in the face of such skepticism?

Up to now I have emphasized that Aristotle argues for the practice of virtue-as-equity and have connected this virtue to practical wisdom; that is, to reasonable assessment of the right thing to do amid all the particulars of a situation. Yet perhaps virtue-as-equity and practical wisdom connote not merely reasonableness. Perhaps they also connote a sense of beauty and proportion. Or, put another way, perhaps practical wisdom is also an aesthetic capacity. The guiding image at the close of the discussion of *philia* is the true self-lover who strives for *ta kala*, for the noble and beautiful. In retrospect, we can see that *ta kala* has been a guiding theme throughout the *Ethics*. In his discussion of the moral virtues, Aristotle insists again and again that we must perform virtue for the sake of *to kalon*, which I have been translating as "noble-beautiful" or "fair." Perhaps this is his answer to our ultimate ignorance about the variety of wholes in which we mysteriously participate. In the end, Aristotle's only injunction is, "Act beautifully on each particular occasion."

Judging beauty is a matter of judging the appropriate proportions of parts within some whole. Likewise, creating beauty is a matter of ordering of parts into a harmony. Clearly, in certain decisive respects, beauty is in the eye of the beholder. This is as true for cultures as much as it is for individuals. But this truism does not mitigate the fact that in order to judge beauty, every beholder must do the work of judging proportionality. The beauty of the human face, for instance, entails a proportionate arrangement of parts—the nose or ears cannot be too big for the whole; the chin cannot be too small or the overall effect is ruined. The same holds true of judging art forms or theatrical performances. In a like way, practical reason has an aesthetic dimension for Aristotle. We must act beautifully in order to act well. Proportionate action can only be seen with reference to the encompassing whole that animates it. In order to be practically wise as a mother, one must do the work of assessing the particularity of one's household: What particular gifts or challenges do the children have? Does one require special attention to flourish? What sort of spouse is present? What unique opportunities and problems exist in that relationship? Every household is non-self-sufficient because it must exist within a particular regime that animates it. So the mother in question has to think carefully about the kind of strengths and weaknesses of her culture's formation in order to raise her children well. That is, in order to create a common good within her particular home, she must struggle to act proportionately, doing her best to insure that each part will be flourishing within the whole of the household, which has its own unique parts, and is at the same time part of a whole religious, social, and political community, and so forth.

If this kind of activity is difficult within the relatively confined whole of the home, with its natural affections urging us to be good, and its relatively confined sphere of action, how much more difficult will right action be in the political regime? Since every regime is decisively different, the demands of practical wisdom will be different in each case. The context in which one is embedded and the demands of that context will insure that what is naturally right to do will vary from place to place (*NE*, 5.7). This process of judging all the particularities within one's encompassing wholes is so difficult and subject to so much particularity, that the general statement, "Act beautifully," is perhaps the best we can do to describe the task of practical wisdom.[37]

As I have noted, after his discussion of equity, Aristotle uses that term to connote goodness generally. He returns to that term often throughout the remainder of the *Ethics*. But he also returns to other terms to describe the ethos of the excellent human being. He employs words like *kalos*, *phronimos* and *spoudaios* at times interchangeably. Perhaps all these terms are needed because each is a dimension of virtue-as-equity. As the *Ethics* proceeds, the best translation is for *epiekeia* becomes "fairness." In a like way, after Aristotle's delineation of authoritative virtue, the best translation for *kalos* is "fair." Recall that initially his audience equated happiness with activities they deemed *kalos*, which they linked with the possession of honor. Honor was desired because it pointed to the resplendent, abundant life they wished for. Honor was the visible sign that the form of their life had a shining attractiveness to it. The "noble *(kalos)* actions" they want are not the same as what we mean by morality, since for us morality does not necessarily involve this element of resplendent beauty.[38] Aristotle's ambitious audience wanted social status and power as a way of creating the conditions for this shining, quasi-divine life.

Part of the drama of the *Ethics* is thus Aristotle's transformation of the meaning of *to kalon*. Throughout the *Ethics* Aristotle took pains to devalue the ethos of honor and redirect that ambition for right action. At the outset of the *Ethics*, his audience identified *to kalon* with a set of vital, shining, attractive actions and forms of life worthy of public celebration. By the end of the *Ethics*, he is still employing the term, but it has a substantively different meaning. *To kalon* still means resplendent, but after the discussion of practical wisdom and friendship, we would have to avoid identifying it with the possession of status and victory in competition. Rather, we would have to identify it with the qualities that shine forth from the person who practices fairness and reasonableness, and who can somehow pick out the appropriate thing to do in each situation given. This means that for Aristotle, what is fair-shining *(kalos)* is the same as what is fair-reasonable *(epiekes)*. Initially his audience thought honor was the most visible sign that they were leading a life worthy of public celebration because its beauty shone forth for all to see. This means that their desire for public praise is a desire for a certain form of life. Aristotle argues that the love of honor is in reality a manifestation of a deeper desire for beautiful-reasonable actions. Ultimately, it is best for an ambitious person to give up the identification of social standing with the good life. This identification is slavish adherence to standards someone else developed. Rather, it is best to devote oneself precisely to a form of life that is beautiful and brilliant—even if that life is despised by conventional standards of success. The community that springs up around the devotion to such a life is at once both satisfying in itself and the condition for the pursuit of the good life.

In English, the term "fair" connotes both virtue and beauty, as does Aristotle's cluster of terms used to articulate right action. Aristotle's ethics is an ethics of being and activity. In the end it is an ethics not only of goodness and truth, but also of beauty, for acting well entails acting proportionately; "fairly." Thus Aristotelian ethics demands attentiveness to the rationality of beauty and the beauty of rationality; it requires the cultivation of thoughtfulness and aesthetic appreciation for action. The practically wise person is one whose form of life shines with the radiance of a life in pursuit of the good, true, and beautiful.

The Negative Way to Virtue-as-Equity

So the recovery of Aristotelian notions of practical rationality entails the reassertion of the central place of beauty in Aristotelian ethics. Yet the Aristotelian emphasis on beauty in ethics should not be an excuse for some kind of proportionalism that justifies actions in terms of their net consequences; thus excusing wrong actions in light of their overall positive effect, or trampling on the weak in the name of a higher good.[39] We should have no illusions about how difficult it would be to discern what is reasonable-fair. Aristotle says over and over in the *Ethics* that it is not easy to be good (1109a29; 1113a33–34; 1106b31–33; 1130a8; 1137a6–7; 1137a12–13). How can we attain such difficult practical knowledge? This may be the only question the *Ethics* really asks. Perhaps individuals come to know right action itself through a negative dialectic. I have argued that Aristotle employs dialectic to reveal the contradictions and paradoxes at the heart of his audience's conception of a happy life. This dialectical method leads to a kind of negative knowledge: we come to know what will not work. This does not end in a nihilistic skepticism that despairs of further inquiry, however. Indeed, the failure of reputable ways of life leads to new views of the nature and scope of human desire. The realization of our own ignorance about how to live provokes wonder about how to live. The failure of our way of life to achieve what we desire reveals that our desires have implications we did not initially see. In desiring honor, for example, Aristotle argues that we are desiring a kind of excellence that initially seemed absurd. Ignorance of and eros for excellence demands a sketch of new forms of life and community that are more adequate to our desires.

One wonders whether Aristotle wants us to apply this process of negative dialectic not merely to the mores of our society, but also to the actions we confront. When deliberating about an action we can be overwhelmed by the crush of things we need to take into consideration: the innumerable factors that make up the context of an action; the unforeseeable, unintended consequences of our actions; the often conflicting or murky demands that actions place on us; the way our habits and viewpoint might lead us to rationalize and misjudge. . . . How are we supposed to judge proportionately, arriving at a reasonable-fair action? Perhaps Aristotelian deliberation proceeds by considering first not right action but wrong action. In this sense, before deciding on a right action, the actor first seeks to discern what actions would have to be ruled out as out of proportion and unreasonable. The right action emerges only through a negative search for it. That is, sometimes a sense for the thing to do emerges only when a thicket of options is closed off. And when the right action emerges, of course, the imperative is always to admit that it is merely the best one can see at the moment, and that if further search uncovers better ways of acting, then a change of course is warranted. Aristotelian ethics emphasizes constant revision and cultivating the conditions for further questioning.

Perhaps this is how an Aristotelian would interpret the Socratic *daimon*. In various places, Socrates claims to hear a sort of voice that turns him away from certain actions. He insists, however, that this voice never urges him forward in a positive way. In short, his *daimon* only tells him what not to do; it never tells him what to do.[40] Right action is illuminated partly by the light cast from a consideration of wrong action. The right thing to do may not be seen with certain clarity. But it can sometimes be pointed to through a pointing away from thoughtless, malicious actions. Perhaps this is why Socrates' *diamon* never gives him positive information.

In this way we could try to relate our actions proportionately to the various wholes in which we participate, including the cosmos itself. This is not merely an intellectual process with no aesthetic dimension. Nor is it merely an aesthetic process with no intellectual dimension. It is a search that involves the whole of our being. It is a search for a form of existence that shines forth beautifully, and that in the end becomes the only argument for its worth.

9
Hortatory Conclusions

Aristotle Tips His Pedagogical Hand

The last book of the *Ethics* is puzzling for several reasons. It seems unrelated to the conclusions offered in the accounts of practical wisdom and friendship, because these emphasized the connection between happiness and a life devoted to practical action. By contrast, *Ethics* 10 argues that *theoria* is the way to happiness. Further, much of the last book of the *Ethics* is about pleasure. But why does Aristotle speak about pleasure in his concluding discussion, rather than tie together the loose threads of a long and complicated argument? Moreover, this account of pleasure is the last in a series of apparently contradictory discussions. From his opening argument that the life of pleasure is fit only for cows, Aristotle concludes by identifying a certain kind of pleasure as the supreme good. Both these accounts of pleasure conflict with the one offered in Book 7. I will explore the problems surrounding the accounts of pleasure first because Aristotle uses his final account of pleasure to summarize and complete the argument as a whole. Aristotle says that the entire book is about pain and pleasure, since they motivate action. So how we understand the relationship of the various discussions of pleasure to each other has large implications for how we read the text as a whole. Fortunately, in Book 10 Aristotle provides the interpretive clues that allow us to understand why he discusses pleasure in such different ways.

Aristotle begins by laying out two opinions: some believe pleasure is the good and others believe it is wholly base (*NE*, 1172a26). But the pleasure knockers are then further divided. Some in this group are convinced that pleasure is really bad.

Others, however, do not think that pleasure is really bad, but think that if they create this impression, people will lead a better life. They argue that since most people become slaves *(douleuein)* to pleasure, they should be driven in the opposite direction to reach the mean (*NE,* 1172a29–33). The disparagement of pleasure is a pedagogical strategy aimed at improving people's lives. The initial taxonomy is clearly incomplete. Not all who disparage pleasure think that it is really base. Some who appear to disparage pleasure do so only to seek to create an impression that it is base, when they know it is not (*NE,* 1172a31–32). These disparagers may belong in the group that holds that pleasure is good.

Yet Aristotle does not think that disparaging pleasure helps people lead better lives. He does not disagree with the notion that pleasure leads people astray; nor does he contradict the assertion that pleasure can enslave. Rather, he argues that disparaging pleasure can backfire (*NE,* 1172a33–34). Actions speak louder than words. If a man who constantly disparages pleasure is seen pursuing it, people will take this to mean that he really thinks that all pleasure is desirable (*NE,* 1172a35–1172b3). Indeed, in some cases, the way we act with regard to pleasure provides the most important evidence for the truth of our arguments. Aristotle says that people did not accept Eudoxus's argument that pleasure is the good because they agreed with his arguments. Rather, since he was extraordinarily self-controlled, they assumed that his arguments did not serve as a justification for his own love of pleasure. His argument gained credence because of his excellent character (*NE,* 1172b15–16). Aristotle concludes that in order to achieve the desired pedagogical effect one must give accounts that are not only useful but true:

> True accounts of pleasure *(oi aletheis ton logon)* are not only useful for knowledge. In addition, they are useful for life. Since they are in harmony with what is, people believe them, and for this reason such accounts urge forward *(protrepontai)* people who have understanding to guide their lives by such accounts. (*NE,* 1172b4–6)

This is where Aristotle reveals his pedagogical strategy. Pleasure does indeed lead us astray. So one must offer useful arguments that steer people away from wrong action. Yet one cannot be so afraid of the negative effects of pleasure that one lies about it. Rather, one must give true accounts of pleasure as a hortatory device that urges people on to right action. The term that Aristotle uses in this regard is derived from the verb *protrepto*, which means "to urge forward." The concluding discussion of pleasure advances the protreptic character of the inquiry. Aristotle's practical intent is to make people good. The various discussions of pleasure advance this goal by urging us forward to a new kind of life through a reconsideration of what is most pleasant. Thus *Ethics* 10 is a hortatory text. It does not aim to lay out systematically the content of a life of contemplation; it does not present a theoretical teaching on the best life. Rather, it aims to urge us forward to reform our lives in line with the arguments that have been advanced in the *Ethics*. In order to understand the implications of the account of pleasure (and subsequently of contemplation, which is the activity Aristotle says yields the best kind of pleasure), we have to read the concluding discussion with its pedagogical intent and hortatory character in mind.

The Accounts of Pleasure

Aristotle belongs not to the group that thinks pleasure is base, but to the group that initially disparages pleasure for pedagogical effect. Clearly there are several different and often conflicting accounts of pleasure in the *Ethics*. Yet these seemingly conflicting accounts must be seen in light of Aristotle's overall pedagogical strategy. Pleasure both motivates and misleads us. The most important thing in cultivating virtue is to learn to find pleasant what is really pleasant and to find painful what is really painful (*NE,* 1172a20–25). Aristotle's *Ethics* is not a treatise which intends to disseminate abstract moralisms to an indeterminate audience but is a dialectical pedagogy with a practical intent. It is an inquiry that begins with his audience's conception of happiness and moves to fuller accounts of a good life. Since the entire discussion in a sense is about pleasure and pain, the various discussions about pleasure are related to the overarching pedagogical intention of the *Ethics* as a whole. Each succeeding discussion of pleasure is a decisive advance over that which came before. The discussions are complementary rather than contradictory, since each advance in the understanding of human excellence allows for an advance in the understanding of pleasure. In turn, each advance in the understanding of pleasure must be related to what came before and to what comes after. The discussions of pleasure are interludes that allow Aristotle to gather up the various threads of the inquiry and show how each new conception of excellence is more in our interest because it is more pleasurable. In this sense Aristotle agrees with Socrates that ignorance of true pleasure accounts for much of what is problematic in human behavior (*Protagoras,* 351c–361c). The pedagogical intent of the *Ethics* is to make us good by attuning us more and more to what is in truth in our interest; it is to make what is most pleasant appear to us as such.

Beginning with Disparagement

Aristotle first mentions pleasure at the beginning of the *Ethics* when he lays out the ways of life that appear to make people happy. The first candidate for happiness is the life of pleasure, and Aristotle's discussion is ambiguous. On the one hand, the audience's own sense of noble action allows him to dismiss the life of pleasure as fit only for cattle (*NE,* 1095b20). Yet at the same time, Aristotle provides powerful evidence that the life of pleasure is quite attractive. Right after his disparaging dismissal, Aristotle says that "many people in high places agree with Sardanapallus" (*NE,* 1095b22), an Assyrian king known for his sensual excesses.[1] I have argued that at least part of Aristotle's audience was led by their love of noble activity to value a life of political domination. While their noble sensibilities might lead them to disparage pleasure in public, many of the people in positions of power to which Aristotle's audience aspire actually want a life of pleasure. Many who desire positions of power actually want to live as the tyrant does. Why does tyranny appear to be so attractive? Apparently, the tyrant can do whatever he wants; he is not restricted by social mores to keep his desire for acquisition or gratification in check; he can create his own context, for he does not have to rely on anyone else to do what he pleases; he is free to maximize his own pleasure, security, and activity. Tyranny appears to be great because it allows one to get pleasure from excessive gain (*NE,*

1130b1–5). Perhaps the contemporary analogue would be the popular obsession with the life of the rock or film star; with the "Lifestyles of the Rich and Famous." Such people are not bound by ordinary constraints, do not have to rely on anyone, are rich and secure, and so they can maximize their pleasure (*NE,* 7.12; cf. 7.14.17ff; 10.4). In extreme cases, the enslavement to pleasure may tempt ambitious people to enslave others. The essence of tyranny is the tyrant's reduction of everyone else to a means that serves his end. This view of life is at once extraordinarily attractive and dangerous. Even as Aristotle disparages pleasure to move the inquiry forward, he hints that there is much more to the story.

The next extended discussion of pleasure occurs in Ethics 3.10 when Aristotle takes up moderation *(sophrosune).* Moderation is the mean with regard to pleasure, and Aristotle begins by discussing what kind of pleasure moderation is about. He draws a distinction between psychic and somatic pleasures. Psychic pleasures include love of learning and love of honor *(philotimia).* Yet people who indulge in these pleasures are not called immoderate (*NE,* 1117b31–32). Rather, moderation deals with tactile somatic pleasures; in reputable opinion moderation is limited to control of eating, drinking, and sex. Since we share these pleasures with the other animals, they appear slavish and bestial to the audience (*NE,* 1118a26). Later Aristotle says that these kinds of pleasure involve pain, and that immoderate people experience pain both when they desire pleasure and when they fail to get what they want (*NE,* 1119a4–5). Immoderate people are like naughty children insofar as they do not obey reason (*NE,* 1119b5–8).

After having seen what comes later in the *Ethics*, this discussion is obviously incomplete. Aristotle's political culture was affected decisively by the drive for honor. However, we have seen that the ambition for honor results in a fundamental ambiguity in how love of honor is praised and blamed. Sometimes, people blame the lover of honor *(philotimon)* for striving for more honor than he should and for trying to get it from the wrong sources. Other times, they praise the lover of honor as a manly man and a lover of what is beautiful *(philokalon).* In a like way, often people criticize the person who does not love honor *(aphilotimon)* for deliberately refraining from the pursuit of honor. Yet at other times they praise the *aphilotimon* because he is measured and self-controlled (NE 1125b11-14). As we have seen, Aristotle says that since there is no name for the mean respecting love of honor, the extremes lay claim to the middle and dispute for the title of virtue. That is, the person who withdraws from the pursuit of honor thinks of himself as a person who is virtuous. At the same time, the person who actively pursues honor identifies virtue with his manly self-assertion. The result is confusion when his audience tries to think and talk about how to relate to honor. From the perspective of the inhabitants of both extremes, the virtue which moderates love of honor appears to be a vice (*NE,* 1125b21–25).

The pleasure that comes from achieving honor is not seen as a vice for many in Aristotle's society. Yet this means that their ambition for honor truncates their notions of pleasure, and thus of moderation. When his audience think of pleasures that require management, they think only of a relatively limited range of physical desires. Consequently, the audience does not think that moderation involves the desire for honor. Their love of honor blinds them to the fact that honor itself might have to be limited. Overgrasping limits popular conceptions of what counts as moderation. For Aristotle's ambitious audience then, moderation is not seen as extending to a host of other psychic and somatic pleasures that may present their own difficulties for engaging in right action. Overindulging in food, drink, or sex can ruin people's lives. Yet overindulging in the nontactile pleasure of sight may present problems as well, as anyone knows who feels the need to slow down at the scene of a bloody accident. Further, from the perspective of Aristotle's audience, overindulging in certain nonsomatic psychic pleasures like honor does not seem to present any problems. Part of the burden of the criticism of the audience's notion of the ethical virtues is to move from a limited horizon of understanding of pleasure to a more comprehensive view. This more comprehensive view is made possible by the way the inquiry undermines prevailing views of excellence to clear the way for new views of human excellence. Aristotle shows why and how the audience's commitment to honor fails on its own terms to satisfy. He uses this failure to introduce his audience to other kinds of pleasure that were not immediately apparent to them at the outset of the inquiry.

Beginning to Recover Pleasure

The account of pleasure given in *Ethics* 7 is transitional. On the one hand, it looks back to the earlier account given in the discussion of moderation. It presents a fuller account because it is not limited to a discussion of tactile somatic pleasure. On the other hand, it looks forward to the final discussion in *Ethics* 10 by introducing themes that will receive their fullest treatment there.

Aristotle is ready for a fuller discussion of pleasure in Book 7 after the dialectical criticism of the particular moral virtues, the articulation of practical wisdom, and the consequent distinction between natural virtue and authoritative virtue. This discussion of pleasure is richer than the previous one because in the interim Aristotle has brought to light new kinds of psychic and intellectual activities that were obscured from view due to the audience's initially limited perspective. He has criticized prevailing accounts of the place of honor and self-assertion in a successful life. He has also argued that since most of us are not good we ought to be critical of our own notions of what is pleasant and right; in a sense we know the content of virtue by knowing what it is not. Further, he has cleared the space for a much fuller account of the place of thought in an excellent human life.

These arguments allow the audience to see their previous commitments in a new light. First, Aristotle is able to discuss somatic pleasure in a new way. In the earlier discussion of moderation, a variety of somatic and psychic pleasures were simply beyond the audience's horizons. Yet after the discussion of practical wisdom and moral strength and weakness, Aristotle is able to point beyond this limited perspective. Aristotle introduces several themes in *Ethics* 7 that are decisive advances over the previous account of pleasure. The first is the distinction between restorative and nonrestorative pleasures. Restorative pleasures are somatic and can be enjoyed only with pain. Interestingly enough, these restorative pleasures are those that reputable opinion identified with moderation: eating, drinking, and sexual activity. For example, hunger is the best sauce. Think of one's relationship with turkey five minutes before and five minutes after Thanksgiving dinner. Indeed, hunger is sometimes induced on Thanksgiving by skipping lunch to heighten the pleasure of the meal. Yet once the pain of hunger is gone, we no longer find it pleasurable to eat. In fact, once we becom stuffed, eating is painful. In a like way, the pain of thirst is the precondition for achieving pleasure in drinking, as anyone knows who has tried to drink more than a few glasses of water a day.

Aristotle points out that these pleasures are subject to strict limits. We cannot engage in them all the time, precisely because they depend on cycles of pleasure and pain that have a definite extent. Further, engaging in these pleasures tends to dissipate and exhaust us. Yet Aristotle points out that there are other kinds of pleasures that do not involve cycles of pleasure and pain since they do not involve bodily sustenance. Some somatic pleasures such as smell belong to this category. Smelling lilacs or fresh cut grass is simply pleasurable; no previous painful anticipation is required. These kind of smells do not wear us out; they invigorate. But the main example Aristotle gives of an activity that does not involve pain and pleasure at this point is *theoria* (*NE,* 1152b36–1153a2).

The pedagogical intention of this discussion is clear: it is both an advance of what came before and an anticipation of what will come later. It is an advance over what came before because the previous discussion of pleasure focused only on a limited range of tactile somatic pleasure. In drawing the distinction between restorative and nonrestorative pleasure, Aristotle redirects his audience's attention away from somatic pleasure to psychic pleasure, particularly the pleasure that comes from intellectual activity. This distinction and redirection have the effect of denigrating somatic pleasure and elevating psychic pleasures, for somatic restorative pleasure is now seen to be a frenzied, wearying cycle of pleasure and pain, whereas psychic pleasure are pleasant because they do not involve pain and becoming (*NE,* 1152b33–1153a7).

The second theme that advances the previous and anticipates the later discussion of pleasure is the argument that pleasures are activities and thus do not involve becoming (*NE,* 1153a14–15). Pleasure appears to be a kind of movement or becoming. For example, the pleasure of eating presupposes a process involving the pain of hunger, which is somehow replaced by the pleasure of eating. The process of hunger-satiation seems identical with the activity of pleasure. Yet Aristotle insists that pleasure does not involve a process, since it is a simple act. This argument is briefly presented in *Ethics* 7, but it is a major theme in Book 10.

The third theme that bridges the and the final discussion of pleasure is the notion that a certain kind of pleasure may in fact be the supreme good (*NE,* 1153b7–1154a7). From the perspective of a culture emphasizing the attainment of honor through noble public actions, indulging in somatic pleasure is a source of shame. So from such a perspective, it would be base to identify pleasure with the supreme good. Yet with the differentiation of restorative from nonrestorative pleasure and with the emergence of a more flourishing conception of human excellence, a new view of pleasure is possible. Aristotle thus is able to introduce the theme that will lead to the startling conclusion in *Ethics* 10: a certain kind of pleasure is the human good. Related to this, *Ethics* 7 introduces the theme of the divine character of certain kinds of pleasure. Aristotle concludes Book 7 by noting that god always enjoys one simple and single pleasure. This pleasure is not merely the human good but also the divine good (*NE,* 1154b26–28). Just as pleasure could not be equated with the human good initially, his conclusion about divine pleasure was impossible to reach from the audience's initially limited perspective. *Theoria* is introduced as a way of allowing human beings to engage in a quasi-divine kind of life.

Hortatory Conclusions

The discussion of pleasure is finally completed only after the discussion of *philia.* Recall that this discussion revealed that the best kind of friendships are most important for human life because they allow us to mutually complete each other; they help us to engage in an abundance of activity and this activity is the human way of being. Interdependence is necessary to actualize our most important human capacities, so friends rather than honor are the most important external good. This new view of the relationship between activity and happiness allows the final discussion of pleasure to advance decisively over those that came before. The concluding discussion of pleasure emphasizes the way pleasure completes activity. This allows us to see both pleasure and activity in a new light.

After a treatment of differing views of pleasure in Book 10,

Aristotle says that what pleasure is will emerge if he takes up the problem again from the beginning (*ap'arches; NE,* 1174a12–13). He does so by comparing pleasure sense perception, particularly to vision. The analogy between the act of pleasure and the act of vision occurs again and again in the final discussion. He uses this analogy to illustrate both that pleasure is a whole not divisible into parts and that pleasure is not contained within an activity, but is somehow superimposed on activity.

An act of vision, Aristotle says, is complete at every instant. It lacks nothing that has to develop later in order to complete the vision. In hearing speech, by contrast, the mind must work to make the sounds intelligible. Hearing is discursive. It requires work to put the parts of the sounds into an understandable whole. This is particularly true of listening to human speech, where syllables, words, and phrases must be related to each other for speech to make sense to a listener. Yet the same does not hold true for sight. When we see, we engage a vision of some whole. And we grasp that whole immediately; the only effort required to have an act of sight is to open one's eyes.

Something similar is true of pleasure, Aristotle says. Each different kind of pleasure is complete at every moment it is actual. There is no pleasure, Aristotle says, that will be made more complete if only it lasts longer. This is why pleasure is not a motion (*NE,* 1174a19). Motion takes place in time and is divisible into parts. For instance, running a race is divisible into parts: legs flex and unflex, steps are taken as we run toward the finish line. We can measure how long it takes to run a race. Yet how long does it take to win the race? Winning happens in a moment; and is complete and perfect at that instant. Running the race was the necessary condition for winning it. Yet winning the race is not coextensive with running it. Running involves motion; winning does not. Winning the race is an event that is somehow superimposed on the act of running it. Aristotle says that motion is possible only in time. Yet what takes place in a moment—like the pleasure of winning—is a whole because it is complete as soon as it happens. In a like way, the enjoyment of winning a race is not divisible into parts. Aristotle concludes that pleasure is not a process. It appears to be so because most of our experience of pleasure is somatic, and in these experiences, a process of movement from pain to pleasure is involved. That process of pain and regeneration, however, is not pleasure itself.

The pain of running the race involved motion and was the condition for the activity of winning and enjoying. But the movement of running the race is not the pleasure of winning it.

Aristotle next considers how pleasure completes activity. Again, his analogy revolves around sense perception. Sense perception is always directed toward something that is perceivable *(pros to aistheton).* Such an act is complete or perfect *(teleios)* when it is well disposed to the most beautiful thing that falls under sense perception (*NE,* 1174b14–17). We will get the most pleasure from an act of sense perception when our sense organs are at their best and when the objects they are perceiving is best. Each sense, each thought, and each beholding *(theorian)* has its own pleasure and is most pleasant when it is most perfect or complete *(teleiotate).* Pleasure is the fulfillment or completion *(teleioi)* of the activity in question (*NE,* 1174b20–33). Aristotle's point can be clarified with an example. Hearing a piece of music will be most pleasant when our ears work well. A deaf person cannot get the same enjoyment out of a musical performance. In addition, however, the pleasure will be greatest when the work of music is best and when it is performed well. No one gets pleasure from bad music badly performed. For Aristotle, pleasure is related both to the person enjoying as well as to the quality of what is enjoyed. Pleasure requires a good condition both of the actor and that which produces pleasure.

However, Aristotle is careful to point out the way this enjoyment occurs. Pleasure completes an activity not as a disposition completes an activity by being in the act, but as a kind of fulfillment *(telos)* that superimposes itself like the bloom of youth in those in their prime (*NE,* 1174b31–33). For Aristotle, the excellence of an act depends only in part on its external performance. In addition, one must answer the question of how *(pos)* the act is performed. The enjoyment of an act is only possible when the action is informed by an excellent disposition *(hexis).* In this sense, the disposition of the actor completes the activity, making it perfect. The disposition of the virtuous person is inseparable from the activity in question; it is in the act. However, this is not how pleasure completes an activity. Rather, pleasure completes or fulfills activity in the same way that young people have a certain abundance to their beauty. Aristotle says that pleasure is a bloom that superimposes itself as an "extra" on top of the activity done. For this reason, Aristotle insists that pleasure is not in the activity as a *hexis* is. Rather, pleasure is a kind of "extra" that "blooms" the excellent act. Indeed, Aristotle says, everyone seeks pleasure because everyone seeks life *(zen)*. All life is a kind of activity. Pleasure is the completion or fulfillment of life. From this perspective, Aristotle says, we do not need to ask whether we seek life for the sake of pleasure or pleasure for the sake of life. The two are interconnected and cannot be separated. There is, he says, no pleasure without activity and every activity is brought to completion by pleasure.

This discussion is related to what I have called the dramatic center of the *Ethics:* Aristotle's account of human being and activity. In his account of *philia*, Aristotle pointed out that everyone desires being, and that being and activity are the same for us. Aristotle emphasized perception and thinking in this discussion. When we act, we perceive that we act (*NE,* 1170a18). The most pleasant life, Aristotle argued, does not consist in having external goods, but by engaging in self-conscious actions that complete one's potential for activity. Life is especially good for the good person because she will be aware of engaging in good acts (*NE,* 1170b3–5). In his discussion of pleasure Aristotle returns to these themes of activity and perception. Pleasure completes or perfects activity. The word used in this discussion is *telos*, which connotes fulfillment, completion, and perfection. Pleasure is the joy superimposed on activities. This joy is happiness. The final discussion of pleasure completes the discussion of the new way of life presented in the account of *philia* just as pleasure completes activity. The account of pleasure is hortatory by hinting at how we might receive an abundant life.

This conclusion allows for a radically different view of pleasure from the one first put forth by reputable opinion. Pleasure is not coextensive with tactile somatic, or restorative, pleasure. For Aristotle, there are different kinds of pleasure, depending on the different activities pleasures attend. This makes possible a new standard that can be used to rank human activities. Those activities are best that are most pleasant to the good person (*NE,* 1176a15–19). The greatest pleasures perfect the activities of those most complete *(teleiou)* and blessed *(makariou)* person (*NE,* 1176a26–30). Aristotle reaches a conclusion that would have been impossible at the outset of the inquiry. The audience initially equated pleasure with Sardanapollus's tyrannical life. The life that maximized pleasure appeared to be one full of power, manipulation, self-assertion, and self-indulgence. Yet at the end of the inquiry, after radically reevaluating his audience's commitments, and after a series of attempts to rehabilitate pleasure by extending the range of its meanings, Aristotle is able to invite his audience to seek those activities that result in the best kind of pleasure. These are radically different from the somatic pleasure of the tyrant. In fact, Aristotle repeatedly says that the kind of pleasure he is speaking about is divine. Aristotle's hortatory conclusion identifies *theoria* as the most divine, pleasant, and therefore the most desirable activity human beings can engage in.

Restorative pleasures dissipate and fragment us. They are limited. They are also nonshareable. Eating, drinking, and sexual activity are private insofar as what is enjoyed cannot be enjoyed by more than one person at the same time in the same way. By contrast, nonrestorative pleasures like pursuit of wisdom integrate us, making us whole within ourselves and with each other. They are abundant, delightful, invigorating, and shareable. Since they are shareable, their common pursuit builds up rather than tears down a common life.

The Fulfillment of Desire

The valorization of *theoria* is the last in a line of reversals that dominate the final three books of the *Ethics.* Initially honor was seen as the highest human good, and the virtue of *philia* was seen to be the least among the moral virtues. By the end of the inquiry, a good friend rather than honor is revealed to be the most important external good. Initially, reputable opinion identified happiness with the possession of a series of manifest, nonshareable external goods. By the end of the inquiry, happiness is identified not with zero-sum goods to be hoarded and fought over but with psychic activities that only increase when shared. Finally, at the outset of the inquiry, respectable opinion held that the life of philosophy was utterly impractical. By the end of the inquiry, Aristotle reverses that opinion by arguing that contemplation—the activity associated with philosophy—is most practical because it is most in our interest.

Aristotle does not describe the content of contemplative activity; all he does is give us a kind of list asserting that contemplation is in the audience's interest because it gets them more of what they initially wanted. A chart could be developed which links the discussion of *theoria* to the human desires that have been revealed in the course of the pedagogy:

Table 9.1.
How the Contemplative Life Fulfills the Audience's Desires

Audience's Initial Desires	*Fulfillment of Those Desires in Contemplation*
1. The audience wanted the "highest good."	1. Contemplation is the highest activity because it is in accord with the highest kind of virtue and what is best in us (*NE,* 1177a12–13).
2. Pleasure is necessary for happiness.	2. Contemplation is the most pleasant activity.
3. The magnanimous man wanted self-sufficiency to be assured so that he could flourish without depending on external contexts.	3. Contemplation is more self-sufficient than other activities, for the wise person needs fewer external goods.
4. Happiness seems to be something desired for its own sake.	4. Contemplation is done for its own sake.
5. Happiness requires leisure.	5. Contemplation is most leisured and also free from weariness. By contrast, the political activities the audience initially valorized are unleisurely.
6. The political life brings power, so it provides security from enemies and enables us to engage in the highest actions.	6. Virtue, *nous,* and the actions of the *spoudaios* do not consist in exercising power (116b18–19). In fact, *nous* far surpasses everything in power (1178a1). Good friends insure security and noble action. It is possible to perform noble-fair actions without being ruler of land and sea (1179a4–5)

Table 9.1 *(continued)*

7. Happiness is connected to honor for two reasons:	7. Happiness is engaging in contemplation for at least two reasons:
a) The political life in which one can show forth one's excellence is most noble *(kalos)* and most active.	a) Contemplation is the activity of *nous. Nous* gives us our notions of what is fair *(kalos)* and divine. Contemplation is the most active activity (1168a5–9).
b) Possessing honor is a way immortalizing oneself; of participating in a divine kind of life.	b) The life of contemplation is more than human. Those who live it only do so by virtue of something divine in them. We should not follow those who advise us to have mortal thoughts. Rather, we should try to immortalize ourselves and do everything we can to live in accord with the highest part of us (1177b26–1178a4).

The discussion of *theoria* completes the practical intent of the pedagogy by showing in what our goodness consists; it meets the intent of the inquiry by arguing that *theoria* satisfies human desire. At the end of the *Ethics*, Aristotle finally returns to the problem of happiness, which motivated the whole work. Happiness is the satisfaction of desire, and Aristotle's argument is simply that the activity of *theoria* satisfies human desire more than any other activity because it gets us more of what we want in wanting anything at all. In this way the concluding discussion of *theoria* realizes Aristotle's pedagogical intent. It is not directed to a systematic investigation of what place contemplation should hold in a person's life. It is not meant to answer the question, "What is the relation of theory to practice?" At the end of protreptic inquiries, it was common to urge participants forward to engage in the activities presented in the course of the discussion. Thus the hortatory conclusion of the *Ethics* is meant to make contemplation attractive to an audience initially suspicious of it. Initially, philosophy seemed unattractive to the audience because it did not seem to be able to help them achieve the noble activity they associated with happiness. So at the end of the *Ethics* Aristotle merely states the advantages of engaging in contemplation.

At the beginning of his discussion of *theoria*, he says that his discussion will be in accord with the account that was given first (*NE,* 1177a18–19). The account at the end of the *Ethics* is in accord with the initial delineation of reputable opinion because it shows the implications of his audience's desire. In wanting the glorious, quasi-divine abundance of noble action, the audience in reality wanted the glorious, quasi-divine abundance that comes with contemplation. Aristotle argues that the audience's desire for happiness is in reality a desire for the satisfaction that comes from *theoria.*

So Why Won't He Talk about Contemplation?

Whenever I teach the *Ethics*, I find students are always frustrated by Aristotle's refusal to give an account of contemplation. Aristotle has taken them on a long, difficult journey into a fundamentally important human question: How can I live in order to be happy? After this journey, he finally hints at an answer, but then refuses to articulate it. Why should the answer to the question he has been asking all along be beyond the scope of the inquiry? (*NE,* 1178a23) After all, the inquiry was directed precisely to finding this answer. On the most important play of the game, Aristotle seems to throw in the towel.

I could venture several hypotheses as to why he refuses to give a description of contemplation. First, it is important for Aristotle's pedagogy and practical intent that he refrain from a detailed account of the nature of contemplative activity. In a decisive sense, giving a picture of contemplation does lie beyond the scope of the inquiry. The scope of the inquiry was defined by its goal: to make his audience good. So the purpose of the inquiry demands that the *Ethics* remain incomplete. The *Ethics* is limited because it must invite the audience to engage in the activity to which it points. Since a protreptic text aims at introducing people to a new way of life, it does not aim at the comprehensiveness of a philosophical system. Its goal is to effect a change in life, so it must end by pointing to that life and exhorting its audience to search for it themselves. The protreptic will proceed and finally conclude by setting up a series of puzzlements. By engaging in these puzzlements, the reader is led through curiosity to wonder. Answers given in protreptic will always yield more questions in order to cultivate the activities toward which it aims. In a text pointing toward the activity of philosophy, it would be especially important to cultivate the practice of questioning. In this way, the philosophical protreptic introduces pupils to the love of wisdom by showing them why and where they ought to look for it. The end of the *Ethics* tells us that our good is the activity of *theoria*, but it does not tell us what that activity is. Thus we are urged forward to continue the search in our own lives. Aristotle leads us to water and invites us to drink. His refusal to articulate the content of a contemplative life is an acknowledgement that he cannot do our drinking for us.

Second, if Aristotle provided a detailed account of *theoria*, it would violate the strict limits he places on the inquiry. The inquiry is meant to be practical, not theoretical. A detailed account of *theoria* would spill over inevitably into a theoretical consideration of the kind of act contemplation is. Since this not the point of the inquiry, it would distract the audience from the practical effect Aristotle seeks to encourage: the questioning of one's own life to see if one is actually being satisfied by one's current practices. The point of the text is to allow us to become good by wondering how to fulfill our desires; the goal is not a theoretical discussion of contemplative activity.

Third, and perhaps most importantly, a theoretical discussion of the nature of contemplative practice might be misleading. Contemplative activity cannot be seen externally. One cannot comprehend it the way one could see the beauty of a painting, because it is not manifest in the same way. Perhaps even more importantly, its worth cannot be judged by conventional standards that extol money, power, and status. Contemplative activity will be inevitably misunderstood. Recall that Aristotle pointed out that respectable opinion bifurcates thought and action. Not only is thought not held to be an action, thought seems to contribute nothing to action. Indeed, reputable opinion asserts that while wise people seem to know big things, their wisdom is useless for the everyday business of living. By the end of this inquiry, we realize the deep reason for this. The goods that most people find utterly serious—honor, power, and wealth—are in reality unserious. The thoughtful activity that most people find impractical and frivolous is in reality most serious because it is the condition for doing anything well.

A life of contemplation requires the cultivation of activities that most people find at best impractical and at worst contemptible. Such a life involves a detachment from the external goods that most of us prize most. It involves fostering peace and balance. This requires setting aside times during the day where one strains every effort to do "nothing" and clear one's mind from fretting about the concerns that constitute the bulk of the so-called practical life. Finally, contemplative activity demands creating a mindfulness and attentiveness to realities that most of us are only dimly aware of because we live so much on the surface of things, valuing as we do size over proportion; volume over value; prestige over excellence; praise over praiseworthiness. In short, perhaps Aristotle cannot speak about what contemplative activity is because so few of us know its content. We may risk diminishing it in an effort to disseminate it. For this reason, I think that Aristotle's sketch of contemplation is an apophatic account of satisfaction insofar as it points to the presence of an activity that is hidden from most of us.

Conclusion: Contemplation, Action, and the Limits of Aristotelian Political Philosophy

The Missing Question

Surely I have missed an essential question: What is the relation of contemplation to action? Aristotle begins the *Ethics* with the question, "What is happiness?" Yet in his answer he seems to advise us to pursue two radically different ways of life. On the one hand, he argues for a life that differs radically from his culture's notion of successful practice. The condition for such a life is an awareness of dependence on one's various communities and a consequent responsibility toward those communities as the condition for one's own flourishing. This is surely an active life, although the activities in question would be very different from conventionally praiseworthy notions. Yet on the other hand, Aristotle concludes the *Ethics* by arguing that since contemplation is the most intrinsically satisfying activity, the contemplative life is best. Yet this seems a life of inactive withdrawal. While the philosophic life is one guided by inactive contemplation, the practical life is one guided by moral activity. Can Aristotle's apparently contradictory advice be reconciled?

Commentators have worked mightily to answer this question.[1] One group simply insists that both emphases are present in Aristotle. They argue that Aristotle believes that a successful life combines some degree of both moral and intellectual virtue. Part of this group argues that Aristotle's teaching is consistent because these different emphases reflect two very different alternatives available to human beings, each with its own attraction.[2] Others argue that the different teachings are presented to different audiences, one of which is attracted to a life of practice and another of which is capable of a life of philosophy.[3] Finally, defenders of the "dominant end" reading argue that Aristotle teaches that contemplation is superior to practical activity, and thus that the philosophic life is superior to the practical or political way of life.[4] To address this question I will first identify problems in the way the debate has been framed. Next, I will provide a sketch of the Aristotelian notion of practical wisdom. Then I will do the same with contemplation. Finally, I will explore how these two activities are related in order to see whether the contradictions presented in the literature are true to Aristotle's own thought.

Interpretive Problems

When we turn to Aristotle's texts to explore this problem, we notice some curious features that seem to block our efforts. First, as I emphasized, Aristotle never provides a systematic account of contemplation in the *Ethics.* Nor does he systematically explore the relationship between contemplation and moral action. The practical intent is to make his audience good, not engage in a philosophical presentation of a problem in the history of ethical theory. The absence of a positive description of the activity of contemplation means that we seem to have no good way to explore its relationship to moral and political action. So when we ask, "What is the relation of contemplation to action?" we are baffled because we do not know the meaning of one of the terms of the question.

Since Aristotle never gives anything approaching a systematic presentation of the content of contemplative activity, we should begin our account by emphasizing that at first sight we may have no idea what he is talking about. Saying anything about the relationship of contemplation to action requires saying something descriptive about both and then seeing how they are related. But the absence of a prolonged discussion of contemplation means that any account of contemplation must be reconstructed from the hints Aristotle gives in the body of the text.

The Way the Problem Appeared to Aristotle's Audience

An interpretive assumption underlies the contemporary debate over the relationship between contemplation and action. Most commentators neglect the pedagogical character of the *Ethics.* For this reason they take Aristotle's characterizations of his audience's view on the subject to be Aristotle's own considered view. However, in confusing Aristotle's view with that of his audience, they adopt the very perspective on theory and practice that Aristotle struggles so mightily to overcome in the *Ethics.* By contrast, I have argued that the *Nicomachean Ethics* is a dialectical pedagogy aimed at making a particular audience good. Thus Aristotle's arguments address a specific set of commitments. If we are to inquire into the relationship of contemplation to action in the *Ethics,* we have to begin by trying to understand how the problem appeared to his audience, since that is where Aristotle would have begun.

Recall that Aristotle opens the *Ethics* by asking what way of life makes us happiest. People derive their conception of happiness from the kind of life they lead, he says. So he sketches several lives and the orientations that give them substance. Activity and contemplation are first distinguished by the commitments stemming from different kinds of lives:

> Cicero reports that Pythagoras answered the question about what he understood the neologism philosophos to mean by comparing the three different types of men who attend festive games: some come to peddle wares for profit, others to achieve honor with their bodily strength, and still others only to gaze at the statues, the athletic accomplishments, and to hear the official speeches. This is true of men generally: some desire money and sensual gratification, others power and the authority of command, but others—the philosophers—choose to contemplate the most beautiful things, *ton kalliston theorian.*[5]

To the politically ambitious audience who desire noble activity and public recognition, the alternative lives are the objects of scorn. The life of the sensual money grubber seems fit only for cows (*NE,* 1095b19–20). The life of the philosopher may be vaguely attractive because it allows one to know many wonderful things. However, it does not issue in noble action, power, reputation, or the ability to protect oneself from the machinations of others. Such a life is impractical insofar as it does not seem to pay attention to the way the real world works. Indeed, as the experience with Socrates shows, pushed to its limits, some citizens will suspect that this life undermines the ethos of the city through its inquiry into human and divine matters. In short, the active life of the politically ambitious citizens that comprise a large part of Aristotle's audience seems better suited to gain the prestige and power that lead to success, conventionally defined.

But the opposition that Aristotle's audience draws between contemplation and practical action breaks down in several ways. First, it assumes that the life of contemplation is an impractical life because it is inactive. Moreover, it assumes that the practical life is the active life, conventionally defined. But throughout the *Ethics* and *Politics* Aristotle argues against this false dichotomy. This is most obvious in *Politics,* 7.2-3, where Aristotle presents a debate between advocates of a politically active life and advocates of a life of quiet withdrawal. Political men hold that the active life is the only one fit for a real man (*andros; P,* 1324a39–40). By contrast, the proponents of political withdrawal insist that the life of a free man is better and different from the life of a political man (*P,* 1325a19–23).

Aristotle adjudicates this dispute in several stages. First he argues that both sides make the same mistake about politics; they both assume that the political life is a life of mastery. Many try to acquire this mastery, sometimes over their fellow citizens, and sometimes over neighboring states (*P,* 1324b32–33). But we have seen that throughout the *Ethics* Aristotle struggles to elevate virtue-as-equity over this conception of virtue-as-virility. The argument is that political life could be improved if one refocused one's desires away from the competitive, zero-sum good of honor to noetic goods that satisfy and do not diminish in the sharing. Politics need not be about despotism and conflict. It could strive to create a convivial and cooperative community. So while advocates of withdrawal are right to argue that it is better to be a free man than a master, they are wrong to assume that all political activity must involve mastery. Indeed, advocates of political withdrawal come close to identifying happiness with a kind of inactivity, for Aristotle argues that they should not praise inactivity *(apraktein)* over activity *(prattein),* because happiness is action *(praxis)* (*P*, 1325a31–34). Advocates of political activity are also partly right and partly wrong. They are right to insist that happiness is a kind of activity, but are wrong to equate the best kinds of activity with despotic rule. They fail to see a kind of rule that is appropriate to free men.

Aristotle concludes that the best way of life for both political bodies and individuals is the practical way of life. But, he insists, "the practical life is not necessarily in relation to others, nor are practical thoughts limited to those which come to be from action for the sake of what results, but much more those that have their end in themselves, and those studies *(theorias)* and thoughts *(diannoeseis)* that are for their own sake. For doing well *(eupraxia)* is the end, and so this too is a kind of practice" (*P*, 1325b14–21). The discussion thus concludes with Aristotle reiterating his earlier insistence that happiness is an activity. Yet at the same time, he extends the meaning of activity to include thought that is done for its own sake. Indeed, this is the most active of all activities according to the conclusion of the *Ethics*, and so the best kind. So he argues that one cannot rest in a false dichotomy between impractical, inactive thought and practical activity. The notion that thought and activity are dichotomous, however, informs the modern framing of the debate as much as it informed the way the debate appeared in Aristotle's time.

The second way the audience's view of the relationship between contemplation and activity breaks down lies in the failure to distinguish between activities and ways of life.[6] Aristotle begins the *Ethics* with the question central to ancient thinking about happiness: Which way of life is best? This is a question about how to orient one's life generally. But answering this question of orientation of a life does not tell us in a straightforward way which actions are best to pursue in particular circumstances. If I decide to become a lawyer, my general orientation will be to the study and practice of law. This orientation will of course inform my life insofar as it will help determine where I work, what kind of work I do, and what kinds of people I associate with. But this decision for a general orientation does not tell me how to discipline my hyperactive child who has just broken an expensive vase, or love a wife suffering with acute depression. The question as to which way of life is best is not coextensive with the question as to how I should act in particular circumstances. In specific circumstances, I may have to ask myself whether I should go to a political meeting or work on a book on Aristotle. That decision may be full of tensions and problems. But those problems can only be deliberated about in the concrete, with attention paid to the particulars of the situation. Am I a tenured professor under no pressure to publish? Or am I a young scholar who has to get a book to press in the next two weeks in order to feed my family? Is the town meeting routine? Or does it have profound implications for the life of my community? The answer to the question, "What should I do tonight?" is not a matter of reminding oneself of the fundamental option one has made to a life and then seeking to maximize that commitment. This is a manifestation of a kind of rule morality that is utterly foreign to the Aristotelian conception of practical wisdom. For an Aristotelian, when deciding what is the right thing to do in such a situation, it would be disastrous to say, "I am a theory-oriented individual. I live a life of theory. Therefore, on this occasion I must maximize theory whatever the cost." Rather, right action depends on thoughtful assessment of a host of factors that one confronts in the unique situation. Saying that contemplation is an intrinsically more satisfying activity to engage in than politics is not the same as saying one should always and everywhere maximize its pursuit whatever the cost to oneself or one's community. Indeed, the inquiry reveals that contemplation is a human activity that, like any other activity, must be chosen in the concrete. Thus practical wisdom must deliberate in the concrete about whether to engage in contemplation just as it deliberates about whether to engage in any other activity. Thoughtlessly making the decision for contemplation regardless of circumstances may even undermine one's ability to contemplate. Since the activity of contemplation has certain material conditions (*NE,* 1178a25), simply maximizing the contemplation may lead to the inability to contemplate. As Salkever notes,

> [I]n theory—that is, on the basis of an abstract and universal consideration of the constitutive potentially or first actuality of human nature—the theoretical life is best; but this theoretical conclusion cannot be translated without considerable distortion into a practical rule, like "Be as theoretical as you can." Just as we should not offer all sacrifices to Zeus, and just as it would be a disastrous error to claim abstractly that the most virtuous people should always have sole political power,

> so it would be wrong to transform the definitive end or possibility of human nature into a developmental stage or practical rule, equally applicable in all particular cases.[7]

The difference between contemplation and action for the sake of what results is not coextensive with the distinction between inactive thought and active morality. Rather, for Aristotle the difference lies in the kind of realities we engage when we do acts of generosity or justice on the one hand and contemplate on the other. So when our practical wisdom tells us to engage in just or generous acts, we aim at a practicable truth; we aim at a kind of truth that inheres in the right action done. This realm of action is necessarily contingent, since we would not be able to make a choice for a just or generous action if the situation we are confronting could not be otherwise than it is. Situations that are not actionable by us are simply beyond our capacity to choose.

On the other hand, when we make a choice to engage in the action of contemplation, we deal with realities that cannot be otherwise than they are, according to Aristotle. They exist in this way and no other. Thus contemplative activity aims at truth just as *phronesis* does. Yet while *phronesis* aims at a practicable truth that inheres in the contingent action, contemplation aims at necessary and unchanging truths. The decision to engage in contemplation is a practical decision because it could be otherwise. On any particular occasion we could choose to engage in contemplation or some other action. Practical wisdom thus must tell us when it is possible and appropriate to engage in contemplation, in the same way as it tells us when to engage in other kinds of activity. Yet it cannot provide us with the intellectual virtues we need to do the activity of contemplation. Nor can it see to the coming to be of the realities that we know when we contemplate. We can decide to get married and have children. We can choose to become active in politics or make room for contemplation in our lives. We cannot choose to become intelligent enough to grasp the intricacies of string theory. Nor can we decide how to structure the spiral galaxies that we contemplate, since these realities are beyond our choice. We can merely know their beauty and inquire into their structure and enjoy this knowing.

In striking ways, the contemporary debate over the relationship of contemplation to action for the sake of what results in the external world proceeds by setting up the same kind of false dichotomies as Aristotle's audience. The framing of the problem in the contemporary literature assumes that there is a gulf between thought and action, not seeing that right action requires thought, that thought is an action, and that it is an action to decide when thought should happen. In each case, the individual may experience all sorts of practical dilemmas in deciding appropriate courses of action. She may find it hard to decide on particular occasions whether to engage in inquiry or work or play with her children. But the tensions and problems involved in these particular decisions do not arise from a gulf between theory and practice. Rather, they involve the hard work of practical wisdom: balancing priorities in the concrete. Aristotle does not think that such practical decisions can be successfully negotiated by subsuming actions thoughtlessly under an abstract rule in the following way: "I am leading a life devoted to theory. I am supposed to maximize that activity. In this instance I am to neglect my responsibilities so that I may engage in theorizing." This rule-bound decision making is foreign to Aristotle's own account of practical wisdom, since that existential virtue is actualized precisely when we judge aright amid the complexities of the situation given to us.

For Aristotle, the political life is not the life of action or practice, whereas the philosophic life is the life of contemplation. Both are active, practical lives insofar as they involve different kinds of activities. The difficult questions about their relationship, therefore, arise not when we reflect abstractly on the relationship between a life of theory and a life of practice. Rather, they arise on particular occasions involving the need for a choice between activities that are at once both attractive and impossible to do at one and the same time. Getting such decisions right, in turn, is not a matter of theorizing the problem correctly. Rather, it involves the cultivation of practical wisdom. Getting such decisions right is a matter of struggling to get them right in each unique case. Since each decision is irreducibly unique, Aristotle will not speak in a general way about the relationship between contemplation and activities for the sake of what results because such an account would in a real sense be useless to the goal of the inquiry—to make people act well in the particular.

Thus Aristotle urges us forward to right action in two

related ways. For those who are philosophically inclined, he urges attention to right action in concrete cases so as to avoid a high-minded amoralism that justifies retreating from the demand to act aright in concrete cases in the name of the "radicalism" of the philosopher. Similarly, he urges those who are politically inclined to infuse their actions with thoughtfulness so as to cultivate the conditions for individual and social flourishing. In saying that contemplation is a superior activity, Aristotle is not advocating an intellectual amoralism that justifies philosophers doing anything in the service of thought. Nor is he saying that political life can be divorced from cultivation of thoughtfulness.

Contemporary Problems in Recovering Aristotelian Contemplation and Practice

Before going on to provide positive accounts of practical wisdom and contemplation, it is worthwhile noting that often the typical contemporary perspective on the relationship between contemplation and practice differs from both Aristotle's audience and Aristotle himself. The matter can be put this way: Aristotle's audience initially assumes that happiness can be found by engaging in noble actions. These actions are done for their own sake and are honorable because they allow men to show forth their excellence. However, Aristotle thinks that such a conception of virtue-as-virility implies a truncated notion of action for several reasons. First, it reduces human excellence to virility. Thus it tends to equate political rule and family systems with mastery simply (*P*, 1252a7–16). Further it does not include thoughtfulness in a conception of right action, nor does it hold thinking to be an activity. However, contemporary people adopt a perspective that differs from both Aristotle and his audience.

For this reason, we need to clear some more ground. I can only briefly sketch the nature of the gulf between Aristotle, his audience, and ourselves. But the story centrally concerns the two great phenomena lying between ourselves and the ancient world: Christianity and modern science. Christianity presents two new ways of understanding the relationship between action and contemplation. First, it conceives God as an omnipotent creator ex nihilo. This image of God makes the cosmos essentially intelligible in a way that is was not for someone who believed that a First Cause acted on prime matter to create the universe. On the Christian account, the world was made through a Logos who is the ground of its intelligibility. On the one hand, this notion accounts for the drive toward contemplative activity in a way that goes beyond anything proposed by Aristotle. It explains the satisfaction gained from contemplative activity by arguing that in knowing and appreciating any particular existent thing, one is knowing some part of God's creative mind. Yet at the same time, this notion of creation elevates making to a status it did not have for Aristotle. The best actions, Aristotle says, are those that are done for their own sake, not for the sake of something else. The Christian notion of creation and the concomitant notion of divine particular providence complicate enormously the understanding of human freedom and practice and the relationship of these to human making. Is human doing an extension of the divine making? Is all human doing a species of divine making? What exactly is the relationship between *poesis* and praxis, now that God is conceived as a creator? Further, what is the relationship of that divine activity to human activity? These questions are substantially different from the ones that drove Aristotle.

A second new problem that Christianity brings to the relationship between contemplation and praxis is the notion that human beings can relate to ultimate, unchanging reality in our contingent actions. Christians insist that when they act lovingly, God acts through them. More radically, they insist that when they act with love, they act not merely upon their neighbors but also upon God himself, insofar as he is present in neighbors (e.g. Matthew, 25:31–46). In short, the doctrine of the Incarnation means that the terms of the theory-praxis distinction got fundamentally changed from the way they appeared to Aristotle. For the Christian, contingent historical events can be the realm where the eternal acts. Indeed, the Christian can and does contemplate particular actions in history like the Crucifixion and Resurrection since they are held to have universal significance. Aristotle emphasizes, by contrast, that one can never engage in contemplation with an object that could have been otherwise.

Modern science also complicates the relationship between *theoria* and praxis. First, early modern thinkers scientize praxis in a way unthinkable to Aristotle. For Aristotle, since human choices operate in the realm of contingency, one cannot expect too much precision from them. They are simply unpredictable because of the element of human choice, and so one can neither master them nor comprehend them with a theory. By contrast, early modern thinkers like Hobbes argue that one can assimilate human affairs to physics if one understands the passions well enough. And if one develops an account of the motivations of human actions with enough precision, one can manipulate the human passions so as to insure a maximally stable commonwealth. Yet this reduces ethics and politics to kinds of making. Several corrolaries flow from this collapse of the distinction between practice and technique. Specifically human activities—politics and ethics—are not seen as noble and for their own sake. They are, rather, forms of making or production that exist for the sake of comfort or security, or whatever other goods human desires may specify. Since, in Vico's terms, we understand only what we make ourselves, it is imperative to remake human society so that we can understand and manipulate it to better suit our interests. In the realm of modern liberal politics and ethics, there is a tendency to elevate technique over both politics and contemplation. Better to lower one's sights and pursue what is humanly actionable through technique.

Second, "theory" in modern scientific terms sometimes comes to be identified with a body of propositions that can be applied to some determinate practice. In everyday speech, we refer to scientific theories, medical theories, political theories, psychological theories, or social theories. We then speak about how to apply these theories to practice to improve human life. Other times, scientific theories are held to reduce complexity to simplicity.[8] However, for Aristotle it is impossible to think of a "theory in practice" because *theoria* does not impinge on practice in such a straightforward way. To get a sense of the gulf separating us from Aristotle, we must to translate *theoria* as "contemplation." It makes sense to us to think about how to apply some theory about subatomic particles to nuclear weaponry. But it makes no sense to speak of the application of the contemplation of the structure of subatomic particles to nuclear weapons. Contemplation is an activity that is useless because it is pursued in a disinterested way. It is not done for the sake of technological application; it is done because such knowledge is simply fun or enjoyable. This does not mean that contemporary Aristotelians must be antimodern technophobes. Aristotle nowhere says that technological application of knowledge is wrong as such. He merely insists that it must be guided by practical wisdom in order to insure human flourishing, and that such knowledge is decidedly different from contemplation. In this sense, while modern thought valorizes technique over contemplation, Aristotle valorizes contemplation over technique.

Another conclusion that flows from this is that contemplation is not knowledge of discursive accounts or propositions. If theory is knowledge of a body of propositions, then it is inactive until it has been actualized by the desire to translate that theory into practice. Knowing the right medical theory to alleviate juvenile diabetes is obviously impractical unless it is put into practice. But this is a different kind of knowledge than contemplative knowing. Contemplation for Aristotle is an activity of beholding. For Aristotle when we contemplate we do not do so for the sake of anything that results in the external world. If we are engaging in theory in order to see how we could apply theory to practice, we are by definition not engaging in contemplation. When we contemplate we are not formulating bullets of theoretical knowledge that can be stored away and called for when needed in practice. Since contemplation is done for its own sake, in a strict sense, it is useless; it has no purpose but pure enjoyment. Thus it is both active and useless in a way that knowing scientific theories is not.

Finally, contemporary citizens do not think in terms of the distinction between theory and practice in the way the ancient world did because we tend to collapse the distinction between doing and making. In contemporary parlance, human action has been systematically reduced to the demands of production. For this reason "activity" is equated with "working for the sake of what results." Increasingly, there is less and less room for the notion that human life gains its meaning in part from actions which have no result other than themselves. Increasingly, citizens in contemporary liberal democracies impose on themselves the requirements of a totalitarian work camp. But this frenzied cycle of work entails that there is no escape from the realm of production. There are only brief respites that can be justified only by referring to their relationship to more work.[9]

The Enlightenment concept "morality" is related to this

drive for productive work. Morality has come to connote a phenomenon with no necessary ties to nature, beauty, or joy. Rather, it is the sphere of autonomous, nonnatural duties, quite often identified with the duty to be productive. Yet from the perspective of an Aristotelian conception of practical wisdom, with its emphasis on the flourishing enjoyment of our natural capacities and the beauty of navigating a difficult choice proportionately, this emphasis on abstract, universally applicable rules is a kind of self-hating torture. Perhaps this is another reason why contemporary inheritors of the Enlightenment do not think in terms of a moral action done for its own sake. Morality is identified with increasing wealth and keeping the peace.

Making a case for contemplation was difficult for a classical audience, and it is hard in a different way for a modern one. Aristotle seeks common ground with his audience by emphasizing a commitment to a life of noble actions done for their own sake. He then questions their notion of successful action in order to come to a fuller notion. This notion ultimately includes contemplation as the most fully actual activity. However, for a modern audience, one could not begin by assuming a commitment to noble action done for its own sake. Rather, one would have to begin by assuming commitments to both doing in the sense of making and to the technological application of scientific theories to practice. One would then have to proceed to undermine these commitments by unveiling their fruits in contemporary life—a life of frantic but often sterile and mindless activity. The latent contradiction in this conception of life is that while it promises fulfillment through productivity and technology, it often results in an empty restlessness. One would then have to articulate an argument to the effect that leisured activity is not the same as loafing. There are human activities that are meaningful without being either work or respite from work, and even today we do these all the time, without being self-consciously aware of it. Only then could one make a case for the satisfying character of activities done for their own sake. Finally, one could expand on that notion of practice to make a case that contemplative activity is happiness. In doing so one would have to overcome the objections not of virile, practical young Greeks. Rather, one would have to deal with the prejudices of inheritors of centuries of scientific progress. To take only one obvious example, it would be easy to object to Aristotle's argument that happiness is the contemplation of realities that cannot be otherwise than they are on modern scientific grounds. We have learned, for instance, that all manner of realities thought previously to be static are in reality dynamic. Darwin and his inheritors tell us that species are not static. Modern astronomy tells us the universe is not static. Modern environmentalists tell us that global warming proves that the earth is subject to the changes we impose on it. If the universe is not what Aristotle thought it was, what makes us think that contemplation is at all possible today? Perhaps there is no such thing as beholding of a reality that cannot be otherwise than it is because all reality in principle is changeable by application of modern scientific techniques. Such problems are so large that they require not a revival of Aristotelianism but rather a new Aristotle.

Practical Wisdom

So far I have merely attempted to clear ground. I have argued that Aristotle's conception of the relationship between contemplation and action for the sake of what results is not what it is generally taken to be in the literature. I have argued further that making a case for Aristotle's teaching on happiness entails understanding the gulf that separates us from him and that gives us such different perspectives on the problem. However, I have not yet given any positive account of the relationship of the activity of contemplation to practice in Aristotle's thought. Such a positive account would have to proceed by saying something positive about Aristotle's conception both of action for the sake of what results and of contemplation.

I have argued that Aristotle seeks to revalue his audience's conception of what a successful human life looks like. Initially, the audience identifies happiness with an active life that allows one to appropriate a set of external goods the possession of which makes one happy. In particular, they think that a life devoted to honor and political power provides opportunities for honorable action. Thus they thought of themselves as refined and practical people who were devoted to acquiring goods that were both tokens of noble action as well as opportunities to engage in noble action. They implicitly devalued the role of thought in a life of action. Thought was considered to be impractical since it could not inform the competition for these external goods and noble activities. By contrast, the practical life is a life of planning, acquiring, and achieving.

Aristotle turns this hierarchy of goods upside down. Honor and despotic power are devalued. Thought and the virtues of friendship are valorized. Friends are the most important external good because they allow one to engage in a set of social practices of which the audience was only dimly aware at the outset of the inquiry: generosity, fairness, evenhandedness, a sense of the need for forgiveness and equity, the desire to deal proportionately with all of one's entanglements. Contrary to the perspective of the great-souled man, interdependence is necessary for completion. This is so because one's own flourishing activity only comes about in large part because of the different excellences of others.

In Aristotle's notion of virtue-as-equity, thought assumes a new and crucial role. Indeed, the intellectual virtue of practical wisdom is the single existential virtue that is required to order all our actions. This virtue is, from the audience's initial perspective, quite passive and reactive. From the audience's initial "refined and practical" perspective, a successful life was devoted to planning for and acquiring power and prestige and opportunities for noble action. But Aristotelian practical wisdom is not merely proactive. It does not consist of formulating a hierarchy of external goods or activities and then seeking plans to acquire or implement them. Clearly, planning is part of life, and it is practically wise to plan. But life is so varied and unpredictable that planning is a source of strife as much as it is of happiness. Indeed, mapping plans on reality can justify all kinds of abuses, since the implicit temptation is to treat the world and its inhabitants as potential obstacles to the successful implementation of one's preferred plan. Moreover, as the dialectical method of the *Ethics* amply demonstrates, what appears to make us happy does not always do so. Correcting one's mistaken impression about what makes one happy is not merely a matter of consistently revising life plans. It may be precisely a matter of giving up this notion in order to take life as it comes. For Aristotle, practically wise activity entails viewing people not as obstacles to be overcome for the successful implementation of one's own life plan. Rather, it entails viewing other people as necessary for one's own happiness because they help one both know oneself and acquire the qualities such as wisdom that make flourishing possible.

Practical wisdom is profoundly reactive, and this for several reasons. It is first of all reactive because right action comes to light only when one tries to be awake to the particular demands each unique situation puts on the actor. Most of the time, we do not create the context of our own choices. And even when we try to act so as to create the context of our choices, our actions have such varied and unintended effects that we cannot possibly comprehend all of them. In other words, any context demanding action act is not of our own making simply. Right action entails reacting to these contexts in each case in as fair and proportionate a manner as our limited wisdom allows. So right action involves not merely planning and frantic activity. It involves a sense of wakefulness and attentiveness to the opportunities the moment presents. In one way, it involves a kind of passivity before or receptivity to the particulars of each situation.

Cultivation of receptivity has certain requirements. Practical wisdom must clear away the distracting clutter of excessive desire for external goods. One cannot become reactive and thoughtful if one is frantically overgrasping. Excessive devotion to honor, power, and profit cloud one's judgement not only by creating a warped sense of priorities. The kind of frenzied, mindless activity that seems to go along with overgrasping destroys the conditions for the cultivation of the attentive mindfulness that is practical wisdom. Thus the excessive desire for external goods can interfere with the desire for psychic goods that are more satisfying. Happiness is the satisfaction of desire. The paradox is that the pursuit of the satisfaction of some desires can become an obstacle to the satisfaction of others. Ridding oneself of commonplace, respectable notions of the place and meaning of activity is a necessary step to flourishing.

This receptivity is also manifest when we accept our loved one's help in knowing ourselves and struggling to become practically wise. One of the reasons the best kinds of friends are our dearest possessions for Aristotle is that they help us to actualize our capacity for practical wisdom by reminding us of our own potentials, limits, and faults. They congratulate us when we go right and correct us when we go wrong. We become practically wise only through a developmental process that demands a receptivity to the gifts they offer us. Receptivity to interdependence is a condition for practical wisdom.

All this means that the problem of appearances intrudes when one speaks about practical wisdom as much as it intrudes when one speaks about contemplation. Practical wisdom may well be misunderstood by devotees of practical action since it demands the cultivation of excellences that do not seem practical from the perspective of reputable notions of success. Wrenching one's desires away from excessive attachment to conventionally respectable priorities may look like impractical idealism. The cultivation of thoughtfulness by gathering oneself up every day and refusing to live a life of frenzied activity and accumulation may look like sheer laziness. To the modern businessperson, the frantically active politician, or today's restless and anxious consumer, practical wisdom may seem anything but practical and wise. If one is frantically busy with getting and spending, one may overlook opportunities for action that constitute sources of deep satisfaction. One would have to provide conditions for inner resources of peace and tranquility that provide the ground for confident engagement of action that many take to be foolish.

Contemplation

A positive description of contemplation would have to proceed from the hints Aristotle gives us in the text. First, he employs a specific term—*theoria*—that was in common use at the time. Aristotle is always mindful of how words are employed in common speech. So one way of approaching a positive account of contemplation is to ask, "Why does Aristotle appropriate this term as a symbol for the activity of contemplation?" We may better understand contemplation if we try to understand how the common use of the term *theoria* lent itself to an evocation of the experience of contemplation. Second, we may get a clearer picture of what contemplation is by putting Aristotle's presentation of it in the context of the Book 10 as a whole. This section of the *Ethics* is dominated by treatments of activity, pleasure, and motion. Further, the metaphor Aristotle consistently employs to describe pleasure is sight. What might these discussions imply about contemplation?

Let me begin by exploring the first point. How was the term *theoria* employed in Aristotle's time? The origin of the word is usually explained by pointing out that *theoria* means "watching" and is related to *theoros,* a spectator at a festival performance. But *theoros* also had a religious connotation: It was the title given to an emissary of a polis who was sent to consult the oracle. Further, the official delegation that a Greek polis sent to a neighboring city-state was called a *theoria.* Sometimes these were sent to take part in sacred rituals and sometimes to honor the neighboring city. This sacred connotation of the term was reinforced by the fact that it reminded the Greeks of the word *theos,* or god.[10] So to Aristotle's audience, to engage in *theoria* was not to do the kind of intellectual work that modern academics do. It was not discursive thought—inquiring into problems, making distinctions, formulating arguments, reading texts, performing experiments, writing articles and books. In coming to terms with what Aristotle means by contemplation we would have to take care not to conflate our own activity as intellectuals with the activity Aristotle is describing. Since he appropriated a term that meant witnessing or seeing, his notion of contemplation implies a kind of beholding—the kind of joyful viewing that one would do at a festival. When one engages in such a beholding, one is on holiday—by definition on a break from the necessities of everyday life. Indeed, the point of festival performances is often to take the spectators outside of their everyday concerns and thus to take them out of themselves.

The hypothesis that contemplation is nondiscursive beholding is buttressed when the discussion of *theoria* is put in context. Ethics 10 has three related emphases. First, there is a discussion of pleasure, wherein Aristotle insists that pleasure is not a motion and does not take place in time. Second, there is an account of the relationship between pleasure and activity, wherein Aristotle argues that different pleasures are abundant blooms of delight that are somehow superimposed on various kinds of activity. Third, there is a presentation of the advantages of contemplative activity. In all three cases, the metaphor of sight appears. Aristotle explains that pleasure is like an act of sight—one does not have to work to enact sight. In a like way, pleasure does not involve motion. Pleasure imposes itself on activities like the bloom of youth, Aristotle says. In saying so he points to an experience of visual beauty as a metaphor for pleasure. Finally, he employs a Greek term that connotes "sight" *(theoria)* in order to evoke the experience of contemplation. In the case of both Aristotle's discussion of contemplation and the way the term is actually employed in his time, contemplation means a kind of beholding.

But this means that contemplation is a receptive activity. When one beholds a festival performance, or becomes lost in viewing the face of one's child, suddenly realizes with pleasure the harmony of a mathematical formula one has worked to understand, or is engaged so deeply by a work of art that one ceases to notice the passage of ordinary time, one suddenly becomes lost in delight and wonder. One is taken outside of oneself. One is invigorated and active. In such events, one both acts and is acted upon. Contemplation in the sense of beholding is a manner of being held by something wonderful and delightful. This being acted upon, however, also demands a certain action, for it presupposes an attentiveness or wakefulness to the reality that holds one:

> What characterizes us inasmuch as we are able to perceive and to understand is our being *awake.* The state of wakefulness has its degrees, as we all know. We can be drowsy and half-asleep. We can be inattentive to what goes on around us. But as long as we are not fully asleep we are *awake,* and we know that we are. . . . This state and manner of being is a state in which we are not closed up but *open.* Wakefulness is openness—the very openness of a huge open door. It is not a state of activity, but rather a state of preparedness, of alertness. This state or manner of being is commonly called in Greek *nous* or *noein.* It is a manner of being which corresponds to the manner of being of any material, any *hule,* and, like the latter, it is only conceivable in relation to what transforms it into a finished product. This transformation and information is brought about by *what* we sense and by *what* we understand. The transformation and information being completed, we are *one* with what we perceive, understand, know. It is not we, in our state of wakefulness, who actively grasp something that is prepared to be grasped. On the contrary, we, in our state of preparedness, are being grasped, molded, formed by what is at work, by the *energeia* of the *eide,* sometimes, nay mostly, through the intermediary of our sensing power.[11]

In this sense, contemplation is an action that we both choose and that befalls us. Falling in love is a similar kind of experience. The expression "falling in love" implies that we do not strictly choose this state. Yet when we fall in love—most of the time unexpectedly and sometimes against our better judgement—we are held by the other in a wonderful way. We are profoundly transformed. Indeed, while we do not strictly choose to fall in love, once we have come to know and love our beloved, we realize, "This is what I wanted all along even though I was not fully aware of it before."

For Aristotle, any perception forms the perceiver. In the act of beholding, we are held by a reality that somehow makes us more like itself. Somehow, beholding a reality makes us adequate to behold it. Continuing with the analogy, when one falls in love, one struggles to become adequate to the beloved. One senses that one must raise oneself out of one's old life in order to be worthy of love. In a like way, the practice of contemplation transforms one's life. Contemplative events are moments of intense pleasure and extreme, abundant life. The fullness that one acquires in them comes all at once from a variety of factors. One is caught up by a glimpse of a meaning and harmony that is larger than oneself. One begins to leave the everyday and ascend to something fascinating and that seems somehow divine. One begins to become aware of a whole in which one participates but which escapes us in its fullness. One senses that this whole is at once present and also absent in that its fullness is beyond one's grasp. This experience holds and fascinates us. It also shapes us. The fascination produced by such an experience can produce a kind of productive tension in one's life, just as the experience of falling in love does. Once one falls in love, one struggles to become worthy of the beloved. Once one becomes used to contemplative activity, one begins to search for ways of becoming more attentive to the situations and realities that might evoke such experiences. One begins to direct one's attention away from everyday concerns with getting and spending, not necessarily because money and status are bad in themselves, but because they are distractions from the attentiveness that is a precondition for beholding. It may not be too strong to say that for Aristotle we become more like what we focus our attention on.

One cannot strictly choose contemplation. Sometimes when one sees a particularly gorgeous sunset one is not impressed.

One can look at a great work of art several times and have nothing happen, only to be enraptured the sixth or seventh time. If contemplation is a kind of delight in beholding, it is an activity that is not chosen, but that befalls one. All one can do through practical wisdom is cultivate the conditions for this beholding to happen. That is, all one can do is persistently cultivate a certain kind of attentiveness, a certain focus for one's attention. This attention has two related directions. It is an attention away from all the activities conventionally defined as happiness. At the same time it is an attention toward a receptive openness to contemplative experiences. So Aristotle might emphasize that there are negative and positive ways of cultivating the conditions for contemplative practice. Negatively, contemplation requires isolation, withdrawal, and specific kinds of abstention. Human beings can engage in different degrees of perception. Paradoxically, certain kinds of perception obscure others. Loud noises interfere with our ability to distinguish softer ones. Bright lights blind us to things in the dark. In a similar way, contemplation demands the cultivation of a kind of inner eye. Perhaps this cultivation involves a deliberate shutting out of all sorts of conventionally respectable activities and goods. In contemporary societies, for instance, the illusions the entertainment and advertising industries bombard us with dull certain sensibilities and capacities. Perhaps the only way to cultivate the attentiveness and inner peace contemplative activity requires is to shut these out as much as possible. A common complaint about modern life is that its frantic pace and the constant buzz of popular culture tend to undermine internal silence. Clearly, one must live in the world. But perhaps abstaining from things like consumerism and television watching is a condition for becoming open to contemplative activity that Aristotle says is the source of our deepest satisfaction.

Yet there may be other ways to cultivate the kind of attentiveness that Aristotle says is necessary for contemplation to occur. In the last Book of the *Politics*, Aristotle describes a program of education for the young. He urges those in charge of young people to introduce them to physical and intellectual activity, and also to music, the spoken and written word, and other forms of art such as sculpture. He insists that an adequate introduction to such activities demands that students cannot remain passive consumers of culture. His educational program in music does not consist in merely taking them to performances, for example. He says, rather, that the young person must learn how to make music to understand music. Aristotle's reflections on cultural education are his last words in the philosophy of human affairs. Why does he close with an injunction to teach young people how to make music and art as a propaedeutic to something larger? Perhaps the cultivation of contemplative practice requires much more than mere abstention from the noise and frantic pace of everyday life. Perhaps it requires, positively, participation in such creative processes. Perhaps one needs to produce shapes and forms for the eye to see. Painting or sculpting requires attentiveness to the form one is seeking to represent. It requires mindfulness of the process through which that form is represented. It requires a focus that is more heightened than usual. The same could be said for working with the written word. Writing well requires deliberate attention to the word that captures exactly what the writer is seeking to convey. Writing and performing music also require a focus on harmonies, mood, other performers, and a host of other facts.

At this point it is clear that the problem of appearances intrudes as much when discussing contemplation as it does when discussing the requirements of practical wisdom. From a perspective informed by most prevailing cultural standards, directing one's attention in this way appears to be massively impractical. It does not help one acquire the external goods related to fortune. Indeed, creating the conditions for contemplation requires precisely withdrawing from the pursuit of such goods so that one can be free to engage in more satisfying activities. However, while from the perspective of the contemplative, this withdrawal is merely a means to the end of the abundant activity of contemplation, from the perspective of Aristotle's audience it will seem to be an impractical, unmanly withdrawal from political life due to fear of healthy competition. From the perspective of some contemporary citizens, it will appear to be an impractical, lazy withdrawal of a loser who cannot hack the stresses of a global economy.

Contemplation and Its Effects on Practical Wisdom

After all this clarification, perhaps the notion of the priority of contemplation still does not sit well. It seems to denigrate human work and human making. After all, someone will object that the valorization of contemplation produces the kind of quietude that excuses inaction in the face of injustice or suffering. Should not the priority be placed on human doing in order to protect our actions from a self-absorbed tendency to contemplation that blinds us to the effects of our own injustices on our fellow human beings, and increasingly, the earth itself? Finally, is not this elevation of contemplation a justification for a "contemplatocracy" of truth holders who assert the right to determine for the rest of us how to live? Thus is not the elevation of contemplation an excuse for the worst kind of irrational domination justified in the name of truth?

To address such pressing questions adequately requires investigating the ways contemplative activity informs other forms of human action. An Aristotelian might speak of a mutual interplay between practical wisdom and contemplation. How does contemplation inform practical wisdom? It does not do so in any straightforward way. Contemplative activity does not provide a set of clear and distinct rules for conduct. What does it do? For Aristotle, we become what we attend to. Attending to virtuous action somehow habituates us to excellence. In a like way, contemplative activity habituates us to a certain mode of being that gives new focus to our lives. Attentiveness to other modes of activities changes us in similar ways. Falling in love informs one's day-to-day actions. It does not do so in any straightforward way. Being in love does not provide any special access to practicable insights or rules of conduct. Rather, being in love informs one's actions decisively by reorienting one's entire perspective. Being in love alters radically one's way of looking at and relating to the beloved. Or to take another example, the relation of contemplation to action for the sake of what results is like the relationship the religious person believes to hold between prayer and daily life. She who abides continually with God in prayer acts rightly in particular situations. Prayer does not provide a set of specific rules. Nor does it give practicable insights straightforwardly. Yet believers think that it alters their perspective and thus enables them to become more and more adequate to excellence.[12] In much the same way, contemplative activity does not produce practicable insights or rules. Rather, it produces fruits in one's life that have a profound effect on one's everyday activity.

From this perspective, perhaps Aristotle's argument that

contemplation is the highest human activity not merely fosters contemplative activity but also cultivates a certain understanding of human making and doing. Aristotle's valorization of contemplation entails a priority on receptivity. Elevating receptivity has a humbling effect on our view of human action. Contemplative practice provides a certain ironic distance from the most conventionally respectable human activities. It provides a perspective that informs one's sense of one's place in the universe. By consistently engaging in contemplative practice one realizes that one creates neither oneself nor the conditions for one's own fulfillment. The person who is aware of such dependence cannot conceive of himself as a self-created demiurge whose projects and desires are the most important reality. For Aristotle, even one's own virtue is the result of interdependence and difference. Since human beings are developmental creatures that require human community to actualize their own potentials, it makes no sense to treat one's surrounding community as an opportunity for despotism. Rather the receptivity that practical wisdom cultivates entails a recognition that one's own achievements are a result of one's prior reception. In this sense before we can act or make aright we must be open to receiving. Further, one's ability to engage in contemplative action depends on receptivity to realities one does not make. Contemplation helps cultivate the conditions for genuine practical wisdom by disposing the whole person to be aware of his or her dependence on receiving.

This perspective fosters certain priorities. Contemplation cultivates right action by encouraging us to respect and be responsible to the encompassing contexts on which we depend, including our family, local communities, religious organizations, larger state, and the earth. In contrast to the great-souled person striving for self-sufficiency, the contemplative person is aware of the fact that he constantly requires realities outside of himself to exist and flourish. The fruits of contemplative action include recognition of dependency and a willingness to be responsible to what we depend on.

Ironically, while some of the literature on Aristotle's treatment of contemplation worries that his valorization of contemplation undermines the conditions for right action, an Aristotelian might argue that his priority protects human action from the ill effects of thinking that our own projects are the most important reality. Aristotle's ethics is an ethics of being and activity, not having. Aristotle begins from what is first for us and proceeds to what is first in itself. That is, he begins from our own commitments and dialectically clarifies them in order to uncover a more flourishing way of life. What is revealed is that if we are committed to our own projects of accumulating money, power, and status, our lives will be sterile. Aristotle's ethics does not begin with an ontology of human nature that he develops a priori and then employs to inform human conduct with a set of exceptionless rules. However, Aristotle's inquiry does lead to a kind of ontology: the priority of being over having. Receptivity to the world as it has been given is the condition for making sure that our own desires and projects are not elevated to the status of the most important reality.

An emphasis on receptivity over activity entails the notion that our lives are not given meaning when we implement our life plans on a more or less recalcitrant reality. Aristotle thinks that we are simply not the most important beings in the universe, and so we should not act as if our proactive plans are the most significant reality. When reality is seen as the non-self-created context within which one lives and acts, one's actions can be conceived as a kind of transitive receiving and returning. Human beings are transitive partners in a community of being wherein what is received is the condition for acting and in turn the act is a grateful return. This is the ultimate meaning of Aristotle's ethics of being and activity. The priority of being is not merely a temporal priority; it is an existential priority. From this perspective, it does not make sense to speak of applying theory to practice. Rather, the emphasis would be on how right action is an extension of the receptivity embodied in contemplation. For an Aristotelian any exercise of genuine practical wisdom is the fruit of contemplation in discrete action.

In this way contemplation cultivates practical thoughtfulness about political reality. I have argued that Aristotle does not set out to answer a set of specific political problems systematically in the *Ethics* and *Politics.* Still less is he interested in supplying the theoretical ground for a set of universally applicable rules. Rather, he wants to make people good (*NE,* 1094b11; 1103b27; 1179b1–4). Specifically, he employs dialectic to question the most respected opinions (*T,* 100b21ff) of a given human community to foster the habits of critical reflection needed to deliberate well about politics. Since *endoxa* set the terms of political debate in a given regime, questioning them clears the ground for new ways of speaking and acting. Thus Aristotle's political philosophy aims to supply us with a set of questions and revisable standards for examining our lives and the political regimes we inhabit. The critical awareness of our presuppositions and blind spots shocks us out of the self-satisfied complacency that stifles thought. For example, I argue that Aristotle brings to light our overgrasping for external goods like honor, power, and wealth and the way this overgrasping undermines political community. This encourages thoughtfulness insofar as it makes us aware of our lack of justice. In doing so it provides the conceptual tools we need to explore better ways of acting in particular situations. In short, contemplation helps us raise and interrogate political questions so that we can deliberate about them well in the concrete.

How does the priority of receptivity to reality affect human making? Human making receives its proper limit for Aristotle in its end. The end of human technology is to transform part of the world. Yet how do we infuse this making with wisdom so that we do not ruin the world in the process of transforming it? For Aristotle, if we lose a sense of wonder and thanksgiving in the face of the world we will prioritize making over receiving. Grateful reception of the world is the condition for responsible use of it. Disinterested contemplation of the wonders of being which stems from an attitude of receptivity prevents our making from becoming a domination that serves only our own narrow ends. Dominance for the sake of our own goals, for example, leads to the destruction of the earth's goods and thus our good because it ruins the contexts on which we depend for a flourishing life. Such an attitude also leads to the reduction of other human beings to the means for our ends in political practice.

The contemplative life is a life spent in enjoying and preparing for contemplation. Yet when Aristotle assigns this activity the status of the highest available to us human beings, he is not advocating the rule of monkish contemplatives who, because they know the structure of reality, can order human society well. First of all, as I have emphasized, contemplative activity does not provide straightforward practicable insights. For an Aristotelian, any argument that contemplation could be applied to practice in a straightforward way so as to justify the political power would be immediately suspect. By contrast, Aristotle insists that experience with practical matters and prudence are necessary for right action in specific situations. In addition, since the contemplative requires a kind of isolation and withdrawal to cultivate its conditions, it is not clear that such a person would want to rule in the first place. Indeed, insofar as any claim to be worthy of rule expresses a desire to rule, that claim is evidence that the claimant is unfit to rule. Any attempt to elevate unformed human desires to the status of the principle of judgement will be severely criticized from a contemplative perspective. Rather, the imperative in the contemplative life is to employ an attitude of observation and attentiveness. This allows a detachment; a perspective to dialectically inquire into human actions to uncover their contradictions and paradoxes. In addition, contemplation points to limits of political activity. The activity of politics is not the only way to transform human desires for happiness. Politics may have a dignity that is not usually ascribed to it by the person who overgrasps for power. Politics may be able in certain unique circumstances to provide a context where members of the community care for each other's good and thus achieve a measure of flourishing. But that transformed notion of political activity both presupposes and leads to an attitude of openness to the world that is embodied in a contemplative attitude that transcends politics. In this way Aristotle protects us from those claiming to own the truth.

Practical Wisdom and Providing for Contemplation

In turn, how does practical wisdom see to the coming to be of contemplation? If contemplation is an experience of delightful beholding, then it cannot be chosen at will. It does not come when we bid. Indeed, such experiences are often unexpected. The same holds true with other activities, however. We long to fall in love. But when we meet and become attracted to the beloved we experience joy partly because he or she comes unbidden as pure other and pure gift. We do not choose or make our beloved. Rather, we accept the new life he or she provides and struggle to make ourselves adequate to that new life.

Perhaps in a like way practical wisdom does not strictly choose contemplation, and this in several senses. Obviously, as Aristotle says, we cannot make the objects of contemplation; we do not make a magnificent natural vista that takes our breath away; we do not create the beauty of a powerfully simple mathematical formula. Moreover, when we reflect on our experience of abundant delight at beholding the wonder of such realities we realize that we do not create the delight that attends such experiences. Somehow, as Aristotle says, this pleasure is something added to our activities like the bloom on a flower. Yet in another sense we do choose such activities. We choose them insofar as we are attracted to them and cultivate the conditions in our lives so that they might arise when the conditions are right. We choose them in the sense of accepting them with joy when they come to be. When we fall in love, we realize our beloved is what we wanted all along; they fulfill our heart's longings. When we become used to such activities, we begin to realize that we need to reorient our perspective in order to help foster the conditions under which they might arise. In a sense, we have to be open to looking for contemplative moments to happen so that we may recognize them for what they are and enjoy them when they present themselves.

If my reflections are more or less on target, perhaps what practical wisdom does is enable adults to live as a very small child. Young children are not bothered by their mortality, inasmuch as it is beyond their horizons. If their basic needs are met, they have no anxieties about where their next meal is coming from or whether their possessions will be taken away. Their characteristic activities are playfulness and wonder. They take delight in the extraordinary character of ordinary objects. They ask simple questions with profound implications about all manner of realities. They take each day as it comes and take joy in their growing and learning. In this sense, very young children live as Socrates did.

Aristotle does not give conflicting advice at the end of the *Ethics.* Tensions will arise in specific situations where one is torn about what kind of activity to choose. But again, this problem cannot be resolved by referring the problem to a tension between two incompatible lives defined in the abstract. However, there is no question that there is a tension between the life of a practically wise person and the life of a practical person conventionally defined. Indeed, from the perspective of conventional priorities, Aristotle's practically wise person may well appear childish and impractical because his or her priorities will be so at odds with prevailing wisdom. This is a tension not in the life of an individual, but between specific individuals and the particular social and political organizations they inhabit. Thus there is no tension between "theory" and "practice" in the abstract. There are only tensions specific human beings experience on particular occasions. Articulating the tension between the demands of a life of "theory" and "practice" for an Aristotelian could only happen on discrete occasions. It would entail wondering, for instance, whether someone who at first glance appears to be impractical has insights into the human condition that are far more practical than respectable individuals. Creating unease with the respectable is a fruit of Aristotle's pedagogy.

An Aristotelian would say that philosophizing about human affairs entails not mapping abstract dichotomies onto choices, but being observant and reflective about the meaning of what people are actually doing. Is a bureaucrat shuffling paper doing praxis? Is a professor editing her work? Is a professor engaged in praxis when preparing a lecture? When working through a particular inquiry? What are we doing when we walk our dog or taking exercise? Is driving a doing or a making? What is watching a particular television show? Is it a leisurely praxis, a contemplative activity, or merely resting up for more work?

Aristotle refuses to spin out a theoretical account of the relationship between contemplation and practice because their relation is only manageable in the concrete. Managing these tensions in specific cases is infinitely more difficult than resolving theoretically the relationship between theory and practice in the abstract. In fact, positing a dichotomy between theory and practice skirts precisely the difficult practical questions. By developing rubrics like "theory" and "practice" and then thinking within them, we may be led to miss opportunities to be attentive to and reflective on what is right to do in specific instances. In the end, Aristotle's only advice is to encourage us to struggle to become practically wise.

Human Limits and the Limits of Aristotelian Political Philosophy

Aristotle argues for the possibility of a satisfaction that transcends the ethos of his culture. Contemplation is presented as the most fully divine, complete, superabundant, excellent action that is with our grasp. Yet at the end of the *Ethics* Aristotle, too, asserts limits. In doing contemplation, we participate somehow in a process of immortalization and live a divine kind of life. Yet, Aristotle says, we get tired and fall asleep. He seems puzzled by this. It would be wonderful if human beings could persist in contemplation, but in the end, some weakness or wickedness in our nature prevents us. I pointed out earlier that sleep was homologized to death in ancient cultures. In saying that we must submit to sleep, Aristotle points to the limits of the satisfaction held out by contemplation.

There is an apocryphal story about Aristotle's life that dramatizes his relationship to these limits. When he went to bed, the story goes, he would grasp a bronze sphere—apparently symbolizing the cosmos—and extend it over a pan next to his bed. As soon as Aristotle fell asleep the sphere would slip out of his hand and hit the pan, waking him so he could get up for more work.[13] This procedure would be repeated over and over. Human life is a struggle to remain awake amid the temptation to various forms of sleep. Remaining awake allows us to live in amazement at what unfolds before us. Remaining awake allows for a kind of satisfaction that surpasses even the glorious abundance of achieving distinction among our peers. Aristotle may try to fight against human limits by refusing to submit to sleep. But eventually he had to submit to this most fundamental human limit. The way of life Aristotle holds out has a quasi-divine character. The philosopher longs for divinization. Yet perhaps to his deep sadness, while there is a longing to become a god there is no avenue available to divinity. The philosopher tastes divine life through contemplative practice but this cannot last.

Aristotle clearly thinks that his pedagogy is subject to strict limits. The problem of the limits of the audience is one of the first Aristotle brings up in the *Ethics* (*NE,* 1.3, especially 1095a1–15). The question is whether those who are listening to the *Ethics* are adequate to judge aright the phenomena of which it speaks. This is a question of competence, Aristotle insists. He argues that we are competent to judge only that which we know (*NE,* 1094b28–1095a4). If we have no experience with a particular way of life or a specific practice, we lack criteria to evaluate it critically. We gain a deeper appreciation of the skill required of a major league baseball player if we try to hit fastballs. We gain a deeper appreciation of the skill of a concert level cellist if we have played the cello. One result of this experience is a better capacity to judge musical performances. Analogously, Aristotle thinks that critically evaluating a way of life requires some lived experience of it.

Aristotle's text is meant to invite and initiate us into another mode of being. His text is meant to be a mediator between the reader and the way of life it seeks to convey. The text is meant to be transparent for this way of life, and in this sense it cannot help but fail to present an adequate picture of the reality to which it points. Thus the classical philosophers insist on the inability of the written word to convey the content of philosophy (e.g., *Phaedrus* 275c–e; *Seventh Letter* 341b–342, 314c). In light of Aristotle's comments about competence and judgement, it seems that part of our task in reading a book like the *Ethics* is to explore our relationship to the way of life Aristotle is presenting to see if we are adequate to it. Approaching it with this hermeneutic of humility helps prevent us from dismissing his account out of hand without really knowing what we are dismissing. Keeping alive the question as to whether we are adequate to the way of life to which the text points allows us to be critically open to his arguments. In other words, a text that tries to change our lives demands the question, "Have I participated in the way of life the text proposes through consistent practice (or at least imaginatively though sympathetic re-creation)?" So part of the task of Aristotle's readers is to see if their own way of life limits their receptivity to the text.[14] This is true even if we wish ultimately to reject the way of life the text seeks to promote, for rejecting it thoughtfully demands the capacity to evaluate it critically.

This means that there are strict limits to Aristotelian formation. The problem might be described as one of receptivity. Are those of us who participate in Aristotle's course of instruction adequate to live the way of life to which he calls us? The life of philosophy is particularly difficult and requires enormous spiritual resources. Thus the limits of Aristotle's pedagogy can be found by exploring the problem of receptivity.

In arguing dialectically for the superiority of philosophy to virtue-as-virility, Aristotle is playing a dangerous game. In order to show the superiority of philosophy, he must show how philosophy meets in a fuller way the desires implicit in a pursuit of honor. To do so, he must expose the psychic motives underlying the pursuit of honor. The drive for honor is a flight from death and a flight to noble life. At the heart of this lust for honor is the insecurity of the human condition. Yet this pedagogical strategy reveals the human situation in terrifying clarity. Uncovering the motive for honor means uncovering the fear of death that drives it on. Indeed, the shadow of death hangs over every mortal project (e.g., *P,* 1257b40ff). Most of us, however, want to retreat from this kind of clarity into the security of human projects like cultivation of honor, political power, and money. These goods, Aristotle says, promise to render our lives more secure by promising to help us manage "good and bad fortune" (*NE,* 1129b4–6). By contrast, philosophers live like very small children who, because they do not fret about great wealth, reputation, or despotic power, are free to be radically open to wonder.[15] Their practice of death allows them to let go of the obsessive concern with self and its self-protective projects, which liberates them to live a divine life.

Yet often some compensation must be offered to live with the clarity that Aristotle seeks to promote. Here is the problem: it seems that the philosopher has no compensation to give, other than the experience of fullness enjoyed in pursuing wisdom. While in old age Aristotle says he loves the myth, in his ethico-political writings he steadfastly refuses to engage in mythical speculation that might assuage the anxieties of his audience over their mortal condition. Aristotle is a true skeptic. He must suspend judgement in order to foster the conditions for his inquiry. Refusing to assert certain knowledge over questions like the ultimate rationality of human action, the self-sufficiency of human desire, or the fate of individual human beings after death is the condition for keeping these questions open. Insistence on ignorance entails that the comfort of myth is not an option; that would close off the wonder that is required to do philosophy. Yet his seriousness entails that the comfort of a life of retreat from clarity about our mortal condition is not an option, either. Rather, for the philosopher, the only consolation for the anxieties produced by clarity about our mortal condition is the suspension of judgement itself. In the *Phaedo,* for example, Socrates argues that he cannot be afraid of death, for he does not have the requisite information to make an informed judgement about it one way or the other. He simply does not know whether it is a great blessing or a great curse, and since this matter is not a subject of deliberation for him the only logical thing to do is refuse to worry about it. Skepticism demands suspension of judgement, and in this suspension lies freedom from fear.

However, not many are capable of suspending judgement in this way without experiencing extreme anxiety. Most of us are tempted to two unphilosophic alternatives. On the one hand, we could opt for the comforts of rebellion by judging human life to be absurd. Yet nihilistic skepticism is unphilosophic because it allows our knowledge of ignorance to betray our love of knowledge. That is, the fact that we are aware that we do not know comprehensively the meaning of the universe does not of itself warrant the claim that the universe has no meaning. If we assert this conclusion, we close ourselves off from a search into meaning because we pretend we already know the answer to our question. On the other hand, we might opt for the comforts of supposed certainty; we could tend to irrational dogmatism or unwarranted speculation. Yet this allows our love of knowledge to betray our knowledge of ignorance.[16] That is, we may desperately want to know the meaning of the universe, but this longing does not in itself provide its own satisfaction. Aristotle thinks we simply do not have enough evidence for either of these options. The only alternative is genuine questioning.

Philosophy is the practice of death because in so doing we let go of the attachments that stand in the way of contemplative activity. But this life must be subject to severe strains. It is unclear whether most of us are really adequate to it. For this reason, philosophy can never effectively reform society on a large scale. The limits of the audience point to the limits of the social effectiveness of the way of life Aristotle seeks to promote. Indeed, philosophy may be socially dangerous to be true to itself, since it must reveal the human predicament in a way that provokes anxiety and yet consistently refuse to offer any speculations that could ease that anxiety. Indeed, the perspective on human affairs gained from the practice of death will lead to an unconcern with all those human projects aiming at the relief of anxiety.

I began this book by observing that we are in a time of transition, when mature people sit back and reflect on what came of Aristotelianism can be understood as part of that attempt at reflection. But in the end, Aristotelians may have to admit the limits of Aristotle's account: The revival of classical philosophy alone cannot provide the resources that we need. To be true to their skepticism, Aristotelians must continue their search.

Notes

INTRODUCTION

1. Vaclav Havel, "The Hope for Europe," *New York Review of Books* (20 June 1996): p. 38. Havel struck the same theme in his 1990 Address to Congress (*Congressional Record—House,* 21 February 1990, H392–95). See also his *Summer Meditations,* trans. Paul Wilson (New York: Vintage Books, 1993). For accounts of Havel's political philosophy and rhetorical strategy in dealing with Western audiences, see Peter Lawler, "Havel on Political Responsibility," *The Political Science Reviewer* 22 (1993): 20–55; Peter Lawler, "The Dissident Criticism of America," in *The American Experiment: Essays on the Theory and Practice of Liberty,* ed. Peter Lawler and Robert Schaefer (Maryland: Rowman and Littlefield, 1994), 123–63.

2. This brief list is far from exhausting the possibilities. For Aristotle as a defender of participatory democracy, see, for example, Sheldon Wolin, *Politics and Vision* (Boston: Little, Brown and Company, 1960), 57–58; Hannah Arendt, *The Human Condition* (Garden City, New York: Doubleday and Company, 1959), 30. For Aristotle as a critic of democracy, see, for example, Ellen Meiksins Wood and Neil Wood, *Class Ideology and Ancient Political Theory: Socrates, Plato, and Aristotle in the Social Contract* (New York: Oxford University Press, 1978). For contrasting views of Aristotle's consistency on the best life for human beings, see J. L. Ackrill, "Aristotle on *Eudaimonia*" in *Essays on Aristotle's Ethics*, ed. Amelie Rorty (Berkeley: University of California Press, 1980); Richard Kraut, *Aristotle on the Human Good* (Princeton: Princeton University Press, 1989); Gerald Mara, "The Role of Philosophy in Aristotle's Political Science," *Polity* 19 (1987): 375–401; Martha Nussbaum, *Fragility of Goodness* (Cambridge: Cambridge University Press, 1986), appendix to part 3; John Cooper, *Reason and Human Good in Aristotle* (Indianapolis: Hackett Publishing Company, 1986); Aristide Tessitore, *Reading Aristotle's* Ethics: *Virtue, Rhetoric, and Political Philosophy* (Albany: State University of New York Press, 1996); Walter Thompson, "Aristotle: Philosophy and Politics, Theory and Practice," *American Catholic Philosophical Quarterly* 68 (1994): 109–24.

3. Leo Strauss, *The City and Man* (Chicago: University of Chicago Press, 1964), 50–51. See also 59. Other prominent scholars have argued convincingly for the necessity of interpreting Plato in light of the dialogue form. Apart from Strauss's many students, there is Eric Voegelin, *Plato and Aristotle* (Baton Rouge:

Louisiana State University Press, 1957), 10–13; the excellent but neglected Robert Cushman, *Therapeia* (Chapel Hill: University of North Carolina Press, 1958), xvii; 6, 8, 100, 251, 305; Hans-Georg Gadamer, *The Idea of the Good in Platonic-Aristotelian Philosophy*, trans. P. Christopher Smith, (New Haven: Yale University Press, 1986), 70ff. For a more recent treatment which seems to owe an unacknowledged debt to Strauss, see Robert Wardy, *The Birth of Rhetoric: Gorgias, Plato, and Their Successors* (London and New York: Routledge, 1996), 53–54. See also Kenneth Sayre, *Plato's Literary Garden: How to Read a Platonic Dialogue* (Notre Dame: University of Notre Dame Press, 1996).

4. One example will suffice to illustrate the conventional way of reading Aristotle. In her *Fragility of Goodness*, Martha Nussbaum presents thoughtful and well-received accounts of Plato and Aristotle. Her treatment of Plato avoids mistaken readings by paying attention to the interpretative problems posed by the dialogue form. Thus she devotes separate chapters to each dialogue considered. This method stays true to the integrity of the dialogue; insofar as each is a single dramatic inquiry, it would be wrong to try to ascertain Plato's thought on a particular issue by extrapolating from several dialogues with no regard for audience, dramatic presentation, or context. However, when she reaches Aristotle, Nussbaum writes, "The structure of this section will differ from the structure of the Plato section, much as Aristotle's philosophical writing differs from Plato's. That is, it will move from problem to related problem, rather than from complex multi-voiced dramatic work to work" (237). This method assumes that Aristotle's works are not single inquiries with an integrity and structure that must be respected, but rather treatises setting forth straightforward conclusions about a variety of topics. So, for example, Nussbaum tries to articulate Aristotle's account of the problem of the appearances by discussing passages taken from the *Nicomachean Ethics*, *Politics*, *Physics*, *deCaelo*, and *On Generation and Corruption*, without taking into account audience, context, or mode of presentation (240–47). This is typical of the interpretive paradigm that dominates Aristotelian studies.

5. I will use "philosophy of human affairs" throughout to designate Aristotle's inquiry in the *Nicomachean Ethics* and *Politics*. This is Aristotle's own term for the inquiry (*NE,* 1181b15).

6. Aristotelians have been ingenious in doing so. Some argue Aristotle presents two inconsistent teachings on the good life (see, for example, Cooper, *Reason and the Human Good*, chapter 3). Others argue that his teaching in Book 10 is consistent with the *Ethics* as a whole, and thus the product not of the mature Aristotle, but rather of an earlier Platonist Aristotle, or some student editor, or perhaps both (see, for example, Nussbaum, *Fragility of Goodness*, appendix to part 3). Still others argue that his teaching is intended to be apparently inconsistent, and that the inconsistency reflects a difference in the audience to whom the respective teachings are addressed (see, for example, Tessitore, *Reading Aristotle's* Ethics, chapter 1).

7. See, for example, Richard Bodéüs, *The Political Dimension of Aristotle's* Ethics, trans. Jan Edward Garret (Albany: State University of New York Press, 1993); Stephen Salkever, "Women, Citizens, and Soldiers: Plato and Aristotle on the Politics of Virility" in *Essays on the Foundation of Aristotelian Social Science,* ed. Carnes Lord and David O'Connor (Berkeley: University of California Press, 1991) 165–90; Paul A. VanderWaerdt, "The Political Intention of Aristotle's Moral Philosopy," *Ancient Philosophy* 5: 77–89.

8. Pierre Hadot, *Philosophy as a Way of Life,* trans. Michael Chase (Oxford: Blackwell Publishers, 1995), 64.

9. As Hans-Georg Gadamer emphasizes, "Dialectic is not so much a *techne*—that is, an ability and knowledge—as a way of being." *Idea of the Good*, 39.

10. Hadot, *Philosophy as a Way of Life*, 83.

11. For an overview of my understanding of how Aristotle employs protreptic, see Thomas W. Smith, "The Protreptic Character of the *Nicomachean Ethics*," *Polity* 27 (1994): 307–30.

12. For this account of ancient protreptic, see Mark Jordan, "The Protreptic Structure of the *Summa Contra Gentiles*," *The Thomist* 50 (1986): 173–209.

13. Joel Litz, "Reflections on and in Plato's Cave," *Interpretation* 21 (1993–1994): 115–34.

14. Stewart Umphrey, *Zetetic Skepticism* (Wakefield, N.H.: Longwood Academic Press, 1990), 19–23).

15. Werner Jaeger, *Aristotle* (Oxford: Clarendon Press, 1948), 68–71.

16. James Jope, "The Didactic Unity and Emotional Import of Book 6 of *De rerum natura*," *Phoenix* 43 (1989): 16–34.

17. See Mark Jordan, "Protreptic Structure." See also Martin Jaffe's excellent interpretive essay in Thomas Aquinas, *The Literal Exposition on Job*, trans. Anthony D'Amico (Atlanta: Scholars Press, 1989).

18. For general information on the *Protrepticus* and an attempt at reconstruction, see Anton-Hermann Chroust, *Aristotle:* Protrepticus: *A Reconstruction* (Notre Dame, Ind.: University of Notre Dame Press, 1964).

19. This view of the text is gaining currency: "Though Aristotle does not use the dialogue form of his own teacher, Plato, his work is, like Plato's, often aporetic, without a clear answer. A statement that appears as an assertion may be considered more like a challenge with a hidden question mark that turns the assertion into a field of exploration, to be questioned, to be tested by what we observe, by what we hear out companions say. The difficulty with much of the scholarship on Aristotle has often been the tendency to turn sentences posed as problems into Aristotelian dogmas when in fact Aristotle's writings retain the aporetic character of his teacher. To ignore the aporetic elements is to lose a sense of the subtlety of his analysis and the important qualifications that he raises about his own claims." Arlene Saxenhouse, *Athenian Democracy: Modern Mythmakers and Ancient Theorists* (Notre Dame, Ind.: University of Notre Dame Press, 1996), 116–17. In this regard, see also Hadot, *Philosophy as a Way of Life*, 105–6.

20. Jonathan Barnes, "Aristotle and the Method of Ethics," *Revue Internationale de Philosophie* 34: 430–51; J. D. G. Evans, *Aristotle's Conception of Dialectic* (Cambridge: Cambridge University Press, 1977); Gadamer, *Idea of the Good*; W. F. R. Hardie, *Aristotle's Ethical Theory* (Oxford: Oxford University Press, 1968), 37–45; Bernard Jacob, "Aristotle's Dialectical Purposes," *Interpretation* 21: 135–67; Nussbaum, *Fragility of Goodness*, chapter 8; G. E. L. Owen, "*Tithenai ta Phainomena*" in S. Mansion, *Aristot et les problèmes de méthod* (Louvain: Publications Universitaires de Louvain, 1961), 85–91; Timothy Roche, "On the Alleged Metaphysical Foundation of Aristotle's *Ethics*," *Ancient Philosophy* 8 (1991): 49–62.

21. See, for example, Terence Irwin's translation of the *Nicomachean Ethics* (Indianapolis: Hackett Publishing Company, 1985).

22. This term is sometimes translated as "commonplaces," implying that a *topos* is an argument that is commonplace, or that is generally held to be true by most people most of the time. See E. S. Forster's translation of the *Topics* (Cambridge: Harvard University Press, 1989).

23. Indeed, some scholars conclude that Aristotle employs rhetoric in the *Ethics*. The assumption of this account is that there is no real distinction between dialectic and rhetoric in Aristotle's treatment of human things. For this line of argument, see Tessitore, *Reading Aristotle's* Ethics.

24. Hadot, *Philosophy as a Way of Life*, 92.

25. Gadamer, *Idea of the Good*, 99.

26. Ibid., *Idea of the Good*, 99–100.

27. Nussbaum, *Fragility of Goodness*, 10–12. See also her chapter 8 generally for her account of the way dialectic works to clarify the opinions of the audience. Interestingly enough, Nussbaum seems to get her conception of Aristotelian dialectic from the anti-Aristotelian, John Rawls. See his *Theory of Justice* (Cambridge: Harvard University Press, 1971), 46–53 for a discussion of "reflective equilibrium," which is an account very similar to Nussbaum's of the goal and method of moral theory.

28. Nussbaum, *Fragility of Goodness*, 10–11; chapter 8.

29. Jurgen Habermas, "A Review of Gadamer's *Truth and Method*," in his *Understanding Social Inquiry* (Notre Dame, Ind.: University of Notre Dame Press, 1977), 357.

CHAPTER 1. THE POLITICAL CHARACTER OF ARISTOTLE'S PEDAGOGY

1. Aristotle's pedagogical project cannot be reduced to contemporary concepts of education, in the narrow sense of mastering a specialized discipline or training for a career. Rather, since Aristotle wants to foster not merely intellectual excellence, but also thoughtful moral action, I am employing the term "formation" to characterize his goal, rather than "education," which currently has a more narrow connotation. Further, "habituation" has too passive a connotation for the process Aristotle describes.

2. Paul A. Rahe, *Republics Ancient and Modern* (Chapel Hill: University of North Carolina Press, 1992), 24.

3. "The American Constitution is not the same thing as the American way of life. *Politieia* means the way of life of a society rather than its constitution. Yet it is no accident that the unsatisfactory translation 'constitution' is generally preferred to the translation 'way of life of a society.' When speaking of constitution, we think of government; we do not necessarily think of government when speaking of the way of life of a community. When speaking of *politeia*, the classics thought of the way of life of a community as essentially determined by its 'form of government.' We shall translate *politeia* by 'regime,' taking regime in the broad sense in which we sometimes take it when speaking, e.g., of the Ancien Régime of France. The thought connecting 'way of life of a society' and 'form of government' can provisionally be stated as follows: The character, or tone, of a society depends on what the society regards as most respectable or most worthy of admiration. But by regarding certain habits or attitudes as most respectable, a society admits the superiority, the superior dignity, of those human beings who most perfectly embody the habits or attitudes in question. That is to say, every society regards a specific human type (or a specific mixture of human types) as authoritative. When the authoritative type is the common man, everything has to justify itself before the tribunal of the common man; everything which cannot be justified before that tribunal

becomes, at best, merely tolerated, if not despised or suspect. And even those who do not recognize that tribunal are, willy nilly, molded by its verdicts. What is true of the society ruled by the common man applies also to societies ruled by the priest, the wealthy merchant, the war lord, the gentleman, and so on. In order to be truly authoritative, the human beings who embody the admired habits or attitudes must have the decisive say within the community in broad daylight: they must form the regime. When the classics were chiefly concerned with the different regimes, and especially with the best regime, they implied that the paramount social phenomenon, or that social phenomenon than which only the natural phenomena are more fundamental, is the regime." Leo Strauss, *Natural Right and History* (Chicago: University of Chicago Press, 1953), 136–37.

4. David Cohen, *Law, Violence, and Community in Classical Athens* (Cambridge: Cambridge University Press, 1995), 23.

5. For an account of the relationship between Aristotelian and modern social theories arguing that the Aristotelian variety is more encompassing, see Bernard Yack, *The Problems of a Political Animal* (Berkeley: University of California Press, 1993), 43–50.

6. "Since we cannot ever become virtuous by our own individual efforts, the shaping or habituating influence of law and custom is a necessary condition for the development of virtuous or flourishing personalities; it is biologically impossible for us to hope to skip over culture or to replace it with a set of rational principles. Thus music education, which trains us to be pleased by and, whenever we can, to emulate the right kind of exemplary characters or personalities, is the most significant, though not the most pressing, part of political life. But this process of socialization is sufficient only to the extent that the conventions that inform it are in turn informed by a true conception of the human good *and* by a solid grasp of local circumstances. Just as a personality or a way of life may be based on a mistaken perception of what it means to live well, so may a *polis* or culture. Thus there may be a difference between a good human being without qualification and a good citizen of a particular city." Stephen Salkever, "Aristotle's Social Sciences," in *Essays on The Foundations of Aristotelian Political Science,* ed. Carnes Lord and David O'Connor (Berkeley: University of California Press, 1991), 12. See also his *Finding the Mean: Theory and Practice in Aristotelian Political Philosophy* (Princeton: Princeton University Press, 1990), 65ff.

7. Indeed, as Bodéüs points out, Aristotle analyzes education in the same terms that he analyses "comprehension" *(sunesis),* presented in *NE,* 6 as an exclusively critical capacity *(kritike monon).* Bodéüs, *Political Dimensions,* 104–6.

8. So Richard Bodéüs has argued that since one's own regime is formative, education in the Aristotelian sense must proceed by forming the political leaders of the regime so that they will, in turn, form fellow citizens properly through law. Thus Bodéüs concludes that Aristotle's goal in the *Ethics* and *Politics* is to guide the work of legislators so that they can enhance human flourishing in their political communities. In short, for Bodéüs, Aristotle's practical goal is to teach the art of lawmaking (*NE,* 1180a33–34). When Aristotle says he wants to make us good, he means that he wants to make us good lawmakers. Aristotle's task is to form legislators who will put into practice Aristotelian insights. "Put into perspective this way, Aristotelian ethics, far from describing an individual ethics alien to politics, presents, on the contrary, the essential body of learning with which the lawgiver must fortify himself when legislat-

ing." So for Bodéüs, the aim of Aristotle's pedagogy is political; it is to change individuals so as to allow them to participate vigorously in politics so that the regime itself can be changed to better form individuals. Bodéüs, *Political Dimensions*, 123. Bodéüs's work has been corrected and expanded in important articles by Paul VanderWaerdt. See especially his "Political Intention," 77–89.

9. Since the cause of civil strife is injustice, the best way to avoid it is to make regimes more and more just. So, for example, Aristotle tells both democracies that tyrannize over the minority and oligarchies that tyrannize over the majority to moderate their rule in the direction of justice by mixing their deficient regimes together. He tells tyrants to moderate their rules in the direction of stewardship, for by caring for their subjects justly they can make their reign more stable (*P,* 5.12). In every case, regimes are made more stable by drawing them more toward moderation (*P,* 1313a18–19).

10. For this point, see Paul VanderWaerdt, "The Plan and Intention of Aristotle's Ethical and Political Writings," *Illinois Classical Studies* 15: 244ff.

11. See for example, Carnes Lord, "The Character and Composition of Aristotle's *Politics*," *Political Theory* 9 (1981): 459–78; Christopher Rowe, "Aims and Methods in Aristotle's *Politics*," in *A Companion to Aristotle's* Politics. ed. David Keyt and Fred Miller (Oxford: Basil Blackwell, 1991): 70–72.

CHAPTER 2. THE PROBLEM OF AUDIENCE

I owe much of my account of Aristotle's treatment of his audience's perspective on action to David O'Connor, "The Ambitions of Aristotle's Audience" in *Action and Contemplation: Studies in the Moral and Political Thought of Aristotle*, ed. Robert Bartlett and Susan Collins (Albany: State University of New York Press, 1999), 107–29.

1. For a good discussion of the texts in question, see Bodéüs, *Political Dimensions*, 97ff.

2. Strauss, *Natural Right and History* (Chicago: University of Chicago Press, 1953), 151–57; Strauss, *The City and Man* (Chicago: University of Chicago Press, 1964), 27–28; Strauss, "On Classical Political Philosophy," in *What is Political Philosophy?* (Chicago: University of Chicago Press, 1959), 78–82.

3. Strauss, *The City and Man*, 25–26.

4. Tessitore, *Reading Aristotle's* Ethics, 17.

5. Ibid., 104–7.

6. Friederich Nietzsche, *On the Genealogy of Morals*, trans. Walter Kaufmann, (New York: Vintage Books, 1967), 33.

7. It could be argued that the discussion of justice in *Ethics* 5 reveals that the audience is wholeheartedly committed to virtue because the text asserts that the virtuous life is the lawful life. Yet I think this text points to the same ambiguity latent in a commitment to noble action. Specifically, Aristotle says that the ruling element in each regime determines the content of virtue because it always acts on some determinant conception of what the good is (*NE*, 1129b12–18). Yet since Aristotle emphasizes repeatedly in the *Ethics* and *Politics* that actual rulers are invariably partial, their conceptions of virtue will also be partial. Thus while rulers will stick to their insistence that their laws foster virtue, Aristotelians have every reason to suppose that in fact they foster faction, dominance, and even despotism.

8. O'Connor expands on this point as follows: "Aristotle is usually read

as if he presupposed a moral decency that refuses to see anything attractive about tyranny. This view seems to be based on the well-known passages in the *Nicomachean Ethics* where Aristotle points to three qualities he presupposes in his audience. First, the audience must accept the variety and variability of what counts as noble and just, the subject matter of political science (*NE,* 1094b11–1095a4-9). . . . Second, they must be able to change and control their desires in light of instruction (*NE,* 1095a4–9). Third, they must not be dazzled by highfalutin accounts of the good or by dialectical sharpness, sticking to their convictions (which Aristotle in the immediate sequel calls "the 'that'") sometimes even in the face of arguments to the contrary (*NE,* 1095a22–28). None of these three qualities presupposes much by way of particular moral commitments. Aristotle is primarily concerned that his audience have developed some judgement and discretion, and take direction well. There is no reason to think that a man who burns with ambition and wonders if tyrants can live successful lives, for example, must also fail to be a good listener, or be unable to put into practice what he learns." "The Ambitions of Aristotle's Audience." 110–11.

9. "*Eudaimonia,* the condition which indicates the goodwill of a supernatural being, occasionally requires the translation 'happiness,' but it was more often applied to material wealth, sometimes to high standing and honor, and rarely to a state of mind. . . ." K. J. Dover, *Greek Popular Morality in the Time of Plato and Aristotle* (Indianapolis: Hackett Publishing Company, 1974), 174.

10. Henry George Liddle and Robert Scott, eds., *An Intermediate Greek-English Lexicon* (Oxford: Clarendon Press, 1990), 322.

11. Jean-Pierre Vernant, "Death with Two Faces," in *Reading the Odyssey: Selected Interpretive Essays,* ed. Seth Schein (Princeton: Princeton University Press, 1996), 61.

12. Here it might be argued that Odysseus does not leave Calypso for glory, for his immortality is already assured. After all, men like Menelaos have survived the expedition and remember his deeds at Troy. Consequently, it could be argued that Odysseus leaves Calypso not for immortality among men but only for home and hearth. However, this confuses the perspective of the reader with that of Odysseus. While the reader knows that Odysseus is celebrated for his deeds at Troy, Odysseus himself does not at the beginning of the story. In fact, as he journeys home he takes care to become his own bard to the Phaiakians, singing praise to his actions both to guarantee safe passage home and to insure his memory. In addition, as long as Odysseus remains alive, he has the opportunity to participate in the substance of divine immortality through shining deeds. Staying in Calypso's cave is like death inasmuch as there are no opportunities for noble deeds there.

13. See Jean-Pierre Vernant, "The Refusal of Odysseus," in *Reading the* Odyssey*: Selected Interpretive Essays,* ed. Seth Schein (Princeton: Princeton University Press, 1996), 185–90.

14. For an excellent interpretation which emphasizes the centrality of the theme of home in the *Odyssey,* including home as a consolation for Odysseus's choice for mortality, see Wendell Berry, *The Unsettling of America: Culture and Agriculture* (San Francisco: Sierra Club Books, 1977), 123–31.

15. I owe this point to Edward Goerner, "Political Culture: Classical Aristocratic Virtue" (Notre Dame, Ind.: University of Notre Dame, 1983).

16. I am using Robert Fitzgerald's translation of the *Iliad* (Chicago: University of Chicago Press, 1951), 206. See also *Iliad* 9. 318–323. An even more emphatic assertion of the same point comes in the *Odyssey,* when Achilles says

he would rather be a farmer's slave alive on earth than king of the dead. See *Odyssey* 11, 570–81.

17. Robert Vacca, "The Theology of Disorder in the *Iliad*," *Religion and Literature* 23 (1991), 17.

18. Rahe, *Republic: Ancient and Modern*, especially 198–202.

19. Josiah Ober, *Mass and Elite in Democratic Athens* (Princeton: Princeton University Press, 1989).

20. Ober, *Mass and Elite*, 84–85; Salkever, "Politics of Virility," 165–90.

21. Thucydides, *History of the Peloponnesian War*, trans. Rex Warner (New York: Penguin Books, 1954), 402–3.

22. Ibid., 404. Of course, this speech immediately precedes the conquest of Melos and the slaughter of its residents.

23. "The more success, the more *arete*; and the person who has the most *arete* of all, in a city that contains one, is the tyrant . . . for *arete* is manifest first and foremost in one's prosperity and that of one's *oikos* [household] and *philoi* [loved ones], and in the qualities which serve to produce or maintain that prosperity; and who more than the tyrant has fulfilled the requirements of *arete*?" A. W. H. Adkins, *Moral Values and Political Behaviour in Ancient Greece: From Homer to the End of the Fifth Century* (New York: W. W. Norton and Company, 1972), 67–68.

24. I use "virtue-as-virility" because of the centrality of manliness to the conventional Greek understanding of human excellence. I use "virtue-as-equity" because Aristotle argues for the identification of equity *(epiekeia)* with the whole of excellence. Indeed, after his treatment of equity in *NE*, 5, he uses *epiekeia* as a synonym for "goodness" throughout the rest of the *Ethics* (see, for example, 1137a35–1137b1, where he says that many people use *epiekeia* as a synonym for "goodness." See also 1107b11; 1158b23; 9.4 generally; 1166a10; 1167b5; *P*, 1308b27; 1452b34). MacIntyre goes so far as to say that for this reason we ought to translate *epiekeia* as "reasonableness." *Whose Justice? Which Rationality?* (Notre Dame, Ind.: University of Notre Dame Press, 1988), 119–20.

25. Thucydides, 405.

26. My distinction between virtue-as-equity and virtue-as-virility differs substantially from Alasdair MacIntyre's distinction between the goods of effectiveness and the goods of excellence. The difference for MacIntyre between these two goods is that the good reasons for action in the case of the goods of excellence will have force for us only insofar as we care about or understand the goods specific to that form of activity. On the other hand, the goods of effectiveness begin not from a conception of the good, but from an understanding of the self as directed toward something by way of need or desire, whose achievement will satisfy. (MacIntyre, *Whose Justice? Which Rationality?*, 30–46). In the case of my distinction, however, the difference between these conceptions of virtue is not that one is motivated by desire and the other by some conception of the good. Rather, both are motivated by attractions to modes of existence experienced as good. The choice here is not between good and desires, but between a desire for different kinds of goods. Indeed, it seems highly un-Aristotelian of MacIntyre not to emphasize that every desire is a desire for some object or way of life experienced as good (*NE*, 1094a1–3; *P*, 1252a1–6).

27. In Plato's *Republic*, Gyges was a Lydian shepherd who found a ring making him invisible. He immediately contrived to meet and kill the king, marrying his wife and ruling as a tyrant in his stead. For him, it was best to appear to be virtuous and in reality be vicious.

28. Adkins, *Moral Values,* 139–40.

29. See his use in this passage of "it appears" *(phainetai)* and "it seems" *(dokei)* at *NE,* 1095b31–32.

30. Of course, virtue-as-equity cannot overcome fortune. But since human beings are always subject to suffering, disease, unjust treatment by their fellows, and ultimately death, it is not clear that virtue-as-virility can overcome it either. Machiavelli argues for a transvaluation of values because classical notions of virtue-as-equity cannot overcome fortune. From an Aristotelian perspective, the question is whether one should suffer or do wrong. Even on the rack, Aristotle says, the best man will not have done the worst things. Thus he will avoid utter misery. Aristotle's problem with Machiavelli's critique is that Machiavelli is more afraid of death than of doing wrong.

31. Mircea Eliade, *Myth and Reality* (New York: Harper and Row, 1963), 126; Walter Burkert, *Greek Religion,* trans. John Raffan, (Cambridge: Harvard University Press, 1985), chapter 4. As Eliade points out, this homology was common to many ancient cultures. For the Jewish people, sleep was comparable to death (see Job 3:13–15; 3:17). Early Christians accepted and elaborated on this homology of death and sleep: *in pace dormit*; *dormit in somno pacis*; *in pace Domini dormias.* For this reason, in ancient cultures awakening from sleep had a therapeutic connotation. See, for example, Gorgias's objection to Socrates awakening of the people against their will at *Gorgias,* 505d. Or, witness Socrates' insistence that Athens needs him around, and if they strike him dead, they will sleep on the rest of their lives, unless the god sends them another gadfly to rouse them from slumber (*Apology,* 30e).

32. So while Tessitore has cleared important ground in articulating the importance of audience in Aristotle's *Ethics,* his account is plagued by univocal treatments of terms such as "morality," "virtue," "nature," "philosophy," "and "friendship." For example, his univocal understanding of nature leads him to identify what is conventional with what is quasi-artificial; that is, "not fully natural" (*Reading Aristotle's Ethics,* 81). Or witness his denigration of political friendship because it is "friendship *only in an analogous sense. . . .*" (89, my emphasis). Here Tessitore's use of the qualifier "only" and his resulting assertions about the necessary divergence between philosophy and politics make it clear that he does not understand the meaning of analogy or its importance for Aristotle's treatment of political things. Analogical terms are those that resist both definition and the application of a single account that does not vary from one context to another, yet still demand employment in diverse contexts in spite of acknowledged differences in meaning. In short, analogical language is necessary for realities that are both different and alike. So Tessitore is right to say that for Aristotle political friendship is different from philosophic friendship. Yet he is wrong to miss that Aristotle's treatment of friendship entails that they are similar as well (see 73–74). Tessitore's treatment is univocal because it points to differences in meaning without attending to similarities. Perhaps this univocity forces him to posit a necessary divergence between philosophy and politics. In much the same way, his discussion of morality and virtue are univocal, thus forcing him to miss the possibility that Aristotle's audience might have held equivocal conceptions of virtue.

33. Cohen, *Law, Violence, and Community,* 62.

34. As Ober has pointed out, for example, elites in Athens could only succeed politically by appealing to the convictions of the masses: "When they addressed the demos, or a fraction of it, the members of the educated elite participated in a drama in which they were required to play the roles of common

men and to voice their solidarity with egalitarian ideals. This drama served as a mechanism of social control over the political ambitions of the elite. Only if they played their demotic roles well were the elite political orators allowed to 'step out of character' and assert their claims to special consideration" *Mass and Elite in Democratic Athens*, 191.

35. This complacency and smugness would have been compounded if Aristotle's audience were young. For a sketch of the problems persuading young people, see *R*, 1389a2–b12.

36. With slight changes, this translation is taken from W. R. M. Lamb, *Lysis, Symposium, Gorgias* (Cambridge: Harvard University Press, 1973), 391. Of course, this passage is delightfully ironic, since Socrates hung around the market all day and showed remarkable courage in battle at Potidea. For this, see *Symposium*, 220b–221e. Compare with 223d.

37. Socrates wanted to know the meaning of the cosmos. As Jacob Klein says, "The term 'world' or *kosmos* in Greek as well as in English, does not mean—and never meant—simply the sum total of all existing things. It means rather the peculiar way in which the diverse parts are suitably arranged to form one whole or a 'universe'. An account of the wholeness of all that is implies of necessity an account of the intrinsic order (taxis) which makes the whole a whole." See his "Aristotle: An Introduction," in *Lectures and Essays by Jacob Klein*, ed. Robert E. Williamson (Annapolis, Md.: University of Maryland Press, 1978), 187–88.

38. These examples from modern science are somewhat misleading as a way of illuminating the failure of pre-Socratic science because ancient science was not divided up into discrete areas of inquiry as modern science is. Part of the reason pre-Socratic science could promise a comprehensive knowledge of the cosmos was that it did not divide the inquiry up into parts, but rather sought to understand the universe as a whole, for example, by reducing it to its most basic elements. Indeed, it seems that the contemporary division of science stems from a realization that the whole must be divided into discrete parts in order to investigate it profitably, because the whole is inaccessible to us simply. Thus Socrates' failure to achieve knowledge of the order of the universe through pre-Socratic science led him to initiate the philosophical method of *diaresis* or division, which modern science inherits. Thus the fact that modern scientists still operate under this paradigm implies they realize on some inchoate level that a grand theory of the whole is impossible through their own methods.

CHAPTER 3. APPROACHING THE VIRTUES

1. For this point see W. F. R. Hardie, "'Magnanimity' in Aristotle's *Ethics*," *Phronesis* 23 (1978), 63.

2. Stanley Hauerwas and Charles Pinches, *Christians Among the Virtues: Theological Conversations with Ancient and Modern Ethics* (Notre Dame, Ind.: University of Notre Dame Press, 1977), 46. The authors also comment, "The deep difference between Aristotle and Christianity is not that the one teaches us to desire happiness and the other does not. Rather, it is to be found in the different accounts of the kind of person we must be if we are to be genuinely happy—which, of course, means what Aristotle and Christians mean by being happy is quite different. In portions of his *Nicomachean Ethics* Aristotle suggests we can be happy only if we achieve a self-sufficiency that guards us against outrageous fortune." Hauerwas and Pinches, *Christians Among the Virtues*, 15.

3. "[T]he essence of pagan virtue assumed by Aristotle served to elevate its possessor. Likewise, the friendship of virtue, by creating equality and similarity among its participants, cannot but at the same time place distance between them and others who do not share it, or do not share their virtue." Hauerwas and Pinches, *Christians Among the Virtues*, 46.

4. "Although this person [the magnanimous man] must only seek honours as rewards for a true exercise of virtue, he is still primarily motivated by this seeking for public acclaim . . . . Not only does the magnanimous man seek to be liberal, he seeks to outshine others in liberality, which implies a competition for limited economic resources. He prefers to be a benefactor rather than receive benefit, and if this sounds possibly 'Christian,' one must note that he also remembers his giving rather than his receiving, and is encouraged to be 'haughty' to those above him in station, but to 'hold back' to those below. The jealousy of munificence shows that Aristotle's ideal of virtue is not perfectly separable from a heroic pursuit of honor. Excellence is still in some measure 'effectiveness,' which can emerge only from engagement in an *agon* [conflict or competition]." John Millbank, *Theology and Social Theory: Beyond Secular Reason* (Oxford: Blackwell, 1990), 352.

5. Ibid., *Theology and Social Theory*, 359–60.

6. Hauerwas and Pinches, *Christians Among the Virtues*, 28.

7. John Casey, *Pagan Virtues* (Oxford: Clarendon Press, 1990), 208. Harry Jaffa, in his excellent *Thomism and Aristotelianism* (Westport, Conn.: Greenwood Press, 1979), also praises Aristotle's praise for the magnanimous man. In some respects, his criticism of christianity mirrors Casey's, although the focus of that criticism is on Thomas and how Thomas's christianity forces statesmen to uphold exceptionless rules of conduct that interfere with decent politicians in their struggle to do what is right. For a critique of this account, see my "The Order of Presentation and the Order of Understanding in Aquinas' Account of Law," *Review of Politics* 57:4 (winter 1995): 607–40.

8. Hadot, *Philosophy as a Way of Life*, 105.

9. "We are led by Aristotle's remarks on the differences between inquiries [i.e., between inquiries directed to knowing what virtue is and inquiries which aim at making us good] about the limits imposed on the present practical study by the nature of its object and end. As for the former, we are told that we can expect only as much precision as the subject matter will admit. . . . (*NE*, 1094b12–27; 1103b35–1104a11; 1107a28–32). As for the latter, might it be the case that the treatment of some problems will extend only so far as is necessary to insure right action?" Thompson, "Aristotle: Philosophy and Politics, 112.

10. Socrates appeals to the same experience of moral weakness when he divides the soul into rational and irrational parts. See *Republic,* 437cff, especially 440c, where Socrates talks about the "faction" of the soul which has warring parts with different arms. See also *Phaedrus,* 246ff.

11. Aristotle complements his example of physical paralysis by comparing the reason-having element of the soul to someone listening to a father. But the same kinds of problems apply here. We do not always listen to our fathers. Indeed, often when we are children, we do not understand the rationale behind his commands—even when such commands are perfectly reasonable to an adult, as when one tells a two-year old, "Don't go off with strangers." A small child can obey such a command, but does not necessarily comprehend its rationale. So even when they "listen to reason" and "do the right thing" it is not clear that children really possess reason in the full sense. By implication we are led to ask whether we adults possess reason in the full sense as well.

12. MacIntyre, *Whose Justice? Which Rationality?*, 112.

13. Aristotle thinks that this work is extraordinarily difficult and dangerous. As evidence of this, he gives a citation to Homer's *Odyssey* (9.90–170). In the scene to which he refers, Circe is telling Odysseus how to navigate between Scylla and Charybdis. Now academics are fond of setting up dichotomies between the twin dangers of the Scylla of this and the Charybdis of that in order to argue for their own more moderate account, so it is necessary to recall exactly what Odysseus's choice requires. Circe tells him that he cannot kill either monster, and both will do him damage. But Charybdis's maelstrom will swallow his entire ship, while Scylla will only kill six of his men. He must sail more toward Scylla, for it is better to lose six men than to lose his ship. The implication is clear. The middle way is not at all easy to hit, and human beings, in their effort to reform their own lives and regimes, will go astray. There is no choice but to navigate between the extremes, but nevertheless, we have to proceed knowing exactly what the pitfalls are. Aristotle concludes this section by reiterating just how difficult virtue actually is (*NE*, 1109b12ff).

CHAPTER 4. CRITICIZING THE MORAL VIRTUES

1. It is difficult for us to imagine just how much of classical Greek life was bound up with war. "Small landholders and craftsmen with their own armor on their backs were liable to be called up from the city's muster rolls for military service any summer after their eighteenth birthday until they turned sixty. In the fifth and fourth centuries, battle broke out in the Greek world nearly two out of every three years, so the chances were good that a man would have to leave his farm, take up his arms, fight in repeated engagements, and fall wounded or die one summer's day in battle." Victor Davis Hanson, *The Western Way of War: Infantry Battle in Classical Greece* (Berkeley, University of California Press, 1989), 31.

2. "Those who are able effectively to defend the group . . . must unite themselves in courage, strength, wealth, and high-birth; and since these are the qualities of which society holds itseld to be in most need, they are denoted by *agathos*, *esthos*, and *arete*," Adkins, *Moral Values*, 73.

3. See Rahe, *Republics Ancient and Modern*, 34.

4. This argument against the usual practice of courage is substantially the same as that which appears in the Platonic dialogues. In the *Phaedo*, for example, Socrates argues that all brave men—except philosophers—are brave only by virtue of dread and cowardice. Brave people, he says, only endure death because they fear evils greater than death (68d). Likewise, in the *Laws*, the argument is that shame—understood as fear of public opinion—is the motive for courage for most people (646e–649d).

5. Aristotle's audience would have had intimate knowledge of the requirements of hoplite warfare. In the phalanx, there were no elite troops with highly specialized skills; everything depended on unit cohesion and protecting the men next to you. The line was only as strong as its weakest links. Therefore, excessive risk for individual glory would be extremely dangerous for the group. "Any reckless departure from the line by individuals in quest of personal success was of little value: the resulting penetration in the enemy line was hardly worth the gap left behind. Aristodemos apparently was the most courageous of the Greek hoplites at the battle of Platais, yet after the victory the Spartans passed him over in awarding the prize for valor, since 'in a frantic state he left

the formation to show all his brave deeds.' Indeed, such a departure from the formation to meet the enemy in a single display of martial prowess was the worst thing any soldier might do" Hanson, *The Western Way of War,* 168.

6. See, for example, *Apology* 28b–d. In this regard, see also *Gorgias,* 452d–e; 463d–467b; 481b–522e; *Republic,* 345e–347e; 357a–368c; 473c–592b. As we shall see, in the *Ethics,* Aristotle presents the activity of *theoria* almost solely in terms of the way it satisfies the desire for honor. See also, for example, *P,* 1252b27–1253a39.

7. Clearly, this is not much of a limit. Recently I read news stories of advertising executives promoting the idea of launching into outer space giant billboards that could be seen by millions on earth. Monetary value, apparently, can be put on the heavens.

8. Cohen, *Law, Violence, and Community,* 68–70.

9. Ober, *Mass and Elite in Democratic Athens,* 227. For the same point, see Adkins, *Moral Values,* 64 and 121–6.

10. Cf. Mark 12:41–44.

11. Tyrants take too much from the wrong sources. They appear to be generous because they give away external goods to hold onto their power. But Aristotle insists that they are not extravagant because what they give away cannot be in excess of the amount they possess, since they insist that they possess everything (*NE,* 1120b25–27). Contrary to appearances, tyrants are stingy. Indeed, they are compared to pimps who live off the misfortune of the people they exploit. To compare tyrannical power to pimpery is obviously to devalue it.

12. Compare this with Machiavelli's treatment of liberality: "And for the prince who with his armies lives on plunder, sack, and ransom, who handles what belongs to others, it is necessary that he exercise liberality; otherwise he will not be followed by his soldiers. And of that which does not belong to you or your subjects, you can be a very great giver, as were Cryus, Ceasar, and Alexander; for the spending of what belongs to others does not take away your reputation but adds to it. It is only the spending of what is yours that hurts you. And there is nothing that consumes itself so much as liberality, for you lose the faculty for using it all the while that you use it, and become either poor and despised, or, to avoid poverty, rapacious and hated. And above all other things, a prince ought to guard against being despised and hated, and liberality conducts you to one or the other. Therefore, it is far wiser to have the name of stinginess, which begets an infamy without hatred, rather than to be necessitated, by wanting the name of liberal, to incur the name of rapacious which begets an infamy with hatred." *The Prince,* trans. Leo Paul S. de Alvarez (Prospect Heights, Ill.: Waveland Press, 1980), 98.

13. Clearly, Aristotle is not a Christian. Yet, in reading Aristotle's treatment of generosity, I cannot help but be reminded of the following passage from Augustine, who at the time is seeking to revalue Roman conceptions of manly self-assertion: "Remove justice and what are kingdoms but gangs of robbers on a large scale? What are criminal gangs but petty kingdoms? A gang is a group of men under a commander, bound by a compact of association, in which by the plunder is divided according to an agreed convention.

"If this villainy wins so many recruits from the ranks of the demoralized that it acquires territory, establishes a base, captures cities and subdues peoples, it then openly arrogates to itself by the title of kingdom, which is conferred on it in the eyes of the world, not by the renouncing of aggression but by the attainment of impunity.

"For it was a witty and a truthful rejoinder which was given by a captured pirate to Alexander the Great. The king asked the fellow, 'What is your idea, in infesting by the sea?' And the pirate answered, with uninhibited insolence, 'By the same as yours, infesting the earth! But because I do it with a tiny craft, I'm called a pirate: because you have a mighty navy, you're called an emperor." *City of God,* trans. Henry Bettenson (New York: Penguin Books, 1972), 139.

14. See Cohen, *Law, Violence, and Community*, 64–66.

15. "Men take vengeance because they fear shame and desire to preserve and enhance their reputation as well as because of the pleasure which its contemplation and exaction bring. They also take vengeance because in such societies it is the only way to deter others from harming them. Wilson, in his study of nineteenth-century Corsica, described the 'cultural imperative' to ensure protection through deterrence by not letting any insult pass without retaliation. A man who did not retaliate was a *rimbeccu,* defined in a Corsican trial to mean 'a social outcast, an object of scorn, whom anyone can insult with impunity because he lacks by the courage to retaliate against such insults.'" Ibid., 67.

16. The helplessness experienced by Meno is not the only response to *aporia,* but it may be the response typical of a young self-consciously virile person.

17. This recalls Plato's account in the *Laws* that life is serious play: most people are serious about unserious matters, and unserious about playful matters. But since playful matters are the best, we ought to be most serious about play (653ff).

18. Criticizing Rorty's notion of irony, for example, MacIntyre states, "Ironic detachment involves a withdrawal from our common language and our shared judgments and thereby from by the social relationships which presuppose by the use of that language in making those judgments. But it is in and through those relationships . . . that we acquire and sustain not only our knowledge of others, but also that self-knowledge which depends on the confirmatory judgments of others. So, if my ironic detachment is genuine and not mere pretense, it involves me in putting in question not only my communal allegiances, but even what I have taken to be my self-knowledge. I am to find a vantage point quite outside those relationships and commitments that have made me what I now am. But what might this be?" *Dependent Rational Animals: Why Human Beings Need the Virtues* (Peru, Ill.: Open Court Publishing, 1999), 152–53.

19. Stephen G. Salkever, "Lopp'd and Bound: How Liberal Theory Obscures the Goods of Liberal Practices," in *Liberalism and by the Good,* ed. Bruce Douglas and Gerald M. Mara (New York: Routledge, 1990), 88–89. I think it is imperative also to distinguish irony from satire in order to clarify what irony is. Satire is more serious than irony; it sits in judgement of others and thus presupposes a perspective above those the satirist is judging. By contrast, irony implies that the ironist is embedded in the same kind of foolishness as everyone else. Irony implies commiseration and identity; satire implies superiority.

CHAPTER 5. GREATNESS OF SOUL

1. Alasdair MacIntyre, for instance, finds Aristotle's account of magnanimity "appalling." See his *Short History of Ethics* (New York: Collier Books, 1966), 79 and 76–81 generally. This assessment continues in his more recent

writings. "Notice that to these virtues of giving must be added virtues of receiving: such virtues as those of knowing how to exhibit gratitude, without allowing gratitude to be a burden, courtesy towards the graceless giver, and forbearance towards the inadequate giver. The exercise of these latter virtues always involves a truthful acknowledgement of dependence. And they are therefore virtues bound to be lacking in those whose forgetfulness of their dependence is expressed in an unwillingness to remember benefits conferred by others. One outstanding example, even perhaps the outstanding example of this type of bad character and also of a failure to recognize its badness is Aristotle's *megalopsychos*, about whom Aristotle remarks approvingly, that he 'is ashamed to receive benefits, because it is a mark of a superior to confer benefits, of an inferior to receive them' (*Nicomachean Ethics* 1124b9–10). So the *megalopsychos* is forgetful of what he has received, but remembers what he has given, and is not pleased to be reminded of the former, but hears the latter recalled with pleasure (12–18). We recognize here an illusion of self-sufficiency, an illusion apparently shared by Aristotle, that is all too characteristic of the rich and powerful in many times and places, an illusion that plays its part in excluding them from certain types of communal relationships." *Dependent Rational Animals*, 126–27. I shall argue that MacIntyre is exactly right to recognize the illusion of self-sufficiency at the heart of greatness of soul, but wrong to attribute that attitude to Aristotle. Indeed, because MacIntyre reads this section of the *Ethics* as a treatise, he misses its rich irony.

2. Hardie, "Magnanimity in Aristotle's *Ethics*," 70.

3. Jaffa comments on this passage as follows: "If then magnanimity is especially concerned with honor, and the highest kind is that which we render to the gods, and it is the highest kind that the magnanimous man aims at, then it is for something divine that the magnanimous man strives." *Thomism and Aristotelianism*, 116.

4. Martin Ostwald, trans., *Nicomachean Ethics* (Indianapolis, Ind.: Bobbs-Merril, 1962), p. 97.

5. Liddle and Scott, *Intermediate Greek-English Lexicon*, 114.

6. I owe much of this discussion of eris to Robert Vacca's excellent article on the *Iliad*. See "Theology of Disorder," 1–22.

7. For the theme of the increasing degradation in the treatment of corpses, see Simone Weil, *The* Iliad, *or The Poem of Force* (Wallingford, Pa.: Pendle Hill Press, 1983). See also Jasper Griffin, *Homer on Life and Death* (Oxford: Clarendon Press, 1980), 44–49.

8. In Book 8, some of the gods express anger that Zeus is helping the Trojans win. Zeus warns them about obstructing his plans: "And any one I perceive against the gods' will attempting to go among the Trojans and help them, or among the Danaans,/ he shall go whipped against his dignity back to Olympos;/ or I shall take him and dash him down to the murk of Tartaros. . . . Come, you gods, make this endeavor, that you all may learn this./ Let down out of the sky a cord of gold; lay hold of it/ all you who are gods and all who are goddesses, yet not/ even so can you drag down Zeus from the sky to the ground, not/ Zeus the high lord of counsel, though you try until you grow weary./ Yet whenever I might be strongly minded to pull you,/ I could drag you up, earth and all and sea and all with you, then fetch the golden rope about the horn of Olympos/ and make it fast, so that all once more should dangle in mid air./ So much stronger am I than the gods, and stronger than mortals" *Iliad* 8.10–27.

9. *Griffin, Homer on Life and Death*, chapter 3.

10. The following account of the funeral games and of the reconciliation with Priam is taken from Goerner, "Political Culture."

11. Cohen, *Law, Violence, and Community*, 88.

12. Plato, *Symposium*, trans. Alexander Nehemas and Paul Woodruf (Indianapolis, Ind.: Hackett Publishing, 1989), 48 (204a–204c).

13. "As part of this sum, as an instance of nature, man is only a reed, liable to be crushed at any moment by the forces of an immense and blind universe in which his existence is but a peculiar blind accident, no less blind than would be the accident of his destruction. As a thinking reed, however, he is not part of the sum, not belonging to it, but radically different, incommensurable: for the *res extensa* does not think, so Descartes thought, and nature is nothing but *res extensa*—body, matter, external magnitude. If nature crushes the reed—man—even while crushed, is aware of being crushed. He alone in the world thinks, not because but in spite of his being part of nature. As he shares no longer in a meaning of nature, but merely, through his body, in its mechanical determination, so nature no longer shares in his inner concerns. Thus that by which man is superior to all nature, his unique distinction, mind, no longer results in a higher integration of his being into the totality of being, but on the contrary, marks the unbridgeable gulf between himself and the rest of existence. Estranged from the community of being in one whole, his consciousness only makes him a foreigner in the world and in every act of true reflection tells of this stark foreignness." Hans Jonas, *The Gnostic Religion* (Boston: Beacon Press, 1963), 323.

An analysis of the problem I am pursuing here would not be complete unless it included early Christianity's critical engagement and transformation of the classical culture of honor, as well as of classical philosophy. This is a deeply unsettled problem in political philosophy today, since it is assumed by many sides that since Aristotle uncritically accepts his culture's emphasis on honor, he must be fundamentally anti-Christian, because Christianity criticizes self-assertive pursuit of honor as a species of pride. However, if it is true that Plato and Aristotle are in truth critical of the pursuit of honor, the relationship of classical philosophy to early Christianity would have to be thought through on a new footing. To complete this inquiry would require, for example, a comparison of the criticisms of honor in Plato and Augustine and other Church fathers, for example.

14. MacIntyre, *Dependent Rational Animals*, 83.

CHAPTER 6. JUSTICE, INJUSTICE, AND EQUITY

1. See Dover, *Greek Popular Morality*, 256 and W. K. Guthrie, *The Sophists* (Cambridge: Cambridge University Press, 1971), 60–78.

2. "What is *nomos* is what is 'good for one.' It is more profitable to be *nomos*-acting." Adkins, *Moral Values*, 106.

3. Rahe, *Republics Ancient and Modern*, chapter 1.

4. John Locke, *Two Treatises of Government*, ed. Peter Laslett (Cambridge: Cambridge University Press, 1988), 269; emphasis in the original.

5. "For 'tis with Common-wealths as with particular Persons, they are commonly ignorant of their own Births and Infancies. . . ." Locke, *Two Treatises of Government*, 334.

6. John Rawls, *Political Liberalism* (New York: Columbia University Press, 1993), 194. To be fair to Rawls, he is not completely comfortable with the term

"neutrality" because "some of its connotations are highly misleading, others suggest altogether impractical principles" (191).

7. Theodore Lowi, *The End of the Republican Era* (Norman, Okla.: University of Oklahoma Press, 1995), 15.

8. Quoted in David O'Connor, "Aristotelian Justice as a Personal Virtue" in *Midwest Studies in Philosophy*, vol. 3, ed. Peter French and Theodore Uehling (Notre Dame, Ind.: University of Notre Dame Press, 1988), 49.

9. So *pleonexia* cannot be translated merely as "greed." And "acquisitiveness" does not quite capture the connotation either, as MacIntyre has pointed out (*Whose Justice, Which Rationality?*, 112).

10. See Cohen, *Law, Violence and Community*, 62–63.

11. While in her *Fragility of Goodness* Martha Nussbaum has explored the problem of luck in ancient thought, she does not focus on the social and political problems created by people's tendency to overgrasp for scarce social resources so as to insulate themselves from fate. She emphasizes instead the different ways philosophy tries through reason to manage dependence on fate. Yet since this approach is apolitical it is untrue to Aristotle's framework in the *Nicomachean Ethics* and *Politics*. Her emphasis on managing fate through philosophy seems to make her more of a Stoic than an Aristotelian. See especially the treatment of Stoicism in her *Therapy of Desire: Theory and Practice in Hellenistic Ethics* (Princeton: Princeton University Press, 1994).

12. For a good discussion of the problems of the ancient economy, see William James Booth, *Households: On the Moral Architecture of the Economy* (Ithaca: Cornell University Press, 1993), especially chapter 2.

13. For example, the doctor does not wish to make her patient a little healthy, but as healthy as possible—without limit. However, Aristotle emphasizes that while the end of genuine arts are indeed without limit in this sense, there is a "limit to what exists *for the sake of the end* (*P*, 1257a28, my emphasis). This is not merely a limit on the means directed to the end of the art, although this is part of Aristotle's meaning. In addition, he means that the goods to which the art aims help constitute the practice of the art in such a way as to limit and direct the activities in which the artist engages to bring something into being. In one way, the fruits of an art can be destroyed by overzealous craftsmen who think that the goods they are making are so precious as to justify any practice directed to that goal. For instance a guild which upholds the practice of violin making will be undermined by a member who steals from her fellows in order to make more expensive, better violins. In another way, arts seem to be limited by the fact that they are incapable of helping us to know how to use the goods they produce, or even if such goods ought to be brought into being in the first place. Even when one possesses a true art, such as medicine instead of quackery, that genuine art for Aristotle requires some further excellence in order to make good use of what the art has produced. The study of the art in itself will not result in the wisdom required to use its fruits well. While medicine aims at health, for example, health can be used in a myriad of ways. Some account external to medicine is required to decide how to use the good of health; medical knowledge in itself will not help here. Indeed, as advances in modern medical technology make painfully clear every day, medicine will not tell us when and if health is a good thing to strive for in the first place; it will not tell us when to leave people alone to die in dignity, for instance.

14. David O'Connor, "The Aetiology of Justice," in *Essays on the Foundations of Aristotelian Political Science*, eds. Carnes Lord and David O'Connor(Berkeley: University of California Press, 1991), 163–64

15. See chart in Thomas Hobbes, *Leviathan*, ed. Edwin Castell (Indianapolis: Hackett Publishing, 1994), 160–61.

16. For this taxonomy of passions see Hobbes, *Leviathan*, chapter 11.

17. For the differences between the English liberal tradition of Hobbes and Locke and the German liberal tradition of Hegel, see Francis Fukuyama, *The End of History and the Last Man* (New York: Avon Books, 1992), Part 3.

18. This is the same point Socrates makes in his conversation with Thrasymachus in *Republic* 1. Thrasymachus identified justice with the advantage of the stronger. Socrates, however, easily exposes this defective argument by pointing out that unless a strong person knows his own interest, he may use his power and strength in a way that actually works to his disadvantage. Strength —or money or power generally—requires reflection in order to know how to use it properly. In the absence of such reflection, people struggling for such scarce resources are arming themselves dangerously, at great risk to their own happiness and their society.

19. "It is indeed true that 'It is not from the benevolence of the butcher, the brewer or the baker, that we expect out dinner, but from their regard to their own interest' (Adam Smith, *The Wealth of Nations* 1, ii). And just as the butcher, brewer, and baker generally act with regard to their own interest, so too do their customers. But, if on entering the butcher's shop as an habitual customer I find him collapsing from a heart attack, and I merely remark 'Ah! Not in a position to sell me my meat today, I see,' and proceed immediately to his competitor's store to complete my purchase, I will have obviously and grossly damaged my *whole* relationship to him, including my economic relationship, although I will have done nothing contrary to the norms of the market. Less obviously and less grossly, even if I respond to his condition only by satisfying those minimum requirements that will enable me to rebut quasilegal accusations of irresponsibility—I call an ambulance and the moment the medical technicians arrive I leave—I will still have undermined my relationship to him and his, by my avoidance of my larger responsibility. Market relationships can only be sustained by being embedded in certain types of local nonmarket relationships, relationships of uncalculated giving and receiving, if they are to contribute to overall flourishing, rather than, as they so often in fact do, undermine and corrupt communal ties," Alasdair MacIntyre, *Dependent Rational Animals*, 117.

20. Hobbes, *Leviathan*, 160–61.

21. "Hobbes identified the rational life with the life dominated by the fear of fear, by the fear which relieves us from fear. Moved by the same spirit, Locke identifies the rational life with the life dominated by the pain which relieves us from pain. Labor takes the place of the art which imitates nature; for labor is, in the words of Hegel, a negative attitude toward nature. The starting point of human efforts is misery: the state of nature is a state of wretchedness. The way toward happiness is a movement away from nature: the negation of nature is the way toward happiness. And if the movement toward happiness is the actuality of freedom, freedom is negativity. Just like the primary pain itself, the pain which relieves pain 'ceaseth only in death.' Since there are therefore no pure pleasures, there is no necessary tension between civil society as the mighty leviathan or coercive society, on the one hand, and the good life, on the other: hedonism becomes utilitarianism or political hedonism. The painful relief of pain culminates not so much in the greatest pleasures as 'in the having those things which produce the greatest pleasures.'" Strauss, *Natural Right and History*, 250–51. Of course, an ambiguous attitude toward modern progress is raised to a fundamental principle in Rousseau. This is obvious in the *Second Discourse*, where Rous-

seau says that the first person to enclose a piece of ground was the real founder of civil society. In turn, the attack on civil society is not merely an attack on property but also on the unhappiness caused by the way civil society increases desire. Jean-Jacques Rousseau, *The First and Second Discourses,* ed. Roger Masters (New York: St. Martin's Press, 1964), 141–49. This theme of the problems attending an increase in desire is most fully explored in his *Émile.* The argument there is that since happiness is the adequate fit between desire and satisfaction, any increase in desire causes unhappiness. The educational program is thus devoted to restraining desire, thus delaying the birth of the selfish form of self-love. Jean-Jacques Rousseau, *Émile, or On Education,* trans. Allan Bloom (New York: Basic Books, 1970). This sort of critique can also be found in Aquinas, for he argues that pursuit of artificial wealth engenders infinite desires. See Thomae Aquinatis, *Summa Theologiae* 1–2 (Madrid: Bibliotecha de Autores), question 2, article 1, reply to objection 3.

22. Rahe, *Republics Ancient and Modern,* 93.

23. This strange duality of liberal societies—their material comfort and their anxiety over the harsh insecurity of the cosmos—is nicely captured, for example, in a typical Steven King horror novel. The setting is usually a bucolic, serene, prosperous, apparently content small town. Yet lurking beneath this apparent peace lies some unspeakable horror which breaks the thin veil of civilization revealing the terror underneath it all. The success of this fiction is only partly due to the obvious storytelling skills of its writer. In addition, King's success is due to the fact that this is the way many experience their own lives.

24. Thus there is at once a strange anxiety and sadness that characterizes liberal democratic regimes, as Tocqueville saw. "Uncertain of his place in society now that all ranks have been levelled, no longer finding a guide in tradition now that the links of time have broken, uncertain of his opinions to the extent that he doubts the value of opinion as such, democratic man does not know how to orient his life. Material goods are the sole fixed point, the sole incontestable value amidst the uncertainty of things." Pierre Manent, *Tocqueville and the Nature of Democracy,* trans. John Waggoner (Lanham, Md.: Rowman and Littlefield, 1996), 59. But since material goods remain as unsatisfying as they always have been, democratic man is unhappy despite having many reasons to celebrate. So Tocqueville says that Americans are sad and grave in their pleasures. See "Why the Americans are so Restless in the Midst of Their Prosperity?" in Alexis de Tocqueville, *Democracy in America,* volume 2, book 2, (New York: Harber Collins, 1969), chapter 13

25. Hobbes, *Leviathan,* 155.

26. "The publique worth of a man, which is the Value set on him by the Common-Wealth, is that which men commonly call Dignity." *Ibid.,* 152.

27. Rawls, *Theory of Justice,* 440–46.

28. "[L]iberalism can be seen as the pursuit of rational recognition, that is, recognition on a universal basis in which the dignity of each person as a free and autonomous human being is recognized by all. What is at stake for us when we choose to live in a liberal democracy is not merely the fact that it allows us the freedom to make money and satisfy the desiring part of our souls. The more important and ultimately more satisfying thing it provides us is recognition of our dignity. Life in a liberal democracy is potentially the road to great material abundance, but it also shows us the way to the completely non-material end of recognition of our freedom. The liberal democratic state values us at our own sense of self-worth." Fukuyama, *End of History,* 200.

29. Rawls, *Theory of Justice*, 14–15.

30. Rawls realizes that there will be people in his society who will be possessed by an exuberant love of crime, political power, honor, lordship, holiness, or moral virtue or philosophy. But what can Rawls do with such people except ship them off to prison or call them insane? For example, Rawls implies that Aquinas is "mad" because he refuses to see the aims of the self as heterogenous. Aquinas is a "dominant end" thinker who subordinates all desire to God (*Theory of Justice*, 554). That is, any rationality that departs from Rawls' view is irrationality. Rawls' reductionist account cannot comprehend the audacity of a saint like Aquinas or a nihilist like Nietzsche.

31. For examples of this theme in Western thought, see, for example, Aquinas, *Summa Theologiae*, 2–2. Q. 60, a. 5, ad. 2, where he talks about judges who must go beyond the letter of the law where the letter is defective. John Locke, *Two Treatises of Government*, ed. Peter Laslett (New York: Cambridge University Press, 1988), 374–80 and Jean-Jacques Rousseau, *On the Social Contract*, trans. Judith Masters (New York: St. Martin's Press, 1978), book 4, chapter 6. While the United States is the only modern Western power with no explicit remedy for emergency situations when the law breaks down, she has a long tradition of granting them. In the early 1970s, for example, one government study identified two hundred laws that give the president virtually unlimited power in situations defined in the law or by the president as a crisis. For this point, see Theodore Lowi, *The Personal President* (Ithaca: Cornell University Press, 1985), 6–7. The authors of the *Federalist Papers* assumed that the president might have to suspend the law during times of emergency (for this see *Federalist* #72). For the best American justification of such powers, see Lincoln's Special Message To Congress, July 4, 1861, in Abraham Lincoln, *Speeches and Writings 1859–1865*, ed. Don E. Fehrenbacher, (New York: The Library of America, 1989), 247–61, especially 252ff. For an excellent articulation of the problem, see Edward Goerner, "Letter and Spirit: The Political Ethics of the Rule of Law Versus the Political Ethics of the Rule of the Virtuous," *Review of Politics* 45 (1983), especially 562–63.

32. This is the conclusion reached by many scholars who discuss Aristotle's conception of equity. For a statement of this position, see, for example, Martha Nussbaum, "Equity and Mercy," *Philosophy and Public Affairs* 22 (1993), especially pp. 92–96.

33. "But, if justice must be understood first as prudence, because all public life includes stochastic elements of sometimes major importance, that would place the making, changing, unmaking, and suspension of the laws and their enforcement in a quite different light. The rules of justice themselves would be seen as rule-of-thumb expressions of the prudent; the rigors of our litigious legalisms would be softened; the laws themselves, and statesmen, and law schools and jurisprudents, and philosophers who argue such matters in the public press would care as much for the encouragement of society as a whole, and especially in its political classes, of a taste for the splendor of a life that was marked by the fair and equitable, and finally for more than its splendor, for the substance itself." Goerner, "Letter and Spirit," 574.

34. So from this point on, "equity" is no longer an adequate translation for "*epiekeia*." See, for example, *NE*, 1137a35–1137b1, where Aristotle says that people use *epieikeia* as a synonym for "good." See also *P*, 1308b27, 1452b34, *NE*, 1158b23, and especially *NE*, 9.4, which includes such striking instances as 1166a10 and 1167b5. Alasdair MacIntyre insists that we ought to translate

epieikeia as "reasonableness," which would make sense if it were seen to be the whole of excellence. See his *Whose Justice? Which Rationality?*, 119–20.

35. An example of this kind of ethos can be glimpsed in Abraham Lincoln's life:

> Once it became Lincoln's duty to give an official reprimand to a young officer who had been court-martialed for a quarrel with one of his associates. The reprimand is probably the gentlest record in the annals of penal discourses, and it shows in few words the principles which ruled the conduct of this great and peaceable man:
>
> "The advice of a father to his son, 'Beware of entrance to a quarrel, but, being in, bear it, that the opposer may beware of thee,' is good, but not the best.
>
> "Quarrel not at all. No man resolved to make the most of himself can spare time for personal contention. Still less can he afford to take all the consequences, including the vitiation of his temper and loss of self-control.
>
> "Yield larger things to which you can show no more than equal right; and yield lesser ones, though clearly your own.
>
> "Better give your path to a dog than be bitten by him in contesting for the right. Even killing the dog would not cure the bite."

(Anthony Gross, *The Wit and Wisdom of Abraham Lincoln* [New York: Barnes and Noble, Inc., 1992], 187–88).

CHAPTER 7. TURNING REPUTABLE OPINION UPSIDE DOWN

1. For this account, see Eric Voegelin, *Anamnesis*, trans. Gerhart Niemeyer (Columbia: University of Missouri Press, 1978), especially 69–70.

2. In *NE*, 6, *phronesis* is compared to *aisthesis* five times: 1142a27–30; 1143b14; 1144a29; 1144b1–17; 1143b5. For this point, see Richard Sorabji, "Aristotle on the Role of Intellect in Virtue," in ed. Amelie O. Rorty *Essays on Aristotle's* Ethics (Berkeley: University of California Press, 1980), 149.

3. Voegelin, *Anamnesis*, 63

4. Thompson, "Aristotle: Philosophy and Politics," 114.

5. *Ibid.*, 120.

6. It is striking to note that the anti-Aristotelian John Rawls is one of the originators of this account of "Aristotelian" rationality. See *A Theory of Justice*, 549 and especially section 65, where he discusses the "Aristotelian Principle."

7. Cooper, *Reason and the Human Good,* 96. For similar accounts along these lines, see, for example, W. F. R. Hardie, "The Final Good in Aristotelian Ethics," *Philosophy* 40 (1965), 237; John Finnis, *Natural Law and Natural Rights* (Oxford: Clarendon Press, 1980), 103ff; Richard Kraut, *Aristotle on the Human Good* (Princeton: Princeton University Press, 1989), 156; Sorabji, "Intellect in Virtue," 206.

8. See, for example, my criticism of John Finnis's rule morality in Thomas W. Smith, "John Finnis' Questions and Answers: An Ethics of Hope or Fear?" *American Journal of Jurisprudence* 40 (1995): 27–49.

9. Aristede Tessitore, "Aristotle's Ambiguous Account of the Best Life," *Polity* 25 (1992): 200–209.

10. Thompson, "Aristotle: Philosophy and Politics," 114–15. My account in this paragraph is taken from Thompson's excellent article.

11. Cooper, *Reason and the Human Good*, 87–88.

12. The full sentence reads, "*Skepteon de palin kai peri aretes*" (*NE,* 1144b1). "*Palin*" has a variety of meanings. When used spatially with reference to a place, it connotes "backwards." But with reference to speech, it has the connotation of contradiction, or to go back on one's word, or to retract what has been said. It can also be translated "contrariwise" when setting up oppositions. (*LSJ,* 587). For example, Socrates calls his second speech in the *Phaedrus* a *palinode* (257a). In this speech he takes back what he said in his first.

13. With reference to persons, *kurios* means having power and authority. Thus the usual translation is "authoritative," which I have kept. Yet this translation is misleading, insofar as citizens of liberal democracies are sometimes suspicious of persons claiming authority, homologizing "authority" with "irrational domination." Yet given the fact that Aristotle identifies authoritative virtue with the possession of practical wisdom and natural virtue with mere cleverness, if we read "authoritative" this way we are liable to misunderstand what Aristotle is getting at. When not used of persons, *kurios* means "ratified," "valid," or "legitimate." Thus given the context, Aristotle's use of the term *kurios* must mean "authoritative in the sense of reasonable and legitimate." (*LSJ,* 458).

14. Socrates states that virtue is *phronesis* in several different places. See, for example, *Meno* 88a–89a. *Phaedo* 69a–b.

15. Indeed, modern translators sometimes use "in accord with right rule" to translate *kata ton orthon logon.* As MacIntyre points out, "[T]here are bound to be occasions on which no formulation is available in advance; it is on such occasions that we have to act *kata ton orthon logon* ('according to right reason,' *Nicomachean Ethics* 1138b25), a phrase misleadingly translated by W. D. Ross 'in accordance with the right rule.' (This misreading by someone who is usually a meticulous translator of Aristotle is perhaps not unimportant; for it reflects the large and un-Aristotelian preoccupation with the rules of modern moral philosophers)." *After Virtue: A Study in Moral Theory,* 2nd. ed. (Notre Dame, Ind.: University of Notre Dame Press, 1984), 153.

16. Recall that at the outset of his discussion of the moral virtues, Aristotle asked a series of question. What are the virtues? What do they deal with? How do they operate? Once we address these, he says, we can determine how many virtues there are. The answer, finally, is that there is only one virtue. See *NE,* 1115a4–5).

17. This paragraph is a highly condensed summary of a long articulation of reputable opinion. In this account, Aristotle lays out the reputable opinion about the status and nature of moral strength and moral weakness, which are contrasted according to a variety of criteria:

A. Praise and Blame
   1) Moral strength is good and praiseworthy states of character
   2) but moral weakness is base *(phaulon)* and blameworthy.
B. Following Reason
   1) The morally strong person abides by reason *(logismos)*
   2) but the morally weak person abandons reason.
C. Passion over reason
   1) The morally weak person does bad things at the urging of passion
   2) but the morally strong person knows certain passions are base
D. In what way a person is morally strong or weak
   1) Some run together the self-controlled and the morally strong person, saying that the morally strong person is self-controlled in every respect

2) while others run the morally weak man and the self-indulgent man together.

E. Possession of practical wisdom
1) The practically wise person *(phronimos)* can never be morally weak
2) but the *phronimos* who is clever can.

F. How moral weakness is shown
1) The morally weak person is shown up in situations involving spiritedness *(thumos)*, honor *(time)*, and profit *(kerdous)* because he does the wrong thing in such situations
2) but the morally strong person does the right thing in such situations.

18. Recall that this is exactly the kind of account given at the beginning of the inquiry into virtue. Since most of us are morally paralyzed, we experience action as a conflict between reason and passion, with passion winning much of the time, ignoring the urgings of reason as a child ignores the commands of a father.

19. For a discussion of analogical terms, see David Burrell, *Analogy and Philosophical Language* (New Haven: Yale University Press, 1973).

20. See Aristotle's discussion of the problem of whether one can be unjust to oneself at the end of Book 5. The answer is a qualified yes for Aristotle, for while justice inevitably involves relations to others, in a sense we have relationships with ourselves as well. In order to understand the problem of how to be good to oneself, however, one must understand that it is better to suffer injustice than to do it. Indeed, at the conclusion of Book 5 (*NE,* 1138a28ff) Aristotle reiterates the scheme of Plato's *Gorgias*:

> *Best:* Neither to suffer nor to do injustice
> *Better:* To suffer rather than do injustice
> *Worse:* To do injustice and be properly punished so that reform is possible
> *Worst:* To do injustice and get away with it for in that case there is no possibility of reform. In the case of badness, since pain at doing the wrong act is not present, there is no punishment and thus no possibility of reform.

21. For a discussion of love as a mode of knowledge in classical philosophy see Voegelin, *Anamnesis*, 183ff.

CHAPTER 8. ANALOGOUS COMMUNITIES

1. Nussbaum, *Fragility of Goodness*, 354. Most of the time, I shall simply use the term *philia*, yet when this is awkward, I shall translate the term, using either "friendship" or "love," depending on the context.

2. See, for example, John Cooper, "Aristotle on Friendship" in *Essays on Aristotle's Ethics*, ed. Amélie Rorty, (Berkeley: University of California Press, 1980), 301–40; A. W. Price, *Love and Friendship in Plato and Aristotle* (Oxford: Clarendon Press, 1989); A. D. M. Walker, "Aristotle's Account of Friendship in the *Nicomachean Ethics,*" *Phronesis* 24 (2): 180–96.

3. In Aristotle's own words, "[I]n the primary *(proton)* and authoritative *(kurios)* sense of the term, we call *philia* that which is based on goodness between good people. The other kinds are called *philia* only insofar as they resemble the best kind *(kath 'homoioteta)*" (*NE,* 1157a30-32).

4. MacIntyre, *Dependent Rational Animals*, 108

5. Ober, *Mass and Elite in Democratic Athens*, 229.

6. E. B. White, *Charlotte's Web* (NewYork: Harper and Row, 1952), 163–64. *Charlotte's Web* is the best introduction to Aristotelianism for any age.

7. As MacIntyre points out, this means that Aristotelianism does not accept a hard division between altruism and selfishness: "The kind of life Aristotle is speaking about is not simply altruism. A presupposition of the notion of altruism is a conception of human beings as divided in their inclinations and passions, some of those being self-regarding, others being other-regarding. Altruists are those in whom on occasion at least the other-regarding inclinations and passions prevail over the self-regarding. The altruist is the counterpart to the egoist and there are of course influential accounts of altruism according to which it is either a disguised form of egoism or, in some more sophisticated versions, a transformation of egoism in the interests of satisfying egoism's original goals.

"We do indeed as infants, as children, and even as adolescents, experience sharp conflicts between egoistic and altruistic impulses and desires. But the task of education is to transform and integrate those into an inclination towards both the common good and our individual goods, so that we become neither self-rather-than-other-regarding nor other-rather-than-self-regarding, nether egoists nor altruists, but those whose passions and inclinations are directed to what is both our good and the good of others. Self-sacrifice, it follows, is as much of a vice, as much a sign of inadequate moral development, as selfishness," *Dependent Rational Animals*, 160.

8. Yack, *Problems of a Political Animal*, 28–33.

9. Political theorists are in the habit of claiming that Augustine developed the notion that commonwealths are communities united together by the object of their affection, but in fact Aristotle made the same move as Augustine several hundred years before. "If, on the other hand, another definition than this is found for a 'people,' for example, if one should say, 'A people is the association of a multitude of rational beings united by a common agreement on the objects of their love,' then it follows that to observe the character of a particular people we must examine the objects of its love" Augustine, *City of God*, 19.24. As far as I can see, this is exactly the kind of argument Aristotle employs in *Ethics*, 8–9, although obviously to different ends. Interestingly enough, Augustine, like Aristotle, links justice and love in commonwealths. See *City of God*, 19.21.

10. See Eric Voegelin, *Anamnesis.*

11. This is a theme of Paul Schollmeier, *Other Selves: Aristotle on Personal and Political Friendship* (Albany: State University of New York Press, 1994).

12. By comparing most fathers to cannibalistic Cyclopes, Aristotle implies that they do not provide a context where their wives and children can flourish. It should also be recalled that the Cyclopes were not political. As such, they did not attend to the formation of their household in light of the fact that the household is not self-sufficient. Yet since the interrelatedness of human society renders the household dependent on its larger social and political context, it is not enough to "lay down the law" within one's house in a way that neglects the formative effect of the regime on the household.

13. Yack, *Problems of a Political Animal*, 29–30; 55; 98.

14. This does not mean that Aristotle subsumes the polis into the family, or that the common goods of these communities are the same. The analogical character of *philia* entails that the political community is unlike as well as like the household. So drawing the similarities between family and political life obscures as much as it illuminates. Most obviously, the political community lacks filial ties of natural affection. In addition, Aristotle thinks that most fathers do not care about the formation of their children (*NE,* 1180a29), and politicians fare even worse in his estimation (*NE,* 1180a25; 1180b28–1181a13). If it is difficult to strive for a harmonious family, how much more problematic would it be to strive for a harmonious political community?

15. Yack, *Problems of a Political Animal*, 110–14.

16. See E. A. Goerner, "The Notion of Christendom and the Problem of Justice" *Continuum* 3(1966): 436–53; Finnis, *Natural Law and Natural Rights*, 168; Austin Flannery, *The Sixteen Basic Documents of Vatican II* (Northport, N.Y.: Costello Publishing,1996), 191–92, 195, 256–61; Mary Keys, "Personal Dignity and the Common Good: A Twentieth Century Thomistic Dialogue" in *Catholicism, Liberalism, and Communitarianism: The Catholic Intellectual Tradition and the Moral Foundations of Democracy,* ed. Kenneth Grasso, Gerard V. Bradley, and Robert P. Hunt (Lanham, Md.: Rowman and Littlefield, 1995) 173–95; Thomas Rourke, "Michael Novak and Yves Simon on the Common Good and Capitalism," *Review of Politics* 58 (1996): 229–58.

17. Finnis, *Natural Law and Natural Rights*, 168.

18. Louis Dupré, "The Common Good and the Open Society," *Review of Politics* 55 (1993), 687.

19. Bruce Ackerman, *Social Justice in the Liberal State* (New Haven, Conn.: Yale University Press, 1980), 10–11; John Stuart Mill, *On Liberty,* ed. Aubrey Castell, (Arlington Heights, Ill.: Harlan Davidson, 1947).

20. Hobbes, *Leviathan* , 57–58.

21. Locke, *An Essay Concerning Human Understanding,* ed. Alexander Fraser (New York: Dover Publications, 1959), 350–51.

22. John Rawls, *Theory of Justice*, 395–407; Rawls, *Political Liberalism,* 215, 243–44, 252.

23. Lowi, *Republican Era*, 15, chapter 6; Rawls, *Political Liberalism*, 191–94.

24. Moderation also involves structuring things so that base people will be unable to overreach. Aristotle's silence about the possibility of transforming the desires of the base implies fundamental limits on the possibility of the common good. This recalls his pessimism about the possibility of educating people in virtue in the last chapter of the *Nicomachean Ethics.* See Peter Simpson, *A Philosophical Commentary on Aristotle's* Politics (Chapel Hill: University of North Carolina Press, 1998), 103.

25. Aristotle employs *epiekeia* as a synonym for "goodness" and "reasonableness." See for example *NE,* 1137a35–1137b1; 1107b11; 1166a10; 1167b5; *P,* 1308b27; 1452b34. MacIntyre suggests that we translate *epiekeia* as "reasonableness" *Whose Justice? Whose Rationality,* 119–20.

26. MacIntyre, *After Virtue*, 190.

27. Yack, *Problems of a Political Animal.*

28. Thompson, "Aristotle: Philosophy and Politics," 117–18.

29. MacIntyre, *Dependent Rational Animals*, 131.

30. Hamilton, Madison Jay, *The Federalist Papers,* ed. Clinton Rossiter (New York: Mentor Books, 1961, 78–79).

31. Ibid., 78.

32. Some argue that the Founders followed this Aristotelian prescription in setting up a bicameral legislature in which the excesses of oligarchy would be checked by the excesses of democracy. For such an account, see Paul Eidelberg, *The Philosophy of the American Constitution: A Reinterpretation of the Intentions of the Founding Fathers* (Latham, Md.: University Press of America, 1986), especially chapters 4–8.

33. He admits at the conclusion of the *Ethics* that his arguments will not work on most people (*NE,* 1179b4–20).

34. Abraham Lincoln, "Address to the Young Men's Lyceum of Springfield, Illinois: The Perpetuation of our Political Institutions," in *Abraham Lincoln: Speeches and Writings 1832–1858,* ed. Don E. Feherenbacher, (New York: The Library of America, 1989), 33–34.

35. MacIntyre, *After Virtue,* 191. In turn, for MacIntyre, a practice is "any coherent and complex form of socially established cooperative human activity through which goods internal to that form of activity are realized in the course of trying to achieve those standards of excellence which are appropriate to, and partially definitive of, that form of activity, with the result that human powers to achieve excellence, and human conceptions of the ends and goods involved, are systematically extended. . . . Bricklaying is not a practice; architecture is." *After Virtue,* 187.

36. Aristotle's discussion of when friends should stop being friends is pertinent here. If one becomes virtuous, one will leave behind certain basic elements of one's former life.

37. The foregoing discussion of the relationship between practical wisdom and beauty was suggested to me by my teacher Edward Goerner. In this vein, he says, "[I]n common speech, 'fair' doesn't exclusively mean the arithmetically equal. It is plainly broader than that and refers to any harmony or balance or symmetry and carries the connotation of something that has a pleasing, shining, attractive quality, a certain beauty of the sort that, for example, evokes cries of 'beautiful' from the spectators of a reverse lay-up executed with a smooth, cool, infinitely graceful fluidity of line." "Letter and Spirit," 572.

38. MacIntyre argues that our term "morality" is a holdover from the Enlightenment: "In that period, 'morality' became the name for that particular sphere in which rules of conduct which are neither theological nor legal nor aesthetic are allowed a cultural space of their own. It is only in the later seventeenth century and the eighteenth century, when this distinguishing the moral from the theological, legal and aesthetic has become a received doctrine that the project of an independent rational justification of morality becomes the concern central . . . to Northern European culture." *After Virtue,* 39.

39. For a critique of proportionalism, see John Finnis, *Fundamentals of Ethics* (Washington, D.C.: Georgetown University Press, 1983), chapter 6.

40. See, for example, *Apology,* 31c, 40a–c; *Euthyphro,* 3b; *Republic,* 496c; *Phaedrus,* 242b–c.

CHAPTER 9. HORTATORY CONCLUSIONS

1. This point is made by Ostwald in his translation of the *Nicomachean Ethics,* page 8.

CONCLUSION

1. For overviews of the debate, see David Keyt, "Intellectualism in Aristotle," in *Essays in Ancient Greek Philosophy,* ed. John P. Anton and Anthony Preus (Albany: State University of New York Press, 1983); Tessitore, *Reading Aristotle's Ethics*, chapter 1; Thompson, "Aristotle: Philosophy and Politics"

2. See, for example, Ackrill, "Aristotle on *Eudaimonia,*15–33; John Cooper, *Reason and the Human Good ;* Nussbaum, *Fragility of Goodness,* 373–77.

3. Tessitore, *Reading Aristotle's* Ethics; Tessitore, "Making the City Safe for Philosophy, Book 10," *American Political Science Review* 84 (December 1990): 1251–62.

4. Hardie, "Final Good," 277–95; Kraut, *Aristotle on the Human;* Kraut, "In Defense of the Grand End," *Ethics* 103 (January 1993): 361–74; Carnes Lord, *Education and Culture in The Political Thought of Aristotle* (Ithaca, N.Y.: Cornell University Press, 1982); Amélie Rorty, "The Place of Contemplation in Aristotle's Ethics." in *Essays on Aristotle's Ethics,* ed. Rorty (Berkeley: University of California Press, 1980), 377–94.

5. Nicholas Lobkowicz, "On the History of Theory and Praxis," in *Political Theory and Praxis: New Perspectives,* ed. Terence Ball, trans. Jere Paul Surber, (Minneapolis: University of Minnesota Press, 1977), 13–14.

6. Thompson, "Aristotle: Philosophy and Politics," 120.

7. Salkever, *Finding the Mean,* 146–47.

8. This is the sense in which theory is used by Murray Gell-Mann, *The Quark and the Jaguar* (New York: W. H. Freeman and Company, 1994).

9. The best Aristotelian treatment of this theme can be found in Josef Pieper, *Leisure, The Basis of Culture* (South Bend, Ind.: St. Augustine's Press, 1998).

10. Lobkowicz, "History of Theory and Praxis," 14.

11. Jacob Klein, *Lectures and Essays by Jacob Klein,* ed. Robert E. Williamson (Annapolis, Md.: University of Maryland Press, 1978).

12. This example is taken from Lobkowicz, "History of Theory and Praxis," 17.

13. Cited in Klein, *Lectures and Essays,* 195.

14. This is the set of problems that caused Pierre Hadot to say that classical philosophical texts are really attempts to cultivate a set of spiritual exercises. According to him, returning over and over to a philosophical school's fundamental texts was a way of improving one's practices. See his *Philosophy as a Way of Life,* especially Part 2 and pages 264–76.

15. Cf. Matthew 19:13–30; Mark 10:13–29; Luke 18:15–43.

16. See *Symposium* 204a: "None of the gods loves wisdom or wants to become wise, for they are wise. And no one else who is wise loves wisdom. Yet on the other hand, no one who is ignorant will love wisdom or want to become wise, either. This is because what is especially difficult about being ignorant is that you are satisfied with yourself, even though you are neither beautiful and good nor intelligent. If you don't need anything, of course, you won't desire what you don't think you need."

Bibliography

Ackerman, Bruce. *Social Justice in the Liberal State*. New Haven, Conn.: Yale University Press, 1980.

Ackrill, J. L. "Aristotle on *Eudaimonia*." In *Essays on Aristotle's Ethics*, ed. Amélie Rorty, 7–14. Berkeley: University of California Press, 1980.

Adkins, A. W. H. *Moral Values and Political Behaviour in Ancient Greece: From Homer to the End of the Fifth Century*. New York: W. W. Norton and Company, 1972.

Aquinas, Thomas. *The Literal Exposition on Job*. Trans. Anthony D'Amico. Atlanta: Scholars Press, 1989.

Aquinatis, Thomae. *Summa Theologiae*. Madrid: Bibliotecha de Autores Cristianos, 1985.

Arendt, Hannah. *The Human Condition*. Garden City, New York: Doubleday and Company, 1959.

Aristotelis. *Politica*. Ed. W. D. Ross. Oxford: Oxford University Press, 1986.

———. *Ethica Nicmachea*. Ed. I. Bywater. Oxford: Oxford University Press, 1988.

Aristotle. *Athenian Constitution, Eudemian Ethics, Virtues and Vices*. Trans. H. Rackham. Cambridge: Harvard University Press, 1992.

———. *Nicomachean Ethics*. Trans. Martin Ostwald. Indianapolis: Bobbs-Merril, 1962.

———. *Nicomachean Ethics*. Trans. Terence Irwin. Indianapolis: Hackett Publishing Company, 1985.

———. *Posterior Analytics and Topics*. Trans. H. Tredennick and E. S. Forster. Cambridge: Harvard University Press, 1989.

Augustine. *City of God*. Trans. Henry Bettenson. New York: Penguin Books, 1972.

Barnes, Jonathan. "Aristotle and the Method of Ethics." *Revue Internationale de Philosophie* 34: 430–51.

Berry, Wendell. *The Unsettling of America: Culture and Agriculture*. San Francisco: Sierra Club Books, 1977.

Bodéüs, Richard. *The Political Dimension of Aristotle's* Ethics. Trans. Jan Edward Garret. Albany: State University of New York Press, 1993.

Burkert, Walter. *Greek Religion*. Trans. John Raffan. Cambridge: Harvard University Press, 1985.

Burrell, David. *Analogy and Philosophical Language*. New Haven: Yale University Press, 1973.

Casey, John. *Pagan Virtues*. Oxford: Clarendon Press, 1990.

Chroust, Anton-Hermann. *Aristotle: Protrepticus: A Reconstruction*. Notre Dame, Ind.: University of Notre Dame Press, 1964.

Cohen, David. *Law, Violence, and Community in Classical Athens*. Cambridge: Cambridge University Press, 1995.

Cooper, John. *Reason and the Human Good in Aristotle*. Cambridge: Harvard University Press, 1975.

Cushman, Robert. *Therapeia*. Chapel Hill: University of North Carolina Press, 1958.

deTocqueville, Alexis. *Democracy in America*. Ed. J. P. Mayer. New York: Harper Collins, 1969.

Dover, K. J. *Greek Popular Morality in the Time of Plato and Aristotle*. Indianapolis: Hackett Publishing Company, 1974.

Dupré, Louis. "The Common Good and the Open Society." *Review of Politics* 55 (1993): 687–712.

Eidelberg, Paul. *The Philosophy of the American Constitution: A Reinterpretation of the Intentions of the Founding Fathers*. Latham, Md.: University Press of America, 1986.

Eliade, Mircea. *Myth and Reality*. New York: Harper and Row, 1963.

Evans, J. D. G. *Aristotle's Conception of Dialectic*. Cambridge: Cambridge University Press, 1977.

Finnis, John. *Natural Law and Natural Rights*. Oxford: Clarendon Press, 1980.

———. *Fundamentals of Ethics*. Washington, D.C.: Georgetown University Press, 1983.

Flannery, Austin, ed. *The Sixteen Basic Documents of Vatican II: Constitutions, Decrees, Declarations*. Northport, N.Y.: Costello Publishing, 1996.

Fukuyama, Francis. *The End of History and the Last Man*. New York: Avon Books, 1992.

Gadamer, Hans-Georg. *The Idea of the Good in Platonic-Aristotelian Philosophy*. Trans. P. Christopher Smith. New Haven: Yale University Press, 1986.

Gell-Mann, Murray. *The Quark and the Jaguar*. New York: W. H. Freeman and Company, 1994.

Goerner, Edward. "The Notion of Christendom and the Problem of Justice." *Continuum* 3 (1966): 436–53.

———. "Letter and Spirit: The Political Ethics of the Rule of Law Versus the Political Ethics of the Rule of the Virtuous." *Review of Politics* 45 (1983): 553–75.

———. "Political Culture: Classical Aristocratic Virtue." University of Notre Dame, 1993.

Griffin, Jasper. *Homer on Life and Death*. Oxford: Clarendon Press, 1980.

Gross, Anthony. *The Wit and Wisdon of Abraham Lincoln*. New York: Barnes and Noble, 1992.

Guthrie, William Keith Chambers. *The Sophists*. New York: Cambridge University Press, 1971.

Habermas, Jürgen. *Understanding Social Inquiry*. Notre Dame, Ind.: University of Notre Dame Press, 1977.

Hadot, Pierre. *Philosophy as a Way of Life*. Trans. Michael Chase. Oxford: Blackwell Publishers, 1995.

Hamilton, Alexander, James Madison, and John Jay. *The Federalist Papers*, ed. Clinton Rossiter. New York: Mentor Books,1961.

Hanson, Victor Davis. *The Western Way of War: Infantry Battle in Classical Greece.* Berkeley: University of California Press, 1989.

Hardie, W. F. R. "The Final Good in Aristotelian Ethics." *Philosophy* 40 (1965): 232–47.

———. *Aristotle's Ethical Theory.* Oxford: Oxford University Press: 1968.

———. "Magnanimity in Aristotle's Ethics." *Phronesis* 23 (1978).

Hauerwas, Stanley, and Charles Pinches. *Christans Among the Virtues: Theological Conversations with Ancient and Modern Ethics.* Notre Dame, Ind.: University of Notre Dame Press, 1977.

Havel, Vaclav. "Address to Congress." *Congressional Record—House* (21 February 1990): H392–95.

———. *Summer Meditations.* Trans. Paul Wilson. New York: Vintage Books, 1993.

———. "The Hope for Europe." *New York Review of Books* (29 June 1966): 24–29.

Hobbes, Thomas. *Leviathan.* Ed. Edwin Castell. Indianapolis: Hackett Publishing, 1994.

Homer, *Iliad.* Trans. Robert Fitzgerald. Chicago: University of Chicago Press, 1951.

Jacob, Bernard. "Aristotle's Dialectical Purposes." *Interpretation* 21 (1986): 135–67.

Jaeger, Werner. *Aristotle.* Oxford: Clarendon Press 1948.

Jaffa, Harry. *Thomism and Aristotelianism.* Westport, Conn: Greenwood Press, 1979.

Jonas, Hans. *The Gnostic Religion.* Boston: Beacon Press, 1963.

Jope, James. "The Didactic Unity and Emotional Import of Book 6 of *De rerum natura.*" *Phoenix* 43 (1989): 16–34.

Jordan, Mark. "The Protreptic Structure of the *Summa Contra Gentiles.*" *The Thomist* 50 (1986): 173–209.

Keys, Mary. "Personal Dignity and the Common Good: A Twentieth Century Thomistic Dialogue." In *Catholicism, Liberalism, and Communitarianism: The Catholic Intellectual Tradition and the Moral Foundations of Democracy,* 173–95. Ed. Kenneth Grasso, Gerard V. Bradley, and Robert P. Hunt. Lanham, Md.: Rowman and Littlefield, 1995.

Keyt, David. "Intellectualism in Aristotle." In *Essays in Ancient Greek Philosophy,* 35–50. Ed. John P. Anton and Anthony Preus. Albany: State University of New York Press, 1983.

Klein, Jacob. *Lectures and Essays by Jacob Klein.* Ed. Robert E. Williamson. Annapolis, Md.: University of Maryland Press, 1978.

Kraut, Richard. *Aristotle on the Human Good.* Princeton: Princeton University Press,1989.

Kraut, Richard. "In Defense of the Grand End." *Ethics* 103 (January 1993): 361–74.

Lawler, Peter. "Havel on Political Responsibility." *The Political Science Reviewer* 22(1993): 20–55.

———. "The Dissident Criticism of America." In *The American Experiment: Essays on the Theory and Practice of Liberty,* 123–63. Eds. Peter Lawler and Robert Scheafer. Lanham, Md.: Rowman and Littlefield Inc., 1994.

Liddle, Henry George, and Robert Scott, eds. *An Intermediate Greek-English Lexicon.* Oxford: Clarendon Press, 1990.

Lincoln, Abraham. *Speeches and Writings, 1859–1865.* Ed. Don E. Feherenbacher. New York: The Library of America, 1989.

Litz, Joel. "Reflections on and in Plato's Cave." *Interpretation* 21 (1993–1994): 115–34.

Lobkowicz, Nicholas. "On the History of Theory and Praxis." In *Political Theory and Praxis: New Perspectives.* Ed. Terence Ball, trans. Paul Surber. Minneapolis: University of Minnesota Press, 1977.

Locke, John. *An Essay Concerning Human Understanding.* Ed. Alexander Fraser. NewYork: Dover Publications, 1959.

Locke, John. *Two Treatises of Government.* Ed. Peter Laslett. Cambridge: Cambridge University Press, 1988.

Lord, Carnes. "The Character and Composition of Aristotle's *Politics.*" *Political Theory* 9 (1981): 459–78.

———. *Education and Culture in the Political Thought of Aristotle.* Ithaca, N.Y.: Cornell University Press,1982.

Lowi, Theodore. *The Personal President.* Ithaca: Cornell University Press, 1985.

———. *The End of the Republican Era.* Norman: University of Oklahoma Press, 1995.

Machiavelli, Niccolò. *The Prince.* Trans. Leo Paul S. de Alvarez. Prospect Heights, Ill.: Waveland Press, 1980.

MacIntyre, Alasdair. *After Virtue: A Study in Moral Theory,* 2d ed. Notre Dame, Ind.: University of Notre Dame Press, 1984.

———. *Short History of Ethics.* NewYork: Collier Books, 1966.

———. *Whose Justice? Which Rationality?* Notre Dame: University of Notre Dame Press, 1988.

———. *Dependent Rational Animals: Why Human Beings Need the Virtues.* Peru, Ill.: Open Court Publishing, 1999.

Manent, Pierre. *Tocqueville and the Nature of Democracy.* Trans. John Waggoner. Lanham, Md.: Rowman and Littlefield, 1996.

Mara, Gerald. "The Role of Philosophy in Aristotle's Political Science." *Polity* 19 (1987): 375–401.

Mill, John S. *On Liberty.* Ed. Aubrey Castell. Arlington Heights, Ill.: Harlan Davidson, Inc. 1947.

Millbank, John. *Theology and Social Theory: Beyond Secular Reason.* Oxford: Blackwell, 1990.

Nietzsche, Friedrich. *On the Genealogy of Morals.* Trans. Walter Kaufmann. New York: Vintage Books, 1967.

Nussbaum, Martha. *The Fragility of Goodness.* Cambridge: Cambridge University Press, 1986.

———. "Equity and Mercy." *Philosophy and Public Affairs* 22 (1993): 83–125.

———. *The Therapy of Desire: Theory and Practice in Hellenistic Ethics.* Princeton: Princeton University Press, 1994.

Ober, Josiah. *Mass and Elite in Democratic Athens.* Princeton: Princeton University Press, 1989.

O'Connor, David. "Aristotelian Justice as a Personal Virtue." In *Midwest Studies in Philosophy,* vol. 13, 46–78. Eds. Peter French and Theodore Uehling. Notre Dame, Ind.: University of Notre Dame Press, 1988.

———. "The Aetiology of Justice." In *Essays on the Foundations of Aristotelian Political Science: Politics and Philosophy in Leo Strauss's Aristotle,* 136–64. Ed. Carnes Lord and David O'Connor. Berkeley: University of California Press, 1991.

———. "The Ambitions of Aristotle's Audience." In *Action and Contemplation: Studies in the Moral and Political Thought of Aristotle*, 107–29. Ed. Robert Bartlett and Susan Collins. Albany: State University of New York Press, 1999.

Owen, G. E. L. "*Tithenai ta Phainomena.*" In *Aristot et les problèmes de méthode*, 83–103. Ed. S. Mansion. Louvain: Publications Universitaires de Louvain, 1961.

Pieper, Josef. *Leisure, The Basis of Culture*. South Bend, Ind.: St. Augustine's Press, 1998.

Plato. *Lysis, Symposium, Gorgias*. Trans. W. R. M. Lamb. Cambridge: Harvard University Press, 1973.

Plato. *Symposium*. Trans. Alexander Nehemas and Paul Woodruf. Indianapolis: Hackett Publishing, 1989.

Price, A. W. *Love and Friendship in Plato and Aristotle*. Oxford: Clarendon Press, 1989.

Rahe, Paul A. *Republics: Ancient and Modern*. Chapel Hill: University of North Carolina Press, 1992.

Rawls, John. *A Theory of Justice*. Cambridge: Harvard University Press, 1971.

———. *Political Liberalism*. New York: Columbia University Press, 1993.

Roche, Timothy. "On the Alleged Metaphysical Foundation of Aristotle's *Ethics*." *Ancient Philosophy* 8 (1991): 49–62.

Rourke, Thomas. "Michael Novak and Yves Simon on the Common Good and Capitalism." *Review of Politics* 58 (1996): 229–58.

Rousseau, Jean-Jacques. *The First and Second Discourses*. Ed. Roger Masters. New York: St. Martin's Press, 1964.

———. *Émile, or On Education*. Trans. Allan Bloom. New York: Basic Books, 1970.

———. *On the Social Contract*. Trans. Judith Masters. New York: St. Martin's Press, 1978.

Rowe, Christopher. "Aims and Methods in Aristotle's Politics." In *A Companion to Aristotle's Politics*. Ed. David Keyt and Fred Miller. Oxford: Basil Blackwell, 1991.

Salkever, Stephen. *Finding the Mean: Theory and Practice in Aristotelian Political Philosophy*. Princeton: Princeton University Press, 1990.

———. "Lopp'd and Bound: How Liberal Theory Obscures the Goods of Liberal Practices." In *Liberalism and the Good*, 65–89. Ed. R. Bruce Douglas and Gerald M. Mara. New York: Routledge, 1990.

———. "Women, Citizens, and Soldiers: Plato and Aristotle on the Politics of Virility." In *Essays on the Foundation of Aristotelian Social Science*, 165–90. Ed. Carnes Lord and David O'Connor. Berkeley: University of California Press, 1991.

Saxenhouse, Arlene. *Athenian Democracy: Modern Mythmakers and Ancient Theorists*. Notre Dame: University of Notre Dame Press, 1996.

Sayre, Kenneth. *Plato's Literary Garden: How to Read a Platonic Dialogue*. Notre Dame: University of Notre Dame Press, 1996.

Schollmeier, Paul. *Other Selves: Aristotle on Personal and Political Friendship*. Albany: State University of New York Press, 1994.

Simpson, Peter. *A Philosophical Commentary on Aristotle's* Politics. Chapel Hill: University of North Carolina Press, 1998.

Smith, Thomas W. "The Protreptic Character of the *Nicomachean Ethics*." *Polity* 27 (1994): 307–30.

Smith, Thomas W. "The Order of Presentation and the Order of Understanding in Aquinas' Account of Law." *Review of Politics* 57(4) (winter 1995): 607–40.

———. "John Finnis' Questions and Answers: An Ethics of Hope or Fear?" *American Journal of Jurisprudence* 40 (1995): 27–49.

Sorabji, Richard. "Aristotle and the Role of Intellect in Virtue." In *Essays on Aristotle's Ethics,* 201–20. Ed. Amélie O. Rorty. Berkeley: University of California Press, 1980.

Strauss, Leo. *Natural Right and History.* Chicago: University of Chicago Press. 1953.

———. *The City and Man.* Chicago: University of Chicago Press, 1964.

———. *What is Political Philosophy?* Chicago: University of Chicago Press, 1959.

Tessitore, Aristide. "Making the City Safe for Philosophy: *Nicomachean Ethics* Book 10." *American Political Science Review* 84 (December 1990): 1251–62.

———. "Aristotle's Ambiguous Account of the Best Life." *Polity* 25 (1992): 197–215.

———. *Reading Aristotle's* Ethics: *Virtue, Rhetoric, and Political Philosophy.* Albany: State University of New York Press, 1975.

Thompson, Walter J. "Aristotle: Philosophy and Politics, Theory and Practice." *American Catholic Philosophical Quarterly* 68 (1994): 109–124.

Thucydides. *History of the Peloponnesian War.* Trans. Rex Warner. New York: Penguin Books, 1954.

Umphrey, Stewart. *Zetetic Skepticism.* Wakefield, N.H.: Longwood Academic Press, 1990.

Vacca, Robert "The Theology of Disorder in the *Iliad.*" *Religion and Literature* 23 (1991): 1–22.

VanderWaerdt, Paul A. "The Political Intention of Aristotle's Moral Philosophy." *Ancient Philosophy* 5 (1985): 77–89.

———. "The Plan and Intention of Aristotle's Ethical and Political Writings." *Illinois Classical Studies* 15: 77–89.

Vernant, Jean-Pierre. "Death with Two Faces." In *Reading the Odyssey: Selected Interpretive Essays.* Ed. Seth Schein, 59–72. Princeton: Princeton University Press, 1996.

———. "The Refusal of Odysseus." In *Reading the Odyssey: Selected Interpretive Essays.* Ed. Seth Schein, 180–95. Princeton: Princeton University Press, 1996.

Voegelin, Eric. *Plato and Aristotle.* Baton Rouge: Louisiana State University Press, 1957.

———. *Anamnesis.* Trans. Gerhart Niemeyer. Columbia: University of Missouri Press, 1978.

Walker, A. D. M. "Aristotle's Account of Friendship in the *Nicomachean Ethics.*" *Phronesis* 24 (2): 180–96.

Wardy, Robert. *The Birth of Rhetoric: Gorgias, Plato, and Their Successors.* London and New York: Routledge, 1966.

Weil, Simone. *The Iliad, or The Poem of Force.* Wallingford, Pa.: Pendle Hill Press, 1983.

White, E. B. *Charlotte's Web.* New York: Harper and Row, 1952.

Wolin, Sheldon. *Politics and Vision.* Boston: Little, Brown and Company, 1960.

Wood, Ellen Meiksins, and Neil Wood. *Class Ideology and Ancient Political Theory: Socrates, Plato, and Aristotle in the Social Contract*. New York: Oxford University Press, 1978.

Yack, Bernard. *The Problems of a Political Animal*. Berkeley: University of California Press, 1993.

Index